The Historical Development of Amsterdam 142

Scale and Abstraction 144

5

THE PERFORMANCE OF DENSITY 147

Systematic Review of Density Performance 151

Density and Public Infrastructure 153

Technical Infrastructure 154

Energy Efficiency 154

Surface Water Management 154

Service Infrastructure 155

Recreational Infrastructure 155

Density and Transport 156

Public Transport 156

Walking and Bicycling 157

Motorised Private Transport 157

Travel Behaviour 158

Traffic Safety 159

Density and Economics 159

Productivity, Innovation and Density 160

Density and Property Value 160

Density and Public Finances 161

Environmental Impact of Density 161

Density and Biodiversity 162

Density and Ecological Conditions 162

Density and Climate Change 162

Density and Micro-Climate 164

Social Impact of Density 164

Density and Well-being 165

Density and Social Interaction 165

Density and Social Equity 166

Density and Crime 167

Density and Health 167

Density and Physical Health 168

Density and Air Quality 169

Density and Psychological Health 169

Spacematrix derived Performance Indicators 169

Parking 171

Capacity of the Network 173

Parking Need 175

Parking Performance Index 176

Thresholds of Parking 178

Daylight 179

Any Light versus No Light 180

Real Levels of Daylight 183

Daylight Performance Index 189

Daylight and Spaciousness 192

Air and Noise Pollution 193

Modeling Noise Exposure 195

Modeling Air Pollution 198

Exposures to Noise and Air Pollution 198

Speculations on 'Urbanity' 198

User Intensity 202

Density and Catchment 203

Block Size and Walkability 205

Performance Based Design 207

6

QUALITIES OF DENSITY 209

A Multivariable and Multi-Scalar Definition of Density 210

Performance-Based Description 211

Sustainable Densities 213

The Professional Challenge 214

The Science of Urban Density 216

LIST OF REFERENCES 221

DERIVATION OF FORMULAE 231

SAMPLES FROM THE NETHERLANDS, GERMANY, SPAIN, UK AND SWEDEN 235

DENSITY DEVELOPMENTS AMSTERDAM 273

SPACEMATRIX

SPACEMATRIX

Space, Density and Urban Form

Meta Berghauser Pont
Per Haupt

nai010 publishers

FOREWORD

Meta Berghauser Pont and Per Haupt
December 2020

This book is the result of the cooperation between two architects and researchers with very different geographical origins; Meta Berghauser Pont, who was born in Cameroun and grew up in the east of the Netherlands, and Per Haupt, who gradually moved from rural Sweden to more populated areas in the south. After one decade of living and working in the busy Dutch Randstad and one decade in rural Sweden, we have experienced the pros and cons of physical concentration and desolation both personally and professionally.

The Netherlands, with almost 500 inhabitants per km^2, has one of the highest overall population densities in the world, while Sweden has slightly more than 20 inhabitants per km^2 and represents a country with one of the lowest overall densities.[1] The capital cities Amsterdam and Stockholm, however, have about the same population density, between 4,000 and 4,500 inhabitants per km^2. It is worth noting, though, that Stockholm offers its inhabitants three times more urban green open space per city dweller, which means that the density of the built-up areas in general is slightly higher there.

In our practice as architects and urbanists, we have been studying the potential of urban density as a tool for urban planning and design ever since 2000, when we executed a commission for Bureau Parkstad in Amsterdam, which resulted in the first edition of *Spacematrix* in 2010. Our fascination with density is not primarily normative. We do not claim to know which density is the best, but are driven by the wish to understand the relational logic between density and different spatial and non-spatial properties. In our opinion this is a prerequisite to understand and successfully predict the effects of specific design and planning proposals. Thus, we are interested in demystifying the image of the city by critically examining the possibility of partially redefining the city through numbers.

The aim is not to turn architects and urban designers into technocratic number fetishists, or to provide developers and bureaucrats with shortcuts to making the role of the designer irrelevant. Quite the opposite is true. Equipped with structural understanding of the nature of urban density, the skills of architects and urbanists needed in their daily trade-offs between quantitative requirements, physical constraints and qualitative preferences will be expanded. And it should also empower us as professionals in our cooperation and confrontation with, among others, economists, ecologists, engineers and politicians.

1
UN, National Statistical Offices/UN/Euromonitor International, 2009.

Continuing population growth and urbanization are projected to more than double the global per capita urban land from 100 m^2 in 2000 to 246 m^2 in 2100.[2] With land being a scarce resource and low densities contributing to climate change, especially as a result of increased private mobility, it is not surprising that density is high on the agenda. UN Habitat recommends high densities as one the five strategies for sustainable urban development, but what this means in terms of urban form and building type remains unclear. Some claim that high-rise buildings will solve the density problem,[3] others that 'with smart low-rise solutions there is plenty of space'.[4] We are convinced that understanding the inherent spatial logic of density and its performance is needed to think beyond architectural solutions and start talking performance. This book contributes to this by providing a more fundamental and factual discussion concerning space consumption, density and urban form. We would like to especially highlight the additions made in Chapter 5 of this revised edition, where we present results of a review of more than 300 scientific papers on density and its effects on, for instance, health, biodiversity and economics. This has resulted in a solid knowledge base that provides information on the advantages and disadvantages of densification, and also highlights where gaps in knowledge still exist and more research is needed.

2 Gao, J., O'Neill, B.C. Mapping global urban land for the 21st century with data-driven simulations and Shared Socioeconomic Pathways. *Nat Commun* 11, 2302 (2020).

3 Anonymous, 'Nota tegen rommelig bouwen', *NRC Handelsblad* 28 June 2008.

4 Schreuder, A., 'Wat goed in Breda past, past niet overal in de Randstad', *NRC Handelsblad* 13/14 September 2008, 5.

This book is based on research done at the Department of Urbanism of Delft University of Technology from 2003 until 2010 and since then at the Department of Architecture and Civil Engineering at Chalmers in Gothenburg as well as the Department of Physical Planning at BTH (Blekinge Institute of Technology) in Karlskrona, Sweden.

We would like to thank Han Meyer and John Westrik for their conviction of the importance of the subject and their unshaken faith in our abilities to explore it. Special thanks are due to Erik van der Kooij who has been a true believer in Spacemate since 2000 and has given us the opportunity to test the results in different projects in Amsterdam. Further, the developments during the last ten years wouldn't have been possible without the support of Lars Marcus. We would also like to thank Håkan Ericsson, Hanneke Rolden and Eric Dorsman who have helped us with parts of the fieldwork and for the recent additions using advanced spatial analysis, we thank especially Ioanna Stavroulaki. In Delft we had the opportunity to work with Rudy Uytenhaak, Truus de Bruin-Hordijk and Marjolein van Esch during our investigation of daylight performance in relation to density. In Gothenburg, we worked together with Jens Forssén and Marie Haeger-Eugensson on noise and air pollution in relation to density. And lastly, Per Berg, Victoria Alstäde and Axel Heyman worked with us on the reviews that are the base for the additions in Chapter 5.

We would also like to thank everybody who made the publication of this revised edition of the book possible; Marcel Witvoet (publisher); D'Laine Camp (editor), Studio Joost Grootens (book design), the Department of Architecture and Civil Engineering, Chalmers University of Technology and the Swedish Research Council Formas.

1

THE CONCEPT OF DENSITY

How humans have come to use space over time – in some cases judged as too intensely, in others as not intensely enough – and the problems connected to this, have resulted in discussions concerning the application of the concept of density in urbanism.[1] The use of the concept has varied greatly through modern planning and design. At the beginning of the twentieth century, Raymond Unwin claimed that nothing was to be gained from overcrowding in cities; he proposed a standard density of 12 houses per net acre *maximum*, or 30 houses per hectare.[2] Fifty years later, Jane Jacobs warned that American slums were not only an issue faced in the inner cities, but also in the low-density, dull areas on the fringes. She suggested that a *minimum* of 100 dwellings per net acre (250 dwellings per hectare) was a necessary condition for a vital and participatory city life.[3] Today high densities and the compact city are often seen as prerequisites for sustainable urbanization and economic growth.[4]

The concept of density in urbanism is frequently used to describe the relationship between a given area and the number of certain entities in that area. These entities might be people, dwellings, services, or floor space. However, the simple fact that density is used in, for instance, design requirements, plan descriptions and communication between parties, does not mean that it is used correctly or to its full potential. In the following chapters, we describe the origins and the contents of existing density concepts, the way these concepts have been used to guide the use of space, and their limitations in doing so. We also present an alternative, multivariable approach, and the results it has achieved. Before doing so, this chapter defines the main research questions and the structure of the book.

It is important to make a distinction between urban density used to describe a built environment (*descriptive* use); and urban density used as a norm in the process of planning and designing the city (*prescriptive*, or normative, use). Prior to the twentieth century, density in cities was merely a result of the complex process of city development. Building techniques, legal constraints, traditions, the requirements for economic profitability, etcetera determined the possible resulting densities. However, no conscious use was made of density. As a matter of fact, density as a concept in urban analysis and planning probably did not exist until the second half of the nineteenth

1
With the term 'urbanism' we refer to the intentional ordering and designing of settlements, from the smallest towns to the world's largest cities. Also referred to as urban planning and urban design.

2
Unwin, R., *Town Planning in Practice* London: T. Fisher Unwin, 1909, 320. 1 acre = 0.405 hectare.

3
Jacobs, J., *The Death and Life of Great American Cities* New York: Random House, 1992, originally published in 1961, 211.

4
For example: Hall, P., *Cities in Civilization* London: Phoenix, 1999; Florida, R., *Cities and the Creative Class* New York: Routledge, 2005; Jenks, M., E. Burton and K. Williams eds., *The Compact City: A Sustainable Urban Form?* London: E&FN Spoon, 1996; Lozano, E., 'Density in Communities, or the Most Important Factor in Building Urbanity', in: M. Larice and E. Macdonald eds., *The Urban Design Reader* Oxon: Routledge, 2007, 312-327; Newman, P. and J. Kenworthy, *Sustainability and Cities: Overcoming Automobile Dependence* Chicago: University of Chicago Press, 1999.

Concentrated high-rise development in Hong Kong, China.

Low-rise development in Phoenix, Arizona, USA.

century. During this period, high densities in industrializing cities were argued to be one of the major causes of fires, disease and social disorder. Mainly through critical publications in England and Germany, the awareness of the problem grew among legislators and urban planners. As a result, planning controls were developed that prescribed *maximum* allowable densities.[5] The legislative developments were paralleled by the introduction of a scientific approach to the large city expansions that took place during the economic and demographic boom of the second half of the nineteenth century. In works by Reinhard Baumeister and Joseph Stübben in Germany, density played a role in the discussions of the preferred urban form. At first, the regulation of density was more indirect through prescribed maximum building heights and minimal street widths. Later, mainly through building ordinances, maximum densities were explicitly used to regulate the urban plan.[6]

If the 'regularism' of the second half of the nineteenth century was a means to facilitate the expansions of the industrializing cities by shaving off its most gruesome edges, the later Garden City Movement suggested a totally different urban model. Critics and designers such as Unwin and Ebenezer Howard in England used density to propagate the advantages of decentralized and self-contained smaller cities.

Taking off in the 1960s, extensive discussions took place concerning the issue of urban sprawl and its negative effects on the liveliness of cities, on transportation and the environment. The criticism was not only directed towards the privatized forms of suburban sprawl (low-rise) but also against the relatively low-density, high-rise expansions of the Modern Movement that were built after the Second World War. Compact cities were judged by many to be the best response to counter these developments. In many parts of the world, the affluence of societies has been manifested through increased space consumption. In some cases this has led to calls for regulating the *minimum* densities of redevelopments and city expansions. Since the 1990s, the focus has shifted, and dense and compact urban development is widely adopted by urban planners and policymakers as the most environmentally friendly form of building cities.[7] An expression of this is that it is frequently endorsed in European national and local policy documents.[8] Also, the European Commission's Green Paper[9] (European Commission 2013), UN-Habitat,[10] and the UN-supported Millennium Ecosystem Assessment argue that city compaction is the most environmentally benign strategy for building cities (MA 2005).[11]

During the last century, density has thus been used both to describe the problems of the city (as too dense a century ago, and as too dispersed today) and, based on such diagnoses, as a norm to prescribe alternatives, at times formulated as maximum densities, at other moments as minimum densities.

In spite of the practical advantages of the concept of urban density in urban planning, critics have argued – especially since the revolt in the 1970s against the quantitative methods of modernist planning – that the use of density for anything but statistical purposes is questionable, as it is

5
Churchman, A., 'Disentangling the Concept of Density', *Journal of Planning Literature*, 13 4 1999, 389-411.

6
Rådberg, J., *Doktrin och täthet i svenskt stadsbyggande 1875-1975* Stockholm: Statens råd för byggnadsforskning, 1988.

7
Buys, L., and E. Miller, 'Residential satisfaction in inner urban higher-density Brisbane, Australia. Role of dwelling design, neighbourhood and neighbours', *Journal of Environmental Planning and Management* 55 2012, 319–338.

8
Howley, P.. 'Sustainability versus liveability. An exploration of central city housing satisfaction', *International Journal of Housing Policy*, 10 2010, 173–189.

9
European Commission, *The Green Paper—A 2030 framework for climate and energy policies* 2013, retrieved October 7, 2017, from https://ec.europa.eu/energy/sites/ener/files/publication/GP_EN_web.pdf.

10
UN-Habitat, *Leveraging density. Urban patterns for a green economy* Nairobi: UN-Habitat. ISBN 978-92-1-132463-1, 2012 and UN-Habitat. 2015. Available from https://unhabitat.org/a-new-strategy-of-sustainable-neighbourhood-planning-five-principles

11
MA, *Millennium ecosystem assessment. Ecosystems and human well-being: synthesis* Washington, DC: Island Press, 2005.

perceived as a too elastic concept that poorly reflects the spatial properties of an urban area. Professionals, as well as researchers, hold the opinion that measured density and other physical properties are independent of each other as also can be seen in ❸:

> Very different physical layouts can have similar measured densities. Previous analyses ... show that measured density and other physical factors are quite independent of each other.[12]
>
> Often people confuse density with building type and assume, for example, that detached houses are lower density than attached housing types. While this is generally true it is not always the case. A high-rise tower with large units set on a park-like site may have a lower density than a set of detached houses on small lots.[13]
>
> One of the problems of defining density in operational terms is the relatively weak relationship between density and building type. The same density can be obtained with radically different building types, and the same type can be used to obtain different densities.[14]

Besides the argued lack of relationship between density and form, density is also considered with suspicion because of the confusion regarding the definition of plan boundaries and the scale at which these are measured. Although it is common to distinguish between net and gross density, the definitions vary from place to place:[15] parcel density, net-net density, net and gross residential density, general density and community density are some of the units of measure used. For instance, the population density of the municipality of Amsterdam was 44 inhabitants per hectare in 2000 (excluding water). The density of its urbanized areas, however, was 63 inhabitants per hectare, and the gross residential density – excluding large-scale working areas and green areas[16] – was almost three times higher: 125 inhabitants per hectare.[17]

Notwithstanding the described shortcomings of the existing density concepts, there is a pragmatic need to continue to use density during the process of city building. In general, however, the use of density seems to create some discomfort. For one, we continue to use and require the concept for planning, programming and in the evaluation of urban environments. On the other hand, we are told that the concept of density has very little relevance for the resulting urban form. It is disturbing that the concept comes with a large 'warning disclaimer'. However, what if the definitions and methods that have been used to argue against a relation between density and form have just been ineffective in establishing such a relation?

After an apparent lack of interest in density in urbanism, the concept received renewed attention since the 1990s with the publication of the Urban Task Force in 1999 that seeks to encourage people to move back into cities

12 Alexander, E.R., 'Density Measures: A Review and Analysis', *Journal of Architectural and Planning Research* 10 3 1993, 181-202, 184.

13 Forsyth, A., 'Measuring Density: Working Definitions for Residential Density and Building Density', *Design Brief*, 8 2003, Design Center for American Urban Landscape, University of Minnesota, 4.

14 Lozano, 'Density in Communities', op. cit. note 4, 325.

15 Churchman, 'Disentangling', op. cit. note 5.

16 'Green areas' include parks, sports fields, garden allotments and graveyards.

17 Calculations are based on maps drawn by the authors using historical maps from Amsterdam and population data. For a detailed account of the data and sources, see Berghauser Pont, M. and P. Haupt, *Space, Density and Urban Form*. dissertation TU Delft, 2009, 235–271.

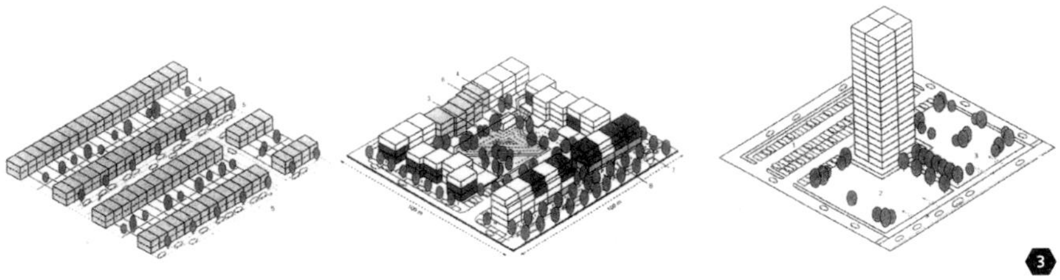

3

Three areas with 75 dwellings per hectare (Fernandez Per & Mozas 2004: 206–207).

and to promote well-designed places that make efficient use of available land and environmental resources.[18] Further, the concept was central to a series of Dutch polemical designs: *Point City* and the publications *Farmax* and *Metacity/Datatown*.[19] Other Dutch examples of the (re)-introduction of density in are the works of, for example, Gert Urhahn and Milos Bobic; Meta Berghauser Pont and Per Haupt; Rudy Uytenhaak. In two publications, *A Pattern Image* and *Strategie voor stedelijkheid*, Urhahn and Bobic describe density as one important element of urban quality.[20] Of more recent date is *Spacemate: The Spatial Logic of Urban Density*, in which the first results of the research at hand were published,[21] and *Cities full of Space: Qualities of Density* which investigates the possibilities of designing and living in more compact cities.[22] In 2015, UN-Habitat launched higher density as one of the five main strategies for sustainable urban development and numerous publication have followed putting density centre stage.[23] Also, attempts were recently made internationally to grasp the relation between density and built form: *Visualizing Density*; *Densité & Formes urbaines dans la métropole Marseillaise*; *DBOOK: Density, Data, Diagrams, Dwellings*; and *Indicateurs morphologiques pour l'amenagement: Analyse de 50 périmètres batis situés sur le canton de Genève*.[24] The number of detailed descriptions in these publications of all facets of the built environment is impressive and useful, but a basic interpretative framework and in-depth research are often lacking. Publications mostly result in an elaborate series of examples. Two recent publications by the London School of Economics and Political Science are exceptions and show, based on the interpretative framework presented in the first edition of this book, density figures in four Asian cities[25] and the relation between density, urban form and energy consumption.[26] This publication, but also other publications in scientific journals as well as

18
Urban Task Force. *Towards an Urban Renaissance.* Final Report of the Urban Task Force chaired by Lord Rogers London, Urban Task Force, 1999.

19
Koolhaas, R., *S,M,L,XL* Rotterdam: 010 Publishers, 1995, 888-893; MVRDV, *Metacity/Datatown* Rotterdam: 010 Publishers, 1999; MVRDV, *Farmax* Rotterdam: 010 Publishers, 1998.

20
Urhahn, G.B. and M. Bobic, *A Pattern Image* Bussum: Uitgeverij THOTH, 1994; Urhahn, G.B. and M. Bobic, *Strategie voor stedelijkheid* Bussum: Uitgeverij THOTH, 1996.

21
Berghauser Pont, M. And P. Haupt, *Spacemate: The Spatial Logic of Urban Density* Delft: DUP Science, 2004.

22
Uytenhaak, R., *Cities Full of Space: Qualities of Density* Rotterdam: 010 Publishers, 2008.

23
UN-Habitat, '*Leveraging*', op. cit. note 10.

24
Campoli, J. and A.S. MacLean, *Visualizing Density* Cambridge, MA: Lincoln Institute of Land Policy, 2007; Fernandez Per, A., and J. Mozas, *DBOOK: Density, Data, Diagrams, Dwellings* Vitoria-Gasteiz: a+t ediciones, 2007; Brunner, C., *Densité & forms urbaines dans la métropole marseillaise* Marseilles: Edition Imbernon, 2005; CETAT, *Indicateurs morphologiques pour l'amenagement: Analyse de 50 périmetres batis situes sur le canton de Geneve* Geneva: Departement des traveaux publics, 1986; LSE Cities, *Resource Urbanisms. Asia's divergent city models of Kuwait, Abu Dhabi, Singapore and Hong Kong* London School of Economics and Political Science, 2017.

25
LSE Cities, *Resource Urbanisms*, op. cit. note 24.

26
LSE Cities, *Cities and Energy. Urban Morphology and Heat Energy Demand* London School of Economics and Political Science, 2014.

policy documents, show how well the first edition of the book *Spacematrix, Space, Density and Urban Form* was received in in the field of urban planning and design, both by academia and practice.

There was and still is clearly a need for further fundamental research on density. This revised version of the first edition that was published in 2010 presents the development of the method to deal with the relation between the quantitative and qualitative aspects of space consumption. This formulation of density based on a multivariable definition has proven to help to establish an effective relation to urban form, and promotes the establishment of a science of density as part of the science of cities. Furthermore, a systematic review of the role densification can play in sustainable urban development gives conclusive answers on the pros and cons of this strategy.

The Broader Context

Besides the mentioned arguments for a revaluation of density, there are presently two general developments in the process of urbanization which can be identified that further legitimize the study of density. First, recent changes in how city building is organized have created a greater need to relate development programmes to spatial qualities. Second, the trend in the increase in space consumption and the environmental, economic and social effects associated with this trend point to the need for research into the relationship between the quality and capacity of space.

Since the 1970s, the traditional hierarchical sequence of the planning process, starting from national, regional and urban planning, continuing on to urban design and architecture, has largely been reversed. Architecture is no longer an extension of planning, but is now often employed to trigger the planning process. In other words, city development has shifted away from normative master and blueprint planning to more strategic and project-based approaches. This has resulted in a process of city development that mainly occurs through negotiations between private and public actors. This shift is often described as a gradual ideological and practical shift from government to governance, implying a growing role for private actors in public policymaking. The government at both national and local levels no longer takes an arm's-length role, but through a new approach to governance has become one of many market parties.[27]

In addition, a greater demand for selling projects that focus on branding and seductive images, something deemed necessary in the current competitive climate, has caused a shift to a project-based design approach driven by aesthetic values.[28] Critics address the superficiality of such a project-based design approach, arguing that the urban development has evolved into little more than large-scale architecture. They posit that to deal with this, instruments are needed to link the instrumentally rational to the image, and projects to a strategy for the city or city region as a whole.[29]

27
See, for example, Harvey, D., 'From Managerialism to Entrepreneurialism: The Transformation in Urban Governance in Late Capitalism', *Geografiska Annaler* 71B 1989, 3-17; Cammen, H. van der, and L. de Klerk, *Ruimtelijke Ordening: Van grachtengordel tot Vinexwijk* Utrecht: Het Spectrum, 2003; Wigmans, G., 'Maatschappelijke trends en gebiedsontwikkeling: Een probleemschets', in: I. Bruil et al. eds., *Integrale gebiedsontwikkeling: Het stationsgebied 's-Hertogenbosch* Amsterdam: SUN, 2004, 30-49; Claessens, F. and E. van Velzen, 'De actualiteit van het stedelijk project', *Stedebouw & Ruimtelijke Ordening*, 87 4 2006, 32-37; Musch, M., 'Polder Ground', *OASE* 52 1999, 16-31; Meijsmans, N., 'The Urban Project on a Regional Scale?', paper presented at the conference *The Urban Project* Delft, the Netherlands 4-7 June 2008.

28
Cammen and de Klerk, *Ruimtelijke Ordening*, op. cit. note 18.

29
Claessens and Van Velzen, 'De actualiteit', op. cit. note 18; Meijsmans, 'The Urban Project', op. cit. note 18; Meyer, H., 'In dienst van de stad onder postmoderne condities/ Working for the City under Post-modern Conditions', in: H. Meyer and L. van den Burg eds., *In dienst van de stad/ Working for the City* Amsterdam: SUN, 2005, 64-68.

The *New Map of the Netherlands*, launched in 1997, shows the enormous scale of new projects that the country faces.[30] From 2,650 projects in 1997, the inventory contained almost 6,500 plans and projects in 2010 and it is not surprising that the epithet 'Projectland the Netherlands' was introduced.[31] However, long-term centralized planning still plays a central role in the Netherlands. In 2008 three National Planning Reports were presented.[32] It is evident that despite the increase of more bottom-up and project-based approaches, the Dutch government still produces planning documents on a macro scale. How these relate to the micro-scale solutions remains unclear. The report *Structuurvisie Randstad 2040*, presented in September 2008, foresees a need for half a million new dwellings in the Randstad, 40 per cent to be realized through densification in cities. At the same time the city of Rotterdam, in *Stadsvisie Rotterdam: Spatial Development Strategy 2030*, proposes projects which focus mainly on the realization of low-rise neighbourhoods to attract middle-class families.[33] To be able to relate the densification goals from the planning report to the proposed low-rise projects in Rotterdam, professionals need new instruments that are able to bridge the gap between the micro-scale level of urban *design* and the macro-scale level of urban *planning*. Such instruments should prevent mismatches between the spatial qualities desired and the development programme foreseen at national, regional and local scale – a mismatch that can have severe qualitative, programmatic and financial consequences. Furthermore, such instruments should facilitate the negotiation process between private and public actors and enable all actors simultaneously to assess programme and urban form. We claim that urban density could play a significant role in doing so.

Another reason why density needs to achieve a more central role in urbanism is that urban space consumption has increased dramatically during the last century.[34] The average population density of Amsterdam fell a factor of 9, from almost 570 inhabitants per hectare in 1880 to around 65 in the year 2000.[35] During this period, the urbanized territory of Amsterdam grew from approximately 560 to 11,500 hectares (a factor of 20), while the population grew from 317,000 to 727,100 inhabitants (a factor of 2.3). The growth of Amsterdam can largely be explained by the increased spatial demands per person,

30
Available at www.nieuwekaart.nl last accessed on 19 May 2008.

31
Metz, T. and M. Pflug, *Atlas van Nederland in 2005: De Nieuwe Kaart* Rotterdam: NAi Publishers, 1997.

32
The report *Samen Werken met Water* by the *Deltacommissie* describes how the Netherlands could become more resistant to flooding. VROM, *Structuurvisie Randstad 2040: Naar een duurzame en concurrerende Europese topregio* The Hague: Ministry of Spatial Planning and the Environment, 2008, presented by the Dutch cabinet on 5 September 2008, aims to make the Randstad an even more internationally competitive environment, and proposes, among other things, an addition of 500,000 houses. The third document is not an official Policy Document, but expresses the intentions of the minister of transport, Camiel Eurlings, for example to invest 4.5 billion euros in the rail network.

33
Municipality of Rotterdam, *Stadsvisie Rotterdam: Spatial Development Strategy 2030* Rotterdam: dS+V, 2007.

34
In a general approach to this problem, one should consider the total human space consumption ecological footprint that is all the cultivated surface needed to satisfy our increasing demands of energy, foodstuff and other natural resources See Rees, W., 'Ecological Footprint and Appreciated Carrying Capacity: What Urban Economics Leave Out', *Environment and Urbanisation* 4 2 1992, 121-130. Accepting the limitations of our discipline, however, we look at this problem only from the perspective of urbanized occupation. The larger context is, of course, always circumscribing this one aspect of the problem.

35
Including housing, green and working areas. Calculations are based on maps drawn by the authors using historical maps of Amsterdam. The sources of maps and population data as well as calculations can be found in Berghauser Pont and Haupt, *Space, Density* op. cit. (note 17).

but only marginally by the growth of the population. This seems to be a general trend in wealthy societies; the number of inhabitants per dwelling unit decreases, dwellings become larger, and the city is less densely built. This was confirmed in a five-year study by the Lincoln Institute where the urban expansion in 30 cities from all over the world is studied, showing a general trend of decreasing densities from the global north to south.[36] The causes of such sprawl of people and activities are complex and the effects multifaceted, but many of the effects are quite generally acknowledged. They include such factors as the increase in car and goods transport, the association of this with the increase in energy consumption, air pollution, noise pollution and the fragmentation in the ecosystems, accompanied by a reduction in the viability of public transport, local amenities and public services, and so forth.[37]

36 Angel, S., J. Parent, D.L. Civco, A.M. Blei, *Making Room for a planet of Cities*, Lincoln Institute of Land Policy, 2011, 23.

37 Couch, C., L. Leontidou and G. Petschel-Held, *Urban Sprawl in Europe: Landscapes, Land-Use Change & Policy* Oxford: Blackwell Publishing, 2007.

This trend of increase in consumption of space calls for further research on the relationship between the capacity and the quality of space. How can more compact approaches accommodate future growth? What qualitative measures (specific technical and design solutions) can be used to compensate for and counteract the negative effects of higher densities? To answer these questions, instruments are needed that make explicit the macro-scale consequences of spatial choices made on project level, and vice versa, instruments that assist in predicting and visualizing the impacts of macro-scale programmes on the micro scale of a project. We claim that urban density can also play a significant role in facing this challenge.

Most recently, not least as a result of the 'urban renaissance' and the publication of the five principles for sustainable urban development by UN-Habitat in 2015, density figures are rising again. In Amsterdam, since 2000, densities started to increase from 63 inhabitants per hectare in 2000 to 74 in 2020, an increase of 17 per cent. This is one of the reasons to publish this revised edition of *Spacematrix, Space, Density and Urban Form*, in which one full chapter is dedicated to discussing the social, economic and environmental effects of densification based on a systematic review of 330 scientific papers. Thus, this revised edition provides not only a *definition* of density capable of reducing the confusion surrounding the concept of density and making it a productive concept in design and planning practice and research, it also gives insight into how density relates to other performances. By performances we here refer to the ability or capacity of the built environment to deliver different results. Examples of performances that to a varying extent are conditioned by density are daylight access, health, segregation and air pollution. Through these performances we are able to suspend our judgements concerning appropriate densities. In addition, the definition of density should enable the development of a *method* that can deal with the current challenges being faced in urbanism. Examples hereof – as sketched earlier in the introduction – are the general trend from government to governance, and from blueprint planning to a more project-based approach, but also the dilemmas of increased urban space consumption.

The method should help to develop a simultaneous understanding of how macro-scale planning ambitions (quantitative and qualitative) relate to micro-scale design projects and vice versa; it should make explicit the macro-scale results of a multitude of micro-scale decisions and spatial developments. Central to all this is the understanding of the variation in density throughout the scales.This book claims to deliver such a definition and method, the Spacematrix, which can be used to uncover the conditionality of density to urban form and performances. The Spacematrix, together with definitions of scale, demarcation of plan areas and derived indicators, offers a solid basis for a method that can be used both in planning and design practice, and for scientific research. The possibilities and specific areas of application will be suggested in the coming chapters. The book aims at reviving the concept of density, to rescue the baby that was thrown out with much of the bathwater said to be fouled by the misconducts of the Modern Movement. This doesn't mean that an old instrument is just taken out of the basement, dusted off and reignited. No, the shortcomings of the existing density-measurement methods in conveying information about urban form and performance are certainly very real, as others have pointed out, and which we will demonstrate further on. Those shortcomings, however, have led many to the conclusion that the concept *as such* is flawed and even dangerous. We insist, though, that the problem with the most commonly used density-measurement methods is rather one of representation and resolution. A too rough a resolution, that is a method that relies on too few variables, turns the concept into a predominately statistical tool. This 'roughness' means that the capacity to differentiate is far too small to make them useful in relation to urban form and performance. At the other extreme of the spectrum, detailed descriptions (or representations) of the built environment tend to be dependent on a large amount of variables and data. Descriptions that are too specific not only make a method complex, but also quickly limit the possibilities to distil generic conclusions. Our research shows that the presented Spacematrix method contains a proper amount and sort of variables, and engages with the suitable levels of scale, to make productive conclusions about urban form and performance. But before unfolding the argument, we will put forward the central hypothesis, formulate a series of questions that need to be answered, and describe the research methods that have structured and guided our search.

Challenges to Understanding Density

The hypothesis central to this book is that urban density does contain valuable information about urban form and the performance of the built environment. If this can be shown to be the case, then urban density has the potential to be effective in developing a method capable of simultaneously articulating quantity and quality, or, expressed in a less abstract way, a method that can relate built programme to urban form and other

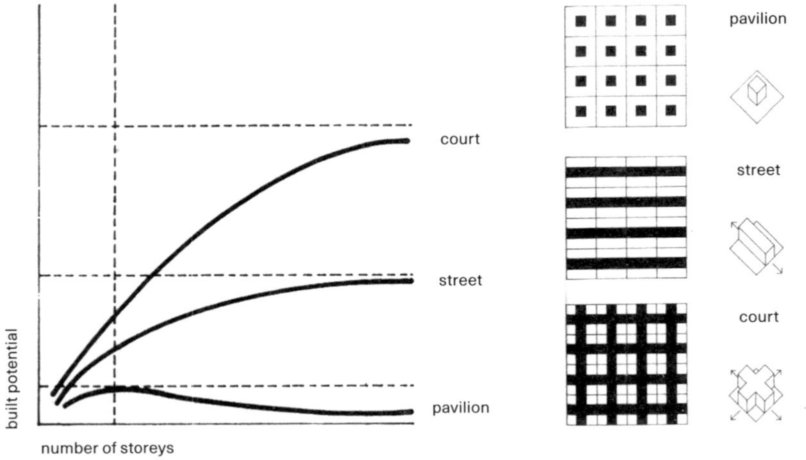

4 Scheme from Martin and March (1972: 36–37).

performances. Such a method should, through its application, be able to contribute to achieving the aims mentioned above, and thus play an important role in current urban practice. To arrive at a significant and productive correlation between urban density on the one hand and urban form and performance on the other, a series of sub-questions needs to be formulated and confronted. The two parts of the hypothesis, quantity and quality, or, more fitting in the present discourse, 'urban density' and 'urban form and performance', both have to be critically examined and (re)defined before being related. For the first part of the assumed correlation – urban density – questions about demarcation of areas, entities of measurement, and levels of scale have to be articulated to arrive at an effective definition of urban density that can be used to make plausible the correlation between density and form: What is measured, how are geographical areas circumscribed, and which levels of scale need to be defined? In this research, to answer these questions we have critically examined and judged the definitions of urban density that have been developed and applied in the past, and more specifically, the indicators that have been, and still are, commonly used to describe urban density. Finally, their capacity to convey information on urban form and performance has been tested.

If the first part of the correlation – urban density – is a complex subject matter, then the second part – qualities of the built environment, in this case understood as urban form and performance – constitutes a challenge of gargantuan proportions. The aim of this research, however, has not been to develop an exhaustive and detailed definition of urban form, but to uncover a general correlation between density and built form, and, with enough precision, suggest conditional dependencies for specific urban types and performances on urban density. To this aim, the description of urban types and the choices of studied performances have sprung out of a mixed process of a relatively autonomous construction of urban types, an inventory of commonsense naming of urban types and their constituent features, and the use of existing formal analytical reductions into basic layout types.

5 Basic typomorphological entities of settlements: streets, plots and buildings (Conzen 1960).

All these together combine into a workable (that is, not too detailed, but also not too inclusive) classification of urban form that later, in the final step of the research, is mirrored in the density data, producing cluster and regularities that can support the hypothesis.

Before taking on the central challenge of relating urban density to form, the book starts with a sweeping description of the historical context of city development that has been extended to cover the last ten years of urban development. This reconstruction of the history of city building in the Netherlands, since the late Middle Ages, is made to underpin the developments signalled as central to the research problem and aim (changes in the city building process and increased space consumption); to trace density developments through urban history; and to reconstruct the wider context in which density evolved from being a result of circumstances to a practically applied, normative concept in city development. The historical context also serves as a source for making an inventory of the definitions and practical applications of density in city development, and it has further served to distinguish some of the differing positions on density in relation to, for instance, sustainability and urbanity. It is by no means an exhaustive reconstruction but intends to capture some decisive transformations. Its brief character makes it vulnerable to criticism for presenting a Eurocentric perspective, or even a 'Dutchcentric' one. This would be a just observation, but in our opinion not a great problem to the later developed method. We would even go so far as to ascribe the developed density method universal aspirations: a universal structure filled with content and applied in ways that differ due to specific contextual circumstances. The historical sketch serves as an illustration of the specific temporal developments in a specific geographical context, namely that of the Netherlands. At times these Dutch density developments are put into a larger context, and planning doctrines, political developments, and density methods and variables from abroad are used to balance the risk of interpreting the Dutch situation in a kind of vacuum. This wider contextualization further serves as a scan of the most commonly used definitions of density and related measurement methods.

In addition to the historical outline, the spatial and demographic developments of Amsterdam were registered to chart the density developments of the city. Different historical maps were used and measured for this purpose, as well as sources on the population development of the city.

Besides unravelling the different historical doctrines and common definitions of density, the research has also relied on knowledge in the field of typomorphology to identify the basic components of the built environment. The work of geographer M.R.G. Conzen, founder of the English school of morphology, was used as a framework. Conzen developed a methodological and theoretical manual to analyse the physical urban plan on different levels of scale.[38] This approach is in contrast to the other morphological schools that are more concerned with architecture (Italian school) and sociocultural aspects of city forming (French school). The studies of typomorphology were combined in the current research with a more deductive, quantitative research approach to come to understand the relationship between urban programmes and spatial properties. The research carried out by Leslie Martin and Lionel March at the Centre for Land Use and Built Form Studies in Cambridge is an example of such a deductive, quantitative approach.[39] Central to their work is the recognition of certain related factors, such as the land available, the buildings located on this land and the roads required to serve them. Rather than a separate 'school' that has little association with the detailed graphical mapping techniques of typomorphology, we see the deductive, quantitative approach as an extension of typomorphology, expanding on the opportunities provided here. The analytical techniques differ, but the research aims coincide: describing and explaining urban form.

The critical examination of the issues mentioned above – the level of scale, the bordering of areas, the definition of entities, the composition of indicators, basic urban form, urban types, performances – has led to a new, multivariable definition of density and a package of practically applicable definitions. The investigation undertaken to make the correlation between density, urban form and other performances plausible has relied on two research methods: empirical and explorative research. We analysed a wide range of samples, from the Netherlands and abroad, and used these to formulate density-based urban types. This analysis of existing built environments

38
Moudon, A.V., 'Getting to Know the Built Landscape: Typomorphology', in: K. Franck and L. Schneekloth eds., *Ordering Space: Types in Architecture and Design* New York: Van Nostrand Reinhold, 1994, 289-311.

39
An institute established at the School of Architecture in Cambridge in 1963.

(empirical research) was combined with design and calculation experiments to explore the limits of the possible design solutions under specific density conditions, and to investigate how different built environments perform in relation to density (explorative research). Both the empirical and the explorative research have been guided and inspired by the two research traditions already mentioned, typomorphology and deductive, quantitative research.

Structure of the Book

The following chapter, 'City Development and Space Consumption', sketches the historical background to the development and use of the concept of density. To understand the circumstances in which the concepts of density were developed and applied in the past, a brief historical account of the developments in Dutch city building and the organization of the planning process is given. A larger international context is used at times to situate the national and local developments. The different concepts developed are discussed as well as the justification for the use of density in urban settings. In some cases, the concepts were based on practical experiences gained from urban projects, in other cases, new concepts were developed for a more polemic and social purpose. This chapter also includes an account of the specific density developments of the city of Amsterdam between 1400 and 2020.

The third chapter, 'Multivariable Density: Spacematrix', looks critically at different density definitions and judges them on the basis of their ability to relate density to urban form. Apart from describing the different concepts employed, such as population density or spaciousness, the chapter also assesses measurement techniques. Issues discussed include the scale of measurement and demarcation of areas. As none of the concepts were assessed as appropriate to describe potential form, a new, multivariable definition of density is proposed called the Spacematrix. The three core indicators applied are Floor Space Index (FSI), Ground Space Index (GSI), and Network density (N). The second portion of this chapter then defines the necessary measurement techniques and introduces additional, useful (derived) indicators.

In the fourth chapter, 'Density and Urban Form', we demonstrate, based on empirical data from various European countries, how this multivariable definition of density indeed can distinguish differences in urban form. This chapter illustrates that the conditions defined by Spacematrix density, combined with real constraints present at a certain place and moment in history, limit the potential urban form to such an extent that it becomes possible to define urban types most likely to emerge under these density conditions. This chapter also includes an account of the mathematical proof of the numbers presented in the book as well as a database with all empirical material used throughout the book, extended in the revised edition with examples from Stockholm, Sweden and London, UK.

In Chapter 5, we discuss the performance of density in detail where we first, present results of a systematic review based on the findings presented in 229 scientific papers. These empirical studies cover topics related to transport, such as modes of transport, trip distance and energy consumption related to transport. Other topics that will be discussed here are effects related to economics, environmental and health effects, social outcomes such as social cohesion and equity, and resource efficiency. Second, in line with the work of Martin and March, the multivariable density matrix is related to qualities of daylight, the distribution of greenhouse gas emissions and noise exposure.

The last chapter, 'Qualities of Density', draws conclusions that offer answers to the questions and problems posed in the first two chapters, based on the results discussed in the third, fourth and fifth chapter. Besides the development of Spacematrix, which defines density as a multivariable and multi-scalar phenomenon, the research addresses the effectiveness of density in the urban planning practice, its academic relevance, and its potential to assist in the efforts to understand and tackle runaway urban space consumption as well as contribute to sustainable urban development.

2

CITY DEVELOPMENT AND SPACE CONSUMPTION

This chapter looks at the history of city development[1] and discusses the role of the differing views on density in this process. The concept of density has acquired both descriptive and prescriptive connotations. On the one hand it is used to analyse problems, and on the other to offer solutions. This chapter sketches the development of density from a mere outcome of complex circumstances (roughly until 1850); through the birth of density as a tool for analysis and diagnosis (1850–1900); via a concept used to propagate alternatives and prescribe maximum densities in order to guarantee certain qualities (1900–1960); to, more lately, an instrument that is used to argue for minimum densities to support amenities and public transport, and produce less unsustainable environments with potential for vital urban interaction.

In addition, this chapter highlights two forces in city development, described briefly in the previous chapter, using a historical perspective. The first relates to the dialectic between an unregulated market and collective intervention[2] and the transition from government to governance; the second focuses on the tension between programme- and image-based planning. These developments are described with the use of examples from Dutch cities, supplemented from time to time by background information on the international context.

We further look at how land use and human space consumption has changed and how this has affected the practice of city development. See ⬟ Density Developments Amsterdam on page 273 where the city of Amsterdam is used to illustrate these historical shifts.[3] Certainly, Amsterdam is just one example. Other cities are of different sizes, have different historical backgrounds, and developed in their own unique ways. Nevertheless, Amsterdam can serve as a suitable point of reference for other larger Dutch cities and for many of the general trends that took place in Europe.

The chapter ends with some critical questions on the effects of these developments and its impact on city development. We highlight the need for a better understanding of the relationship between quantity and quality, or between programme and the performance of the urban landscape.[4]

1
The notion of city development is used to include both intentionally planned developments and more organically generated settlements.

2
Collective intervention through state institutions (municipalities, provinces, ministries), and/or corporativist organizations.

3
The calculations are all made by the authors based on historical maps of Amsterdam and different sources for the statistics concerning the amount of inhabitants (For a detailed account of the data and sources, see Berghauser Pont, M. and P. Haupt, *Space, Density and Urban Form*. dissertation TU Delft, 2009, 235-271).

4
Concerning the use of the term 'urban landscape' we follow the argument put forward in Moudon, A.V., 'Getting to Know the Built Landscape: Typomorphology', in: K. Franck and L. Schneekloth (eds.), *Ordering Space: Types in Architecture and Design* (New York: Van Nostrand Reinhold, 1994), 289–311.

Dutch Density Developments

The subsequent analysis delineates four distinct periods. The shift from one period to the next is sometimes rather imperceptible as ideas of previous periods extend into, and continue to influence subsequent periods. The role density has played is central to this historical examination, whether it has been used as a tool or merely manifests itself as an outcome. The periods described are:

—— *Mercantile Capitalism* (1400–1815). This period stretches from the end of the Middle Ages to the beginnings of the nineteenth century. It sees the birth of Dutch cities and sets the scene for later industrial expansions. Two distinct practices of city development coexist. One concerns public streets laid out by the feudal ruler or municipality, the other individual lots developed by users. Density is a mere outcome.

—— *Liberal-Competitive Capitalism* (1815–1900). During this period the dynamics of the market, industrialization and city growth are only marginally influenced by political and public sector interference. Towards the end of the century, the density concept is introduced. It is used to diagnose and compare cities that quickly have to absorb growing populations, but plays a limited role in the creation of new expansion plans.

—— *State-Managed Capitalism* (1900–1979). This period, starting from around 1900 and extending to the end of the 1970s, is often dubbed as a state-driven planning tradition. The *managerial state* and public institutions dominate, from start to finish, throughout the entire urban development planning process. The term *embedded liberalism* is sometimes used to describe this period and to distinguish it from the previous one. During this period, density is used to prescribe preferred densities. The Garden City Movement in England and the early functionalists in Germany are the first to systematically engage with the concept. The use of density resonates well with the scientific, positivist ideal of the time.

—— *Neoliberal Capitalism* (1979–today). Referred to as the period after the late 1970s when planning practice is to a large extent privatized. The state becomes more of an *entrepreneurial state,* facilitating the demands of private investors and consumers in the marketplace. An urban crisis (unemployment, declining population and budget deficits) defines the first part of this period. The postmodern critique of centralized, modernist planning also tarnishes the reputation of density as a 'technocratic' instrument that had played an important role in the 'crimes' of the earlier period. However, problems of sprawl, mobility and unsustainability, and economic demands for profitable developments turn the attention to the need for minimum densities.

Mercantile Capitalism (1400–1815)

One can distinguish two types of Dutch towns prior to the nineteenth century.[5] A regular pattern of streets developed in a rather short period of time characterized the first type. These towns were established by powerful

5
Rutte, R., *A Landscape of Towns: Urbanization in the Netherlands from the 11th to the nineteenth Centuries* (Delft: Delft University of Technology, Faculty of Architecture, 2004).

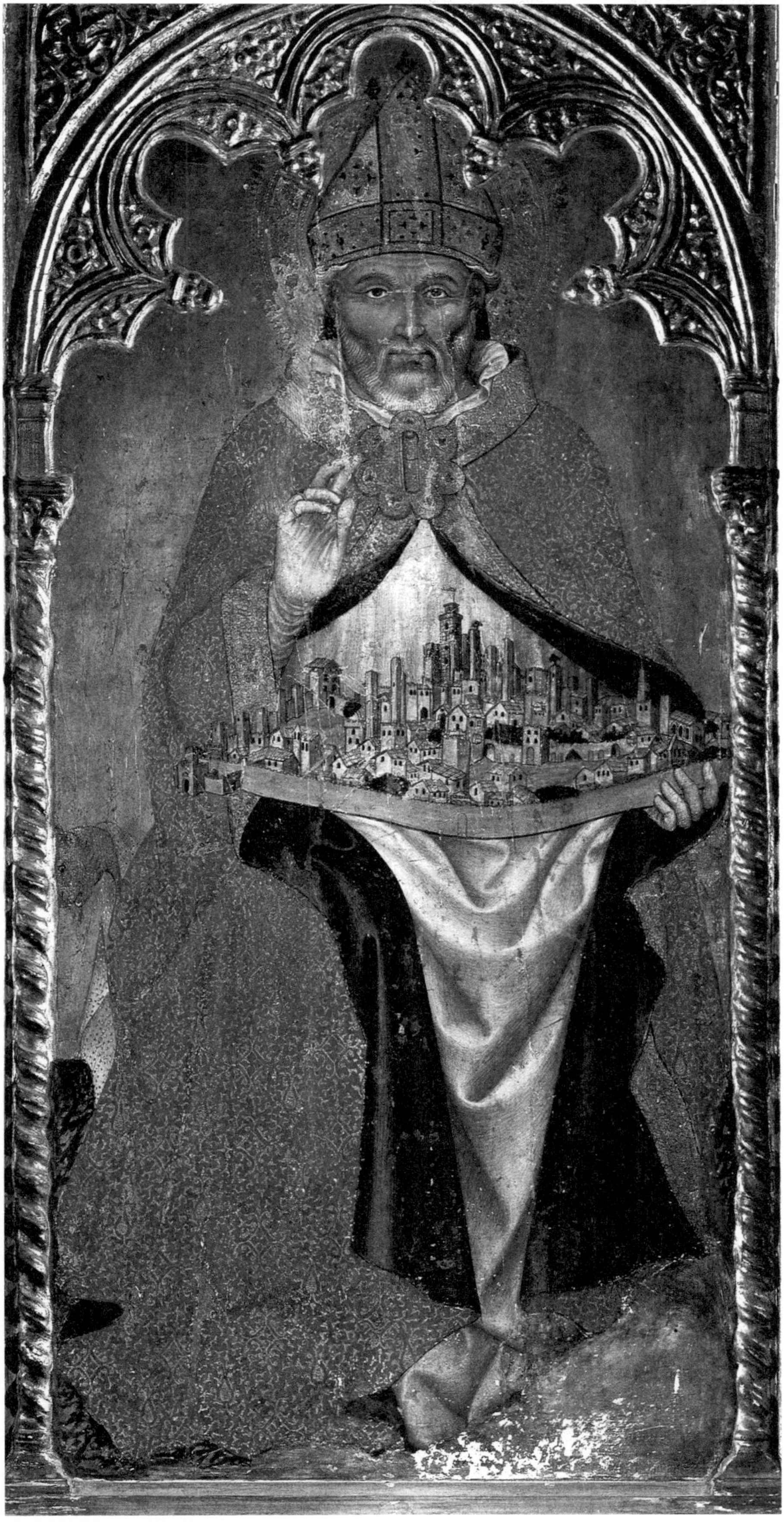

1 The patron saint of San Gimignano (Italy) holds an image of the city crowned by feudal towers, in a fourteenth-century altarpiece by Taddeo di Bartolo (Kostof 1991: 297).

Population density in Amsterdam from 1400 to 2000.

2

Map of Oud-Noord-Beverlandpolder with Colijnsplaat, drawn by Lucas Sinck, 1598.

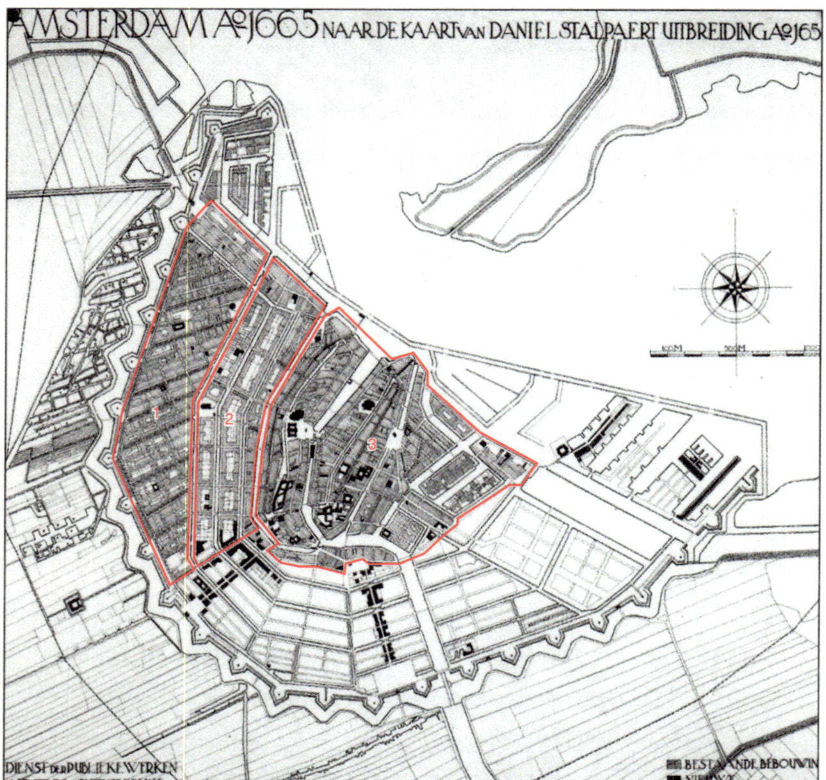

1 Jordaan
2 Grachtengordel
3 Center

3

Amsterdam in 1665; the realization of Grachtengordel and Jordaan (dienst der Publieke Werken, based on the map of Daniel Stalpaert).

rulers (such as counts, bishops, dukes) or through large-scale land reclamation projects. ❷

The second type of late medieval towns are characterized by a gradual urbanization. Growth was driven by a flourishing economy, rising population and increases in commercial activity. Amsterdam is a good example of this type. The initial inhabitants of Amsterdam were farmers who settle on both sides of the Amstel River on terps.[6] In 1300 Amsterdam acquired city rights, but not until after 1450 did large numbers of people settle in the city (more than 10,000 inhabitants).[7] During an economic boom in the first half of the seventeenth centurye – the Golden Agee – the population density grew substantially until it peaked in 1650 at 650 inhabitants per hectare. By the seventeenth century, Amsterdam had grown from being a small town into being one of the largest cities in Europe.[8]

Large-Scale Expansion

At the beginning of the seventeenth century, Amsterdam undertook new expansion plans to combat increasing densification and to facilitate economic growth. The plans cover the Grachtengordel and the Jordaan. ❸ These expansions contain something different in comparison to previous expansions. The Grachtengordel plan incorporated the aesthetic, classicist preferences of that time. This plan results in a regular and symmetrical layout with rectangular blocks and lots, whereby appearance, functionality and profit go hand in hand. The municipality not only designated the building lots, streets and canals, but a new type of land management emerged that influenced the way in which private lots were developed and utilized. The city expropriated the land needed for new expansions and sold the lots. In specific contracts, the city authorities stipulated the requirements concerning the use and types of the development permitted within the plan.[9] The plan was in effect instrumental in sealing agreements between the various parties involved.[10]

The two expansion plans for the Grachtengordel and the Jordaan culminated in zoning plans (functional and socioeconomic) that had never existed before on such a scale in the Netherlands.[11] The first two canals of the Grachtengordel (Herengracht and Keizersgracht) were in effect housing developments, especially for the ruling class. Specific conditions were linked to the lots sold along these canals, so called standards (*keuren*). These standards laid down strict conditions for the building of the houses, including construction time (usually one year) and how the resulting structures should be aligned in the street to ensure a neat row of façades. Height and depth of the houses were also limited to allow for large gardens in the courtyards behind the buildings.[12] These stipulations directly or indirectly had a bearing on the final built form and on density.

The Jordaan area originally arose in a part of the city outside the walls that had sprung up illegally (*de voorstad*, or *faubourgs*). The redevelopment

6
A *terp*, an artificial dwelling hill, is a mound created to provide safe ground during high tide and river floods. The first terp-building period in the Dutch province of Friesland dates from 500 BC.

7
Dijkstra, C., M. Reitsma and A. Rommerts, *Atlas Amsterdam* (Bussum: Uitgeverij THOTH, 1999).

8
Abrahamse, J.A., 'De ruimtelijke ontwikkeling van Amsterdam in de zeventiende eeuw en de opkomst van de stedebouw als wetenschap', in: B. Bakker and E. Schmitz (eds.), *Het aanzien van Amsterdam: Panorama's, plattegronden en profielen uit de Gouden Eeuw* (Bussum: Uitgeverij THOTH, 2007), 24–41.

9
Heeling, J., H. Meyer and J. Westrik, *Het ontwerp van de stadsplattegrond* (Amsterdam: SUN, 2002);

10
Terlouw, E., 'A House of One's Own', *OASE* 52 (1999), 32–77.

11
Abrahamse, 'De ruimtelijke ontwikkeling', op. cit. (note 9).

12
Ibid., 29.

plan, consisting of industry and housing, included the widening of streets and the demolition of some existing structures to align the streets. In this plan no additional standards (*keuren*) were enforced. In 1859 the density of the Jordaan was 830 inhabitants per hectare while the Grachtengordel housed only 270 inhabitants per hectare.[13] When the last bubonic plague struck Amsterdam in 1664, 25,000 people, almost 10 per cent of the population, perished.[14] The poorest and most densely populated areas, such as the Jordaan, were most severely affected.

After 1672, the year of catastrophe (*het Rampjaar*), the Dutch economy stagnated and the market for land and property in the southern part of the Grachtengordel collapsed. No Dutch town or city grew until well into the nineteenth century. Amsterdam even lost a quarter of its population between 1735 and 1815. The area covered by the city remained very much the same, but the diminished population spread out. This translated into a fall in population density in Amsterdam from 650 inhabitants per hectare during the Golden Age of the seventeenth century to 320 inhabitants per hectare by 1815.

13
Based on an 1859 census. Sources: Laloli, H.M., 'Beter wonen? Woningmarkt en residentiële segregatie in Amsterdam 1850–1940', in: O.W.A. Boonstra et al. (eds.), *Twee eeuwen Nederland geteld: Onderzoek met de digitale volks-, beroeps- en woningtellingen 1795–2001* (The Hague: DANS and CBS, 2007); and www.amsterdamhistorie.nl, accessed August 2008.

14
Moll, H., 'Vuile teringstad: Vijf eeuwen besmettelijke ziekten in Amsterdam', *NRC Handelsblad* 31 January 2001.

Liberal-Competitive Capitalism (1815–1900)

Following a period of relative stagnation, the Dutch population began to grow once more during the nineteenth century. Amsterdam had developed into a strong, innovative financial centre and the period saw the completion of a series of major national and international infrastructure projects, such as the opening of the Suez Canal (1869), and the Noordzeekanaal (1876). The middle part of the period has been referred to as the Mini Golden Age and the glorious Age of Capital.[15] In 1815 Amsterdam had 180,000 inhabitants, in 1850 224,000 and by the end of the nineteenth century 510,000. Rotterdam actually tripled its population between 1850 and 1900.[16]

The increases in population prior to 1875 were absorbed into a city that had not grown in size since the seventeenth century.[17] Between 1750 and 1850, the amount of families living in Amsterdam increased by 20,000 to 40,500, while the amount of houses only increased by 900, to 27,600. A doubling of the population thus had to be accommodated in an (almost) unchanged housing stock. Only after the introduction of the *Fortification Law* (*Vestingwet*) in 1875 could the population growth once more be accommodated in (legal) urban expansions outside the fortifications.[18]

Population density in the Jordaan increased between 1859 and 1889 by more than 50 per cent, from 830 to 1,265 inhabitants per hectare.[19] Cheap dwellings were constructed in the courtyards of existing city blocks. This meant that 40 to 60 per cent of the dwellings lacked the required amount of sunlight.[20] In Rotterdam the percentage of the dwellings with more than ten inhabitants increased from 43 per cent in 1840, to 70 per cent by 1849.[21] Despite this process of intensification, street plans were relatively unchanged due to their 'inertia': a high level of resistance from

15
Wintershoven, L., *Demografisch eeuwboek Amsterdam: Ontwikkelingen tussen 1900 en 2000* (Amsterdam: dRO, 2000); Hobsbawm, E., *The Age of Capital: 1848–1875* (London: Weidenfeld and Nicholson, 1975).

16
Cammen, H. van der, and L. de Klerk, *Ruimtelijke Ordening: Van grachtengordel tot Vinex-wijk* (Utrecht: Het Spectrum, 2003), 45.

17
Martin, M. and C. Wagenaar, 'Stadsverfraaing en stadsuitbreiding', in: E. Taverne and I. Visser (eds.), *Stedebouw: De geschiedenis van de stad in de Nederlanden van 1500 tot heden* (Nijmegen: SUN, 1993), 124–129, 124.

4 Living conditions at the beginning of the twentieth century in the Joden Houttuinen, Amsterdam (Gemeentearchief Amsterdam).

an established structure. Structures were often rebuilt to accommodate a higher density within the same street layout, illustrating the robustness of the urban ground plan (*stadsplattegrond*).[22]

Growth Pains

This tendency for higher densities represented one of the factors that led to serious health problems in industrializing cities. The first cholera pandemic in Europe reached London and Paris in 1832. In London, the disease claimed 6,500 victims, in Paris 20,000 of a population of 650,000. Throughout France 100,000 people died of cholera during the pandemic. In 1866, a fourth cholera pandemic led to 21,000 victims in Amsterdam. 5 Just as in 1664 when the bubonic plague struck Amsterdam, the majority of the victims were in the most densely populated areas.[23]

In the second half of the nineteenth century people started to reconsider and criticize the poor living conditions of overcrowded cities. People living in disadvantaged areas with high population densities suffered from the combined effects of a lack of access to daylight, fresh air, clean water and adequate sewerage.[24] Established in 1844 in London, the *Society for improving the*

18
Klerk, L. de, *De modernisering van de stad 1850–1914: De opkomst van de planmatige stadsontwikkeling in Nederland* (Rotterdam: NAi Publishers, 2008), 15. Exception in Amsterdam is the Singelgracht area, added between 1820 and 1860; see Plas, G. van der, 'Amsterdam 1750–1850: van stadsstaat naar hoofdstad', in: Taverne and Visser, *Stedebouw*, op. cit. (note17), 148–159, 159.

19
Based on the censuses of 1859 and 1889. Sources: Laloli, 'Beter wonen?', op. cit. (note 13); and www.amsterdamhistorie.nl, accessed August 2008.

20
Plas, 'Amsterdam 1750–1850', op. cit. (note 18), 150.

21
Cammen and De Klerk, *Ruimtelijke Ordening*, op. cit. (note 16), 45.

22
Rutte, *A Landscape*, op. cit. (note 5), 48; Heeling, Meyer and Westrik, *Het ontwerp*, op. cit. (note 9); Plas, 'Amsterdam 1750–1850', op. cit. (note 18), 149.

23
Moll, 'Vuile teringstad', op. cit. (note 14).

24
Ruijter, P. de, *Voor volkshuisvesting en stedebouw* (Utrecht: Matrijs, 1987), 34–45.

5 1866 cholera map of Amsterdam on which the number of deaths per neighbourhood is registered (Hameleers 2002: 24).

condition of the labouring classes, an organization dealing with public health issues, exerted considerable influence throughout Europe. This was followed by the British *Public Health Act* in 1848. This regulation, and the investments in public works in England (water, sewer, parks, pavement), served as an example for many cities.[25] In Amsterdam, the architect J.H. Leliman designed several dwellings for the working class inspired by the activities of this society.[26] Still, such charitable initiatives were exceptions, as financial returns remained the driving force in town planning. By the onset of the second half of the nineteenth century, a mere 1 per cent of new buildings consisted of such social housing. They remained 'islands in the sea of slums'.[27]

At the same time, more centrally ruled countries implemented grand classicist schemes such as the boulevards in Paris (1851) and the Ringstrasse in Vienna (1857).[28] The oldest parts of Paris were occupied at a density of almost 1,000 inhabitants per hectare.[29] The poor living conditions in the overcrowded city were not only a problem for the poor, as diseases and criminality originating in poor areas quickly spread to the rest of the city.

25 Ibid., 40; Rådberg, J., *Doktrin och täthet i svenskt stadsbyggande 1875–1975* (Stockholm: Statens råd för byggnadsforskning, 1988), 106.

26 De Ruijter, *Voor volkshuisvesting*, op. cit. (note 24), 41.

27 Ibid., 42.

28 Taverne, E., *De wortels van de contemporaine stad*, Reader Architectuur- en Stedenbouwgeschiedenis (Groningen: Rijksuniversiteit Groningen, 2000); Castex, J., J-C. Depaule and P. Panerai, *De rationele stad: Van bouwblok tot wooneenheid* (Amsterdam: SUN, 2003), originally published in 1977 as *Formes urbaines: de l'ilot a la barre*.

29 Rådberg, *Doktrin*, op. cit. (note 25), 40.

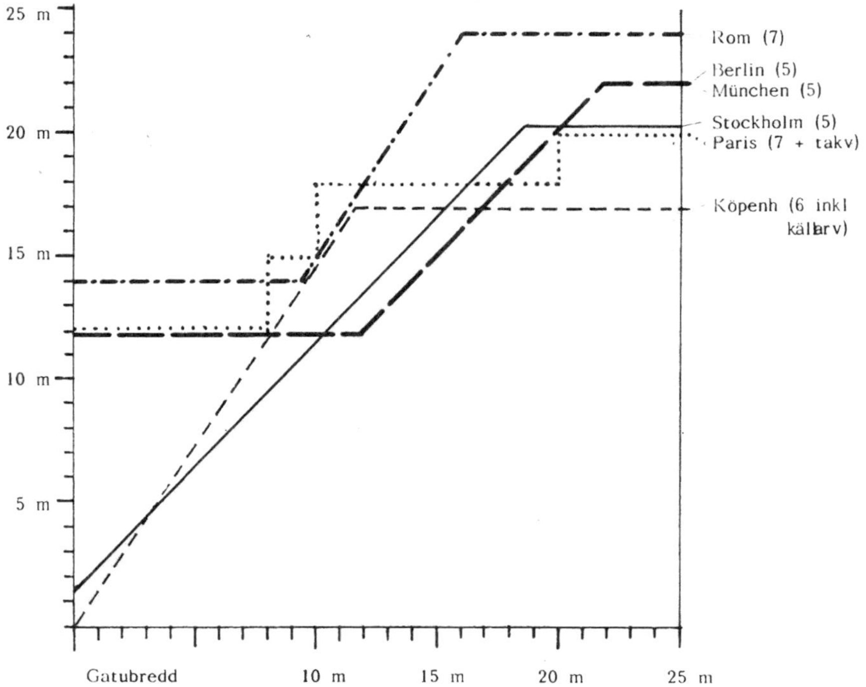

6 Maximum building height in relation to street width in some European cities in 1889; the maximum number of storeys is in brackets (Rådberg 1988: 43).

According to the report from 1855, published by the Royal Institute of Engineers on the request of king Willem III, 'diseases originating from workers districts have a wide influence on the surroundings, and affect all classes, spreading a scourge of disaster to the houses of the more civilized'.[30]

Squalid living conditions affected large segments of society and led to riots and social unrest.[31] Later, after the First World War, this fear was evident in England from the deliberations leading to the Housing and Town Planning Act: 'The money we are going to spend on housing is an insurance against Bolshevism and Revolution.'[32] In 1870, jhr. mr. D.O. Engelen in his dissertation *Over arbeiderswoningen* clearly underlined the interdependence of productivity and good housing in the Netherlands: 'One is starting to recognize that the worker, like the machine, needs a good dwelling to be able to produce well.'[33]

30 Ottens, E., 'De aanloop naar de Woningwet: "de holen der mensen…"', in: J. Keesom (ed.), *Wonen. Woning. Wet. Wij wonene – 100 jaar Woningwet* (Amsterdam: Stedelijke Woningdienst Amsterdam, 2000), 9–40, 24.

31 Hall, P., *Cities of Tomorrow* (Oxford: Blackwell Publishers, 1996), 14–46.

32 Ibid., 71.

33 Cammen and De Klerk, *Ruimtelijke Ordening*, op. cit. (note 16), 74.

Regularism versus Laissez-Faire

In Germany, by the end of the nineteenth century, a scientific approach was increasingly the norm when dealing with the problems of hygiene and social misery in overcrowded cities. Reinhard Baumeister advocated such an approach. With a modern perspective on urbanism he aimed to link the artistic, technical, and economic aspects of city development.[34] He argued in his book *Stadterweiterungen in technischer, baupolizeilicher und wirtschaftlicher Beziehung* (*Urban expansions from a technical, regulatory and economic perspective*, 1876) that municipalities should take an active role in coordinating development. He argued that decisions should be supported

34 Rådberg, *Doktrin*, op. cit. (note 25), 47.

by statistical research, comparative density figures, and systematic survey methods covering population, real estate, and traffic conditions.[35]

35
De Ruijter, *Voor volkshuisvesting*, op. cit. (note 24);
Rådberg, *Doktrin*, op. cit. (note 25), 47.

Baumeister, and his colleague Joseph Stübben, adhered to a rather pragmatic approach to city development. This combined the need for access to daylight and fresh air with practical economic considerations. Although they believed that low-rise solutions resulted in improved living conditions, they accepted the need to increase density in cities. Single-family dwellings were not an option for many people. Standards dealing with the maximum building height, lot size and the distance between buildings came into force to counter some of the negative effects of the increase in density. ❻ Baumeister introduced a normative building ordinance (*Normalbauverordenung*) in 1880 that stipulated a maximum of four storeys and prescribed that the building height should never exceed the street width. Although such rules had earlier been applied during the rebuilding of London (1667), in Paris (eighteenth century) and Barcelona (1859), Baumeister and Stübben can be regarded as the first to systematically engage with urban density (directly and indirectly) in their analyses of the problems of existing cities and prescriptions for new expansion plans. Density does not yet play a role as a norm in specific plans, but is more a tool used in the process. Later, in plans such as the AUP in Amsterdam, density becomes a guiding framework for the plans themselves.

Baumeister and Stübben's convictions that healthy cities should be realized by public authorities required public intervention and land ownership that did not correspond to the views of the conservative-liberal elite in Dutch cities. They perceived entrepreneurs as being the leading force of city development and private property a sacred institution. The state should confine itself to sorting out street width, building alignment and some minimal guidelines covering housing hygiene standards.[36] Two different expansion plans for Amsterdam can illustrate the tension between state-managed and market-oriented development plans. ❼ ❽ One was drafted by Jacobus van Niftrik (1867) and the other by Jan Kalff (1877). Van Niftrik's plan included plenty of public space, a strict division between social classes, and a functional zoning that did not consider the existing distribution of land ownership.[37] In addition, the plan stipulated that the street width should be at least 1 to 1.5 times the height of the highest building to guarantee enough daylight inside the buildings and in the streets.[38] However, these aspects made the plan too expensive and an alternative was drawn up by Kalff, the director of public works in Amsterdam.

Kalff's plan retained the existing pattern of streets and, in contrast to the plan made by Van Niftrik, it respected the distribution of land ownership. The word *expropriation* was not mentioned once during the process, and private developers were frequently able to adapt the street layout to accommodate their own preferences.[39] According to the architect Willem Kromhout, it rendered 'narrow, long and depressing streets', known today as De Pijp (the pipe).[40] The population density in De Pijp was approximately

36
Ibid., 78;
Wagenaar, M., 'Amsterdam 1860–1940: Een bedrijvige stad', in: Taverne and Visser, *Stedebouw*, op. cit. (note17), 218–234, 220.

37
Dijkstra et al., *Atlas Amsterdam*, op. cit. (note 7).

38
De Ruijter, *Voor volkshuisvesting*, op. cit. (note 24), 51.

39
Wagenaar, 'Amsterdam 1860–1940', op. cit. (note 36), 228.

40
De Ruijter, *Voor volkshuisvesting*, op. cit. (note 24), 51. The word *pijpenla* in Dutch is used to describe a long narrow room.
In this case De Pijp is used to describe an area with long narrow streets.

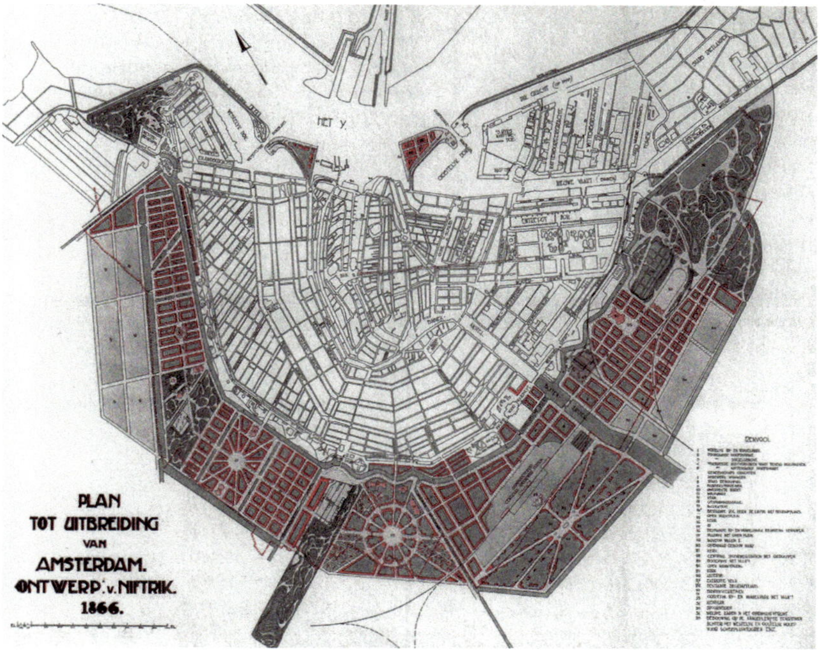

7 Expansion plan for Amsterdam drawn by Van Niftrik in 1866 (De Klerk, 2008: 258).

8 Expansion plan for Amsterdam drawn by Kalff in 1877 (De Klerk, 2008: 259).

700 inhabitants per hectare; less than the Jordaan, but still three times more than in the Grachtengordel.[41] The more aesthetic elements of town planning were largely ignored by Kalff's plan. Almost 60 years later, Cornelis Van Eesteren described it as:

> ... a plan, that by its lack of character is typical of the period of cultural collapse in which it was developed ... The tradition of city development from the seventeenth and eighteenth centuries has been lost; any form of spatial guidance from the state is absent; urbanism is left up to developers and other private enterprises, speculation entered the urban planning process. Neighbourhoods such as 'De Pijp' and the not so very poetic 'Dichterbuurt' are witnesses in stone of the societal and artistic incapability of its time.[42]

In the light of the economic developments of the second half of the nineteenth century, one could interpret the Van Niftrik Plan as expressing the self-secured bourgeoisie ambitions of an ever-expanding economy (The Age of Capital), while Kalff's plan, in contrast, illustrates the choice for a less costly and more pragmatic plan at the beginning of what was to become the Great Depression of 1875–1895.[43]

The Vondelparkbuurt in Amsterdam is a good example of a development where enough means were present to let aesthetic considerations play a central role. This new part of Amsterdam was targeting a different segment of the urban population. In 1864, eight wealthy inhabitants of Amsterdam took the initiative to create a park on the south-western edge of the city. The only urban green area present in the older parts of the city, the Plantage, was to a large extent built upon in 1857.[44] The sale of the lots adjacent to the Vondelpark yielded sufficient profit to commission garden architect Jan David Zocher to design the park. Only the wealthy segment of the city could afford to undertake this kind of privatized urban development. The expansion also had a very explicit programme. Houses were permitted, while workshops or factories were forbidden. The initial development, to only build large villas that would compete with the attractive rural settlements of the immediate surroundings (Gooi, Kennemerland), was never realized because of the higher development costs.[45] Even so, population density in the Vondelparkbuurt was only between 190 and 225 inhabitants per hectare, which was less than a third of the density in De Pijp.[46] It is important, however, not to forget that the Vondelparkbuurt represented an exception. The norm for Amsterdam was the continuing speculation that dominated the housing market in the city, leading to the related problems of overcrowding and poor hygiene.

By the end of the nineteenth century, aesthetic ideas on town planning began to gain influence, especially in Austria and Germany. In 1889 Camillo Sitte published a small polemic entitled *Der Städtebau nach seinen Kunstlerischen Grundsätzen* (*City planning according to its artistic principles*).

41 Based on the dwelling density as mentioned on the 1956 map *Woningdichtheden* ('dwelling densities') from the Dienst der Publieke Werken, Department Stadsontwikkelin in Hameleers, M. (ed.), *Kaarten van Amsterdam 1866–2000* (Bussum: Uitgeverij THOTH, 2002), 270. The dwelling density of the oldest parts of De Pijp was between 190 and 220 dwellings per hectare, and the occupancy rate of Amsterdam in 1958 was 3.5.

42 Municipality of Amsterdam, *Algemeen Uitbreidingsplan van Amsterdam (AUP): Nota van toelichting* (Amsterdam: Stadsdrukkerij Amsterdam, 1934), 7.

43 Hobsbawm, E., *The Age of Empire: 1875–1914* (London: Weidenfeld and Nicholson, 1987).

44 Dijkstra et al., *Atlas Amsterdam*, op. cit. (note 7).

45 Wagenaar, 'Amsterdam 1860–1940', op. cit. (note 36), 228–230.

46 Based on the dwelling density as mentioned on the 1956 map *Woningdichtheden* ('dwelling densities') from the Dienst der Publieke Werken, Department Stadsontwikkeling in Hameleers, *Kaarten*. The dwelling density in the Vondelparkbuurt was between 55 and 65 dwellings per hectare. The occupancy rate of Amsterdam in 1958 was 3.5.

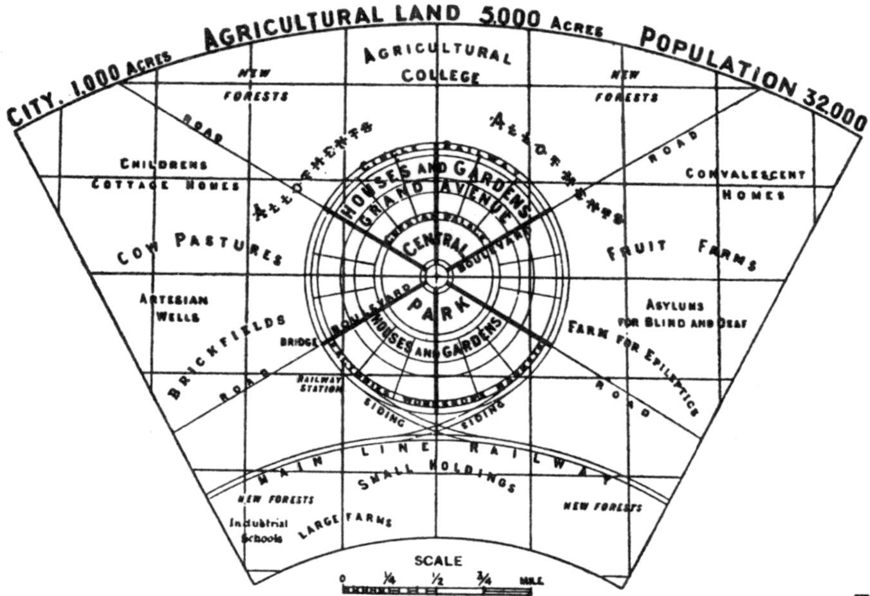

9 Diagram of the Garden City by Ebenezer Howard, 1898 (Kostof, 1991: 203).

This book made him the leading proponent of a new school in town planning.[47] Sitte argued that town planning should be more than only land-use planning whereby streets and lots are determined. In this polemic he expressed his concern about city development leading too often to the creation of wide and straight streets accompanied by monotonous buildings of uniform height. Sitte instead believed in compact urban patterns with narrow winding streets. The ideas of Sitte immediately had an impact in the Netherlands, leading to a discussion about the role of the engineer and the artist in city development.

47 De Ruijter, *Voor volkshuisvesting*, op. cit. (note 24), 53, 162–164.

At about the same time, in 1899 in England, Ebenezer Howard founded the Garden City Association to promote the 'Social City'.[48] This new, decentralized city offered an alternative to the overcrowded and unhealthy cities with their lack of natural environments. In the book *Garden Cities of Tomorrow: A Peaceful Path to Real Reform*, published in 1898, Howard explained his ideas about the ideal town. 9 Garden cities should have a maximum of 30,000 inhabitants and should be built on an area of 1,000 acres (approximately 400 ha). This translates to a population density of 75 inhabitants per hectare. The most important amenities are in clusters at the centre of each town. Housing is located in spacious settings surrounding the centre and industry on the outer ring.

48 Rådberg, *Doktrin*, op. cit. (note 25), 54–57.

State-Managed Capitalism (1900–1979)

Around the turn of the century city development became increasingly influenced by the ideas of the 'Healthy City' (Baumeister), the 'Beautiful City' (Sitte), and the 'Social City' (Howard). In response to rampant

10 Second version of Plan Zuid (1917), Amsterdam, by H.P. Berlage (Taverne 1993: 233).

speculation and poor public health in the city, and the fears of the powerful working-class movement that since 1890 was becoming a factor that could not be ignored, the Housing Act (Woningwet, 1901) and the Long Land Lease Regulation (Erfpachtregeling, 1896) came into force.[49] Through the Housing Act it became not only possible to plan land use on a large scale, but, at the same time, it offered public institutions the means to plan space in a manner that was both socially and aesthetically responsible. Public or semi-public services (local Government Departments and Housing Associations) became not only responsible for the layout of streets and the required infrastructure, but also for large social housing developments. This constituted a qualitative break with the past. At the beginning of the twentieth century, population density fell throughout Amsterdam. This was caused by a combination of a massive home building programme, the demolition of small slum dwellings during the first decades of the century, and a decrease in the occupancy rate from an average of 4.4 persons per dwelling in 1900 to 3.6 by 1938.[50]

Amsterdam's Plan Zuid 10, designed during the first decade of the twentieth century by Hendrik Petrus Berlage,[51] was one of the first examples whereby a public street plan and the architecture of the lots and the buildings represented a synthesis of public planning policy and art, a *Gesamtskunstwerk*.[52] Unlike any previous city expansion plan, it was not a pragmatic exercise using entrepreneurial principles. Plan Zuid embraced both the aesthetic and the social dimensions of Sitte and Howard. The quality of the public space, improved housing for the working class, more schools, and better recreational opportunities; all were central to the plan: 'Plan Zuid was to be the first large-scale demonstration of a modern twentieth-century city, based on social-democratic ideals of social justice and cultural elevation.'[53] Dwellings were larger and occupied by fewer people. More public space had been added (wide streets), and the open spaces within the building

49 De Ruijter, *Voor volkshuisvesting*, op. cit. (note 24); Hall, *Cities*, op. cit. (note 31); Heeling et al., *Het ontwerp*, op. cit. (note 9); De Klerk, *De modernisering*, op. cit. (note 18).

50 Wintershoven, *Demografisch eeuwboek Amsterdam*, op. cit. (note 15).

51 1st plan 1905, 2nd plan 1917.

52 Wagenaar, 'Amsterdam 1860–1940', op. cit. (note 36), 232.

53 Heeling et al., *Het ontwerp*, op. cit. (note 9), 44.

lots were more spacious through private and communal gardens. However, although the density of Plan Zuid with 315 inhabitants per hectare was less than half the density of De Pijp (700 inhabitants per hectare), it was still four times higher than the ideal of 75 inhabitants per hectare proposed by Howard 20 years earlier.[54]

The Garden City Movement

The ideas of Howard and the Garden City Movement were also very influential in alternative housing developments built in other countries during this period. In Germany and France this led to the founding of the Gartenstadtgesellschaft and the Association des Cité Jardins.[55] Despite the call by some for similar changes in the Netherlands, such as by Bruinwold Riedel in his book *Tuinsteden* of 1906, no such association was established here. The architect Jan Leliman explained in 1908 at the opening of an exhibition of the German *Gartenstadtgesellschaft* in Amsterdam the numerous reasons for this. According to him, the problems in Dutch cities were not quite as bad or as widespread as in many other European cities. In addition, the decentralized tradition and legal autonomy of municipalities had made it rather difficult to establish new towns. Last but not least, Dutch planners were not convinced that the ideas of Howard fulfilled a real need.[56] Ideas like those expressed in the regional plan developed by the *Tuinstadcommissie* (the garden city commission) in Amsterdam, which included garden cities located 10 to 20 km from the existing city, were not taken seriously until the 1960s when the policy of new towns was introduced through *The Second National Policy Document on Spatial Planning*.[57]

Some of the ideas of the Garden City Movement did, however, influence Dutch practice. Especially the work of Raymond Unwin, a socialist and self-educated planner, was influential. The Arts and Crafts ideals of William Morris and the historical references of Middle Age communities were combined by Unwin with analytical studies of urban form and land use. The garden suburbs in Letchworth and Hampstead, designed together with Barry Parker, are the most well known. Unwin, best known for *Town Planning in Practice* (1909) and his pamphlet *Nothing Gained by Overcrowding!* (1912), set a norm of 12 dwellings to the net acre (30 dwellings per hectare, excluding all roads) and argued that it was cheaper to build in such low densities. He demonstrated this by comparing two schemes with single-family housing with densities of respectively 30 and 60 homes per hectare.[58] The most important difference, besides the number of dwellings, was the price for infrastructure (streets) needed to access the dwellings. In the first scheme (30 dwellings per hectare) almost £5,000 was needed to construct the street plan, and in the second scheme (60 dwellings per hectare) £10,000. As the total land price (for 5 ha) in both schemes was similar (£5,000), the costs per dwelling would have been £67 and £50 respectively. In other words, the denser scheme was cheaper when measured per dwelling, but the price of

54 Based on the dwelling density as mentioned on the 1956 map *Woningdichtheden* ('dwelling densities') from the Dienst der Publieke Werken, Department Stadsontwikkeling in Hameleers, *Kaarten*, and the average occupancy in 1958 of 3.5 in Amsterdam from Wintershoven, *Demografisch eeuwboek Amsterdam*, op. cit. (note 15).

55 De Ruijter, *Voor volkshuisvesting*, op. cit. (note 24), 184–185.

56 De Ruijter, *Voor volkshuisvesting*, op. cit. (note 24), 187.

57 VROM, *Tweede nota over de ruimtelijke ordening* (The Hague: Ministry of Housing, Physical Planning and the Environment, 1966).

58 Unwin, R., *Nothing Gained by Overcrowding! How the Garden City Type of Development May Benefit Both Owner and Occupier* (Westminster: P.S. King & Son, 1912), 6–8.

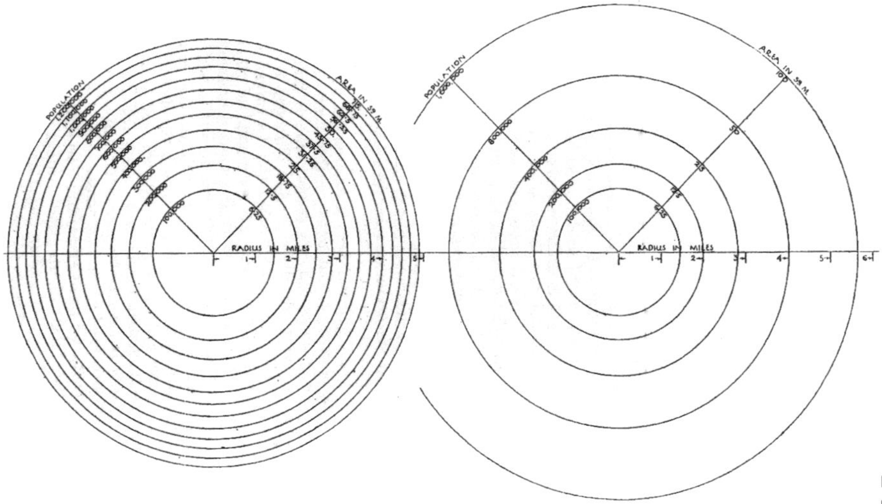

11 Diagram showing the relatively small increase of radius required to provide area sufficient to house a growing population from an average of 25 people per acre (Unwin 1912: 15).

the lots (per m^2) were in the less-dense scheme only 20 pence while in the second scheme this was 30 pence. Unwin argued, therefore, that the economic results of overcrowding are less favourable when the price per square meter of land is considered.[59] Another argument often used against low densities, refuted by Unwin in his pamphlet, was that it took up more land and, therefore, caused an increase in commuter traffic. Unwin used the radius and the surface of a circle to argue that when the radius of a circle was doubled, and thus the distance from the circumference to the centre of that circle, the surface of 'land' added is quadrupled. 11

59 Ibid., 3–10.

Scientific Design

Mathematical reasoning of this kind was used by more urban planners in this period. In the 1920s in Germany, Anton Hoenig is an exponent of this approach. Others included L.H.J. Angenot, Aad Heimans, the people associated with SAR (Stichting Architectuur Research) in the Netherlands (1950s–1960s) and Leslie Martin and Lionel March in England (1960s–1970s). The work of Hoenig is particularly interesting as he introduced the concept of spaciousness (Weitraumigkeit) in an attempt to measure 'urban quality'.[60] This concept stemmed from the Berlin Building Ordinance, passed in 1925. 12 This ordinance defined five different building categories based on building height (*Stockwerksanzahl*; from two to five storeys), and lot coverage (*Ausnutzung der Grundstücks*; from 10 to 60 per cent). For each category the built density (*Ausnutzungsziffer*) could be calculated as the product of building height and lot coverage.

60 Rådberg, *Doktrin*, op. cit. (note 25), 67–72.

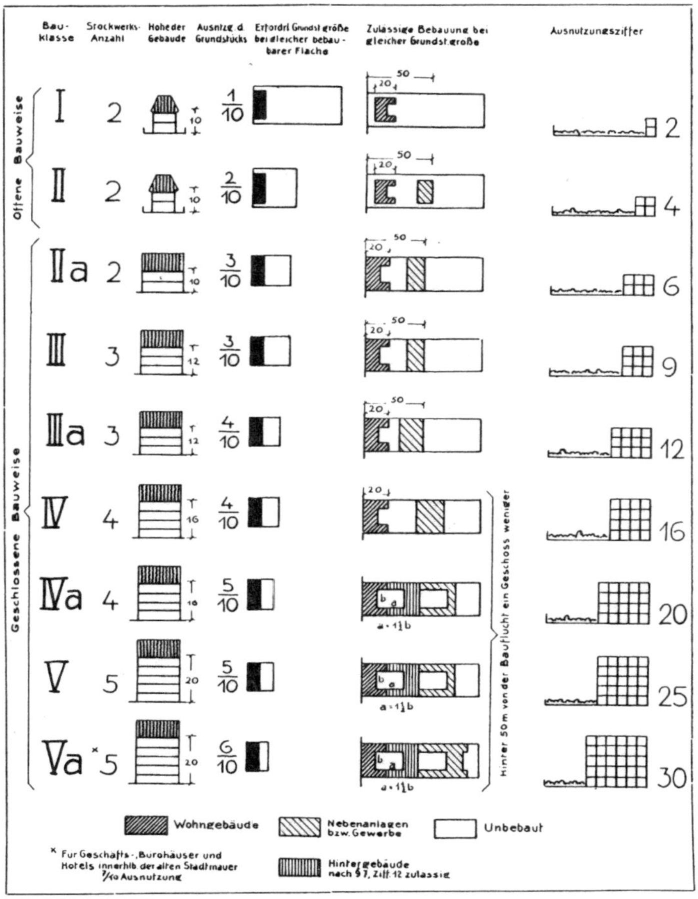

12 Building categories within the construction ordinance of Berlin effectuated in 1925 (Rådberg 1988: 69).

Hoenig used the same definitions given in the building ordinance, but added spaciousness, defined as the ratio between the non-built land and the total amount of building stock. In the article *Baudichte und Weitraumigkeit*, Hoenig discusses the relation between urban density, spaciousness and building height.[61] Put another way, spaciousness expresses the amount of non-built land that each dwelling has at its disposal. Hoenig showed that the lowest and highest building densities in Berlin's building ordinance differ by a factor 15, but when spaciousness is added to the equation, the densities differ by a factor 35. Each square metre of floor area in the highest category (*Bauklasse Va*) has 0.13 m^2 of non-built space available, while in the lowest category (*Bauklasse I*), the figure is 4.5 m^2. Hoenig argued further that quality can only be guaranteed when each square metre of floor area is at least compensated for by one square metre of non-built land. This applied only to the first three categories of Berlin's building ordinance, all of which concerned single-family housing.

In 1933 Le Corbusier presented an alternative to the compact nineteenth-century city and the spacious garden city: *La Ville Radieuse*. This was a model for a 'Green City' with plenty of open space, light, sun and fresh air. Densities were highe – up to 1,000 inhabitants per hectare, comparable

61 Hoenig, A., 'Baudichte und Weitraumigkeit', *Baugilde* 10 1928, 713–715. 'Building density and spaciousness' (authors' suggestion). All measures in the article relate to the lots only and thus do not take into consideration the streets surrounding them.

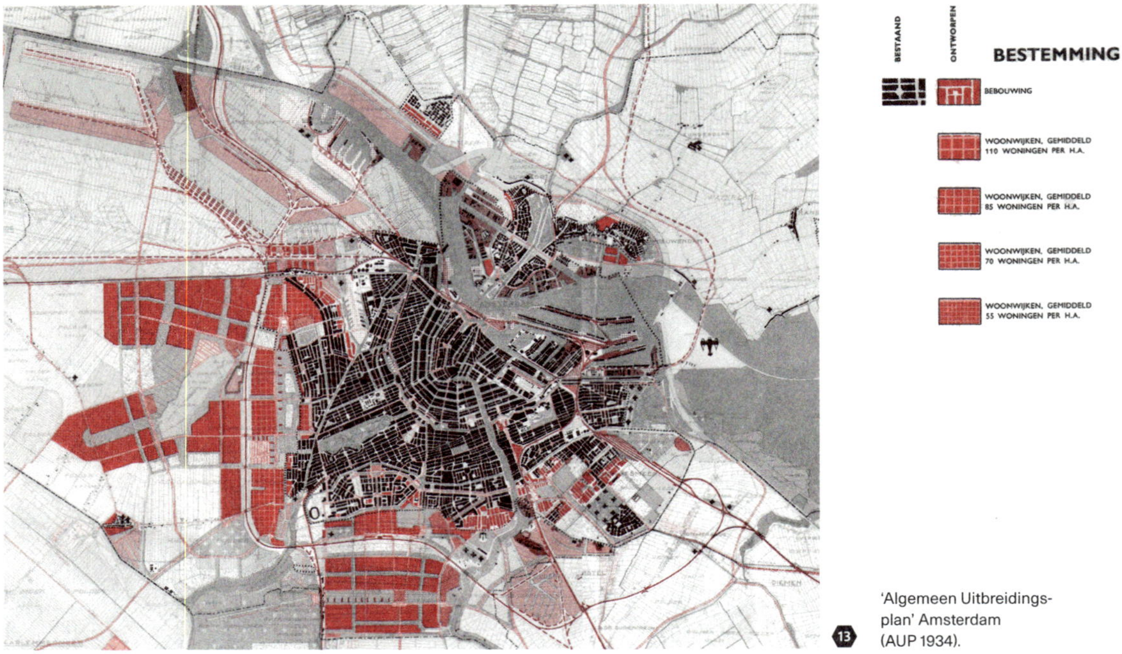

13 'Algemeen Uitbreidings-plan' Amsterdam (AUP 1934).

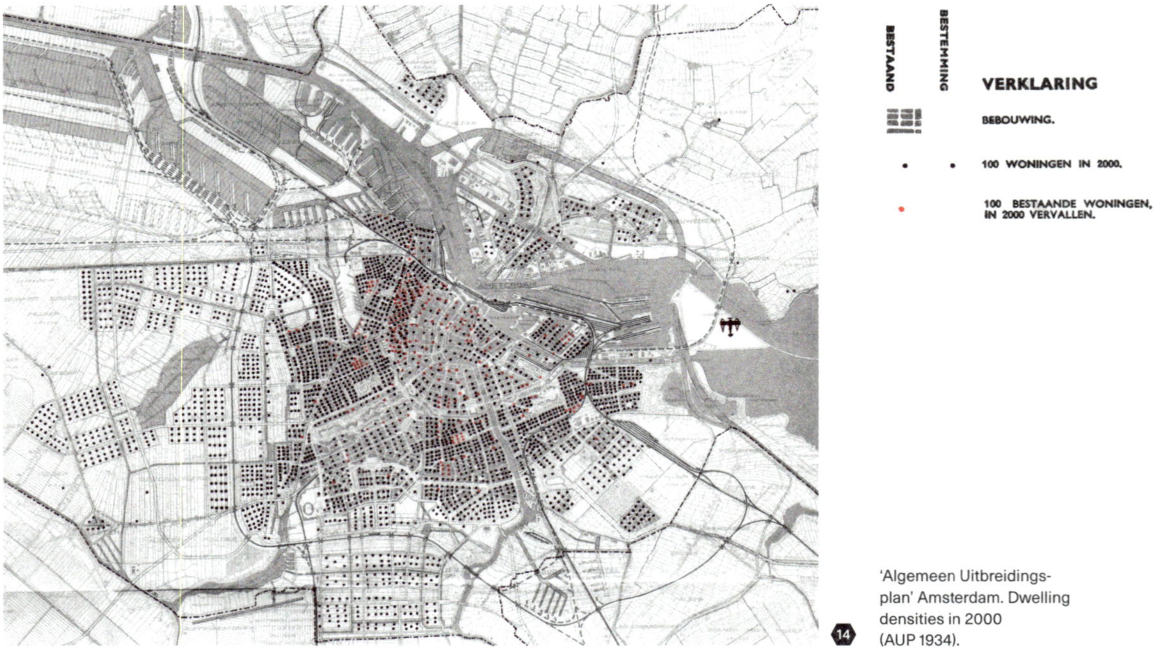

14 'Algemeen Uitbreidings-plan' Amsterdam. Dwelling densities in 2000 (AUP 1934).

to the density of the Jordaan 50 years earlier, which had often been characterized as being heavily overcrowded. The rationale for such a high density was to minimize land use and distances travelled. High-rise buildings were used to realize such high densities. Hoenig used the work of Le Corbusier to illustrate the relationship between density and spaciousness. Le Corbusier's plan for Paris (*Plan Voisin*) consisted of buildings of 60 storeys and 95 per cent of the lots left open. The built density (*Ausnutzungsziffer*) achieved in this way was comparable to the highest building category in Berlin's building ordinance (30). The spaciousness, however, of *Plan Voisin* was three times higher than in Berlin (0.32 compared to 0.13) and, Hoenig concluded, when high densities had to be achieved, better qualities could be realized with high-rise buildings.

This scientific ideal of analysis in planning was important to the international movement CIAM (*Congrès Internationaux d'Architecture Moderne*), founded in 1928 at the initiative of Le Corbusier and Siegfried Gideon in La Sarraz, Switzerland. The CIAM perceived the urban landscape as the sum of collective functions of a city. *Die Funktionelle Stadt* was not determined aesthetically, but functionally.[62] Cornelis van Eesteren, chairman of CIAM from 1930 until 1947, developed a model for the modern functional city in Amsterdam: the General Extension Plan (*Algemeen Uitbreidingsplan Amsterdam* or *AUP*).[63] 13 14 Van Eesteren, with Th.K. van Lohuizen, did not seek to realize an ornamental plan with a formal layout based on intuition or artistic inspiration, but aimed instead to create the appropriate conditions for the modern city based on scientific methods. The AUP was to become a model for the modern functional city. This model included such elements as housing, amenities, industry, roads and parks, all developed based on their own intrinsic rules and ideals. Most of the housing types reflect functionalist views on living; they are oriented towards the sun, have access to fresh air and good housing schemes, and are characterized by the well-known open block structures.[64] Prior to the urban plan, Van Lohuizen undertook a thorough survey that was used to predict the population growth of Amsterdam. A survey of this nature was comparable to the statistical research and demographic prognoses mentioned by Baumeister at the end of the nineteenth century, the scientific method advocated by Hoenig, and, even earlier, to the work on the 1860 expansion of Barcelona by Cerda. Patrick Geddes's call for 'survey before plan' had also influenced Dutch planning through Unwin's 1909 book *Town Planning in Practice.*[65]

Van Lohuizen estimated that the population of Amsterdam would not exceed one million inhabitants by 2000, and satellite cities, as advocated by the Garden City Movement, would not be necessary. This methodology adhered to prevailing optimistic ideas about science and its ability to predict social developments using extensive, often quantitative analysis of human behaviour and socioeconomic phenomena. The exact area required for the extension could be calculated with precision based on the number of houses required (111,200) and the preferred urban densities, defined as the number of dwellings per hectare.[66] Adhering to the ideas of the Garden City Movement, the initial idea was to provide single-family homes on a large scale, including homes for the working class. However, to prevent excessive sprawl and to keep the price of land acceptable, a mix of housing types was suggested. Research into different lot patterns had shown that within a density of 70 dwellings per hectare, 50 to 60 per cent of the dwellings could still be realized as single family homes. With high land prices adjacent to the existing

62
Rådberg, *Doktrin*, op. cit. (note 25), 115–124; Taverne, *De wortels*, op. cit. (note 28), 64; Cammen and De Klerk, *Ruimtelijke Ordening*, op. cit. (note 16), 137.

63
Municipality of Amsterdam, *Algemeen Uitbreidingsplan*, op. cit. (note 42).

64
Engel, H. and E. van Velzen, 'De vorm van de stad: Nederland na 1945', in: Taverne and Visser, *Stedebouw*, op. cit. (note17), 276–282; Hereijgers, A. and E. van Velzen, *De naoorlogse stad, een hedendaagse ontwerpopgave* (Rotterdam: NAi Publishers, 2001); Venema, H., 'Bos en Lommer', in: S. Komossa et al. (eds.), *Atlas van het Hollandse bouwblok* (Bussum: Uitgeverij THOTH, 2002), 112–123.

65
Cammen and De Klerk, *Ruimtelijke Ordening*, op. cit. (note 16); De Ruijter, *Voor volkshuisvesting*, op. cit. (note 24), 200.

66
Municipality of Amsterdam, *Algemeen Uitbreidingsplan*, op. cit. (note 42), 83.

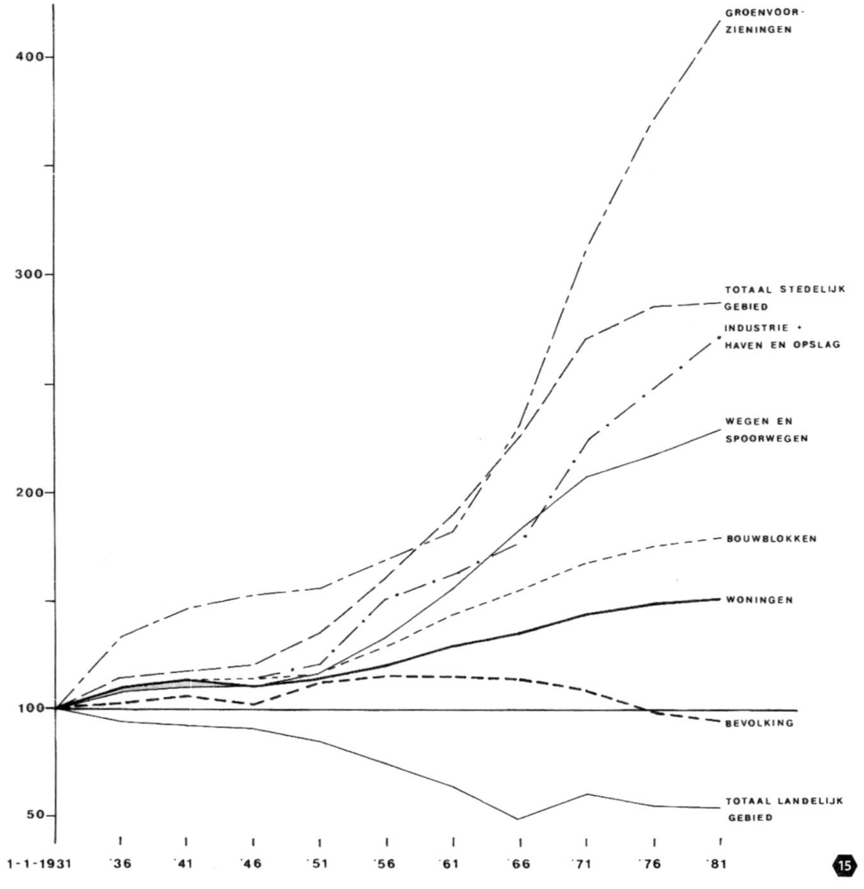

Relative growth of land use in Amsterdam from 1931 to 1981 (1931 = 100) (Hellinga & de Ruijter 1985: 128).

city, densities were higher on central locations (85–110 dwellings per hectare), and lower in the more peripheral areas (55–70 dwellings per hectare).[67] This is probably the first time in Dutch planning practice that density was used in such a prescriptive, normative fashion.

Despite the studies carried out in advance of the realization of the AUP, the actual densities turned out to be lower than were envisaged. The peripheral areas had between 45 and 60 homes per hectare instead of 55 to 70, and there were fewer single-family units than originally planned (32 per cent instead of 50 to 60 per cent).[68] As a result, the envisioned mix of dwellings and commercial activities (shops and small-scale industry) was never actualized for the simple reason that there were not enough people living in the area. The housing shortage just after the Second World War further decreased the amount of commercial activities in favour of dwellings. The idea of concentrated shopping areas, dominant since the 1950s, caused a further specialization in separate living and shopping areas.

There were two important reasons for the fall in densities in the AUP.[69] (15) First, the rate of occupancy had fallen much faster than expected. The expected number of 3.37 in 2000 had already been reached by 1960. In 2000, the rate of occupancy was 1.98.[70] Based only on this decline, space

67
Based on the assumed occupancy rate of 3.37 from Ibid., 82.

68
Based on the dwelling density as mentioned on the 1956 map *Woningdichtheden* ('dwelling densities') from the Dienst der Publieke Werken, Department Stadsontwikkeling in Hameleers, *Kaarten*, 270. The dwelling density in Geuzenveld-Slotermeer was between 45 and 60 dwellings per hectare and the occupancy rate in Amsterdam in 1958 was 3.5. In Slotermeer, 32 per cent of the dwellings were single-family houses, 11 per cent consisted of two-storey houses (so called duplexes) and 57 per cent were multi-family apartments. From Cammen and De Klerk, *Ruimtelijke Ordening*, op. cit. (note 16), 144.

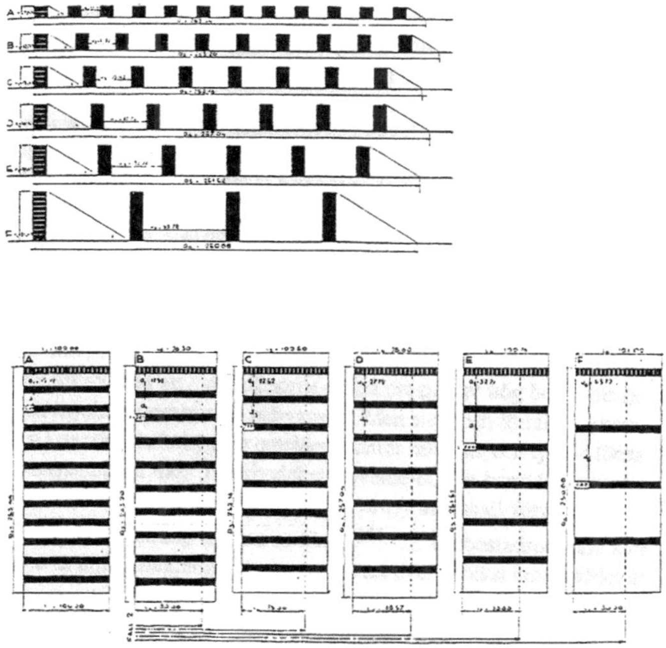

16 Scheme by Gropius (1930), illustrating the relation between building height, sun angle, land use and built density (Rådberg 1988: 83).

consumption for housing rose by 70 per cent from 1960 to 2000. Secondly, economic growth caused a general increase in space consumption. Houses became larger, with wider lots (*beukmaat*), leading to an increase in land use. For instance, single-family housing units in Slotermeer (part of the AUP) had lots of 5.4 m wide, instead of the originally calculated 4.5 m in the AUP. Also, more cars, public buildings (schools), cultural and health facilities, office and industrial areas, and public green space (sport facilities and parks) were needed than had been projected in the plan.

The lower densities in the AUP, in combination with enormous transformations of the housing stock in the centre of Amsterdam and the process of 'city forming' (decrease of housing and increase of shops and work places), made new large-scale expansion areas necessary. Parts of North Amsterdam (Buikslotermeer) and, later, the south-east of the city (Bijlmermeer) were developed in the 1960s with a large proportion of the dwellings in high-rise buildings. The realization of the Bijlmermeer, a vertical garden city planned by Siegfried Nassuth and the municipality of Amsterdam, was the last modernist project in the Netherlands and represented one of the best examples of a plan in which the CIAM ideals and the Green City of Le Corbusier and Walter Gropius were realized.[71] Both had earlier researched the advantages of high-rise buildings. Between 1928 and 1931 Gropius developed his ideas about high-rise developments consisting of 8 to 12 storeys.[72] By using simple schemes (16) he argued that high-rise buildings had many advantages:

— Given the same sun angle and plan area, higher built densities were possible;

69 Hellinga, H. and P. de Ruijter, *Algemeen Uitbreidingsplan Amsterdam 50 jaar* (Amsterdam: Amsterdamse Raad voor de Stedebouw, 1985), 128.

70 Wintershoven, *Demografisch eeuwboek Amsterdam*, op. cit. (note 15).

71 Cammen and De Klerk, *Ruimtelijke Ordening*, op. cit. (note 16).

72 Rådberg, *Doktrin*, op. cit. (note 25), 79–84, 118.

—— Less land was needed to realize the same number of dwellings;
—— Using the same density and available land, improvements in quality (in terms of daylight access, sun, view, and privacy) could be achieved.

In the Bijlmermeer, these arguments were put into practice: the housing density matched that of the AUP (about 45 dwellings per hectare), but as the buildings were higher, more land was available on which to construct large green parks between the buildings.[73] The spaciousness in the Bijlmermeer matched the minimal standard introduced by Hoenig: one square metre of open space for each square metre of floor area. We can thus conclude that the same methodology (mathematical analysis) led Unwin to advocate the advantages of low-rise developments with a maximum density of 30 dwellings per hectare; led Hoenig to argue for a spaciousness of at least 1.0; and was used by Le Corbusier and Gropius to promote high-rise developments in their critique of both the traditional city and the Garden City Movement:

> Le Corbusier ... argued that the evil of the modern city was its density of developments and that the remedy, perversely, was to increase that density. Le Corbusier's solution, whereby an all-powerful master planner would demolish the entire existing city and replace it by a city of high-rise towers in a park [illustrates this].[74]

In the 1960s and 1970s, at the Centre for Land Use and Built Form Studies in Cambridge, Martin and March developed a comparable approach to investigate the relationship between density and urban form. In the first volume of a series of monographs emanating from this institute, Martin and March explained that their approach moved beyond the usual boundaries of architecture to include the measurement of the urban landscape.[75] Similar research existed in the Netherlands. Angenot published the book *Verhandelingen over het vraagstuk van de dichtheid van de bebouwing* (*Discussion on the subject of built density*),[76] Heimans the book *Bebouwingsdichtheid en grondgebruik voor de woningbouw in de stadsuitbreiding* (*Building density and land use in urban housing expansions*),[77] and the SAR (Stichting Architecten Research) developed the tissue method (*weefselmethode*).[78]

Heimans distinguished different types of allotments (from closed to open building blocks) and related these to their dimensions. He stated that one cannot speak of the density of a building type as it was also dependent on the dimensions of the ground plan. Within the SAR method, the type of lot division (tissue models) was central. Two basic models are mentioned: closed blocks and strip developments. The distribution and function of public space (streets, parking and green space) and building height were important elements that needed to be added to characterize tissue models. In the book *Urban Space and Structure*, Martin and March argued that more floor space could be realized in semi-detached housing types in

73 Based on the numbers of dwellings in 2007 of the Bijlmermuseum in which all high rise slabs are still present (area T94c and n, O&S, Amsterdam). The dwelling density was 44 dwellings per hectare in 2007.

74 Hall, *Cities*, op. cit. (note 31), 9.

75 Martin, L. and L. March (eds.), *Urban Space and Structures* (Cambridge: Cambridge University Press, 1972).

76 Angenot, L.H.J., *Verhandelingen over het vraagstuk van de dichtheid van bebouwing* (Alphen aan den Rijn: N. Samsom NV, 1954).

77 Heimans, A., *Bebouwingsdichtheid en grondgebruik voor de woningbouw in stadsuitbreidingen* (The Hague: Ten Hagen, 1965).

78 Stichting Architectuur Research, *Deciding on Density: An Investigation into High Density Allotments with a View to the Waldeck Area, The Hague* (Eindhoven, 1977).

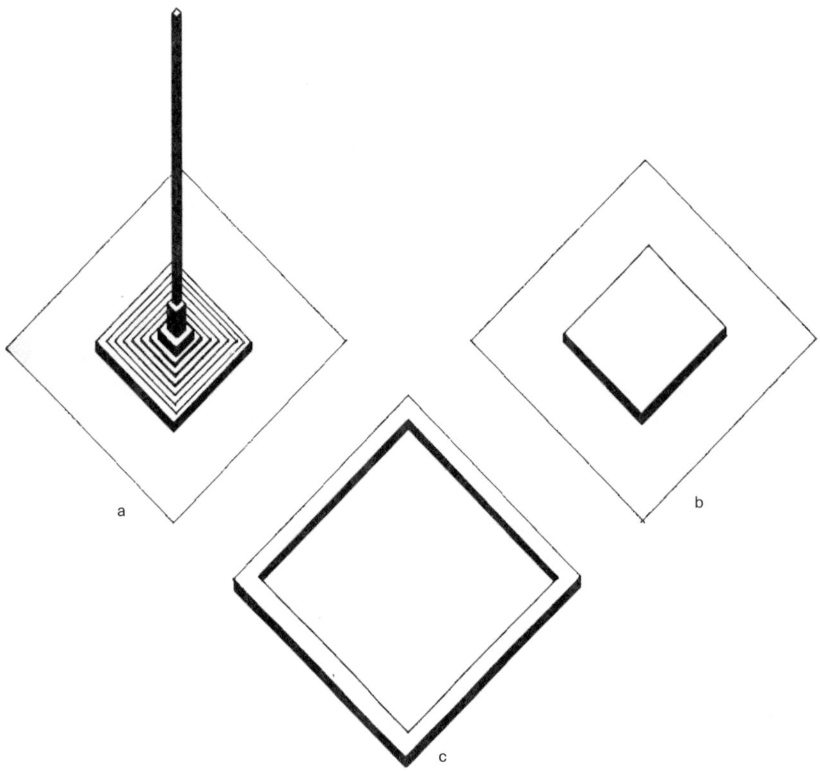

a Each band (with equal width) accommodates an equal amount of built space: in the outermost ring, a building is only one storey high and in the centre 72 storeys are required.
b Two examples showing
c the same built space and plot ratio, whether distributed in a concentrated or a linear form.

17 Housing density in relation to its distribution (Martin and March 1972: 52).

the countryside than with high-rise buildings in inner-city centres.[79] As the city expands with equal-width bands, the outer bands would be able to accommodate more built space than the inner bands. To compensate for this, the same area of floor space in the inner bands had to be achieved in the sky. 17 This choice between central and peripheral dispositions of space was also central in the models of Unwin, as discussed earlier, and the Dutch architect Hans van der Laan.[80] The latter concluded that when cities were built following the concept of peripheral disposition, a large open square could be positioned in the centre, but when the periphery had to remain open, the city would be crowded at its centre.

The three plans discussed in this section, Plan Zuid, AUP and Bijlmermeer, all illustrate clear breaks with nineteenth-century urban planning. These twentieth-century plans relied on the idea that it was possible, and preferable, to create a new (part of a) city by design. These ideas of deliberate city design were supported by the legal instruments embodied in the Housing Act and the Long Land Lease Regulation. Berlage, inspired by the work of Sitte and Howard, viewed the city as a harmonious, three-dimensional artefact. The city could be designed like a building, uniting all levels of scale in a *Gesamtkunstwerk*.[81] In a baroque fashion Berlage strived for visual unity.

79
Martin and March, *Urban Space*, op. cit. (note 75), 51–53.

80
Tummers, L.J.M. and J.M. Tummers-Zuurmond, *Het land in de stad: De stedebouw van de grote agglomeratie* (Bussum: Uitgeverij THOTH, 1997).

81
Castex, *De rationele stad*, op. cit. (note 28); Wagenaar, 'Amsterdam 1860–1940', op. cit. (note 36).

The Sittean picturesque, combined with a baroque composition, puts the plans of Berlage in stark opposition to nineteenth-century pragmatic engineering plans.[82]

The approach of Van Eesteren, in contrast, did not aspire to a final image. Instead, city expansions were designed relying on the ideals of CIAM, with 'a collection of land uses that through their functional relations would become a productive whole'.[83] This also applied to the 1947 Plan for the Reconstruction of Rotterdam by Cornelis van Traa.[84] As with the AUP, but in contrast to Berlage's Plan Zuid, the new plan for Rotterdam did not prescribe any specific architectural form or final image, but offered an open plan of structures. Van Traa's plan was even more radical in its functionalism and flexibility than the AUP.[85] This shift from three-dimensional city development by urban design (for example Sitte, Berlage, 'City Beautiful'), to a two-dimensional functional organization of the city, represented a triumph for the ideas of CIAM. Scientific and technology-based ideals became the main driving force for urban planning:

82 Cammen and De Klerk, *Ruimtelijke Ordening*, op. cit. (note 16), 93.

83 Engel, 'De vorm van de stad', op. cit. (note 64), 277.

84 Klerk, L. de, *Particuliere plannen: Denkbeelden en initiatieven van de stedelijke elite inzake volkswoningbouw en de stedebouw in Rotterdam, 1860–1950* (Rotterdam: NAi Publishers, 1998), 244–247.

85 Cammen and De Klerk, *Ruimtelijke Ordening*, op. cit. (note 16), 182.

> The Plan [for Rotterdam by van Traa] does not only propagate the structuring of space, but also the structuring of time by deliberately leaving options open. That which was smouldering before 1940 had inflamed: on an urban scale, spatial planning as organization of land uses has taken over from urban design [*vormgevende stedebouw*].[86]

86 De Klerk, *Particuliere plannen*, op. cit. (note 94), 247.

Based on scientific urban surveys, the modern city could be planned with great precision. This belief in the possibility to predict population growth, housing needs, traffic patterns, and so forth made spatial planning one of the most important political tools after the Second World War. Peter Hall describes this as 'the golden age of planning'.[87] The Fordist-Keynesian welfare state under construction after the Second World War had planning and state management of the economy at its core: 'Everything was subordinated to growth.'[88] This model, however, must not so much be seen as the opposite of capitalism as such, but as a stabilizing and facilitating apparatus necessary to guarantee future accumulation, although with a different agency compared to the character of the state half a century earlier.

87 Hall, *Cities*, op. cit. (note 31), 324.

88 Henri Lefebvre, quoted in Brenner, N., *New State Spaces: Urban Governance and the Rescaling of Statehood* (Oxford: Oxford University Press, 2004), 131.

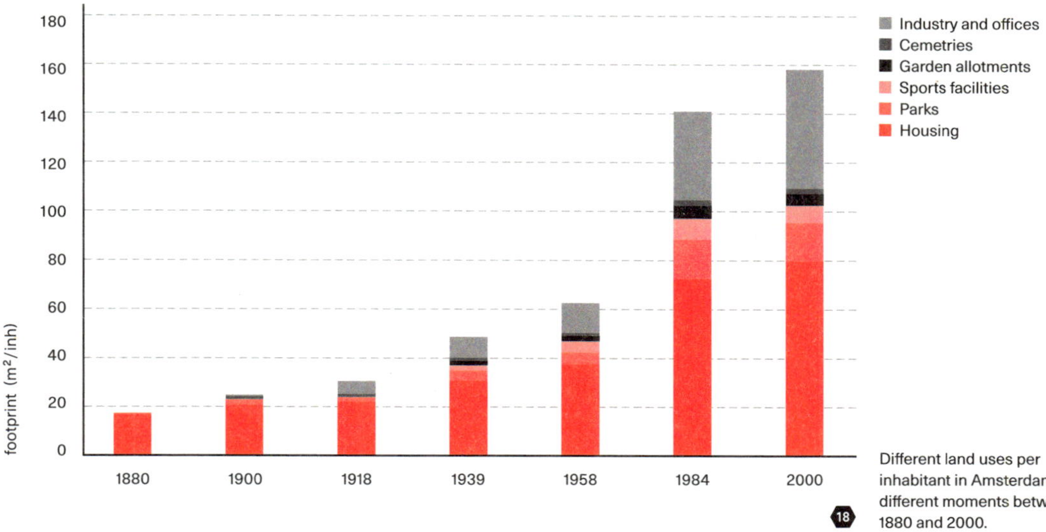

Different land uses per inhabitant in Amsterdam at different moments between 1880 and 2000.

Spatial Policies

Between 1958 and 1984, the population of Amsterdam shrank from 871,580 inhabitants to 676,520.[89] Rotterdam experienced a similar development during this period; falling from 731,000 in 1965 to 555,000 inhabitants in 1984.[90] Still, although the population of Amsterdam decreased by 22 per cent between 1958 and 1984, the urbanized area of Amsterdam grew by 75 per cent, from 5,400 to 9,460 hectares! A large part of this growth came from the harbour, which attracted workers from Amsterdam and the surrounding area. However, even if one only examines the relationship between population decline and growth in the area of housing, the figures show the same trend.[91] The total size of the area occupied by housing grew by 50 per cent during this period, from 3,240 to 4,865 hectares. Statistically speaking, an inhabitant in Amsterdam had 37 m² of residential area at his or her disposal in 1958, and by 1984 this had almost doubled to 72 m² per person.[92] (18) Some of the relatively well-off middle classes escaped from the city to low-density environments and thereby drained cities like Amsterdam and Rotterdam of much tax income and vitality. With fewer taxpayers and citizens in the city centre, the advantages of scale that higher densities offered in terms of amenities, community interaction and transport efficiency were threatened. In turn this led to a further depopulation of the city centre. All over Europe, and even more so in the USA, the trend of suburbanization led to an exodus of the middle class from the cities, especially from the big cities.

Various subsidies in the Netherlands were created to control the rapid (sub)urbanization of the Randstad (conurbation in West Netherlands). One measure was to stimulate the regions furthest away from the Randstad to again make them economically viable. The scale of urban planning was upgraded, with national planning becoming an accepted tool to organize land uses and restore the economic viability of peripheral regions. The first

89
Wintershoven, *Demografisch eeuwboek Amsterdam*, op. cit. (note 15).

90
Bik, M. and D. Linders, *Factsheete – prognose: Bevolkingsontwikkeling Rotterdam 2003–2017* (Rotterdam: Centrum voor Onderzoek en Statistiek, 2003).

91
This excludes large scale green areas and larger working areas such as the harbour.

92
See Berghauser Pont and Haupt, *Space, Density*, op cit. (note 3).

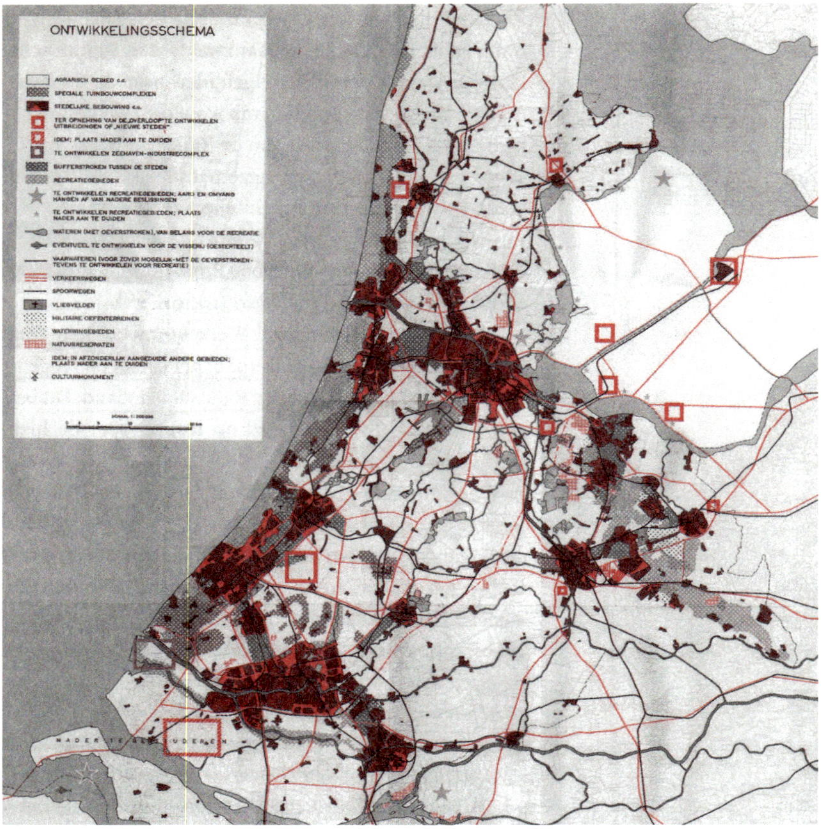

19 'Ontwikkelings-schema Westen des Lands 1980', proposing regional urbanization with satellite towns such as Almere, Hoorn and Zoetermer (van der Cammen & de Klerk 2003: 221).

National Policy Document on Spatial Planning (*Nota inzake de ruimtelijke ordening*) of 1960 was about such an equal distribution of population and economic activities.[93] The juridical and organizational framework for the planning on all different levels of scale was laid down in *The Spatial Planning Act* (*Wet op de ruimtelijke ordening*) of 1965.[94]

The policy was successful, partly due to positive economic developments. Industries in need of cheap labour relocated from the Randstad to the peripheries of the country. The economic boom continued during the 1960s and the Dutch Statistical Institute (*Centraal Bureau voor Statistiek*) predicted in the mid 1960s that the Dutch population would reach 20 million people by the year 2000. This was 7 million more than had been predicted in the *National Policy Document on Spatial Planning* five years earlier.[95] In 1963 the international planner and advisor for the State Service for the National Plan (*Rijksdienst voor het Nationaal Plan*), J.P. Thijsse Jr, presented a plan for the Netherlands in the year 2000. The plan was to accommodate 20 million inhabitants in two huge agglomerations.[96]

An alternative to combat the growth of such huge agglomerations and to react to the laissez-faire character of suburbanization was presented in *The Second National Policy Document on Spatial Planning* (*Tweede Nota over de Ruimtelijke Ordening*): concentrated dispersal (*gebundelde deconcentratie*).[97] New and existing towns and cities (satellite cities, or *groeikernen*)

93 VROM, *Nota inzake de ruimtelijke ordening* (The Hague: Ministry of Housing, Physical Planning and the Environment, 1960); Brenner, *New State Spaces*, op. cit. (note 98), 142–143.

94 VROM, *Wet op de ruimtelijke ordening* (The Hague: Ministry of Housing, Physical Planning and the Environment, 1965); Cammen and de Klerk, *Ruimtelijke Ordening*, 174.

95 Cammen and De Klerk, *Ruimtelijke Ordening*, op. cit. (note 16), 211–212.

96 Ibid., 212.

were to be (further) developed at a distance of 10 to 20 km from the existing larger cities of the Randstad. (19) By assigning areas where urbanization could take place, the demands for suburban living environments could be accommodated, green open spaces would be saved and the size of the Randstad agglomerations would be controlled. Fifty years after its birth, one could conclude that Howard's regional planning model had finally been adopted in the Netherlands. The Dutch approach to new towns, however, had not been implemented to counter the negative effects of overcrowding. Instead it focused, above all, on channelling residential investments into less developed or marginalized areas, on preserving open space within the Randstad's Green Heart, on expanding regional transportation infrastructures, and on managing demographic expansions throughout the whole country.[98] The satellite cities consisted of the expansion of existing towns such as Alkmaar, Hoorn and Zoetermeer and the newly created new towns of Lelystad (1967) and Almere (1975). Although the prognosis for Dutch population growth turned out to be inaccuratee – in 2000 the Netherlands had less than 16 million inhabitants and not the predicted 20 millione – all the space that had been set aside was used up by a rapid increase of space consumption per capita. In an analysis by L. Wijers it is shown that human space consumption over a ten-year period (1945–1955) more than doubled in the new expansion plans, from 80 m^2 to 180 m^2 per person.[99]

97
VROM, *Tweede nota over de ruimtelijke ordening* (The Hague: Ministry of Housing, Physical Planning and the Environment, 1966); Cammen and De Klerk, *Ruimtelijke Ordening*, op. cit. (note 16), 213–217.

98
Brenner, *New State Spaces*, op. cit. (note 98), 156.

99
Cammen and De Klerk, *Ruimtelijke Ordening*, op. cit. (note 16), 225.

Reactions to Modernism

During the last part of the period of state-managed capitalism, some people came to criticize what they saw as the failure of modern planning and architecture. People such as José Luis Sert and Jane Jacobs contributed through their books to a change in the theory and practice of city development. The titles of their publications expressed the urgency of their ideas: *Can Our Cities Survive?* and *The Death and Life of Great American Cities*.[100] Sert reached the conclusion that high density was often mistaken for overcrowding and that the solutions of the Garden City Movement and the high-rise solutions promoted by Le Corbusier and Gropius were to blame for much of the decline of city life. Jacobs argued that modern planning had ignored the complexity of the city and had forgotten that social and economic vitality were essential ingredients for achieving a city that functions well. To arrive here Jacobs propagated a minimum density of 100 dwellings per acre.

Jacobs's conclusions on the devastating effects of modern planning and architecture on existing habitats and cities marked the beginning of a move towards typomorphological research in architecture and urbanism. Anne Vernez Moudon describes the origins and different schools of morphological research in her text *Getting to Know the Built Landscape: Typomorphology*.[101] In Italy, typomorphological studies have their origins in the 1940s with the work of Saverio Muratori, an architect who argued that the roots of architecture were to be found not in the fantastic projections of the

100
Sert, J.L., *Can Our Cities Survive? An ABC of Urban Problems, Their Analysis, Their Solutions Based on Proposals Formulated by the CIAM* (Boston: Harvard University Press, 1942); Jacobs, J., *The Death and Life of Great American Cities* (New York: Random House, 1992), originally published in 1961.

101
Moudon, A.V., 'Getting to Know the Built Landscape: Typomorphology', in: K. Franck and L. Schneekloth (eds.), *Ordering Space: Types in Architecture and Design* (New York: Van Nostrand Reinhold, 1994), 289–311.

modernists, but from within the more continuous tradition of city development emanating from antiquity until the 1930s. The French, and especially the Versailles school, followed the Muratorian philosophy, believing that modernism had created a complete break with the past that could not be repaired. They believed that the roots of architecture had to be rediscovered in past traditions. The shift to the morphological perspective in architecture and urbanism led to an emphasis on the formal and historical characteristics of urban patterns. Demographic surveys, social statistics and abstract zoning diagrams by planners gave way to matters more intrinsic to the design profession such as typologies, historical map analyses and detailed drawings of settlement patterns. And besides, as a reaction to the dominance of the regional scale and the autonomous architectonic structure in modernist planning, the attention also shifted towards the 'intermediate scale'. Especially Manuel de Solà-Morales called attention to the lack of interest in this intermediate scale, or the urban project, in modern planning (Meyer 1999).[102]

102 Ibid.

The counterculture of the 1960s and 1970s was, among many things, a reaction against industrialized mass production, large-scale projects and the wholesale post-war demolition of existing city-centre environments. Plan areas became smaller in the 1970s and the long-term perspectives were replaced by solutions addressing the local problems of the day. This can be described as a transition 'from a technocratic to a sociocratic process'.[103] Concepts such as advocacy planning and urban renewal came to dominate professional discussions. Architects and urban planners affiliated with the Dutch magazine *Forum* heavily criticized functionalist planning as inhumane and argued for a (re)turn to human scale in planning and design. Hall caricatured these rapid shifts of professional attitude from the 1950s to the 1970s in his *Cities of Tomorrow* as follows:

103 Cammen and De Klerk, *Ruimtelijke Ordening*, op. cit. (note 16), 242.

> In 1955, the typical newly graduated planner was at the drawing board, producing a diagram of desired land uses; in 1965, s/he was analyzing computer output of traffic patterns; in 1975, the same person was talking late into the night with community groups, in the attempt to organize against hostile forces in the world outside.[104]

104 Hall, *Cities*, op. cit. (note 31), 334.

Neoliberal Capitalism (1979–today)

In the early 1970s, the economic boom of the Fordist-Keynesian period that had followed the Second World War turned into a worldwide recession.[105] This economic stagnation forced countries and municipalities to cut spending. Furthermore, much industrial production was unable to compete with the emerging Asian economies and sectors such as shipyards and textiles, but also consumer goods, shrank while the service sector grew. The programme of economic reform in China of 1978 instigated after the death of Mao by Deng Xiaoping, and the opening up of new populations for production and consumption with the fall of the Iron Curtain during the 1990s,

105 Brenner, R., *The Economics of Global Turbulence: The Advanced Capitalist Economies from Long Boom to Long Downturn, 1945–2005* (London: Verso, 2006); Harvey, D., *A Brief History of Neoliberalism* (Oxford: Oxford University Press, 2005); Brenner, *New State Spaces*, op. cit. (note 98).

further increased the global competitive character of life at the end of the twentieth century. The global recession of the 1970s, the transition from regional, via national, to global competition between corporations, and the rise of unemployment in the 1980s had a significant impact on the development of Dutch cities. In Amsterdam unemployment more than doubled from a relatively high level of 8 per cent to 17 per cent between 1980 and 1984.[106] Housing associations were privatized and while in 1980 the national housing production in the Netherlands consisted for 90 per cent of social housing, by 2000 this had shrunk to 20 per cent.[107]

106
Brenner, *New State Spaces*, op. cit. (note 98), 179.

107
Cammen and De Klerk, *Ruimtelijke Ordening*, op. cit. (note 16), 405.

After an almost standstill in the housing construction in Amsterdam between 1977 and 1980, the production of social housing quickly increased between 1981 and 1984. These counter-cyclical investments during the severe recession marked the end of a long period of collective investments in housing that started after the Second World War and the beginning of a market-oriented urban governance. Neil Brenner in his book *New State Spaces* summarizes this general shift as a reorientation 'from the managerial, welfarist mode of the Fordist-Keynesian period to an entrepreneurial, growth-oriented, and competitiveness-driven framework during the post-1970s period'.[108]

108
Brenner, *New State Spaces*, op. cit. (note 98), 177.

After the criticism of a centralized and technocratic state paradigm on many levels of society, a reorientation on the social and human scale of the city took place. This period was characterized by urban renewal and regeneration. Political protests and social unrest at the end of the 1960s and beginning of the 1970s led to an increased democratization of the urban process, and advocacy planning paved the way for locally focused 'building for the neighbourhood' (*bouwen voor de buurt*). The need to revitalize the cities after a long period of depopulation and 'urban crisis' was expressed in the *Structure Scheme Urban Areas* (*Structuurschets stedelijke gebieden*).[109] Here the focus was less on collective investments in social housing. These had become too expensive to the bleeding treasuries, and seemed to only reproduce an expensive social structure of low-income groups with little purchasing power to support amenities and with the wrong qualifications to suit the new service economy. The educated middle class that had migrated to the suburbs and smaller towns was what the large cities were in need of. 'People with an above average income [were needed] back in the city.'[110] Gentrification had thus become not only a neighbourhood phenomenon, but was rescaled to play out over whole regions. Such an uneven geographical development became accepted as a fact, and policies that were set up in the 1960s to geographically redistribute wealth were abandoned.

109
VROM, *Structuurschets stedelijke gebieden* (The Hague: Ministry of Housing, Physical Planning and the Environment, 1983).

110
Cammen and De Klerk, *Ruimtelijke Ordening*, op. cit. (note 16), 279.

Spatial Privatization

The socially engaged criticism of the 1960s and 1970s of technocratic planning paved the way for an interactive consensus planning approach. The assumption of the latter was that market forces would increase efficiency, making all those involved sensitive to the wishes of housing consumers and investors. Proximity to 'real life' would enable them to respond more adeptly to social and economic changes. This market orientation was initiated not only because of a general revaluation of private initiative's competence and ability, but also because municipalities and the state simply lacked the resources.[111] It became a pragmatic necessity in the 1980s to invite market parties to participate in the (re)building of the cities to cover (local) government budget deficits. The private sector now operated on an equal footing with the state. This was in stark contrast to the past when developers and private building firms used to be mere minions who executed the grand designs of government and municipal planning agencies.

111
Brenner, *New State Spaces*, op. cit. (note 98); Harvey, *A Brief History*, op. cit. (note 105).

In recent decades private developers and investors have gained a central position in city development through strategic investments in land: 'Attention of all private parties has shifted from buying land that has been prepared for housing development to the purchase of undeveloped land.'[112] In the quarterly bulletin of the *Dutch Bank* (*De Nederlandse Bank*) of March 2008, it was stated that 85 per cent of released land for new housing projects came from private developers and not from municipalities.[113] Private developers have hereby become more powerful in project negotiations with local authorities. They have a greater say on the quantitative goals (number of dwellings to be developed) and qualitative ambitions (type of dwellings, amount of green space, parking options) of such projects. This gradual shift from government to governance has created a receptive environment for a project-based approach, an approach in which public and private partners sign agreements (under private law) *before* the spatial aspects of these agreements become legally binding through zoning plans (under public law). This phenomenon of 'after-zoning' has been criticized for its democratic deficit as most of the project formulation takes place outside democratic institutions.[114]

112
Segeren, A., *De grondmarkt voor woningbouwlocaties* (Rotterdam: NAi Publishers, 2007), 10.

113
Leeuwen, H. van, 'Geef bouwgrond niet aan speculanten', *NRC Handelsblad* 18 August 2008.

114
Meyer, H., 'In dienst van de stad onder postmoderne condities / Working for the City under Post-modern Conditions', in: H. Meyer and L. van den Burg (eds.), *In dienst van de stad / Working for the City* (Amsterdam: SUN, 2005), 64–68.

A more adaptive planning approach was propagated for the first time in the Netherlands in the 1988 national planning policy of *The Fourth National Policy Document on Spatial Planning* (*Vierde Nota over Ruimtelijke Ordening*), and *Vinex; The Fourth National Policy Document on Spatial Planning Extra* (*Vinex; Vierde Nota over Ruimtelijke Ordening Extra*) of 1994.[115] With hindsight, these policy documents officially mark the end of a long tradition of government-controlled housing construction that began with the introduction of the *Housing Act* in 1901.

115
VROM, *Vierde nota over de ruimtelijke ordening* (The Hague: Ministry of Housing, Physical Planning and the Environment, 1988); VROM, *Vierde nota over de ruimtelijke ordening extra* (The Hague: Ministry of Spatial Planning and the Environment, 1994).

Policy Reactions

Despite this shift, the Dutch government has continued to produce spatial policy documents. In 1983 The Third National Policy Document on Spatial Planning (Derde Nota over Ruimtelijke Ordening) introduced the concept of the 'Compact City', aiming to temper the depopulation of the larger cities that was signalled in the 1976 Policy Document on Urbanization (Verstedelijkingsnota).[116] In the *Vinex* report (1994), the policy was formulated

116
VROM, *Derde nota over de ruimtelijke ordening* (The Hague: Ministry of Housing, Physical Planning and the Environment, 1973–1983);

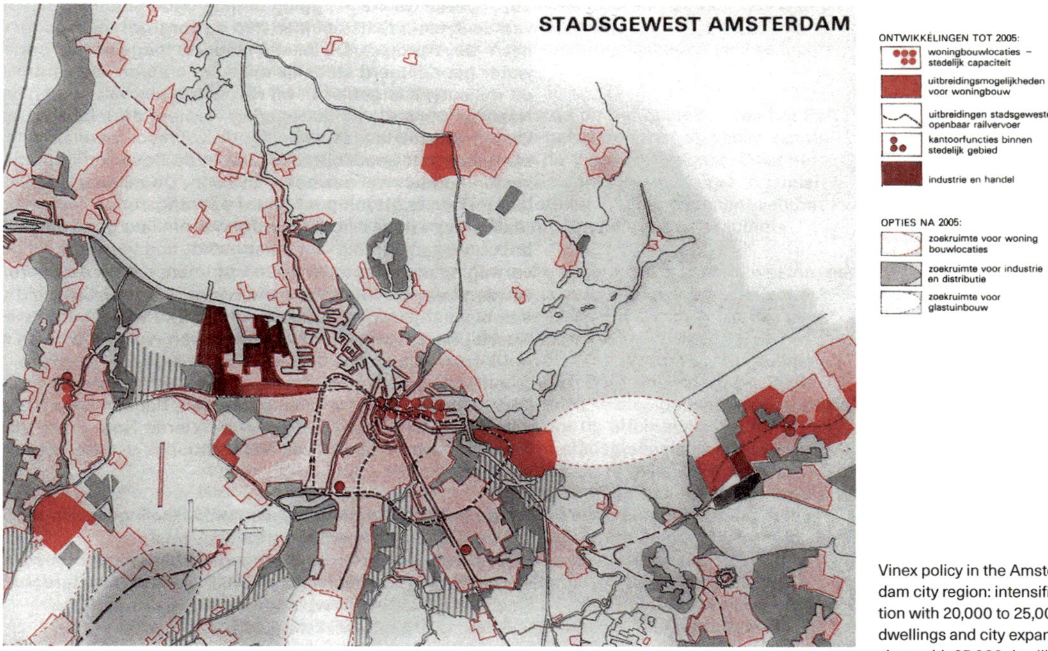

20 Vinex policy in the Amsterdam city region: intensification with 20,000 to 25,000 dwellings and city expansions with 65,000 dwellings (VROM 1994: 46).

as follows: to build preferably within existing cities through intensification, or, if not possible, adjacent to existing cities to accommodate suburban living environments. Between 1995 and 2005, 455,000 houses were needed according to the survey underpinning the *Vinex* report. In Amsterdam (including Almere) more than 100,000 houses were foreseen of which 35 per cent were projected as 'infill' projects and 65 per cent in areas adjacent to the city. 29 An example of the first strategy of this policy was the development of the South Bank of the IJ in Amsterdam (IJ-oevers). Cities, together with private developers, tried to create top locations to attract both real estate investments and economically viable activities in high-density mixed developments. The density of the IJ-oevers in Amsterdam was 90 dwellings per hectare (200 inhabitants per hectare) and although these numbers were higher than those realized earlier in the AUP and Bijlmermeer, they were still far lower than the minimum density for vital cities of 175 dwellings per hectare proposed by Jacobs in the 1960s.[117]

The suburban expansion De Aker in the western part of Amsterdam is a good example of the second Vinex strategy of developments adjacent to existing cities. As is the case in most of the other extension areas of that period in the Netherlands, De Aker consists of mostly single-family housing (more than 70 per cent) and has a density of approximately 35 dwellings per hectare.[118] This is similar to the density proposed by Unwin and it could, according to Jacobs, be viable and safe and even ecologically sustainable (although heavily car dependent), but it would not generate city liveliness or public life for the simple reason that there would not be a sufficient concentration of inhabitants.

117
Java island, KNSM island, Borneo and Sporenburg (O+S Amsterdam). AUP had 50 dwellings per hectare in 2007 and the Bijlmer 45 dwellings per hectare (O+S, 2007). Based on 100 dwellings per acre (Jacobs, *The Death*, op. cit. (note 100), 211) and $T_f = 0.3$, thus $0.3 = 1 - (FSI_f / 100)$.

118
Based on the amount of dwellings and inhabitants in 2007 (O+S Amsterdam), the population density is 103 inhabitants per hectare in 2007.

21

Design sketch for Kattenbroek in Amersfoort. Example of the conceptual, image-based urbanism of the 1980s (Ashok Bhalotra).

Preparations for a *Fifth National Policy Document on Spatial Planning* (*Vijfde Nota over Ruimtelijke Ordening*) at the end of the 1990s included a national inventory of spatial claims for all functions that needed to be accommodated until 2030.[119] For infrastructure, housing and businesses alone, an extra 200,000 hectares of land would be required, an increase of 45 percent.[120] Following market research, housing needs were noted for green suburban areas with low densities and urban areas with higher densities. As was the case already in the *Vinex* report, *The Fifth National Policy Document on Spatial Planning* inclined towards a compromise to accommodate both claims. Alongside the continuation of a liberalized housing policy, it argued for the liberalization and decentralization of spatial planning. Although *The Fifth National Policy Document on Spatial Planning* was never approved, the following report, *The Spatial Planning Policy Document* (*Nota Ruimtee – Ruimte voor Ontwikkeling*) of 2004, formalized these ambitions with an even clearer choice for decentralization.[121] Spatial planning and design became key instruments for contributing to a better economic performance in the current globalized and competitive environment.

119
VROM, *Vijfde nota over de ruimtelijke ordening* (The Hague: Ministry of Spatial Planning and the Environment, 2001).

120
Cammen and De Klerk, *Ruimtelijke Ordening*, op. cit. (note 16), 423.

121
VROM, *Nota ruimtee – ruimte voor ontwikkeling* (The Hague: Ministry of Spatial Planning and the Environment, 2004).

The Image of the City

Parallel to changes in spatial planning, the architecture policy of the government was summed up in the Memorandum Belvedere.[122] Here, in line with the transition from a predominately industrial production society to a de-industrialized consumer society, with its postmodern 'aesthetification of life', the image of the city in terms of cultural heritage, identity and

122
RACM, *Nota Belvedere* (The Hague: The National Service for Archaeology, Cultural Landscape and Built Heritage, 1999).

spatial quality dominated. This shift from planning to design matched the increased emphasis on competition between cities:

> It was an approach that saw the city largely in design terms and it accorded well with another theme from the 1980s and 1990s: marketing them like cars or kitchens, which was part and parcel of globalization in an era where the old locational advantages had blown away.[123]

123
Hall, *Cities*, op. cit. (note 31), 416.

This development corresponded to a more general reorientation from planning to design. Technical content gave way to form, instrumental engineering was replaced by image design, or 'seduction engineering'. Of course, the rationality of engineering, technology and economics remained keys to success, but the carefully produced imagery became more central to the sales effort of plans and projects.

The interest in morphology and premodernist city development mentioned earlier are good examples of this shift. The use of morphology in analysis and design corresponded with the scaling down of urban planning. This was in contrast to the earlier all-encompassing blueprint expansions and the mechanist functionalism that expressed the view that form was merely a result of technique, economy, programme and organization. The 'postmodern turn' in urbanism was illustrated by the renaissance of more romantic humanist architects such as Sitte, the 'City Beautiful' movement, and the birth of the New Urbanism movement, the latter labelled by Michael Sorkin 'the Opus Dei of urban design'.[124] With New Urbanism, traditional urban form and the cultural significance of the city development received a greater emphasis.[125]

In the Dutch practice 'culturee – in the sense of image and image productione – again received a position in spatial planning when the mainly on programming and containment fixated planning was substituted by one concerned with seduction and inspiration'.[126] In the policy report *Nota Wonen. Mensen, wensen, wonen* citizens were defined as consumers with different lifestyles that needed to be matched with a suitable object in an appropriate setting.[127] These could then be translated into a series of urban environment types (*stedelijke milieutypen*). Urban and architectural 'qualities' were looked after by detailed image and quality plans (*beeld- en kwaliteitsplan*) and supervisors (quality coordinators) to adequately enhance the image. In a way, this marked a return of blueprint planning, this time not as a programme, but as the image quality of a plan.[128] One of the best known examples of such an image-based plan was Kattenbroek in Amersfoort (1990) where the architect Ashok Bhalotra used metaphors and themes to diversify the image of a neighbourhood with some 4,500 homes. 21 Despite the diverse image, the programming of the area is rather uniform: almost 80 per cent of the housing stock consisted of single-family homes in a homogenous density of 30 dwellings per hectare.[129]

124
Sorkin, M., 'The End(s) of Urban Design', *Harvard Design Magazine* fall 2006/winter 2007, 5–18, 12.

125
Harvey, D., 'New Urbanism and the Communitarian Trap', in: W.S. Saunders (ed.), *Sprawl and Suburbia*, A Harvard Design Magazine Reader (Minneapolis: University of Minnesota Press, 2005).

126
Taverne, E., 'Kan de erfgoed de ruimtelijke ordening redden?', in: F. Claessens and H. Engel (eds.), *OverHolland 2* (Amsterdam: SUN, 2005), 107–110, 107–108.

127
VROM, *Nota wonen: Mensen, wensen, wonen* (The Hague: Ministry of Spatial Planning and the Environment, 2000).

128
Cammen and De Klerk, *Ruimtelijke Ordening*, op. cit. (note 16), 309–310, 360–361.

129
Municipality of Amersfoort, *Amersfoort in cijfers* (Amersfoort: Onderzoek en statistiek, 2006).

Urbanity and Sceptics

'Urbanity' (*stedelijkheid*) is another concept that, next to 'spatial quality', achieved an important status in defining the ambitions for city extensions and transformations during the 1990s. In the Netherlands different books and reports were published trying to define urbanity, for instance *Strategie voor stedelijkheid*; *Structuurplan Amsterdam: Kiezen voor stedelijkheid*; and *Stedelijkheid als rendement: Privaat initiatief voor publieke ruimte.*[130] The concept tends to be very elastic and there is little consensus on how it should be defined. François Barré described two related meanings of urbanity in the article 'The Desire for Urbanity'. The first was morphological and described the physical space of the city and its conditioning aspects for urbanity. The second was socioeconomic and concerned the actual use of the city.[131]

Gert Urhahn and Milos Bobic emphasized 'complexity' as the main attribute in their 1996 book *Strategie voor stedelijkheid*. Their emphasis was on the spatial, physical and strategic conditions that stimulate the socioeconomic complexity of life. This adherence to complexity was also expressed by Heeling, et al. in *Het ontwerp van de stadsplattegrond*:

> The urbanity of a city is primarily determined by the degree to which the spatial configuration is able to contain a large pluriformity of land use, economic activity, institutions, life forms, cultural life styles and social relations. The more complex and pluriform the city is, the more it will be experienced as urban.[132]

Jacobs, Richard Sennet and Marshall Berman discussed the civic dimension of urbanity in terms of public interaction and accessibility. Both Sennet and Berman emphasized the need for spaces in which public urban life can flourish.[133] Jacobs saw vitality, diversity and concentration as being central to urbanity: 'Dense concentrations of people are one of the necessary conditions for flourishing city diversity.'[134] She added the need for high lot coverage (60 to 80 per cent) as a condition for urban vitality to indirectly force people into the public streets and parks and so increase social interaction. Jacobs suggested a minimum density of 175 dwellings per hectare to arrive at a vital and diverse urban landscape.[135]

The emphasis on urbanity as an attractive part of city life fit in well with two problems that cities were confronted with in the 1980s: competition with suburbia, and a general degeneration of city economies as a result of recession and de-industrialization. Cities reinvented their identities in what, somewhat tautologically, was seen as the essence of the city: *urbanity.* Cultural sociologist Anton Zijderveld claimed in the Van Eesteren lecture in 1992 that:

> Urbanity has the same function as a management culture to a corporation or an administration. Cities without urbanity have no

130
Urhahn, G.B. and M. Bobic, *Strategie voor stedelijkheid* (Bussum: Uitgeverij THOTH, 1996); Municipality of Amsterdam, *Structuurplan Amsterdam: Kiezen voor stedelijkheid* (Amsterdam: dRO, 2003); Lengkeek, A., *Stedelijkheid als rendement: Privaat initiatief voor publieke ruimte* (Haarlem: Trancity, 2007).

131
Barré, F., 'The Desire for Urbanity', *Architectural Design* 11/12 (1980), 4–7.

132
Heeling et al., *Het ontwerp*, op. cit. (note 9), 101.

133
Meyer, H., F. de Josselin de Jong and M.J. Hoekstra (eds.), *Het ontwerp van de openbare ruimte* (Amsterdam: SUN, 2006); 10–13.

134
Jacobs, *The Death*, op. cit. (note 100), 205.

135
Density as dwelling units per net acre of residential land, excluding public streets. If public streets are included, this corresponds to approximately 175 dwellings per hectare (with 30 per cent of the land used for streets).

face and lack propulsion. There is then a lack of administrative legitimacy and conviction and the economy is adrift, not capable to attract the necessary investments.[136]

136
Quoted in Cammen and De Klerk, *Ruimtelijke Ordening*, op. cit. (note 16), 361.

Following the politically tumultuous 1970s, this re-branding of the city and its way of life partially helped to stem the exodus from the physically and economically decaying cities to the suburbs. Furthermore, the postindustrial boom of services led to a focus on innovation, financial services, entertainment, leisure and tourism. These were all activities that for many were inherently connected to urbanity.[137] For Dutch cities, these urban ambitions contributed to the realization of compact inner city (re)developments, such as Zuidas and the IJ-oever projects in Amsterdam, The Resident in The Hague, and Kop van Zuid in Rotterdam. The enthusiasm for the concept probably also contributed to some increase of densities in more suburban developments such as Noorderhof in Amsterdam and Brandevoort in Helmond. However, with around 50 dwellings per hectare these areas were still far from vital if we are to believe Jacobs.

137
Florida, R., *Cities and the Creative Class* (New York: Routledge, 2005);
Hall, P., *Cities in Civilization* (London: Phoenix, 1999);
Municipality of Amsterdam, *Structuurplan Amsterdam*, op. cit. (note 130);
Urhahn and Bobic, *Strategie*, op. cit. (note 130).

Despite a consensus in recent decades on the positive effects of the concepts of urbanity and spatial quality on city development, some people were critical of these concepts.[138] What kind of vitality and intensity was actually being striven for when all parties unite around the flag of 'urbanity'? Was it the friction and 'accident and mess' that seemed to be an important part of Jacobs's urban vitality? Or was it the concentration of retail outlets and gentrification, the nice front of diversity and 'cappuccino urbanism'[139] that led to a less diverse social reality? The main points of Jacobs's criticism on the monofunctional sleep city and her plea for street vitality and people power seemed to have been lost along the way.

138
E.g. Brenner, N. and N. Theodore, *Spaces of Neoliberalism: Urban Restructuring in North America and Western Europe* (Oxford: Blackwell Publishing, 2002);
Davis, M. and D.B. Monk (eds.), *Evil Paradises: Dreamworlds of Neoliberalism* (New York: The New Press, 2007);
Sorkin, M. (ed.), *A Theme Park: The New American City and the End of Public Space* (New York: Hill and Wang, 1992);
Sorkin, 'The End(s)', op. cit. (note 124).

139
Saunders, W.S., 'Cappuccino Urbanism, and Beyond', *Harvard Design Magazine* fall 2006/winter 2007, 3.

The Battle for Growth

Throughout much of the twentieth century private financers, developers and construction companies had been viewed with some suspicion. They were central actors during the housing boom at the end of the nineteenth century and were seen by many as profiteers, contributing little to the common good. A rather statist top-down approach had in the 1960s and 1970s forced most of the private initiatives to the periphery of spatial and urban development. In the 1990s the economy was no longer seen as the enemy but rather as the motor for social and spatial transformations. The economic reality had to be accepted and growth stimulated with the help of the creativity of, among others, architects and urban designers. Ranking Randstad, a research project initiated at the Faculty of Architecture of Delft University of Technology, illustrated this by recognizing the struggle of cities in a competitive global economy. The programme examined how 'spatial quality and spatial characteristics account for the competitive/ comparative advantages/disadvantages in various city-regions'.[140] The right spatial

140
www.ranking-randstad.net, accessed October 2008.

interventions in combination with appropriate fiscal and social policies could attract improvements in corporate investments, tourism, expatriates and well-educated immigrants. This would result in a higher ranking and, one supposes, sustained economic growth.

If we are to believe Rem Koolhaas, the affirmative stance of the neoliberal epoch had made urban planning and design meaningless and even undesirable as it intervened in the self-organizing power of cities.[141] Apart from producing marketing imagery the most the urban designer could achieve was to engage with the physical components that made the flows of people, money and goods possible. In this way urban designers became spatial engineers, optimizing the techniques of physical organization. The machinery that needed greasing was different from the rationally organized city of Le Corbusier, though. If *La Ville Radieuse* attempted to fetter the beast of corporate profit and individual desire through embedded capitalism, Koolhaas's *Generic City* was created by the beast and was proud of it. The title of a book by Crimson reflected the *zeitgeist* of such an extremely ironic and hedonistic pragmatism: *Too Blessed to be Depressed.*[142]

141
Koolhaas, R., *S, M, L, XL* (Rotterdam: 010 Publishers, 1995), 1248–1264; Haupt, P., 'Adriaan Geuze, Rem Koolhaas och staden som inte längre finns', *Arkitektur*, 1 1996, 68–73.

142
Crimson, *Too Blessed to Be Depressed: Crimson Architectural Historians 1994–2002* (Rotterdam: 010 Publishers, 2002).

Runaway Space Consumption?

Predictions in the past about future land use in the Netherlands have often been inaccurate. This was also the case with the prediction of a dramatic increase of the Dutch population from 12 million in 1966 to 20 million inhabitants by 2000 that The Second National Policy Document on Spatial Planning used as its point of departure.[143] However, it transpired that the space that had been reserved was still needed to accommodate the Dutch population. Part of the explanation for this can be found in the fact that anticipated occupancy rates were too high. For example, the calculations in the surveys undertaken in the 1930s for the AUP were based on an estimated 3.37 inhabitants per dwelling by 2000. The real level in Amsterdam in 2000 was 1.98 inhabitants per dwelling.[144]

Predictions of demographic developments and their influence on city growth and contraction remain dubious. A lesson that a city like Amsterdam could draw from past experience, however, is that its urban footprint[145] has been exponentially increasing since the end of the nineteenth century. Amsterdam's urban footprint

143
VROM, *Tweede nota*, op. cit. (note 57). The Netherlands had 15,864,000 inhabitants in 2000, and 16,500,000 in March 2009 (CBS).

144
Wintershoven, *Demografisch eeuwboek Amsterdam*, op. cit. (note 15).

145
The urban footprint is defined as the total amount of land needed for housing fabrics (areas dominated by dwellings), urban green (parks, sports fields, garden allotments and graveyards) and working areas divided by the total amount of inhabitants.

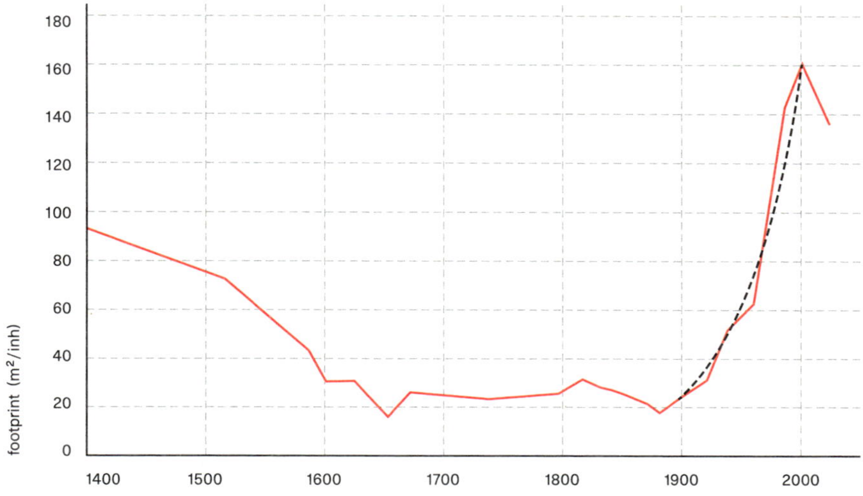

22 Urban footprint for the city of Amsterdam from 1400 to 2020.

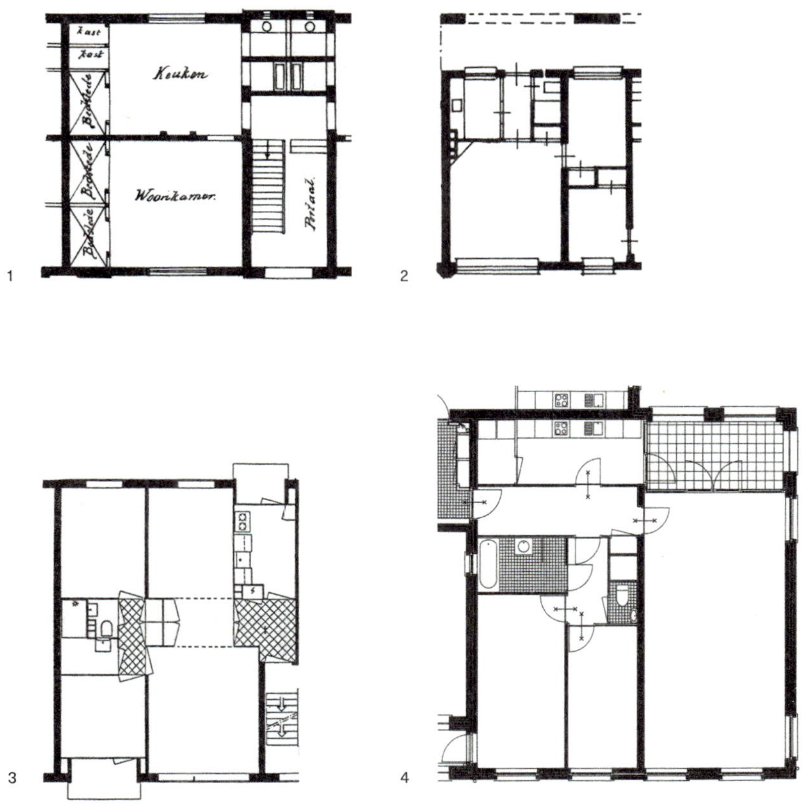

1 One-room apartment 1876, Amsterdam: 30 m²
2 Two-room apartment 1926, Mathenesserhof Rotterdam: 50 m²
3 Four-room apartment 1958, Sloterhof Amsterdam: 80 m²
4 Three-room apartment 1998, Wolveschans Leek: 120 m²

23 Floor plans of four dwellings, scale 1:200 (Kloos 2000: 15; Floet 2001: 247, 399, 440).

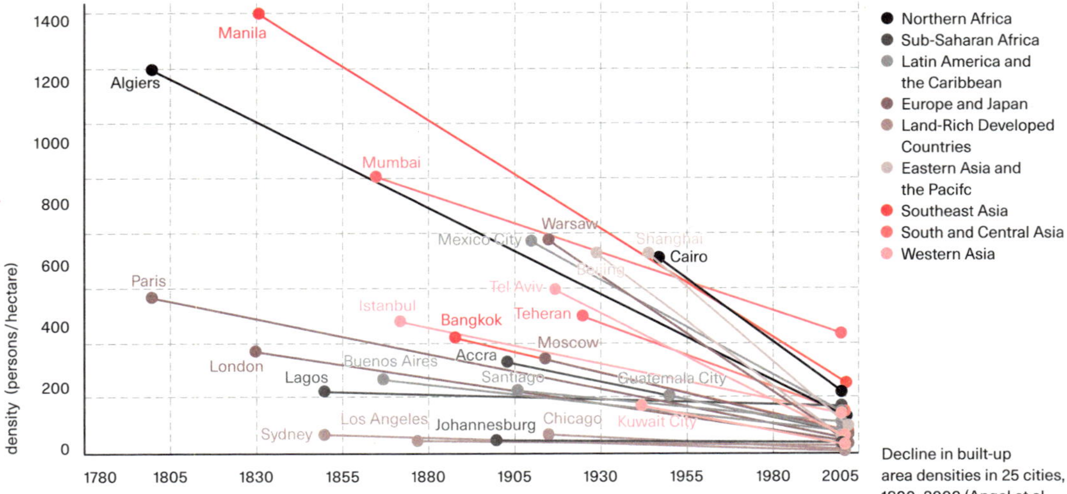

Decline in built-up area densities in 25 cities, 1800–2000 (Angel et al. 2011: 23).

increased with a factor 6.4 during the twentieth century.[146] This is comparable to an annual growth of 1.9 per cent, and equivalent to a doubling of the urban footprint every 37 years. 22 Expressed another way, one could say that every new generation in Amsterdam since 1900 has had the double amount of urban space at its disposale – or lives half as denselye – as their parents.[147]

People during the twentieth century tended to live in ever-smaller households,[148] in larger houses,[149] at greater distance from each other and from their places of work. 15 23 The increase in individual housing allocations, the functional zoning of cities into separate areas for housing, green space (for example parks, graveyards and sport fields), offices and industries, and the increased use of the car (wider streets with more parking facilities) have since 1900 all contributed to an increased urban footprint.

This trend of increased space consumption is not a phenomenon unique for Amsterdam or Europe. Angel has shown that most cities have grown faster in size than in population and, as a result, have decreased their density.[150] This decrease in density is not only true for the period between 1800 and 2000, but recent developments also indicate that, despite the urban renaissance, in cities in Asia, North and South America and Europe, densities decreased between 1990 and 2000. 24 However, through the detailed analysis of Amsterdam, we are able to reveal a trend break. In Amsterdam, since 2000, densities have started to increase, from 63 inhabitants per hectare in 2000 to 74 in 2020.

146
In 1900, each person in Amsterdam had 25 m^2 of city at his or her disposal; in 2000 this was 157 m^2 per person. See Berghauser Pont and Haupt, *Space, Density*, op cit. (note 3), 235–271.

147
Ignoring a temporary interruption in population increases during the 1970s and 1980s.

148
The occupancy rate in Amsterdam in 1900 was 4.37 persons per dwelling; in 2000 this was 1.98. From Wintershoven, *Demografisch eeuwboek Amsterdam*, op. cit. (note 15).

149
The amount of rooms per dwelling can serve as an indicator for size. In 1899, 75 per cent of the dwellings in the Netherlands had less than three rooms. In 1989, only 12 per cent had less than three rooms. From CBS, *Historie bouwnijverheid vanaf 1899* (The Hague: Statistics Netherlands, 2008).

150
Angel, S., J. Parent, D.L. Civco, A.M. Blei, *Making Room for a planet of Cities*, (Lincoln Institute of Land Policy, 2011).

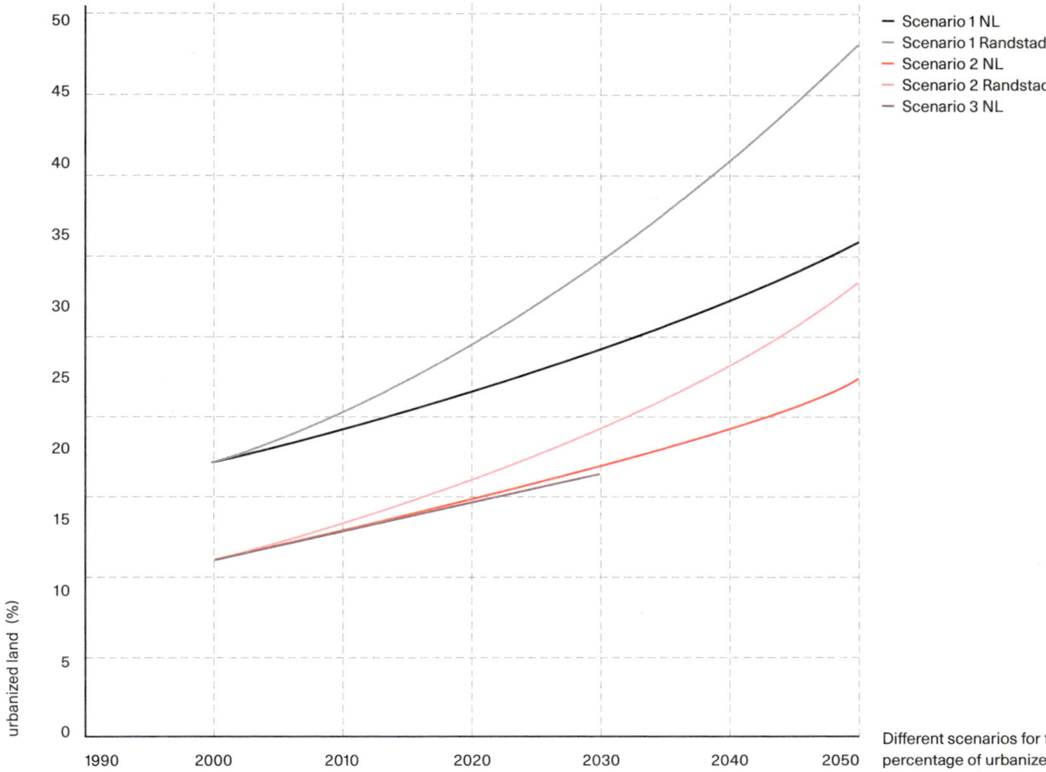

25 Different scenarios for the percentage of urbanized area in 2050 (Berghauser Pont and Haupt 2009: 64).

Scenario's for Space Consumption

Based on the changes in land use in the past, and considering the twentieth-century developments in Amsterdam as a point of reference for the Netherlands as a whole, the continuation of the micro-scale trends described abovee – people living in larger houses, with less people in lower densitiese – could theoretically result in a situation in 2050 whereby more than 30 per cent of the country would be covered by urbanized areas. This should be compared to 12 percent in 2000.[151] In the Randstad almost 50 per cent of the area would be urbanized, compared to 19 per cent in 2000. (Scenario 1 in 25) Even when a less polemic, and perhaps more realistic scenario is set out, one based on the growth of the land use in the Netherlands between 1993 and 2000, we still arrive at a substantially larger amount of urbanized areas by 2050: 22 per cent for the country as a whole and 33 per cent of the Randstad. (Scenario 2 in 25) This last scenario corresponds almost exactly to the trend described in *The Fifth National Policy Document on Spatial Planning*.[152] (Scenario 3 in 25) The Netherlands Institute for Spatial Research predicted in a recent report, *Demographic Decline and Spatial Development*, that a number of Dutch municipalities would soon experience a decrease in population.[153] However, in a situation where this coincides with economic growth and a continuation of current behaviour patterns, the increase in spatial footprint may well outpace any population decrease. People

151
Housing, working areas, and infrastructure. Based on Schuit, J. van der, et al., *Ruimte in cijfers 2006* (The Hague: Netherlands Institute for Spatial Research, 2006). This calculation assumes zero population growth. See Berghauser Pont and Haupt, *Space, Density,* op cit. (note 3), 247, for further details.

152
VROM, *Vijfde nota*, op. cit. (note 119).

153
Netherlands Institute for Spatial Research, *Demographic Decline and Spatial Development: Planning for the Consequences of Population Changes, Summary* (The Hague, 2006), available online at: http://rpb.ddg5.tamtam.nl/upload/documenten/summary_demographicdecline.pdf (accessed 19 November 2008).

will continue to prefer bigger houses in the countryside and many of them will be able and willing to pay for them.

The issue of rapid urbanization, conflicting spatial claims, and 'spatial chaos' has recently been placed at the top of the political agenda in the Netherlands by the media.[154] A Christian Democratic Party (CDA) report argued for the creation of an additional 5 million parking spaces in the Netherlands between now and 2020, and the policy report *Structuurvisie Randstad 2040* predicted the addition of 500,000 dwellings within the Randstad.[155] The number of parking spaces suggested in the first report would correspond roughly to the whole area of Amsterdam.[156] The half million new homes that have been proposed for the Randstad would cover an area almost three times the size of Amsterdam, if constructed at an average density of 30 dwellings per hectare.[157] When lower densities are chosen, such as proposed in the study *Waterland 2020* for the provincial executive of North Holland, the increase in urbanized land would reach even higher values. This study suggested that the countryside may be saved from the periods of overproduction crisis of agriculture in the Netherlands by people looking for big houses at very low densities.[158] The introduction of a variety of traditional housing types at low densities in rural areas, it is claimed, would not substantially influence the quality of the landscape in any negative way. Critics of these ideas suggest that sprawl and suburbanization go hand in hand with car mobility, social segregation and a decline in public services.[159] The increased mobility that accompanies sprawl undermines the overriding aim of curbing energy consumption and the emission of greenhouse gases. After all, it is no secret that both the SUV (Sports Utility Vehicle) and sprawl are the last in line for a green energy label. Furthermore, the insecurity of food prices, competition with food crops and the increasing demand for meat in the world has already begun to ameliorate the agricultural crisis in the Netherlands. Food production may not be characterized by surpluses and subsidies in the near future, but by increases in demand and necessity.[160] Any general agricultural crisis is then difficult to apply as an argument in favour of transforming arable land into housing estates.

Economic bubbles expand and burst. The spatial bubble, fed by financial abundance and the transformation of finance capital into fixed capital in the form of

154
The Netherlands Environmental Assessment Agency (MNP), NOVA (TV news magazine produced by NPS and Vara), and the Netherlands Architecture Institute (NAi).

155
ANP, 'CDA wil 5 miljoen extra parkeerplaatsen', *de Volkskrant* 1 July 2008; VROM, *Structuurvisie Randstad 2040: Naar een duurzame en concurrerende Europese topregio* (The Hague: Ministry of Spatial Planning and the Environment, 2008), presented by the Dutch cabinet on 5 September 2008.

156
The amount of space needed per car is estimated to be 25 m^2, resulting in a need for 12,500 ha of parking space (5 million cars x 25 m^2). The urbanized territory of Amsterdam was 11,475 ha in 2000.

157
With a housing density of 30 dwellings per hectare on the scale of the fabric (the average density of most suburban areas in the Netherlands), the amount of land needed to accommodate 500,000 dwellings is 16,667 ha fabrics. Considering all other land uses (parks, infrastructure, working areas, etcetera), the land needed on city scale is then approximately 33,000 ha (based on the same ratio between fabric area and total area as in the case of Amsterdam).

158
Province of North-Holland, *Bouwen voor Waterland 2020* (Haarlem, 2004).

159
Carbonell, A. and R. Yaro, 'American Spatial Development and the New Megalopolis', *Land Lines*, 17 (2) 2005; Couch, C., L. Leontidou and G. Petschel-Held, *Urban Sprawl in Europe: Landscapes, Land-Use Change & Policy* (Oxford: Blackwell Publishing, 2007).

160
See for instance FAO's initiative on Soaring Food Prices, 30 May 2008.

built landscapes, risks bursting.[161] Many parts of the world may run into huge difficulties when / if real estate values deflate and transportation costs become prohibitive. Sprawl might have a short-term attraction and deliver much consumer satisfaction, but in the long run one could certainly argue that it is unviable. In his polemic on Robert Bruegmanns pro-sprawl book *Sprawl: A Compact History*, James Howard Kunstler undermines this blind idolization of the consumer:

> His book fails entirely to acknowledge the fact that we are entering a permanent global energy crisis that will put an end to the drive-in utopia whether people like it or not ... The stark truth of the situation is that we are simply going to have to make other arrangementse – and I'm sorry to have to repeat that this will be the case whether we like it or not. Suburbia will be coming off the menu. We will no longer be able to resort to the stupid argument that it is okay because we chose it.[162]

Density and Sustainable Urban Development

Given the urgency of climate change, emission reductions and depleted world carbon fuel supplies, we have to reconsider current trends in urban land use. In low-density cities in North America energy consumption per inhabitant for transport is far higher than the same energy used by Europeans, and even more so when compared to very high-density cities in Asia. (26) North Americans are almost totally dependent on the private car, while the Japanese in general cluster in higher densities and are able to sustain a more efficient public transport network.[163] Denser urban environments certainly do not automatically mean less transport and energy consumption. Distances between homes and places of work, regulations and fiscal policies probably have far greater impacts on car use than the mere physical layout of cities and regions.[164] However, if the argument is turned around, one has to admit that dense settlements are a necessary prerequisite if we are to aspire to a radical cut in car and lorry transportation. Only dense settlements offer feasible circumstances for the large investments needed for a more energy-efficient and environmentally responsible movement of goods and people. Such settlements are also the only environments that can be successful when it comes to healthy and sustainable modes of transportation, such as walking and cycling. Also, proximity and mixing of functions seem to be a prerequisite for lower mobility and energy consumption. The urban patterns that are appropriate for such goals are those with a qualified urban density and a balanced mix of functions.[165]

The trigger for the critical density analyses of planners and architects of the Garden City Movement and the early modernists a century ago was rapid industrialization. Such problems of too much in too little space seem a long way off today (except for road congestion), as they have largely been displaced from the command centres of our global economy to booming

161
Harvey, D., *The Urbanization of Capital* (Baltimore: John Hopkins University Press, 1985), 1–31. As of September 2008, the real estate markets in many countries are contracting. Prime examples are Spain, Ireland, UK, Denmark, the USA and Dubai. See articles on the subject in *The Guardian*, *The Financial Times*, *The Economist*, etcetera from winter 2008 / 2009.

162
Kunstler, J., 'Review of Sprawl: A Compact History', *Salmagundi* 152 (Fall 2006), 175–183; Bruegmann, R., *Sprawl: A Compact History* (Chicago: University of Chicago Press, 2005).

163
Newman, P. and J. Kenworthy, *Sustainability and Cities: Overcoming Automobile Dependence* (Chicago: University of Chicago Press, 1999); Nozzi, D., *Road to Ruin: An Introduction to Sprawl and How to Cure It* (Westport: Praeger Publishers, 2003).

164
Neuman, M., 'The Compact City Fallacy', *Journal of Planning Education and Research* 25 (2005), 11–26.

165
Kann, F. van and W. Leduc, 'Synergy between regional planning and energy as a contribution to a carbon neutral societye – energy cascading as a new principle for mixed land-use'. Paper presented at the SCUPAD conference (Salzburg, Austria, 2008).

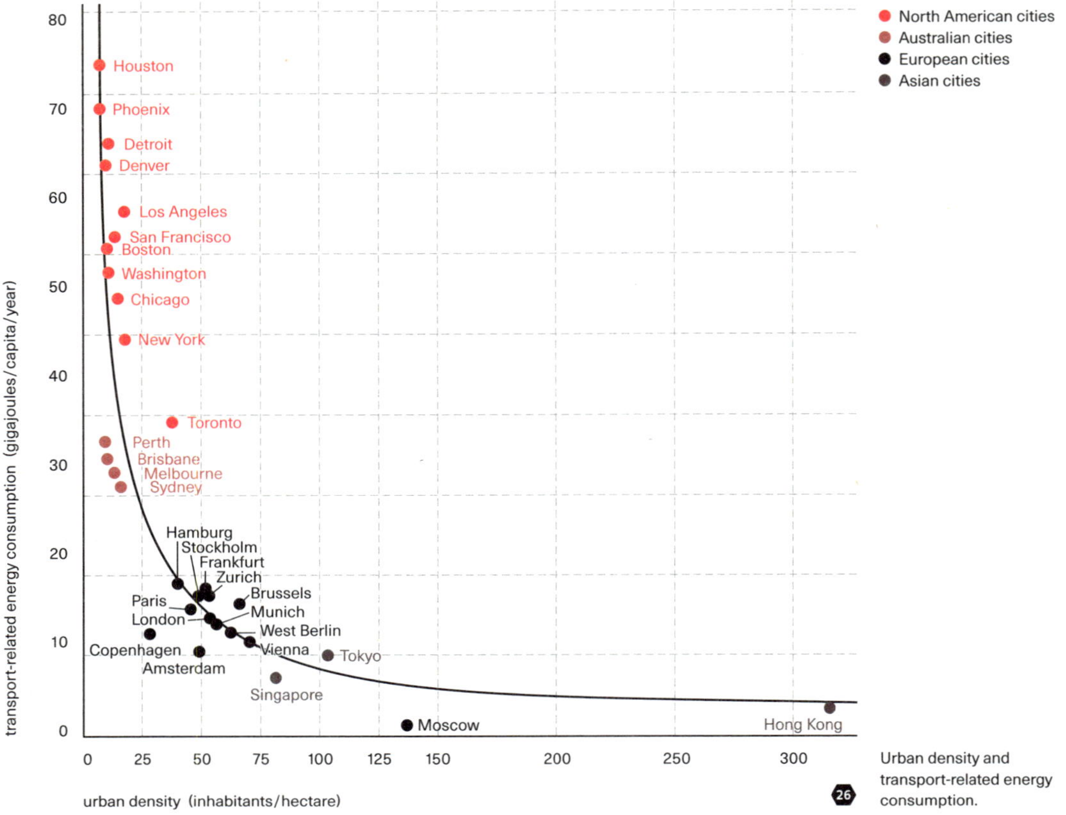

Urban density and transport-related energy consumption.

production zones elsewhere in the world. There, as Mike Davis describes in his book *Planet of Slums*, urbanization is taking place that dwarfs the growth pains of Western Europe a century ago, the period when the concept of density was introduced.[166] In the Netherlands the challenges facing spatial planning and design are quite the opposite of those that confronted planners and architects a century ago. Our affluence has brought with it suburbanization and sprawl that seem to threaten the very vitality of cities, aggravate social segregation and feed burgeoning car mobility. As mentioned earlier in this chapter, trends towards intensification have been evident in many urban developments during the last couple of decades (for example the waterfront developments in Amsterdam and Rotterdam, and the Zuidas in Amsterdam). The average space consumption per capita hereby seemed to increase less rapidly than it did a couple of decades ago. Nevertheless, these developments were mostly targeting high-end consumers and businesses. They were not addressing the vast stretches of less appealing industrial areas and suburban expansions that were added to the Netherlands each year. Sorkin, in his article *The End of Urban Design*, pointed to an important polarization 'between inevitabilism and nostalgia' in American cities over the last decade.[167] On the one hand the sprawl of traditionalist suburbia (in the New Urbanism social and aesthetic fashion) with low, but not very low densities, and, on the other gentrified inner-city developments with many of

166
Davis, M., *Planet of Slums* (London/New York: Verso, 2006).

167
Sorkin, 'The End(s)', op. cit. (note 124).

the characteristics of 'urbanity' and with high, but not very high, densities.

A strong consensus has emerged among experts and policymakers that we need to use land more efficiently and sustainably. Since the 1990s, the compact city approach has been the main planning strategy used to cope with the fierce competition between land uses as a result of global urbanization and is regarded as one of the main strategies for sustainable urban development.[168] This has resulted in an increase of density in Amsterdam of 17 per cent between 2000 and 2020. It is argued to provide, through densification and compact building, several environmental gains, especially related to the reduction of greenhouse gas emissions, innovation and economic growth.[169] However, there are also negative effects associated with higher density, not least when it comes to environmental degradation.[170] The strong dichotomy between, on the one hand, the positive effects of density on transport and economics and, on the other, the negative effects on ecology, social issues and human health, is striking. It also formulates a challenging task for urban planners and designers to balance these two spheres (the system and the lifeworld), while at the same time acknowledging the need for some form of densification to handle current urbanization rates.[171]

Therefore, although current urbanization rates require some form of densification, there is need for a better understanding of its trade-offs. At the beginning of the twentieth century the threat of social upheaval and revolution made housing and urban reform a necessity. During a period of political turmoil Le Corbusier in 1923 spelled out the options at the beginning of that century: 'It is a question of building which is at the root of the social unrest of today: Architecture or Revolution.' At the beginning of the twenty-first century, as we face climate change, social and spatial inequalities and serious degradation of the ecological system, this might be restated as a choice between Urbanism or Meltdown.

168 Haaland, C. and C. K. van den Bosch, 'Challenges and strategies for urban green-space planning in cities undergoing densification: A review', *Urban Forestry & Urban Greening*, 14:4 (2015), 760–71.

169 Ahlfeldt, G. and E. Pietrostefani, *Demystifying Compact Urban Growth: Evidence From 300 Studies From Across the World* (London and Washington: Coalition for Urban Transitions, 2017).

170 Gren, Å, J Colding, M Berghauser Pont and L Marcus, 'How Smart is Smart Growth? Examining the Environmental Validation Behind City Compaction', *Ambio* 48 (2018).

171 Berghauser Pont, M. Y., P. G. Berg, P. A. Haupt, A. Heyman, 'A systematic review of the scientifically demonstrated effects of densification', *IOP Conf. Ser.: Earth Environ. Sci.* 588 052031 (2020).

Reinvented Density, Different Doctrines

In this chapter we have discussed changes in the process of city development, focusing on changes in the role state institutions played and the role of density in planning. During the first part of the twentieth century an active role of the state was accepted in response to dealing with public health issues. Density was used to diagnose this situation and propagate alternatives. Interventions and legislation countered the negative effects of overcrowding and laissez faire capitalism. Still, this interventionism was fairly modest compared to the state-managed economies that took form after the Second World War. Coordinated planning and state investments played an important role in the Keynesian growth strategy, peaking in the 1960s and coming to an end in the crises of the 1970s. With the neoliberal shift in the 1980s and 1990s, liberals of a less fundamentalist charactere – those ascribing to the Third Way social-democracy of the 1990se – argued that many of the direct impacts of inevitable reforms (read deconstruction of the welfare system) would be softened by trickledown effects of economics and win-win situations. Instead of striving for more healthy and social cities, urban designers produced marketing imagery to attract investments.

Today, it seems difficult to plea for direct public intervention in spatial and urban planning, since the current managerial state is just one of many forces that determine the direction of future space consumption. Furthermore, decentralization, competition between cities and the fragmentation of urban developments into separate competing urban projects described by Brenner, Harvey, and so forth, run against such public activism on all levels, be it national, regional or global. At the end of the nineteenth century private developers were the drivers of city development when the practice of speculation was flourishing. They had at the end of the twentieth century, again, assumed centre stage, following an interval of 75 years of more or less continuous state management. Today private and public actors work together in project based agencies. Such projects are, to use the words of Harvey, 'concerned with the construction of place (the image of a specific place) and the enhancement of property values rather than the amelioration of conditions (housing, health, poverty, etc.)'.

However, the quick turns of the most recent crisis of capitalisme – acknowledged not only by its sternest critics, but by just about everyone – makes fundamental reconsideration of the neoliberal spatial strategies of the last decades necessary. A post-neoliberal path will certainly, at least temporarily, include more state intervention (so far mostly in the form of the socialization of private losses) and collectively formulated guidelines and regulations to once again save capitalism from itself. That the de-financialization of large swaths of society will bring about fundamental changes in the realm of fixed capital, that is, the physical development of cities and countryside, seems quite self-evident.[172] Whether it will lead to a more democratic society or further strengthen the corporative character of the state is an open question. In both cases, a larger involvement of state institutions will mean that new instruments are (again) needed to reconnect national, regional and urban planning with urban and architectural design.

Whatever the political and economic constellation will be in the near future – a return to neoliberalism, a solidification of state interventions, or

172
Sassen, S., 'Too Big to Save: The End of Financial Capitalism'. Available online at HTTP: http://www.opendemocracy.net, accessed 24 November 2009;
Harvey, D., *The Urbanization*, op. cit. (note 160).

other not yet imaginable arrangementse – some urgent issues will need to be responded to. As we discussed before, an infinite urban growth cannot be sustained in a finite world. Even if many parts of the world spatially seem able to absorb almost endless urban expansions, the associated consequences for transportation, energy consumption, climate change and loss of arable land will be immense. The need for density discussions today can be likened to the one a century ago, but with some fundamental differences. Then, attempts were made to describe and understand the problems of the industrializing cities (for example diseases) and their causes (such as overcrowding), alternatives were suggested (for example the Garden City), and instruments created and implemented, often in the form of maximum densities. Today, overcrowding, extreme poverty and human misery have moved from Manchester to Manila (where legally binding maximum densities would be part of radical emancipation!). The proximity of production and consumption, wealth and poverty, that earlier was present in one and the same city in Western Europe (for instance the Jordaan next to the Grachtengordel), structure many developing metropolises today. At the same time, large swaths of affluence here and predominant production there have created new problems (such as exploitation of humans, climate change, pollution, resource scarcity), driven by overconsumption of resources (transport, goods, energy, humans) and space (sprawl). If industrialization took off with urbanization and overcrowding, the fossil-fuel-driven economic growth and developments in transport techniques of the last century have dispersed and thinned out our cities. The consequences of the present overconsumption and overshoot of the earth's resources, as well as possible responses (such as (re)intensified cities, compact villages, rural self-sufficiency), should be investigated through, among other things, the concept of density. A future step would be to further integrate density into the legal process of contracting, plan making and zoning documents. Instead of the maximum densities that are often (indirectly) prescribed, a shift to minimum densities should in many cases be made, taking into consideration its trade-offs. The ambitions for intensifying Dutch cities are present, mainly as part of the limitation of development costs and creation of 'urbanity'. However, other, more urgent, reasons (such as survival) to consciously and more firmly guide, plan and regulate the exploitation of space should give the question a very high priority. Carbon taxing and rationing are being discussed in some countries, and cars and buildings have to confirm to tightening CO_2 and energy performance requirements respectively. Why should one of the most fundamental conditions, the spatial stage set, or the urban plan, be exempt of such regulations? This rather naive question surely shortcuts many reality constraints and vested interests, but still, it should be of great importance to speculate about and develop appropriate instruments that can be part of such a shift.

In this chapter we have shown how the dominating emphasis in urban planning during the twentieth century in the Netherlands shifted from quantifying urban developments through scientific surveys and mathematic reasoning (Unwin, Hoenig, Van Eesteren and Lohuizen, Martin and March) to grasping the qualitative aspects of city development in terms of urban form, identity and urbanity (Sitte, Berlage, Jacobs, Urhahn, Bhalotra). Morphological research at one stage became part of the answer, but as this approach focused mainly on the traditional city (read the one before the modernist takeover), this often resulted in preservationism, selectively extracting elements and symbols of the city to create a culture of 'niceness'.

When considering quantity and quality too much in isolation, the primacy of one may be to the detriment of the other. To arrive at more sustainable urban developments we need to reconcile spatial quality at the micro level (variation in built environments, housing typologies, public spaces, micro-climate and so forth) to the structural effects on society as a whole (programme, mobility, socioeconomic effects, integration / segregation, energy consumption). Gains can be made if quantity and quality can be engaged simultaneously.

3

MULTIVARIABLE DENSITY: SPACEMATRIX

As Arza Churchman describes in *Disentangling the Concept of Density,* there is not one accepted measure of density in, or shared by, different countries.[1] In general, density measures vary according to the manner in which numerators and denominators are defined.[2] Some countries define density using the number of people per given area (population density), while others define it using the number of dwelling units or the building mass per given area (Floor Space Index, or land use intensity). It is important to realize that one can translate one density measure into another by making assumptions or applying known statistics, such as dwelling size and occupancy rate. A purely physical density, such as FSI, can be translated into a more socially relevant form of density, such as dwelling and population density. A variety of land units, including acre, hectare, square mile and square kilometre can be used for denominators. These measures are not difficult to convert.

More important – and problematic – is the definition of the boundary of an area, as this, to a large extent, determines the outcome of density calculations. Although it is common to distinguish between net and gross density, the definition of net and gross varies from place to place, and has been a source of great ambiguity. This book aspires to formulate a clear set of definitions for these boundaries. Most important, however, is to be consistent when comparing different areas.

Related to the discussion of boundaries is the issue of scale and averages. An average density does not necessarily mean that the whole area has a uniform density. The larger the area over which the density is measured, the more heterogeneous it is likely to be. Moreover, as the scale increases, the amount of non-built land (roads, railways, green areas and water) also increases in relative terms, and density, be it population density or another measure, decreases. Thus, the definition of the denominator – the total area of the land – in the quotient is crucial when determining density.

The first part of this chapter critically assesses the density measures introduced in Chapter 2 and their ability to describe built form. We demonstrate that existing density indicators have a programmatic and statistical character and are indeed, as is discussed in Chapter 1, inadequate in describing central spatial properties of urban landscapes. The second part of this chapter presents a method designed to simultaneously assess different

1
Churchman, A., 'Disentangling the Concept of Density', *Journal of Planning Literature*, 13 4 1999, 389–411.

2
The numerator A is the number above and the denominator B is the number below the line in a vulgar fraction A / B.

density variables and describe spatial properties with more precision. The use of this method is demonstrated with the help of the examples from Amsterdam used in the previous chapter. Chapters 4 and 5 then further discuss in greater detail the relationship between urban density, urban types and performance.

Perceived Density

Before discussing different measuring methods, it is important to realize that density can be approached in different ways. One important distinction is between physical density and perceived density.[3] Depending on a range of individual and sociocultural factors, a person (inhabitant, visitor) will evaluate and react differently to perceived density. The concept of 'crowding' highlights, in this case, a negative evaluation of perceived density.[4] An example: a shy person from a rural area will react in a specific manner to a busy inner-city street; this reaction might be described as a feeling of 'crowdedness'. On the other hand, the reaction of a streetwise metropolitan dweller to the same physical and social situation might be described as the joy of 'urbanity'.[5] He or she might appreciate the pace of the city and enjoy the random, social forms of intercourse.

Although these more multifaceted aspects of density are of great importance to the evaluation of design and understanding people's reactions to different urban environments, in our research we limit ourselves primarily to physical density as defined by Ernest Alexander.[6] We return to the distinction between perceived and physical density in Chapter 5 in a discussion of the issue of performance as it relates to density.

3 Rapaport, A., 'Toward a Redefinition of Density', *Environment and Behaviour* 7 2 1975, 7–32.

4 Churchman, 'Disentangling', op. cit. note 1.

5 This concept will be further discussed in Chapter 5.

6 Alexander, E.R., 'Density Measures: A Review and Analysis', *Journal of Architectural and Planning Research* 10 3 1993, 181–202.

Physical Density

Different physical density measures have been used to describe and prescribe human space consumption. In this section we describe the most conventional methods used to measure density and draw conclusions about their effectiveness in describing urban form. The measurement methods discussed are:

- Population and dwelling density;
- Land use intensity;
- Coverage;
- Building height;
- Spaciousness.

Population and Dwelling Density

Population density can be expressed in terms of the number of people or households in an area, while dwelling density measures the number of dwellings in an area. Families vary in size (social and historical spread)

1 Associated architects and developers playing with miniature Rockefeller Centers: '... combine the maximum of congestion with the maximum of light and space' (Koolhaas 1994: 178).

and a household can range from a single person to multiple family units. Population density calculations are used to plan for new schools, retail, utilities and the transit expansion needed for an area. As social transformations generally are quicker than physical transformations, the population density of an area can have changed through history even if the number of dwellings has remained the same. Dwelling density is thus the more robust of the two and is often used in descriptions of urban developments.

Raymond Unwin stated in his 1912 pamphlet *Nothing Gained by Overcrowding* that density should be limited to 12 dwellings per acre (30 dwellings per hectare).[7] Frank Lloyd Wright, on the other hand, proposed in Broad Acre City an ideal density of one dwelling per acre (2.5 dwellings per hectare).[8] In the Netherlands, Cornelis van Eesteren and Th.K. van Lohuizen were the first to use dwelling density in a planning document. They studied the relationship between dwelling type and density and arrived at a density that would allow for feasible land use in combination with the construction of as many single-family houses as possible.[9] Research into different allotment patterns had shown that with a density of 70 dwellings per hectare, 50 to 60 per cent of the dwellings could be constructed as single-family houses.[10] In the

7 Unwin, R., *Nothing Gained by Overcrowding! How the Garden City Type of Development May Benefit Both Owner and Occupier* Westminster: P.S. King & Son, 1912.

8 Wright, F.L., *The Disappearing City* New York: W.F. Payson, 1932.

9 Municipality of Amsterdam, *Algemeen Uitbreidingsplan van Amsterdam AUP: Nota van toelichting* Amsterdam: Stadsdrukkerij Amsterdam, 1934.

10 Hellinga, H. and P. de Ruijter, *Algemeen Uitbreidingsplan Amsterdam 50 jaar* Amsterdam: Amsterdamse Raad voor de Stedebouw, 1985.

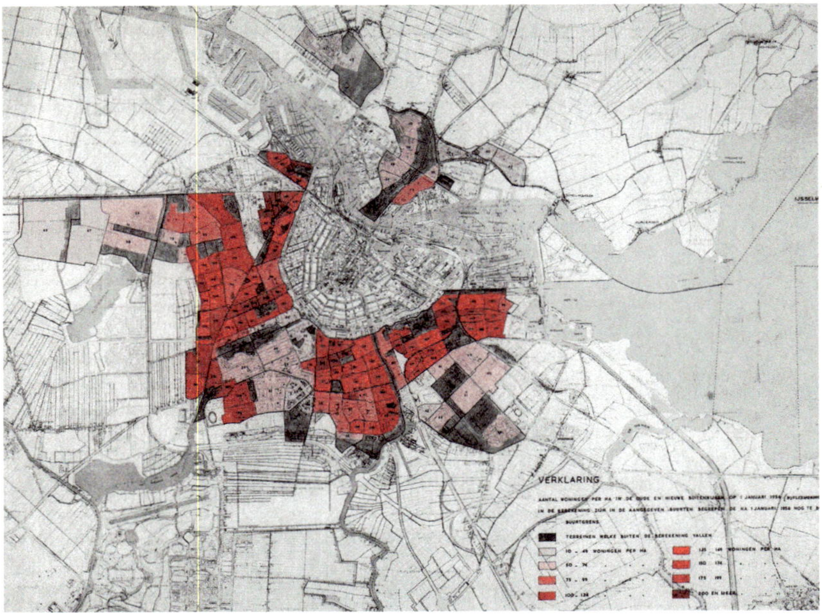

❷ Dwelling density in the old expansion areas on 1 January 1956 (1956, k226-9 and 226-10 in Hameleers 2002: 270).

Netherlands, this ratio between the number of dwellings and a hectare of land was recommended as a standard for measuring density in 1942.[11]

In most cases a differentiation is made between net and gross density, or between net residential density, neighbourhood density (*wijkdichtheid*) and city density (*generale dichtheid*).[12] Net density mostly excludes all public streets and residential density usually describes the portion of the neighbourhood used solely for housing. Gross, or neighbourhood density, also covers neighbourhood facilities such as primary schools and grocery shops, and city density adds the more general amenities, such as a city library, hospitals, etcetera.

A residential area is in the Netherlands often defined as a unique combination of street systems, lot patterns and building configurations (size and shape) and is delineated by boundaries drawn in the middle of the streets surrounding the lots and buildings.[13] The gross density, or neighbourhood density, was calculated by adding the amount of land needed for amenities to serve the population in a residential area.[14] The 1956 density map of Amsterdam, ❷ which applied Van Lohuizen's method for calculating density, included the residential area, the neighbourhood facilities and the main roads, and thus corresponds to the gross density, or neighbourhood density.[15] The definition of the neighbourhoods (*buurten*) used today by the Dutch municipalities and Statistics Netherlands (CBS) are similar to the boundaries set in 1956, although the exact borders are often revised to match municipal borders. The effects of these different definitions for measured density are enormous and make comparisons between areas difficult. ❸

The previous chapter referred to a series of areas in Amsterdam as representatives of different periods in the history of city development in the Netherlands. We will use these again here to demonstrate the different

11
Angenot, L.H.J., *Verhandelingen over het vraagstuk van de dichtheid van bebouwing* Alphen aan den Rijn: N. Samsom NV, 1954.

12
Alexander, 'Density Measures', op. cit. note 6; Angenot, *Verhandelingen*, op. cit. note 11; Churchman, 'Disentangling', op. cit. note 1; Forsyth, A., 'Measuring Density: Working Definitions for Residential Density and Building Density', *Design Brief*, 8 2003, Design Center for American Urban Landscape, University of Minesota; Rådberg, J., *Doktrin och täthet i svenskt stadsbyggande 1875–1975* Stockholm: Statens råd för byggnadsforskning, 1988.

13
Angenot, *Verhandelingen*, op. cit. note 11.

14
Ibid.

15
Ibid.

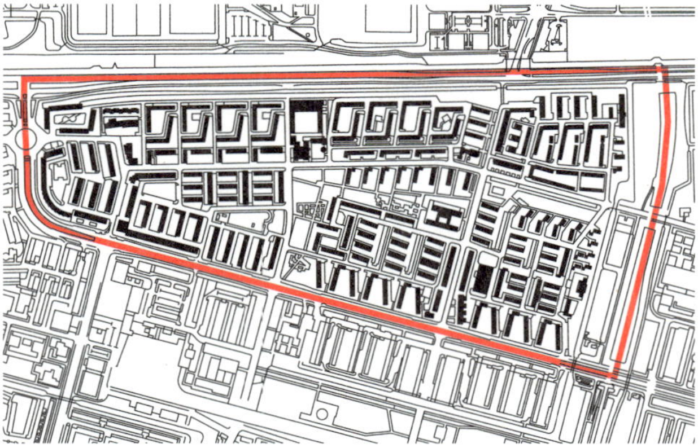

1 Bureau for Research and Statistics in Amsterdam: 40 dw/ha

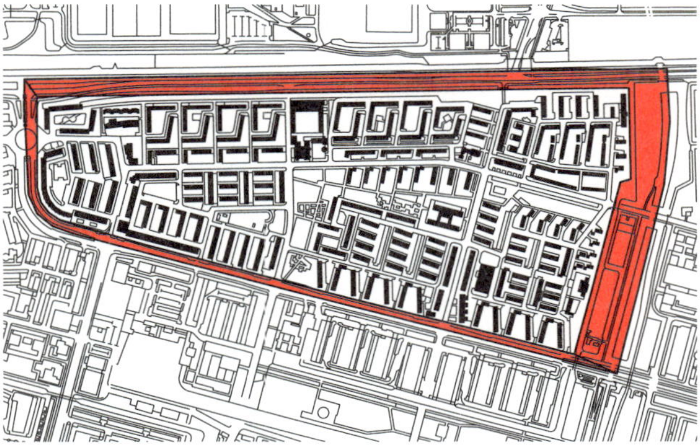

2 Van Lohuizen: 50 dw/ha

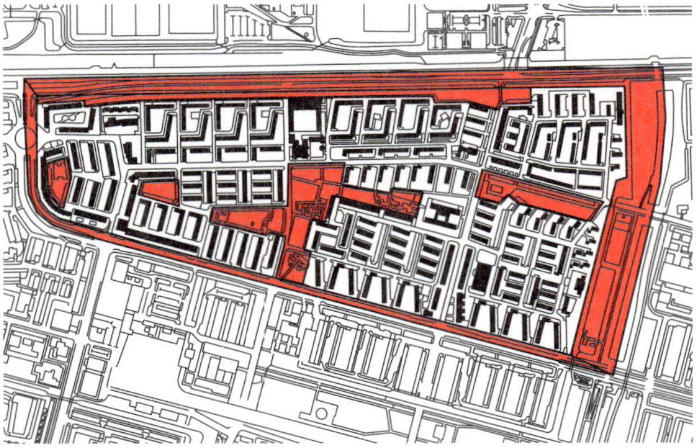

3 Van Lohuizen excluding larger green areas: 60 dw/ha

3 Dwelling density in Slotermeer Noord, Amsterdam, calculated based on three different boundary definitions (in red the subtracted area).

density measures. The Jordaan (seventeenth century) and De Pijp (nineteenth century) had among the highest population densities in Amsterdam. The former had 1,265 inhabitants per hectare in 1889, the latter 700 inhabitants per hectare at the end of the 1950s.[16] During the same periods, two other areas were built for the well-to-do inhabitants of Amsterdam: Grachtengordel (seventeenth century) and Vondelparkbuurt (nineteenth century). These had, respectively, densities of 270 (Grachtengordel in 1889) and 200 (Vondelpark in 1958) inhabitants per hectare. One reason for the difference in density between Jordaan and De Pijp, on the one hand, and Grachtengordel and Vondelparkbuurt, on the other, is that the first two areas, built for immigrants and the working class, contained large numbers of small dwellings, inhabited by large families. The dwellings in Grachtengordel and Vondelparkbuurt were much larger. A family was allowed to construct only one house per lot. Later, when the economic situation changed, dwellings were subdivided or transformed into offices, thus changing the population density. Today, especially in the Grachtengordel, more people work in the area, resulting in a decrease in population density.[17] A different type of transformation has taken place in the Jordaan and De Pijp. Small dwellings have been united into larger ones and industries have been moved to the periphery of the city. Relatively few people now work in these areas.[18] Also, the average number of people per dwelling (occupancy rate) in Amsterdam decreased from 4.36 towards the end of the nineteenth century to 1.97 in 2000.[19] ❹❺ demonstrates how the transformations in Grachtengordel and Jordaan brought about less extreme differences in population density.

The changes in population density in these four examples occurred without much change in the layout of the urban fabric. We can therefore conclude that there is little relation between population density and urban form. ❻ demonstrates that the high-rise development in Bijlmermeer has a lower dwelling density than the garden city of Betondorp, which comprises low-rise housing. ❼ The same dwelling density can thus be achieved through very different urban forms, and we can therefore question Alexander's conclusions, presented in a graph, which show a relationship between dwelling types and net dwelling density.[20] ❽ The reasons that dwelling and population density demonstrate a weak relation to built form are threefold: the occupancy rate of dwellings differs, the size of the dwellings differs and the amount of non-residential space is not taken into account when expressing dwelling density.

Of course, the differences in the numbers of inhabitants influence such characteristics of an area as the user and traffic intensity, or the potential for different programmes, etcetera. In short, the quality of life in an area is dependent on the dialectic relation between the physical environment and the social activities taking place. However, these variations take place in a physical context that is largely characterized by stability and robustness.[21] A monofunctional working area does not physically

16
Based on the dwelling density as mentioned on the 1956 map *Woningdichtheden* 'dwelling densities' from the Dienst der Publieke Werken, Department Stadsontwikkeling in Hameleers, M. ed., *Kaarten van Amsterdam 1866–2000* Bussum: Uitgeverij THOTH, 2002, 270; and Laloli, H.M., 'Beter wonen? Woningmarkt en residentiële segregatie in Amsterdam 1850–1940', in: O.W.A. Boonstra et al. eds., *Twee eeuwen Nederland geteld: Onderzoek met de digitale volks-, beroeps- en woningtellingen 1795–2001* The Hague: DANS and CBS, 2007.

17
The ratio between people living and working in the Grachtengordel is 1:1.5 and in Vondelparkbuurt 1:0.6. Source: O+S, Statistics for the areas A02c and V47d available online at www.os.amsterdam.nl 2007.

18
The ratio between people living and working in the Jordaan is 1:0.3 and in De Pijp 1:0.2. Source: O+S, Statistics for the areas A06c and V24d available online at www.os.amsterdam.nl 2007.

19
These numbers are averages for the whole city, based on Wintershoven, L., *Demografisch eeuwboek Amsterdam: Ontwikkelingen tussen 1900 en 2000* Amsterdam: dRO, 2000.

20
Alexander, 'Density Measures', op. cit. note 6, 193.

21
Heeling, J., H. Meyer and J. Westrik, *Het ontwerp van de stadsplattegrond* Amsterdam: SUN, 2002; Rutte, R., *A Landscape of Towns: Urbanization in the Netherlands from the 11th to the 19th Centuries* Delft: Delft University of Technology, Faculty of Architecture, 2004.

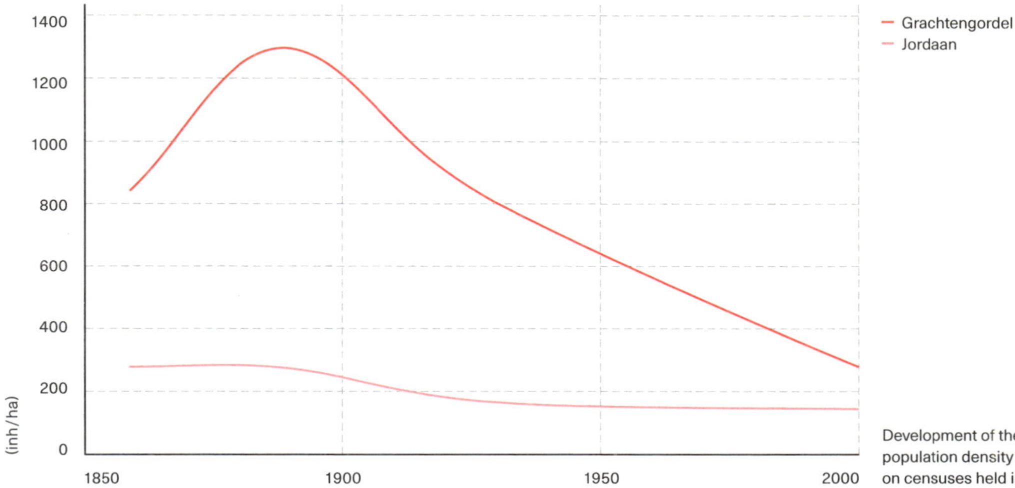

4 Development of the population density based on censuses held in 1859, 1899 and 1930 (Laloli, 2007), and statistics (O+S 2007).

5 Aerial and street view of Grachtengordel and Jordaan.

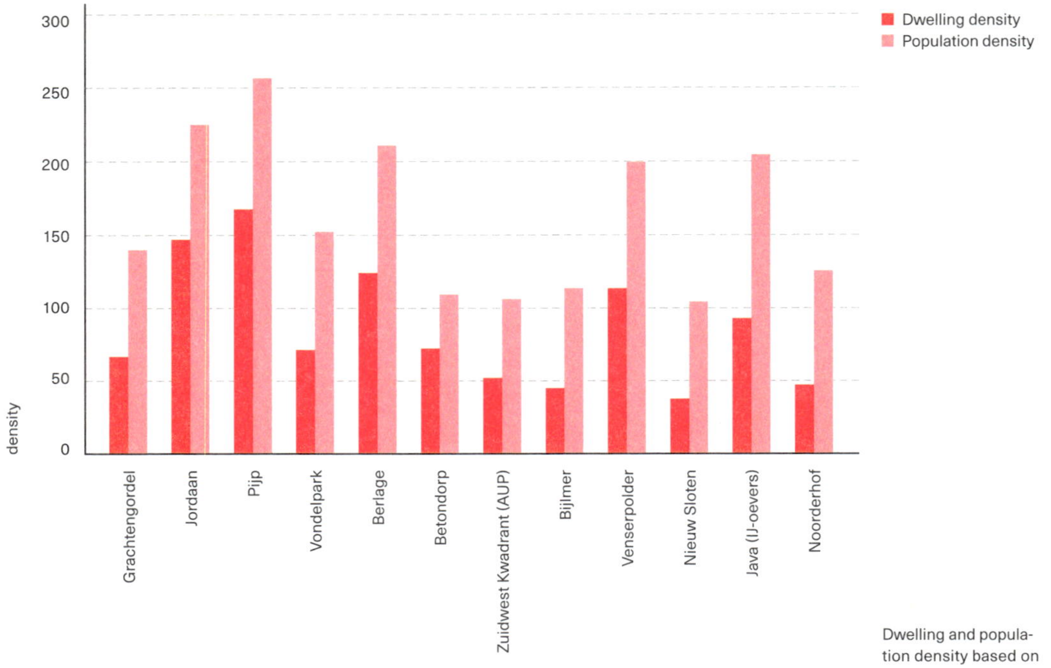

6 Dwelling and population density based on statistics from O+S Amsterdam (2007).

7 Aerial and street view of Bijlmer and Betondorp.

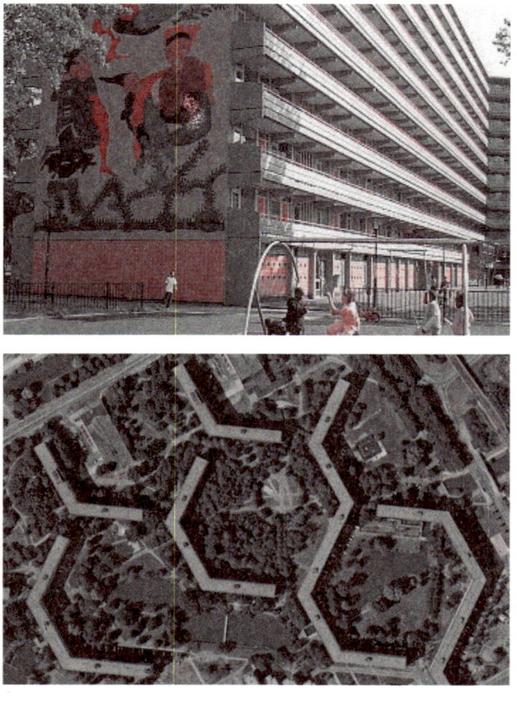

Bijlmer [NL] 112 inh/ha and 44 dw/ha

Betondorp [NL] 108 inh/ha and 70 dw/ha

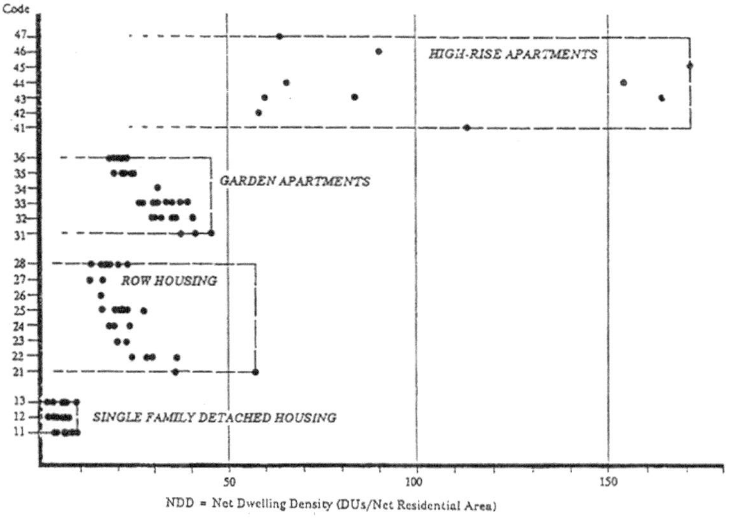

8 Distribution of Net Dwelling Density (dwelling units per net residential area) by dwelling type (Alexander 1993: 193).

transform during the night although it is crowded during the day and empty at night. Its physical form can certainly change, but occurs in time spans measured in decades and centuries, rather than days and years.

Land Use Intensity

Today, population and dwelling densities are still widely used in the urban profession. The Dutch Ministry of Spatial Planning and the Environment (VROM) for instance, uses households per hectare as a classification of urban environments.[22] Another, purely physical, density measure only recently became more popular in the Netherlands: the Floor Space Index (FSI).[23]

The 1925 Building Ordinance of Berlin made use of the so called *Ausnutzungsziffer* (exploitation number).[24] This variable expresses the relation of the amount of built floor area to the area of a plan. This is one of the first examples in Europe of the use of a more neutral indicator that combined *all* floor space to describe and prescribe density, independent of its use. In 1944, the British Ministry of Health suggested using the building bulk (floor area) as the numerator, expressed as floor-space-index, or FSI.[25] It was particularly to be used in areas dominated by commercial buildings. An international conference in Zurich in 1948 established this index as the common standard in Europe. A comparable term used in New York City's Zoning Resolution is the floor to area ratio (FAR), which expressed the building bulk in relation to lot size.[26]

22 In the most recent National Policy Document on Spatial Planning, VROM, *Nota ruimte – ruimte voor ontwikkeling* The Hague: Ministry of Spatial Planning and the Environment, 2004, and in the report VROM, *Nota wonen: Mensen, wensen, wonen* The Hague: Ministry of Spatial Planning and the Environment, 2000, five urban environments are defined with a density for working and living, expressed in households and work places per hectare.

23 Municipality of Amsterdam, *Structuurplan Amsterdam: Kiezen voor stedelijkheid* Amsterdam: dRO, 2003; Municipality of Rotterdam, *De Rotterdamse woonmilieuprofielen-atlas* Rotterdam: dS+V, afdeling Wonen, 2003; Municipality of Amsterdam, *Meten met twee maten: Referentieplannen bebouwingsintensiteit* Amsterdam: dRO, coördinatieteam Optimalisering Grondgebruik, 2001; Urhahn, G.B. and M. Bobic, *A Pattern Image* Bussum: Uitgeverij THOTH, 1994.

24 Rådberg, *Doktrin*, op. cit. note 12, 68.

25 Angenot, *Verhandelingen*, op. cit. note 11.

26 City of New York, *Zoning Handbook: A guide to New York City's Zoning Resolution* New York, 1990. Probably this term was not established in the first resolution of 1916. The introduction of the *Zoning Handbook* states that the current resolution, in which FAR is mentioned, came into effect in 1961.

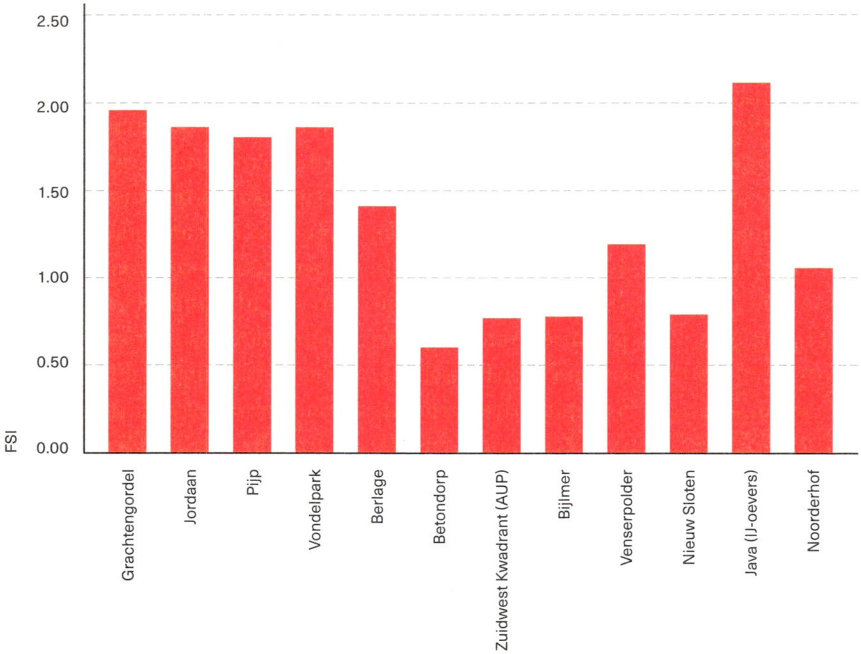

9 Intensity (FSI) of a selection of urban fabrics.

10 Aerial and street view of Zuidwest Kwadrant and Nieuw Sloten.

Zuidwest Kwadrant 2 [NL] FSI 0.78 and 51 dw/ha

Nieuw Sloten [NL] FSI 0.77 and 36 dw/ha

Under the guidance of the *Central Service for Reconstruction and Public Housing* (*Centrale Directie van de Wederopbouw en de Volkshuisvesting*), the Land Index was developed in the Netherlands in 1949 to measure built density.[27] This quotient uses the ratio of the land area (in the numerator) to the floor area (in the denominator), and is inversely equivalent to the *Ausnutzungsziffer*, FSI or FAR. This measure has, however, never been widely accepted in the Dutch urban profession. The number of dwellings per hectare has remained popular. The first time FSI was used in an official Dutch planning document was, as far as we have been able to trace, in the 2003 *Structuurplan Amsterdam*.[28] In this document, built environments are defined by, among other things, density measures, expressed as FSI.[29] This plan was preceded by two studies by Bureau Parkstad in Amsterdam,[30] and the report *Meten met twee maten* in which a distinction was made between lot FSI, net FSI and gross FSI.[31] The boundary of the net plan area was defined by the urban project and therefore sometimes took into account streets, water and green areas, but on other occasions consisted of only a single lot. This makes comparisons risky. The gross plan area was calculated by drawing a boundary line 30 m from the borders of the lot or, when adjacent lots were in close proximity, by drawing the boundary exactly in the middle of the lot lines. To a large extent, both definitions are arbitrary and were criticized in an expert meeting organized by the municipality of Amsterdam in 2001.[32]

When assessing the samples from Amsterdam,[33] we see that the four oldest areas (Grachtengordel, Jordaan, De Pijp and Vondelparkbuurt) have a similar FSI although the population and dwelling density, as we have seen in the former paragraph, differs significantly. (9) When comparing the FSI with the spatial characteristics of these areas, it appears thus that FSI expresses form in a better way than population and dwelling density.

However, other samples show that although FSI takes all functions into account, it is not nuanced enough to convey urban form. The typical post-war open block structures of Zuidwest Kwadrant (part of the AUP), the high-rise developments of the Bijlmermeer and the single-family houses of Nieuw Sloten have identical built intensities (FSI), but they differ greatly in terms of urban form. (7) (9) (10)

27
Angenot, *Verhandelingen*, op. cit. note 11.

28
Municipality of Amsterdam, *Structuurplan*, op. cit. note 23.

29
Ibid. Another physical measure mentioned in *Structuurplan* is Ground Space Index, or coverage. This measure is discussed in the following paragraph.

30
Permeta architecten, *FSI-GSI-OSR: Atlas Westelijke Tuinsteden, instrumentarium voor verdichting en verdunning*, commissioned by Bureau Parkstad Amsterdam, 2001; Permeta architecten, *FSI-GSI-OSR als instrumentarium voor verdichting en verdunning: Case study Nieuw West*, commissioned by Bureau Parkstad Amsterdam, 2000.

31
Municipality of Amsterdam, *Meten*, op. cit. note 23.

32
Persons present at the meeting: I. Kleijnjan coordinatieteam Optimalisering Grondgebruik, dRO, K. van Zanen & L. de Laat authors *Meten met Twee Maten*, dRO, M. Berghauser Pont Permeta architecten, E. van der Kooij & G. de Boo dRO, R. Meertens & J. Westrik Delft University of Technology, L. Vrolijks Urhahn Urban Design, J. Harts URU, University Utrecht, C. Maat OTB, Delft University of Technology, M. de Koning Gans RPD, A. Oude Ophuis Tauw, F. de Jong SEV, C. de Boer Slotervaart/Overtoomse Veld, D. Dicke EGM, M. Simons, C. de Koning, R. Mertens, N. van Eeghem, and M. van Kessel dRO.

33
Based on calculations and field work by the authors. Areas are defined as urban fabrics consisting of a reasonably homogenous urban pattern of streets and islands building or urban blocks and thus rather similar to the definition of net residential density. However, all functions are expressed in the total amount of floor area. Floor area is defined as gross floor area of buildings as described in the Dutch standard NEN 2580.

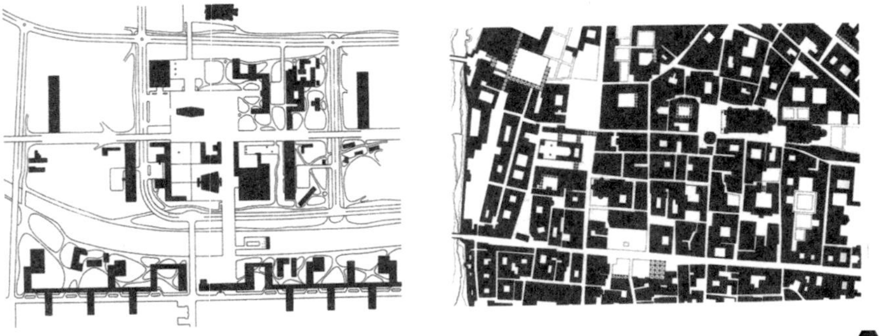

11 Figure-ground analysis from 'Collage City' by Rowe and Koetter (1978).

Coverage

The concept of coverage was frequently used throughout the twentieth century to express the relationship between built and non-built land. Colin Rowe used the figure-ground analysis to visually represent coverage as the distribution of (built) mass and open space.[34] He used this representation to decode two opposite doctrines at the core of modern and traditional planning: the first an accumulation of solids in an endless floating void, the other dominated by mass and cut through by voids. 11

In Germany, the coverage measure was applied to limit the negative effects of solid urban patterns. Reinhard Baumeister, Joseph Stübben, Karl Hoepfner and Anton Hoenig all worked with the concept of coverage and in 1925 it became part of the official planning policy in the Building Ordinance of Berlin.[35] Coverage was actively used even earlier in planning. The expansion plan of Barcelona by Ildefonso Cerdà is a good example. Here the coverage was restricted to a maximum of 50 per cent of the lots to guarantee good hygienic conditions.[36] This was, however, to a large extent ignored during implementation and, over time, coverage reached almost 90 per cent in many areas. Interestingly, Jane Jacobs argued in 1961 for high lot coverage (between 60 and 80 per cent for the building blocks). This was to bring people out into the public streets and parks, and to create a lively city.[37] Jan Gehl recently used the same argument for a high degree of coverage in his study for Ørestad Syd in Copenhagen.[38]

The 1916 New York City's Zoning Resolution restricted the amount of ground that could be covered by buildings.[39] In the Netherlands, coverage is used in zoning plans (*bestemmingsplannen*) to regulate maximum utilization of an area.

When we look at the areas with identical FSI values discussed in the former section – namely Zuidwest Kwadrant, Bijlmermeer and Nieuw Sloten – we observe that the coverage (or Ground Space Index, GSI) differs. In fact, GSI can be said to be a better standard with which to distinguish the spatial differences of these samples. 12 However, a part of Plan Zuid by Hendrik Petrus Berlage and Noorderhof, an area in Amsterdam designed by Rob Krier and Christoph Kohl in 1999, have similar GSI values although the spatial characteristics are remarkably different. 13 The land use plan

34 Rowe, C. and F. Koetter, *Collage City* Cambridge, MA: MIT Press, 1978.

35 Rådberg, *Doktrin*, op. cit. note 12.

36 Busquets, J., *Barcelona, the Urban Evolution of a Compact City* Rovereto: Nicolodi, 2005, 130.

37 Jacobs, J., *The Death and Life of Great American Cities* New York: Random House, 1992, 214.

38 Presentation of Jan Gehl's studies by Jan Christiansen, city architect of Copenhagen, at the conference *Scale, Form and Process. Scales in Urban Landscapes*, Aarhus School of Architecture, Department of Landscape and Urbanism, Aarhus, Denmark, 23–24 February 2006.

39 City of New York, *Zoning Handbook*, op. cit. note 26.

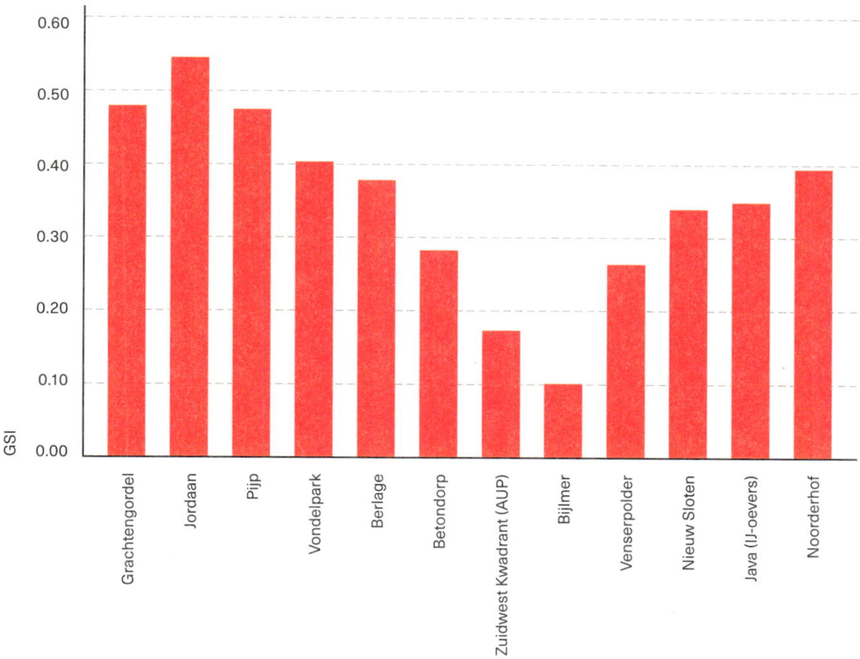

12 Coverage (GSI) of a selection of urban fabrics.

13 Aerial and street view of Berlage, Plan Zuid, and Noorderhof.

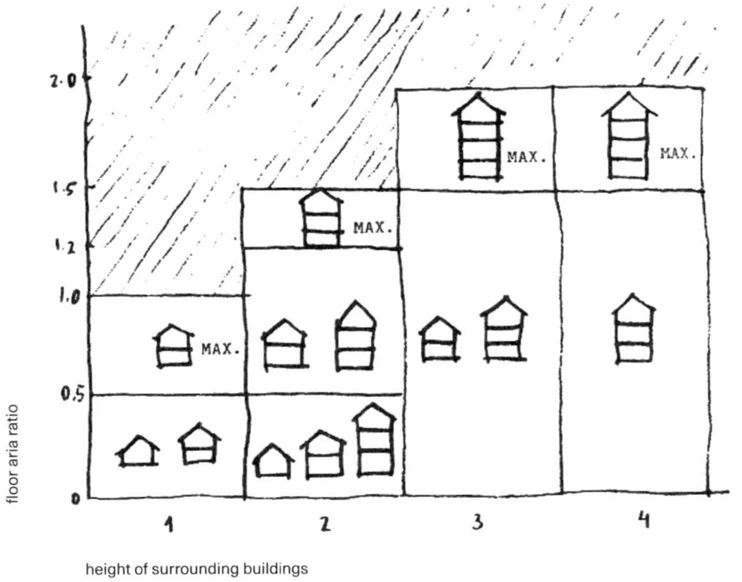

(14) Relationship between the maximum heights of the buildings, based on the height of the adjacent buildings and the floor area ratio (FAR), according to Alexander (1977: 476).

of Noorderhof is composed of small blocks with low-rise housing and little public space. Plan Zuid is composed of rather big blocks with apartment buildings of four to five storeys and wide streets. We conclude from this that coverage alone also has a rather weak relation to urban form.

Building Height

In most European countries at the end of the nineteenth and the beginning of the twentieth century, building height and street width were regulated through ordinances.[40] In Paris, the Ordinance of 1902 regulated that buildings of seven storeys, plus attics, were allowed on streets of at least 20 m width. In Berlin, the maximum height was five storeys. In the Netherlands in 1878, Jacobus van Niftrik argued that streets should be 1 to 1.5 times wider than the highest building on a street.[41] His plan for the expansion of Amsterdam, in which he put this approach into practice, was never executed. It was perceived as too expensive, partly due to its wide streets. Baumeister and Stübben went even further and proposed to also relate building height to the size of the courtyards.[42]

The relation between street width (or court size) and building height was also a factor in the studies of Walter Gropius. He argued that by planning for higher buildings, one could provide more open space without losing out on the number of dwellings (and population density). Later, Christopher Alexander, arguing against the modernist high-rise developments, introduced psychological arguments to subject all buildings to height restrictions.[43] (14) Based on evidence from the *British Medical Journal* and Newman's experience since the early 1970s of carrying out and analysing 'Defensible Space' projects, Alexander claimed that 'there is abundant

40
Rådberg, *Doktrin*, op. cit. note 12, 43, 106.

41
Ruijter, P. de, *Voor volkshuisvesting en stedebouw* Utrecht: Matrijs, 1987.

42
Rådberg, *Doktrin*, op. cit. note 12, 48, 51.

43
Alexander, C., et al., *A Pattern Language: Towns, Buildings, Construction* New York: Oxford University Press, 1977, 114–119.

evidence to show that high buildings make people crazy'.[44] To protect people from becoming crazy, Alexander advocated limiting the height of the majority of buildings in any urban area to four storeys or less, no matter how dense the area.

44
Ibid., 115.

When looking at samples from Amsterdam with the same average building height, say two storeys, we find examples ranging from villas in a spacious layout to compact old villages. We can thus conclude that building height alone does not contribute much to an understanding of density and urban form or to the relation between the two. Of the Amsterdam samples, the Bijlmermeer has the highest buildings. 15 Despite the height of the buildings, the FSI is similar to Nieuw Sloten. Here the floor space is evenly distributed over the area, while in the Bijlmermeer it is concentrated to leave large amounts of open green space. 16

Spaciousness

Hoenig was the first to systematically study the density and spaciousness of the urban environment.[45] In his article *Baudichte und Weiträumigkeit,* he introduced the concept of *Weiträumigkeit,* or spaciousness, defined as the relationship between open space and total floor area, as a measurement of the quality of an urban plan.[46] Spaciousness is equivalent to the Open Space Ratio (OSR) mentioned in the New York City's Zoning Resolution.[47] OSR was used as an instrument to stipulate that a development must provide a certain amount of open space on a zoning lot in specified districts. It can be viewed as an expression of the trade-offs between the desire to maximize the building bulk (programme or FSI) and the public and private demand for adequate open space.

45
Rådberg, *Doktrin*, op. cit. note 12, 68–70.

46
Hoenig, A., 'Baudichte und Weitraumigkeit', *Baugilde* 10 1928, 713–715.

47
City of New York, *Zoning Handbook*, op. cit. note 26.

At the level of a lot (or building block), Hoenig proposed a minimum of one square metre of open space for every square metre of built floor area. He believed that when this standard was met, the area could be described as spacious (*weiträumig*). Built areas with less open space were not acceptable and were described as cramped or crowded (*engräumig*).

In Amsterdam, the only example that, on the scale of the building block, meets the spaciousness standard proposed by Hoenig is the Bijlmermeer. The other Dutch areas analysed have lower figures. In Berlin, however, most low-rise samples built from the 1920s to the 1960s fulfil Hoenig's requirements.[48]

48
Based on all empirical data used in the research for this book (Berghauser Pont, M. and P. Haupt, Space, Density and Urban Form (Delft: 2009), 273–295.

Two samples, Venserpolder and Noorderhof, with similar OSR values, consist of respectively large building blocks of 4.5 storeys high and small blocks of 2.5 storeys. 17 18 We can thus conclude that OSR alone does not contribute much to the understanding of urban form. However, it does reveal the character of the areas in terms of pressure on the non-built space. If all of the inhabitants of the dwellings in these houses would go out onto the streets and into the courtyards at the same time, each person would have the same amount of open space at his/her disposal in both samples.

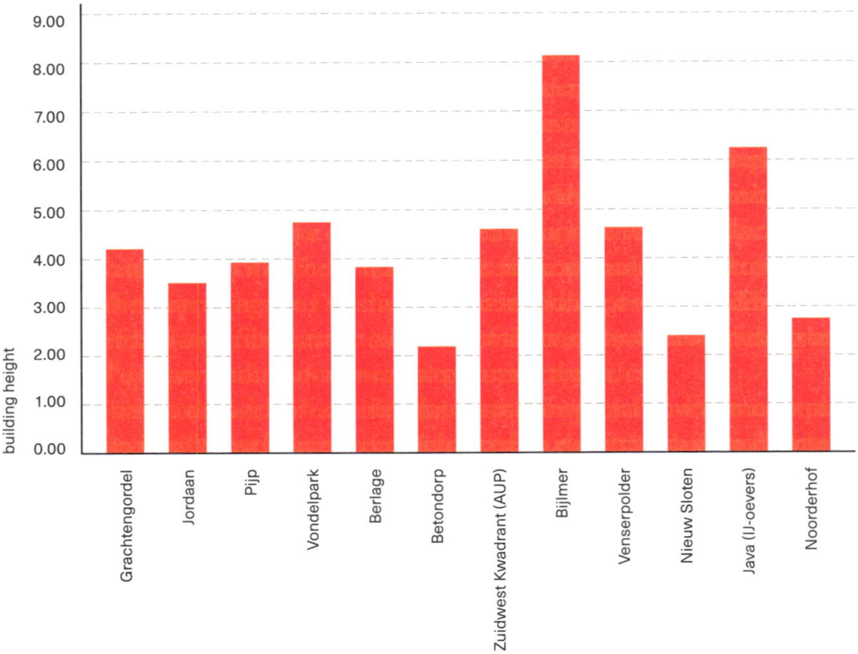

15 Building height (L) of a selection of urban fabrics.

18 Aerial and street view of Nieuw Sloten and Bijlmer.

Nieuw Sloten [NL] L 2.31 and FSI 0.77

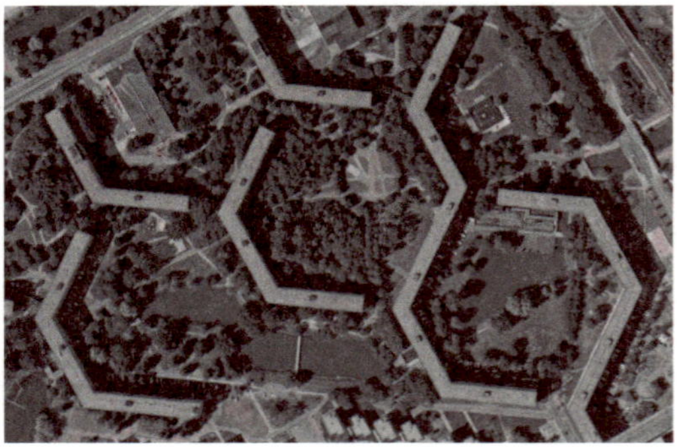

Bijlmer [NL] L 7.92 and FSI 0.76

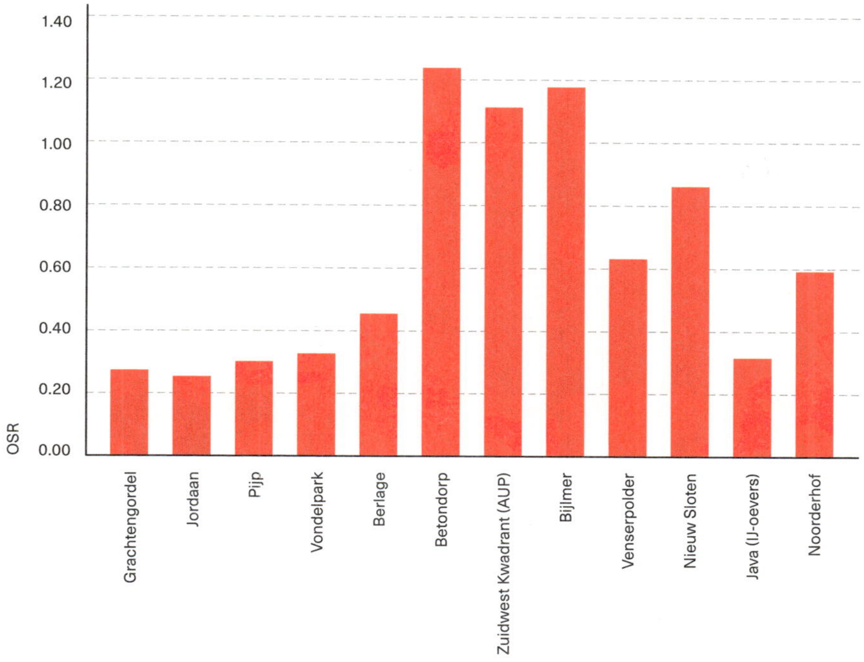

17 Spaciousness (OSR) of a selection of urban fabrics.

18 Aerial and street view of Venserpolder and Noorderhof.

Density Measure	*Year*	*Use*	*Norm*
Population density			
Inhabitants per hectare	1899	Howard	< 75 inh/ha (district)
	1933	Le Corbusier	1,000 dw/ha
Dwelling density			
Dwellings per hectare	1909	Unwin	< 30 dw/ha (island)
	1934	Van Eesteren	55–110 dw/ha (fabric)
	1961	Jacobs	> 250 dw/ha (island)
Land use intensity			
Ausnutzungsziffer = FSI × 100	1925	Building Ordinance Berlin	20–300 (lot)
Land Index = 1 / FSI	1949	Central Service for Reconstruction and Public Housing	
Floor to Area Ratio (FAR)	1961	New York Zoning Resolution	maximum FAR (lot)
Floor Space Index (FSI)	2003	Structuurplan Amsterdam	minimal FSI (fabric)
Coverage			
Coverage = GSI × 100	1961	New York Zoning Resolution	maximum coverage (lot)
	1860	Cerdà	< 50% (lot)
	1925	Building Ordinance Berlin	0.10–0.60 (lot)
	1961	Jacobs	0.60–0.80 (island)
Ground Space Index (GSI)	2003	Structuurplan Amsterdam	minimal GSI (fabric)
Building height			
Building height	1961	New York Zoning Resolution	maximum height
Amount of stories	1667	Rebuilding Law London	
	1880	Baumeister	< 4
	1902	Ordinance Paris	< 7 + attic
Spaciousness			
Weitraumigkeit = OSR	1928	Hoenig	> 1.0 (lot)
Open Space (Ratio) = OSR × 100	1961	New York Zoning Resolution	minimal OSR (lot)

19 Examples of density measures used through history.

Evaluation of Density Measures

As we have discussed, population and dwelling density have some serious shortcomings when it comes to establishing a relation with urban form. When working with dwelling density, the floor space allocated to employment is not taken into account. It is further impossible to determine whether people reside in large or small dwellings. In addition, issues of health and hygiene, which led to the introduction of the concept of density in urbanism, are not only influenced by the number of people residing in an area. Also relevant are dwelling size, building height and the distance between buildings. In 1880, the Jordaan had a dwelling density of 1,265 inhabitants per hectare. The area more than once faced high death rates due to diseases; in 1664 from the bubonic plague and in 1866 as a result of a cholera outbreak.[49] The bad living conditions (read: high population density) were perceived as part of the reason that the area was so badly affected by these pandemics. But were the pandemics caused by high population density or by the fact that a large number of people were living in small and cramped dwellings? Is it possible to imagine such a circumstance, a ratio of 1,265 people per hectare, without the problems that European cities encountered

49 Moll, H., 'Vuile teringstad: Vijf eeuwen besmettelijke ziekten in Amsterdam', *NRC Handelsblad* 31 January 2001.

50 The FSI in the Jordaan is assumed for this calculation to be unchanged FSI = 1.89. The population density in 1889 was 1,265, in 2007 it was 222 inhabitants per hectare. Other functions within the area were not taken into account.

1 The four solutions are identical in terms of FSI, GSI, OSR and L
2 The four solutions are identical in terms of FSI, but differ in terms of GSI, OSR and L

1

2

20 Children's game, illustrating the relation between FSI, GSI, OSR and L.

at the end of the nineteenth century? In the Jordaan, in 1880, the space allocation was 15 m^2 of floor area per inhabitant. In 2007, this had increased to 85 m^2.[50] Accommodating a density of 1,265 persons per hectare with the same amount of floor area per person, as is thought to be appropriate today, would result in a FSI increasing from 1.9 to 10.8![51]

We observe that land use intensity (FSI or FAR) is more effective but still does not allow us to differentiate between different spatial layouts. The same can be said about the other density indicators discussed here. All are, to a certain degree, informative, but none can be used on their own to adequately describe spatial properties as a step towards defining urban types with the use of density. This conclusion corresponds with the opinion commonly held by professionals, as well as researchers, as mentioned earlier.

An alternative approach is to use more variables to describe an urban area. The New York City's Zoning Regulation contained three indicators of density: FAR (or FSI), coverage (GSI) and population density. In Barcelona, both building height and coverage were considered and the building ordinance in Berlin of 1925 mentioned *Ausnutzungsziffer* (FSI), *Ausnutzung der Grundstücks* (GSI) and *Stockwerksanzahl* (building height). More recently, a combination of different indicators have been used to differentiate between various development patterns.[52] These approaches highlight the advantage of using a multivariable approach to density.

An example of a multivariable approach to density can be illustrated by looking at a children's game in which a circle is divided in two, three or

51
Derived from the situation in the Jordaan in 2007: FSI = 1.89 and population density of 222 inhabitants/ha.

52
CETAT, *Indicateurs morphologiques pour l'amenagement: Analyse de 50 perimetres batis situes sur le canton de Geneve* Geneva: Departement des traveaux publics, 1986; Rådberg, *Doktrin*, op. cit. note 12; Yoshida, H. and M. Omae, 'An approach for analysis of urban morphology: methods to derive morphological properties of city blocks by using an urban model and their interpretations', *Computers, Environments and Urban Systems*, 29 2005, 223–247.

four pieces. This game is portrayed in ⓴. In the first instance, the pieces are positioned in such a way that four full circles are constructed. In terms of intensity (FSI), coverage (GSI), height (L) and spaciousness (OSR) these solutions are identical (1, 1, 1, and 0 respectively). In the second case, the same pieces are stacked on top of each other. The first solution, consisting only of one piece, is identical to the one in the first picture. The second solution consists of two pieces stacked on top of each other, resulting in a halving of the GSI (0.5) and a doubling of the height. Also, the OSR has changed from zero to 0.5. The FSI, though, remains the same (1.0). The other two solutions in the second picture, still with the same FSI, have both different GSI, L and OSR values (third solution: 0.33, 3, and 0.67; fourth solution: 0.25, 4, and 0.75). We suggest that such a combination of indicators is needed to better relate density to potential urban form.

A shortcoming of this combination of density indicators, however, is their focus on the built mass and the absence of a reference to size. In the example of the children's game nothing indicates the size of the wooden pieces. For all we know, they could represent a villa or an industrial shed with identical density measures. By introducing network density, we can add the non-built space more profoundly and arrive at an abstract indication of size of the urban grain.

Network Density

Network density is defined by us as the amount of network per area unit, and is expressed as metres of network (length) per square metres of ground area (surface). This measure is related to Metric Reach as introduced by Peponis et al. (2008)[53] and defined as the total street length covered by all paths extending out from one point. Reach is a measure of connectivity or relatedness and, as we argued above, also a measure to indicate the grain of the urban fabric. Different from reach, in network density the total street length is divided by the area covered by these streets. The type of network included should be made explicit (motorized, bike, pedestrian, or a combination). To justify the choice of network as a fundamental characteristic of urban areas, the following section looks at the basic elements of the urban ground plan as defined in morphological and quantitative research.

We use the arguments of Conzen, the founder of the British school of morphology, in defining the main research entities of the urban landscape. The spatial entities identified by Conzen as essential to the town plan (or ground plan) are the street system, the lot pattern and the building configuration. These three entities are similar to the distinction made by Jan Heeling, et al. in *De Stadsplattegrond* between the public streets (street system) and private islands (consisting of lots and buildings) or between the layer of movement and occupation.[54] ㉑ The combination of streets and a series of islands surrounded by these streets constitute *the urban fabric*, or tissue. The main task of a designer, according to Heeling, et al., is to combine these two in the best possible manner.

53
Peponis, J., S. Bafna and Z. Zhang, 'The connectivity of streets: reach and directional distance', *Environmental and Planning B: Planning and Design*, 35 2018, 881–901.

54
Heeling, et al., *Het ontwerp*, op. cit. note 21.

1 New York
2 Paris

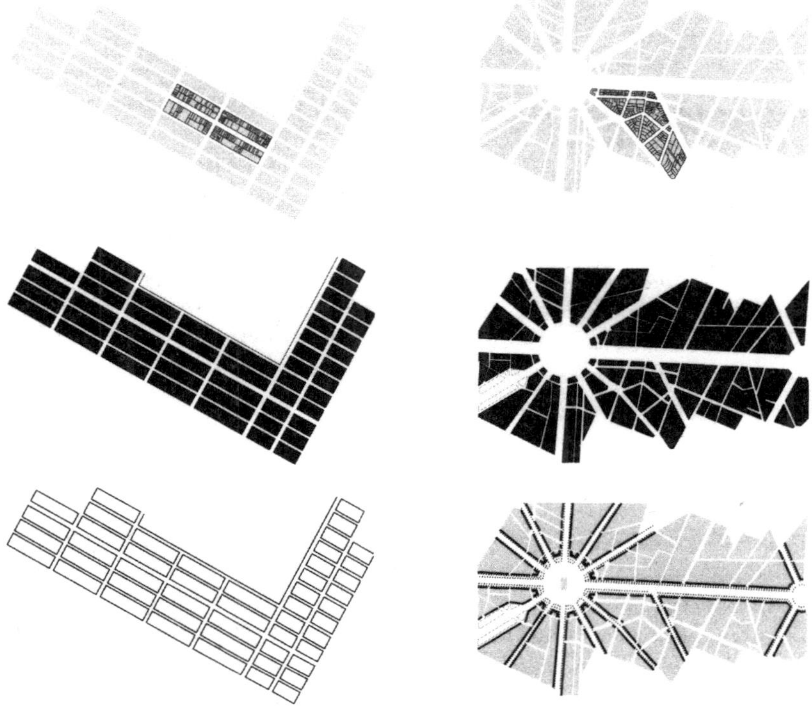

1 2

21 Entities of the ground plan: lots, islands and network (Heeling et al. 2002: 102).

Conzen and Saverio Muratori describe the lot as the most conservative entity within a morphological complex.[55] Heeling, et al., on the other hand, focus more on the public street pattern and its relation to the private islands. As Erik Terlouw illustrates, the lots in most Western European towns founded in the twelfth and thirteenth centuries developed in a way known as the 'burgage cycle'.[56] The lots of the original layout (approximately 650 m^2)[57] were divided lengthwise and the backside of lots and the alleyways, connecting the front- and backside, were developed resulting in smaller lots (of approximately 150 m^2). The street pattern, however, remained mostly intact and was more resistant than the lots. This robustness of the network (and the islands defined by the network) makes it appropriate to view network and islands as the basic entities of the town plan.

The mutual dependence of streets and islands is important in understanding the ground plan. Street space, to use the words of Stephen Marshall, constitutes 'the basic core of all urban public space forming a contiguous network by which everything is linked to everything else. This continuum is punctured by lots of private land.'[58] For one, built floor space generates movements and causes flows (people, cars, etcetera) that need to be facilitated by the network. In addition, the open space of the network enables light to access the buildings and influences privacy, depending on the profile width and the size of the islands. Compactly developed islands can be compensated for by wide street profiles and vice versa. This whole interrelatedness of network, islands and building bulk should thus be at the core of a new definition of density.

55
Moudon, A.V., 'Getting to Know the Built Landscape: Typomorphology', in: K. Franck and L. Schneekloth eds., *Ordering Space: Types in Architecture and Design* New York: Van Nostrand Reinhold, 1994, 289–311.

56
Terlouw, E., 'A House of One's Own', *OASE* 52 1999, 32–77, 65–67.

57
Standard lot of 3 × 15 rods = 11.30 × 56.50 m = 640 m^2.

58
Marshall, S., *Streets & Patterns* Oxon: Spon Press, 2005, 13.

Much has been researched and written on the role and character of the network in the urban landscape at different scale levels.[59] One perspective can be historical or morphological, another more technical (traffic engineering), or more concerned with the function of the network as a public space. Here it is important to note, however, that we do not aspire in this book to provide any exhaustive description of the form and/or function of the urban network, but to focus on its primary measurements and its relation to built density. Neither will we focus on its configurative properties as discussed extensively in Space Syntax research,[60] but instead highlight the local properties that affect the potential for these kinds of movements within reasonable ranges of walking distance,[61] but also the sizes of the islands and thus potential uses of them.

The function of the public (street) network in a city or town is thus two-fold. For one, it facilitates the different modes of movement taking place in the urban fabric and provides access to the islands. It also defines the urban layout by dividing land into public and private land. We follow here the line of reasoning employed by Leslie Martin and Lionel March, Heeling, et al. and Marshall.[62] They argue that the street grid (network) and the ground plan are the framework for urbanization.

The measurements of the network and the grain of the urban fabric, as mentioned by Manuel de Solà-Morales are decisive in establishing the relationship between general form and built content: smaller blocks (or islands) provide the greatest proportion of public ways and overall exposure ratio (façade length to area).[63] Jacobs argues for small blocks to stimulate city liveliness.[64] Amis Siksna underlines Jacob's arguments in the article *The Effects of Block Size and Form in North American and Australian City Centres*.[65] He argues that in cities with small- or medium-sized blocks, the street layout remains intact, whereas in cities with large initial blocks, the layout is modified by the addition of streets and alleys, creating smaller blocks and sub-blocks. Size thus matters, and the most fundamental measurements in the urban plan are related to the network.

Adding network density as a primary indicator of the density concept increases its capacity to indicate important primary measurements of the urban landscape and describe important aspects of urban form. We demonstrate later that combining the network and built density allows us to introduce measures to an otherwise scale-less density concept. In addition, it enables the analysis of a range of properties that are characterized by the relation between serviced and served, between network and islands, lots and buildings.

Network density at the level of the urban fabric can be viewed as a specific example of a general *transition density* concept. With transition density we refer to the level of concentration of borders of different entities in a certain area. A border demarcates two locations. A fundamental change takes place when this border is crossed. The intensity of transitions in an area can be described as transition density. In a dwelling, the walls separating

59
See e.g. Bach, B., et al., *Urban Design and Traffic; A Selection from Bach's Toolbox/Stedebouw en verkeer; een selectie uit de gereedschapskist van Bach* Ede: Crow, 2006; Calabrese, L.M., *Reweaving UMA: Urbanism, Mobility, Architecture* Rotterdam: Optima Grafische Communicatie, 2004, Marshall, *Streets & Patterns*, op. cit. note 57; Meyer, H., F. de Josselin de Jong and M.J. Hoekstra eds., *Het ontwerp van de openbare ruimte* Amsterdam: SUN, 2006; Rofé, Y., 'Space and Community: The Spatial Foundations of Urban Neighborhoods', *Berkeley Planning Journal* 10 1995, 107–125.

60
Hillier, B. and Hanson, J., *The social logic of space* Cambridge: Cambridge University Press, 1984.

61
Peponis, et al., 'The connectivity of streets', op. cit. note 53.

62
Martin, L. and L. March eds., *Urban Space and Structures* Cambridge: Cambridge University Press, 1972, 6–27; Heeling, et al., *Het ontwerp*, op. cit. note 21; Marshall, *Streets & Patterns*, op. cit. note 57.

63
Solà-Morales, M. de, 'Towards a Definition: Analysis of Urban Growth in the Nineteenth Century', *Lotus*, 19 June 1978, 28–36.

64
Jacobs, *The Death*, op. cit. note 37, 178–186.

65
Siksna, A., 'The Effects of Block Size and Form in North American and Australian City Centres', *Urban Morphology* 1 1997, 19–33.

different rooms constitute the borders of transition, in a building these are the façades, in a building block these transitions are the borders of the lots. At the level of the urban fabric this can be defined as the public network (a zone of transition defined by street width), and at the level of a district, the edges of the urban fabric that constitute the district define the transitions between one fabric and another (precise definitions of the different scales follow later in this chapter). In this research we focus on the transition density on the level of the urban fabric, that is, network density.

Multivariable Definition of Density

We suggest that a multivariable density concept consisting of the three fundamental indicators intensity (FSI), compactness (GSI) and network density (N) can offer a method that is specific enough to allow for the definition of urban types, as well as economic enough to ensure that excessive amounts of data can be managed without drowning in too many over-detailed definitions. We maintain that this multivariable density model is a balanced concept that can be positioned between the too detailed – and thereby non-generic – and the too abstract – and thereby too inclusive – representations, and can distinguish between basic spatial properties. In the next section, we will demonstrate these three main indicators, which are both effective enough to be able to differentiate (by constructing types) and economic enough to fit the adagio of Occam's razor: whenever something can be described in more fundamental terms, it should be done so.[66]

66 Stanford Encyclopedia of Philosophy, author's interpretation.

To be able to compare areas and plans, it is important to agree upon accurate and generally accepted definitions. In this section, we suggest a consistent set of equations and variables that can be used in this multivariable density approach.

Four Variables to Calculate Density

The four variables needed to calculate the basic indicators FSI, GSI and N, are:

- Base land area (A);
- Network length (l);
- Gross floor area (F);
- Built up area, or footprint (B).

In the following sections we formulate workable definitions for these variables.

Base land area (A)

The definition of the unit of analysis and its boundaries can be defined in various ways. This is of particular importance in cases where areas are to be compared or used as references and when correlations, or associations, between two indicators are tested, but also for the description of an area in general. There are roughly three ways of defining area boundaries:

- *Administrative boundaries* that define, for instance, cadastral units, postal units[67] or other institutional units such as municipalities and neighbourhoods;
- *Projected boundaries*, such as an arbitrary grid of cells, often used in GIS applications;
- *Generated boundaries* based on, for example, morphological characteristics.

67
Postal areas are defined by the Dutch postal service; CBS, *Kerncijfers postcodegebied 2004* The Hague: Statistics Netherlands, 2006.

One of the advantages of administrative boundaries is that most statistical data is available for these units. That was the reason that VROM, the Ministry of Housing, Spatial Planning and the Environment, recently used the four-digit postal code areas to identify deprived areas (*probleemwijken*), neighbourhoods judged as having socioeconomic problems.[68] This method can be criticized as inadequate, as postal areas and neighbourhoods often do not coincide. The system of postal codes was developed in 1978 to economize the sorting of letters. Today, it is also used to analyse postal areas as in the example mentioned. However, area measurements such as the four-digit postal code areas, have an inbuilt 'ecological fallacy' well known in geography as 'The Modified Area Unit Problem' (MAUP), which basically means that statistics are arbitrary since the definition of the 'area' is subjective.[69] The main issue of concern related to the MAUP is the scale effect, which is attributed to variation in numerical results, owing strictly to the number of areal units used in the analysis. The larger the area of aggregation and the greater the diversity in the aggregated parts of that area – the more the variation is lost in the calculation making the results more abstract and less relevant for urban planning and design. If, instead of postal areas, morphologically defined neighbourhoods had been chosen to define deprived areas, the selection would probably have looked different. Furthermore, the methods used to define them differ from one municipality to the other.[70] In rural areas, boundaries mostly follow the topography of the landscape; in urban areas socioeconomic criteria are more important for determining the boundaries.

68
Kamerstuk 24 april 2007, Ministry of Housing, £Spatial Planning and the Environment.

69
Openshaw, S., P.J.A. Taylor, 'A million or so correlation coefficients: three experiments on the modifiable areal unit problem', *Stat. Appl. Spat. Sci.*, 21 1979, 127–144; De Jong, T., and D.J.M. van der Voordt eds.. 2002. Ways to study and research urban, architectural and technical design. Delft: Delft University Press.

70
Meer, A.J. van der, *Gemeentegrenzen Nederland 1795 – heden,* dissertation OTB Research Institute, Delft University of Technology, 2007.

Projected and generated boundaries have the same problem, but are at least more open to be adjusted in accordance to the research question. The main difference between the two is that the first, the projected boundary, aims to control the geography and its content 'top-down', while the second, the generated boundary, analyses it 'bottom-up'.

In our opinion, the third method of drawing boundaries is more suitable when relating density to spatial properties. By letting the matter itself define its boundaries, the artificial straightjacket forced upon that which is analysed is minimized. This requires, however, a sensitivity to local morphology and changes in density gradients when establishing the boundaries. Definitions of morphological properties that define the border, such as walls, plots or networks, and of the amount of homogeneity required of the components that make up the aggregation at hand, can help guide the demarcation. Besides defining the morphological boundaries based on such properties, the areas can also be depicted based on accessibility where the boundary is generated based on the reach from a specific point and thus describes what we could call a 'walkable neighbourhood'.[71] This approach is more easily translated into algorithms that make the analysis of entire cities and regions possible using geographical information systems (GIS). Furthermore, it makes it possible to change the distance that defines the walkable neighbourhood and apply it, for example, to the quarter-hour city that was launched by the mayor of Paris, Anne Hidalgo, in 2020. The idea of the quarter-hour city is that every resident can meet their essential needs within a short walk or bike ride from their home, but the same method could be used to measure the density within the boundaries of the quarter-hour city.

In relation to the MAUP, it is important to clarify another aspect: the difference in density at different scale levels. In his dispersal and concentration theory, Taeke De Jong paid particular attention to the nature of different scales.[72] The larger the area and the greater the variation in parts of the area, the more statistical in nature the index (dwellings per hectare or FSI) will become. In addition, the more variation is lost in the calculation, the more abstract and less formally relevant the result is. It is for this reason that a study by the University of Geneva defines an upper and lower range for the size of an urban fabric: between 0.5 and 8 hectares.[73] In the BYGG report of 1962, this range was set between 1 and 3 hectares.[74] We do not use such limits as our conclusions depend more on the consistency, or homogeneity, of the urban fabric than on the size of the area. The Bijlmermeer example discussed earlier, for instance, measures more than 30 hectares, but consists of only two large high-rise slabs in a park surrounded by streets. It would be incorrect to exclude this example solely because it is considered to be too big. Working with densities means accepting the arrogance of the average – because of its productive advantages – but at the same time elaborating on the (more or less) divers characteristics of the components that constitute this average.

Knowledge of the differences in density at different scale levels is of great importance. When working at a small scale, for instance at the scale of a building or lot, or at a larger scale, such as the whole city or region, new components can be constructed as aggregates of smaller components. In most cases this is accompanied by the addition of a certain surplus, or tare space. Tare space is commonly defined as the difference between gross and net areas. Later we provide a definition of tare space which is solely characterized by densities at different scale levels. We will later also return to ways to gauge homo- and heterogeneity on different levels of scale.

The units and aggregations of analysis we use in this book, illustrated by two schemes representing respectively a traditional closed perimeter building block (left) and a modernist open building block (right), are as follows (22):

71
This method of defining the unit of analysis relates directly to the measure reach that we discussed earlier when introducing network density. A more extended discussion about this method in relation to density calculations cane be found in the paper Berghauser Pont, M., and Marcus, L., 'Innovations in measuring density. From area and location density to accessible and perceived density', *Nordic Journal of Architectural Research* 2014.

72
Jong and Voordt, *Ways to Stud*, op. cit. note 69..

73
CETAT, *Indicateurs morphologiques pour l'amenagement: Analyse de 50 périmetres batis situes sur le canton de Geneve* Geneva: Departement des traveaux publics, 1986, 23

74
Rådberg, *Doktrin*, op. cit. note 12, 11.

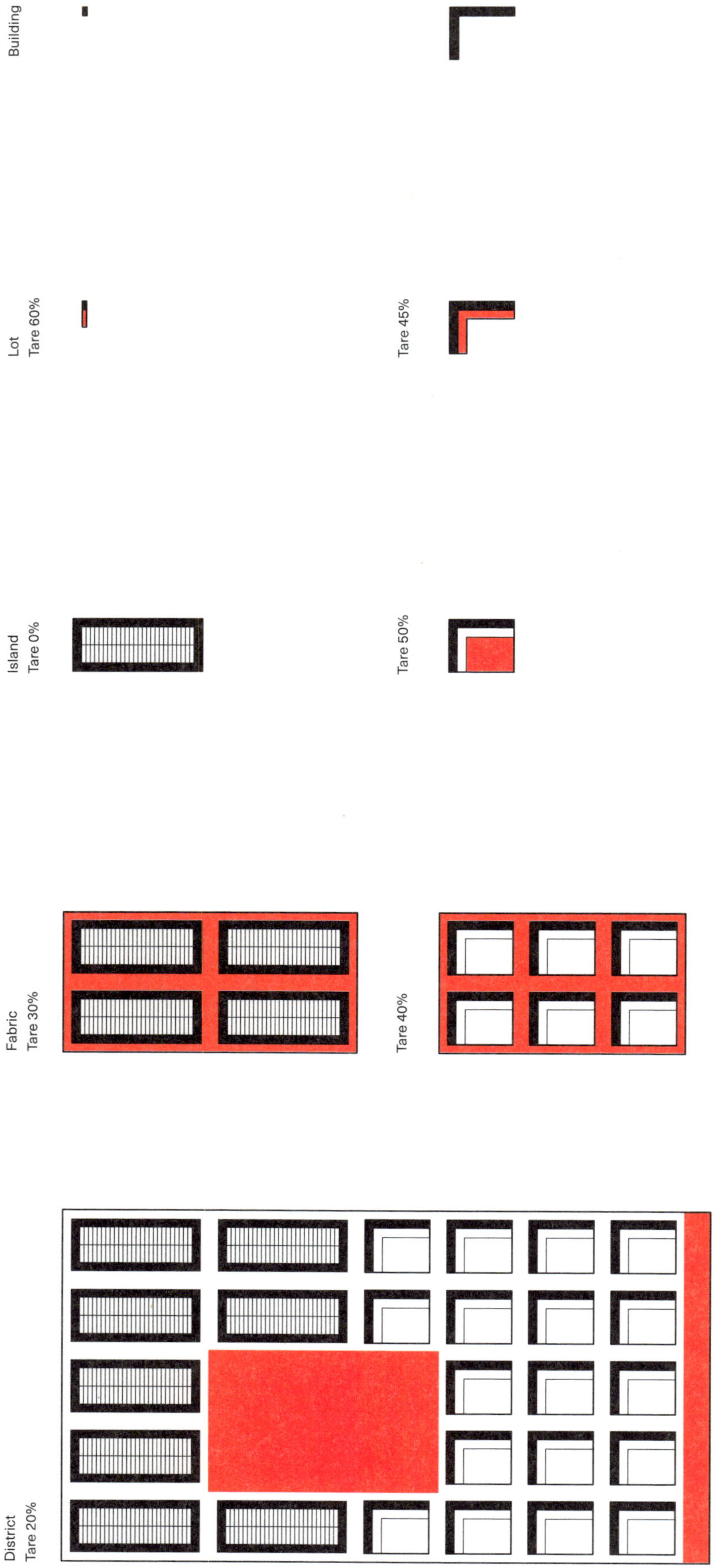

22 Tare space of the areas at each level of aggregation.

— *Building.* The area of the building is the same as the built area or footprint. The borders of the built area are defined by the edges of the building footprint. We use the definitions as published in the Dutch standard NEN 2580.[75]

— *Lot.* The area of the lot (also referred to as parcel or plot) is the sum of built and non-built (predominately private) areas designated for building. The non-built area is the tare space between *building* and *lot*. In residential areas, these non-built areas (tare space) are mostly used for gardens. In some cases, the lots comprise built areas only and thus correspond to the building; no tare space is added. The borders of the lots are defined by the legal boundaries specified in the cadastre.

— *Island.* The area of an island,[76] also referred to in the traditional city as an urban block, comprises the lots and, in some cases, non-built space not designated for building. These non-built spaces constitute the tare space between the *lot* and *island*. Some examples include playing fields, small squares or parking areas. The border of an island is defined by the surrounding public streets. When there is no bordering street, the periphery of the island is set by the lot boundaries.

— *Fabric.* The area of the fabric is similar to the scale and definitions used for a *plan unit,* as described by Conzen, and the *tessuto,* as used by Gianfranco Caniggia.[77] The urban fabric consists of a collection of islands, as well as the network that surrounds these islands and is required to access the islands. These access streets primarily serve to access the private lots and buildings.[78] Circulation streets on the other hand are primarily used to move from one urban fabric to the other or across the city. When linear green or water elements such as the canals in the Grachtengordel in Amsterdam are part of the street pattern, these are considered as part of the network as well. The network area constitutes the tare space between *island* and *fabric*. The boundaries of the fabric are drawn in the middle of the access streets. In circumstances where there is no street, the boundaries of the fabric are set by the lot boundaries. The size of the fabric is determined by the level of homogeneity (spread) of the different islands within that fabric.

— *District.* The area of the district is similar to the *town plan* introduced by Conzen or the neighbourhood (*buurt*) defined by Van Lohuizen. The district is composed of a collection of fabrics and large-scale non-built areas not included in the fabric itself, such as circulation streets,[79] parks, sports fields and larger water areas. These constitute the tare space between *fabric* and *district*. The boundaries of the district are drawn in the middle of the circulation streets. In cases where the access streets are also used for circulation, the boundary of the district coincides with that of the fabric.

75
NEN, *NEN 2580: Areas and Volumes of Buildings – Terms, Definitions and Methods of Determination* Delft: NEN, 2007.

76
According to Panerai, P., 'De schaal van het bouwblok', in: S. Komossa et al., *Atlas van het Hollandse bouwblok* Bussum: Uitgeverij THOTH, 2002, 11–14, the ancient Romans called their urban blocks *insulae*, or island, reflecting the topological containment of buildings and land parcels lots within a continuum of public space primarily constituted by the system of public streets.

77
Moudon, 'Getting to Know', op. cit. note 54.

78
'Access streets' are defined following Buchanan, C.D., *Mixed Blessing: The Motor in Britain* London: Leonard Hill, 1958.

79
Ibid.

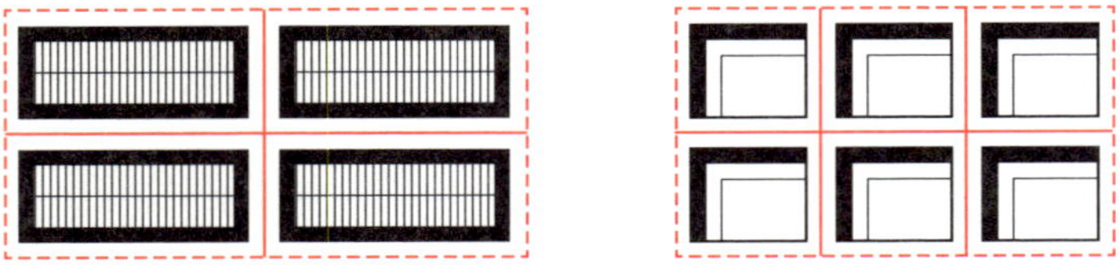

23 Interior and exterior streets of two urban fabrics.

Network Length (l)

At the scale of an architectural object, the network of, for instance, a multifunctional high-rise tower consists of stairs, corridors, elevators and other spaces needed for pedestrian circulation within the building. At the scale of the district, the network consists of circulation streets, rails, roads, canals and so forth. At the scale of the urban fabric, which is the focus of this book, the network is the access street, which in older parts of the city coincides with the circulation street. In functionalist plans, different modalities are often separated, and access streets do not coincide with circulation streets. A common characteristic of physical networks is that they function as access to the areas served. In the case of the urban fabric the street (that is, network) gives access to an island, in the case of a building the corridor (that is, network) gives access to a dwelling or a room. The network can be defined for all sorts of modalities, each of them taken separately or all together. It is important, however, to make the selection explicit, whatever modalities are used. For the samples of this book the car network was used to define network length.

In addition, one must differentiate between internal and external networks 23. 'Internal network' refers to all networks that do not coincide with any fabric demarcation. 'External network' refers to the network divided in half by a fabric demarcation. Only half of the external network contributes to the fabric as the other half 'belongs' to the surrounding fabrics. In practice, this implies that the entire network length inside a sample is measured and to this measure is added half of the network that circumscribes the sample.

Gross Floor Area (F)

The definition used here is taken from the Dutch standard NEN 2580.[80] The basic rule is that the gross floor area of a building is the sum of all surfaces, measured per floor, along the perimeter of the partitions that surround the building, including underground floor area and floor area under a pitched roof 24. Voids and wells are not included as long as the area is greater than 4 m^2. Occasional niches or recesses and irregular protrusions do not have to be taken into account, as long as the area is less than 0.5 m^2. Exterior spaces, such as loggias, balconies, uncovered walkways, roof terraces, etcetera are not included in the gross floor area calculation of a building. In addition,

80 NEN, *NEN 2580*, op. cit. note 71.

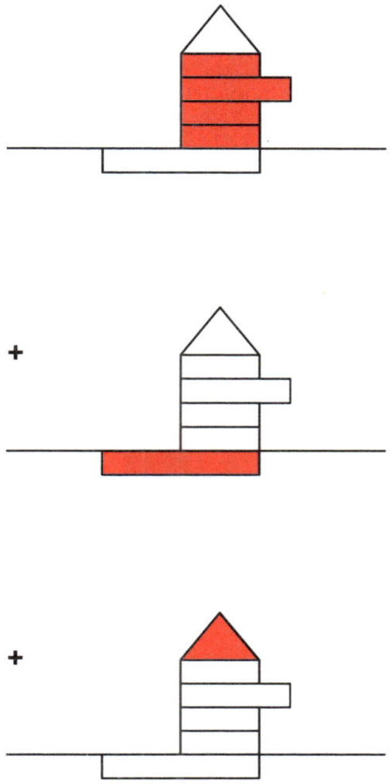

24 Calculation of gross floor area (F).

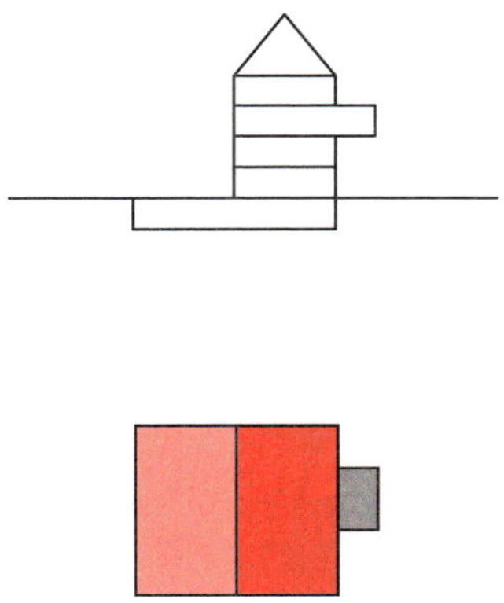

25 Calculation of built area (B).

open fire escapes and emergency stairways are not included when calculating the gross floor area.

Built Area or Footprint (B)

When establishing the built area, the same definitions outlined above for gross floor area are used. The built area is thus defined as the floor area, measured at ground level along the perimeter of the dividing partitions of the building, and excludes overhanging or underground built areas. 25

Basic Indicators[81]

Network Density (N)

The density of the network, N, refers to the concentration of networks in an area, in our case the fabric. The density of a network is defined as network length per square metre of base land area (m/m^2), and is calculated as the sum of the whole internal network and half of the length of the network used to demarcate the base land area. The unit of the outcome is metre of network per square metre of fabric area.

81 For an extensive argumentation of the construction of the formulae, see ● Derivation of Formulae on page 231.

❶ $$N_f = [\sum l_i + (\sum l_e / 2)] / A_f$$

l_i = length of interior network (m);
l_e = length of edge network (m);
A_f = area of fabric (m^2).

Building Intensity (FSI)

FSI reflects the building intensity independently of the programmatic composition and is calculated as follows for all levels of scale as described earlier:

❷ $$FSI_x = F_x / A_x$$

F_x = gross floor area (m^2);
A_x = area of aggregation x (m^2);
x = aggregation (lot (l), island (i), fabric (f), or district (d)).

Coverage (GSI)

GSI, or coverage, demonstrates the relationship between built and non-built space and is calculated as follows for all levels of scale as described earlier:

❸ $$GSI_x = B_x / A_x$$

B_x = footprint (m^2);
A_x = area of aggregation x (m^2);
x = aggregation (lot (l), island (i), fabric (f), or district (d)).

Derived Indicators

We can derive a series of indicators by using the basic ones defined earlier, FSI, GSI and N. These will contribute to describing the spatial properties of urban areas and explore the potential of densities in relation to urban form and performance. We elaborate on these issues in the following chapter, using the indicators introduced here. The derived indicators point to an abstract quality and should not be interpreted in a literal way. The first two we will discuss are building height and spaciousness and both concern the relation between the built and non-built space.

Building Height (L)

The average number of storeys (or layers), L, can be arrived at by ascertaining the intensity and coverage or, FSI and GSI, for the aggregation x. If more floor area is developed in a certain area, without changing the footprint, L will increase. If the building height should remain constant, then FSI and GSI have to increase.

4 $$L = FSI_x / GSI_x$$

Spaciousness (OSR)

The variable OSR, or spaciousness, is a measure of the amount of non-built space at ground level per square metre of gross floor area. This figure provides an indication of the pressure on non-built space. If more floor area is developed in an area (with the same footprint), the OSR decreases and the number of people who will use the non-built space increases. The unit of OSR is m^2/m^2.

5 $$OSR = (1 - GSI_x) / FSI_x$$

Tare (T)

One important feature of density is its characteristics at different levels of scale. The difference in base land area (A_x) between two levels of scale define the tare (T_x), also often described as the difference between net and gross. If T describes the tare between, for instance, fabric (x) and island (x − 1), then T can be arrived at through:

6 $$T_x = (A_f - \Sigma A_{x-1}) / A_x$$

x = aggregation x;
x − 1 = level of scale of the components of which aggregation x is composed.

If the coverage or intensity is known for both fabric and island, then tare can be defined purely through density indicators. In the case of the fabric, the following applies:

7 $T_f = 1 - GSI_f / GSI_i$

8 $T_f = 1 - FSI_f / FSI_i$

The relationship between tare and built densities on different levels of scale can be generalized as follows:

9 $T_x = 1 - GSI_x / GSI_{x-1}$

10 $T_x = 1 - FSI_x / FSI_{x-1}$

As the amount of privately issued land, PIL is the negative, or the remaining part, of tare, PIL can be expressed as follows:

11 $PIL = 1 - T_f$

12 $PIL = GSI_f / GSI_i$

13 $PIL = FSI_f / FSI_i$

Grain of the Network and Street Profile Width (w and b)

Network density can be used to calculate an indicative grain size (w), or the distance from street to street in a square grid of the urban fabric, using the following formula:

14 $w = 2 / N_f$

A high network density (N) corresponds to a small mesh of the urban layout and a low N to a large grain. Combined with the tare of the fabric (T_f), one can arrive at the profile width (b). The relationship between these variables can be described as:

15 $b = 2[1 - \sqrt{(1 - T_f)}] / N_f$

or, combined with 7:

16 $b = 2(1 - \sqrt{(GSI_f / GSI_i)}) / N_f$

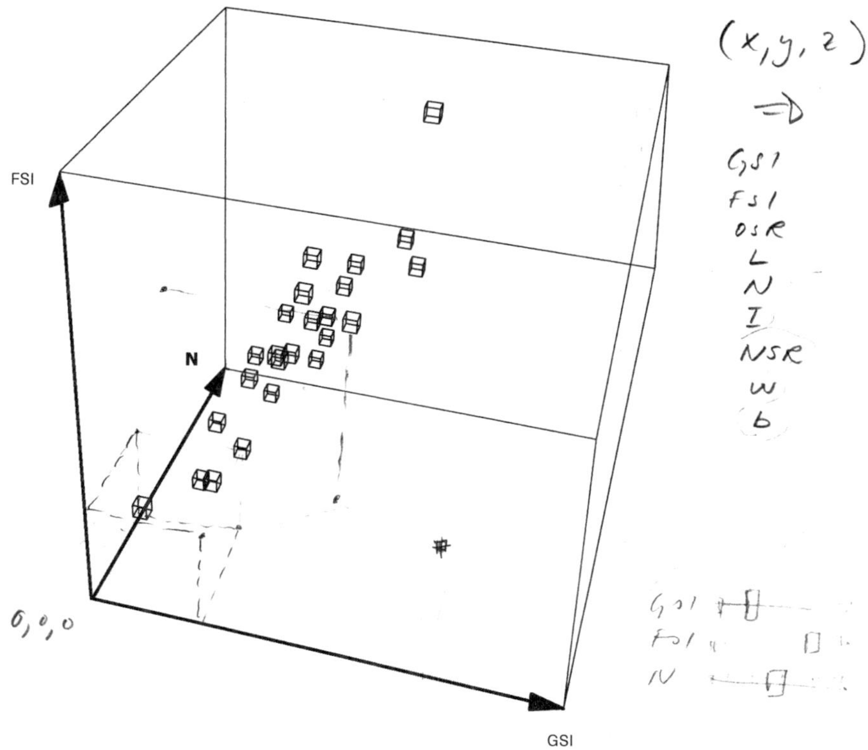

26 Spacematrix. The FSI on the z-axis gives an indication of the intensity in an area and the GSI on the x-axis reflects its compactness. The N on the y-axis provides us with information concerning the area's network.

Representation of Density

Spacematrix

To be able to simultaneously assess the three main indicators FSI, GSI and N, a three-dimensional diagram has been constructed, the Spacematrix: FSI on the z-axis expresses the built intensity of a certain area, GSI on the x-axis is an indicator of the compactness of the built environment, and N on the y-axis describes the network density, and is as such an indicator of size of the urban layout. 26 For every selection of an urban landscape, all entities of its composition can be positioned in the Spacematrix. The position of a district, for instance, is composed of a cluster of fabrics, which are composed of a series of islands, and so on. All the necessary information of the derived indicators described above is present through the position of all parts (absolute and relative). This means that an area can be represented by many mediators, such as maps, photos or text, but also through its density fingerprint, expressed as a series of positions in the Spacematrix. This spatial DNA of an area offers much data (absolute and relative) to analyse and make explicit certain spatial properties of the area. These can serve as input for the understanding of and speculation on other, non-spatial properties.

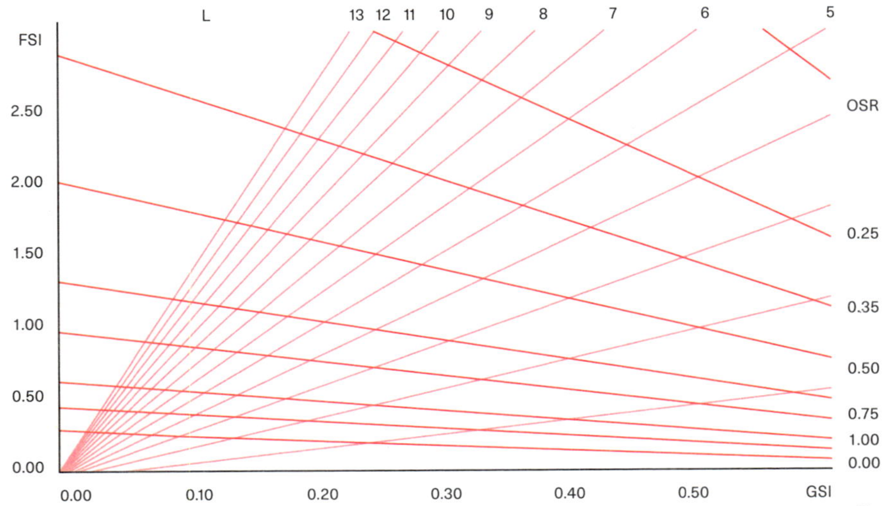

27 Diagram FSI (GSI) or Spacemate.

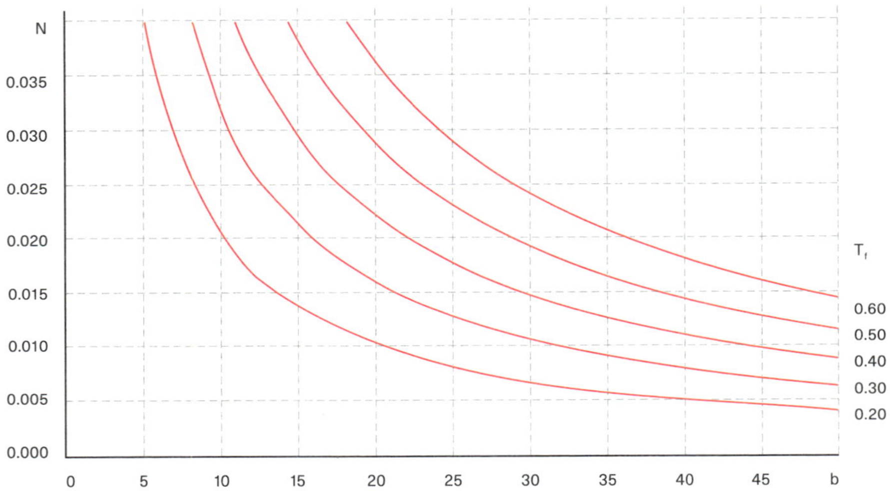

28 Diagram N_f(b).

Separate projections of the Spacematrix are in the present context necessary due to limitations in data management and representation (and thus communication) of the results. The projection FSI (GSI) in the Spacematrix, the Spacemate, is shown in 27. Here FSI on the y-axis gives an indication of the built intensity in an area and GSI on the x-axis reflects the coverage, or compactness, of the development. The OSR and L are gradients that fan out over the diagram. OSR describes the spaciousness (or pressure on the non-built space), and L represents the average number of storeys.

Based on 15, another diagram can be constructed with network density (N_f), profile width (b) and tare space (T_f) as shown in 28. The N_f on the y-axis denotes the network density of the urban layout, and b on the x-axis the profile width of the streets. The tare space as a percentage of public space in a fabric is shown as gradients in the diagram. With two known indicators the third can be derived from the diagram.

(17) $$T = 1 - (1 - b \times N / 2)^2$$

(18) $$PIL = (1 - b \times N / 2)^2$$

Scale and Variation

Two aspects of the urban landscape that can be gauged with the help of the Spacematrix are scale and homogeneity. The multivariable density of the different aggregations – building, lot, island, fabric and district – convey not only absolute values of the different aggregations, but also the relative values in the form of tare. A fabric composed of a certain amount of islands will be positioned at a position closer to the origin of the diagram (lower GSI and FSI) than the average of the islands. (29) (30) The (relative) distance between the two describes the amount of tare present as network in the fabric. In fabrics composed of high-density islands and scarce public network (narrow alleys and large blocks), the resulting fabric will have a position relatively close to that of the islands. In a case where islands are surrounded by a vast space of (modern) infrastructure, the positions will be further apart. In the first example little tare is added to the islands as in the second a large amount is added. This is true at all levels of scale.

Besides the scalar composition that can be gauged through the Spacematrix (and the Spacemate), the amount of homogeneity versus heterogeneity of the aggregations can be represented. Every aggregation can be represented both as an average of its components and with specific values for every single component that form the aggregation. The average is the density value of a certain level of scale, the specific values of the components form a larger or smaller cluster around this centre of gravity. In the case of pure repetition, and thus absolute homogeneity, the positions of every component and the average coincide. The heterogeneity of an area is represented by the size of the spread, or cluster, of components. The character of the spread can of course differ in pattern, from a single deviation from a large bulk of relative homogeneity, to a symmetrical and balanced spread of the components. (31)

The complete data picture can thus be said to form the DNA, or spatial fingerprint, of a specific area. A fabric will in the Spacematrix be characterized both by the average values determining the positions of the different scale levels (district, fabric, island, lot and building), and by the size of the spread of the individual components. Some of the indicators are directly present through positions in the Spacematrix. Examples of these are GSI, FSI, N, L, OSR and w. Others achieve their value through the relative values of the different levels of scale. Examples of these are tare and profile width (T and b).

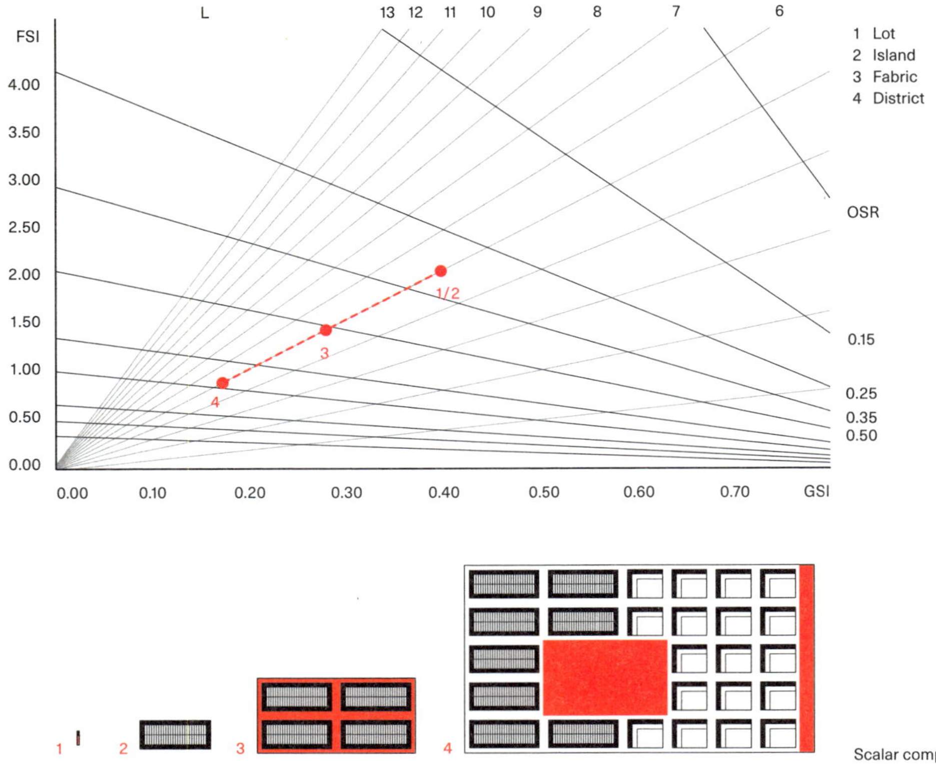

29 Scalar composition of scheme representing a traditional closed perimeter building block.

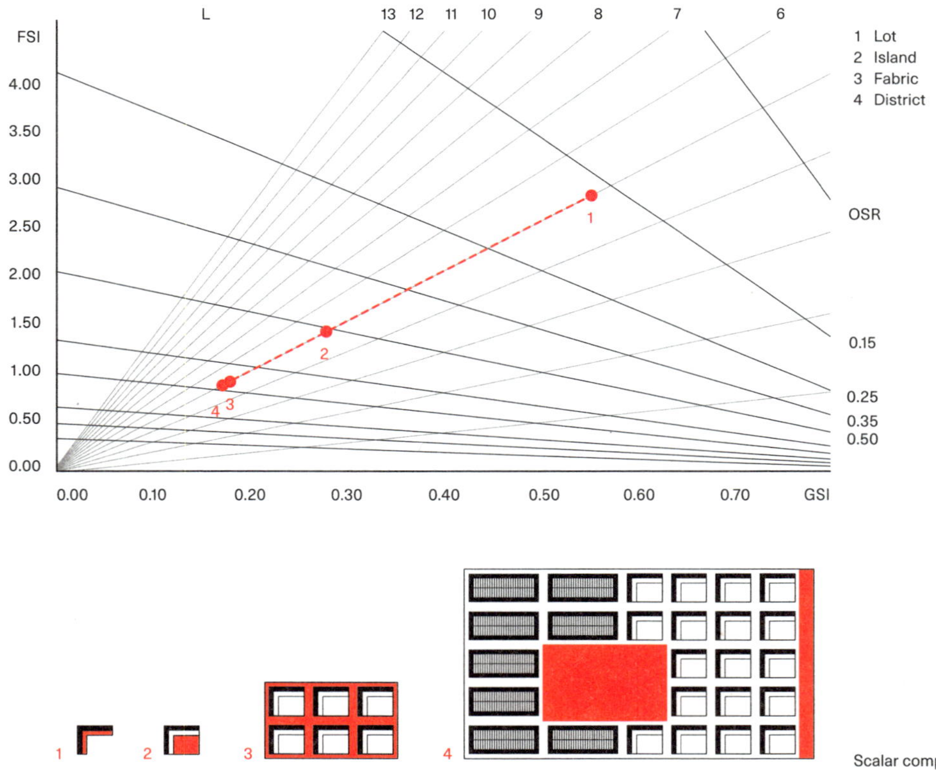

30 Scalar composition of scheme representing a modern open building block.

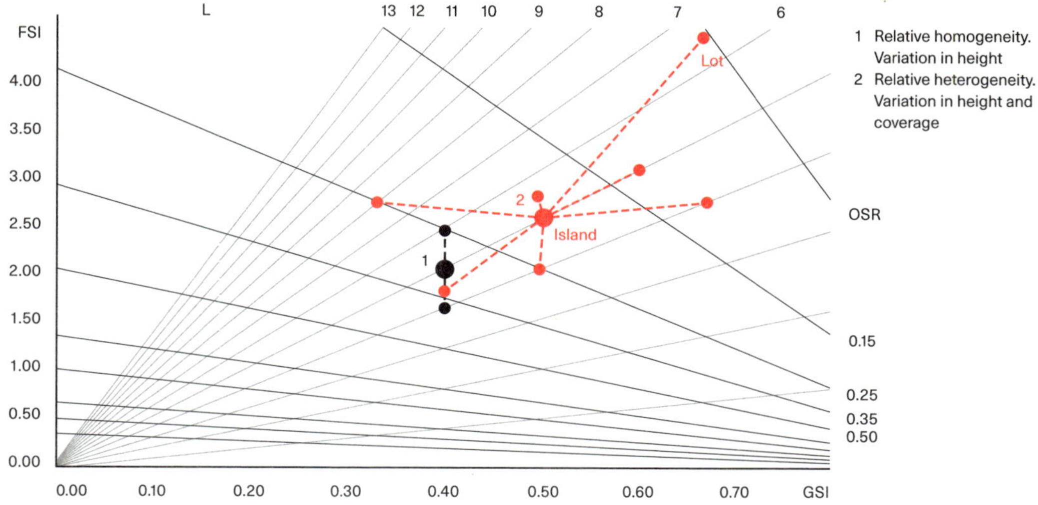

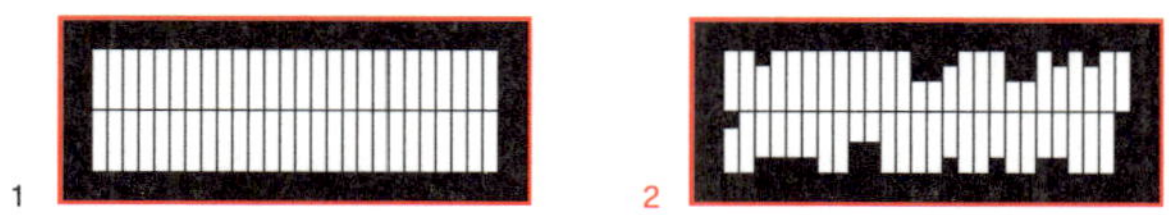

31 Two traditional closed perimeter building blocks with differing variation.

Density Calculations of Four Examples

To illustrate the differentiating potential of Spacematrix, we can use four of the samples from Amsterdam discussed earlier: Grachtengordel, De Pijp, Betondorp and Zuidwest Kwadrant. 32 33 34

Grachtengordel and De Pijp

The Grachtengordel (1613) and De Pijp (1875) are both examples of fabrics with traditional building blocks composed of many individual lots. In the case of the Grachtengordel, these lots were developed individually, while in De Pijp building developers sought to pack as many dwelling units as possible into relatively small blocks. The Grachtengordel was developed as an extension of the medieval city, which, due to the economic growth at the end of the sixteenth century, had become overcrowded. The urban fabric is characterized by an orthogonal and rational layout of streets, canals and blocks and is not based on the underlying landscape or the adjacent older fabric. De Pijp, on the other hand, was shaped by the existing landscape. This resulted in a smaller grain, and because of speculation, a lack of canals or other costly elements. Despite the similarities in building type, the network patterns are rather different in terms of size: measurement of the islands and the width of the street profile differ significantly.

Grachtengordel [NL]

De Pijp [NL]

32 Two examples: Grachtengordel and De Pijp.

Betondorp [NL]

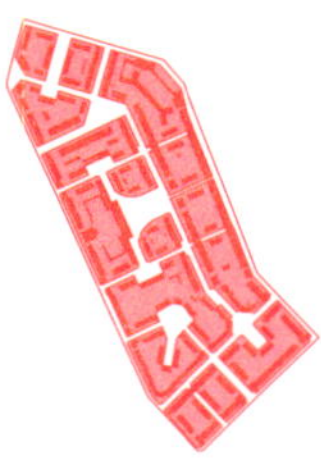

Zuidwest Kwadrant 2 (Osdorp) [NL]

33 Two examples: Betondorp and Zuidwest Kwadrant (Osdorp).

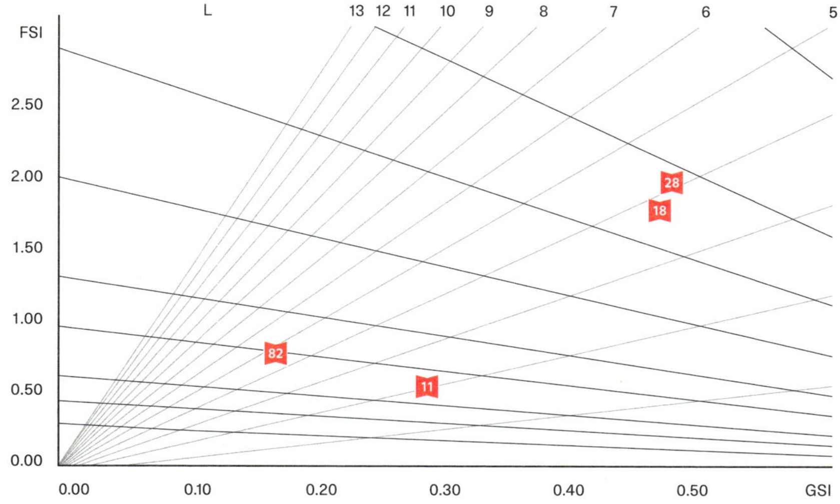

[NL] 11, 18, 28, 82

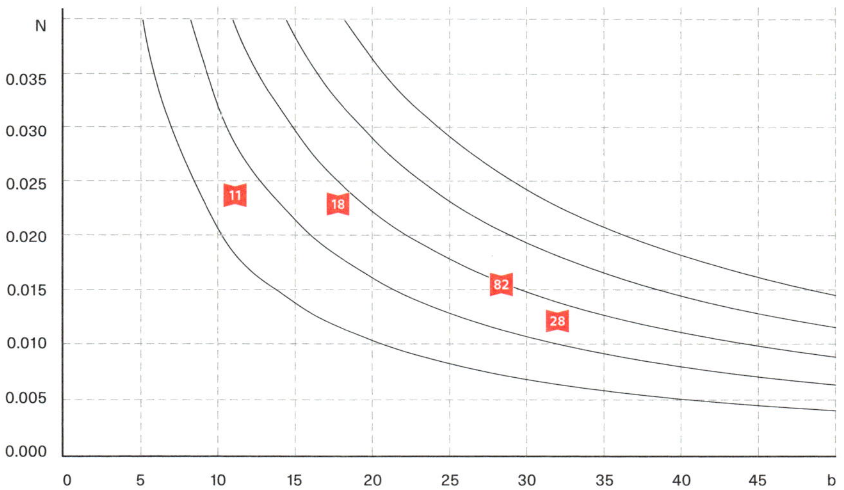

[NL] 11, 18, 28, 82

Four examples in the two diagrams: FSI (GSI) or Spacemate and N_f (b). For an overview of all samples, see Samples from the Netherlands, Germany, Spain, UK and Sweden on pages 235–271.

34

The residential density in Grachtengordel is 65 dwellings per hectare and in De Pijp 165 dwellings per hectare.[82] This confirms the conclusion that dwelling density has a weak relation to building type. The Spacemate density (FSI and GSI) of the Grachtengordel and De Pijp is, however, fairly similar. Both have an FSI_f of approximately 2.0 and, with almost 50 per cent of the fabric built upon, a GSI_f of 0.50. At the scale of the island the values are similar as well.[83] As the built densities (FSI and GSI) are similar at the scale of the fabric and the island, the tare space is the same in both cases: approximately 35 per cent of the fabric is used for access streets. In the case of the Grachtengordel, this public (tare) space is concentrated in a few wide streets (including canals). In De Pijp the tare space is evenly distributed over the fabric, resulting in a lot of narrow streets. This difference becomes clear

82
The following argument is based on statistics from O+S, Amsterdam. Available online at www.os.amsterdam.nl 2007.

83
$FSI_i = 3.00$ and $GSI_i = 0.74$ for Grachtengordel and $FSI_i = 2.84$ and $GSI_i = 0.75$ for De Pijp.

when network densities and profile widths are compared. In the Grachtengordel N is 0.012 and b is 32 m, while in De Pijp N is twice as high and b more narrow (0.023 and 18 m respectively).[84] Both morphological similarities and differences can thus be expressed using the three indicators FSI, GSI and N.

84
The grain size of the two samples is 164 m in the Grachtengordel and 87 m in De Pijp.

Betondorp and Zuidwest Kwadrant

Betondorp was developed in the early 1920s when Amsterdam was struggling with a housing shortage. The dwelling density of this low-rise development is similar to the Grachtengordel, with 70 dwellings per hectare. The Spacemate density, however, is much lower: the FSI_f is 0.58 and thus almost a fourth of the FSI_f in the Grachtengordel and De Pijp. In Zuidwest Kwadrant in Osdorp, the closed (perimeter) blocks of the inner city have been transformed into half-open blocks that allow light, air and green space to penetrate the islands and the buildings. The dwelling density of 50 dwellings per hectare is lower than in Betondorp. The FSI_f, is, however, higher: 0.75. As both areas, Betondorp and Zuidwest Kwadrant, are rather monofunctional (housing), this can only be explained by the difference in dwelling size. The coverage (GSI) in Betondorp is 0.30 while in Zuidwest Kwadrant only 0.15, leaving large amounts of non-built space. The lower coverage in Zuidwest Kwadrant is compensated for by the higher buildings that create a higher FSI than in Betondorp. Again, the multivariable approach is valuable when discussing urban form. When looking at network density, it is interesting to note that Betondorp and De Pijp have similar values, indicating that the grain of the urban layout is similar in both cases. Betondorp, however, has narrower streets (11 m). The Grachtengordel and Zuidwest Kwadrant both have larger islands and wider streets. Although the building types are different here, the street patterns show structural similarities in terms of grain size and street width.

DENSITY AND URBAN FORM

In the following sections, the Spacematrix method and its definitions are used to investigate the correlation between density and urban form.

The hypothesis is that urban density exercises limitations that to a significant degree determine the conditions for urban form. These limitations develop in the context of constraints. Some are geometrical and physical, others are individual (preferences, biography and talents of the designers), or collective (professional doctrines) and many are societal (rules, laws, levels of material wealth and acceptable standards). The multivariable approach to define density suggested in the previous chapter, in combination with the constraints present at a certain place and moment in time, exert specific limitations on the potential possibilities for urban form. This occurs to such an extent that it is possible to predict the urban fabric types that are most likely to occur under given density conditions.[1]

This chapter starts with an introduction to the two methods that have been used to investigate the relationship between urban form and density. These methods are, respectively, explorative and empirical.

Prescribing and Describing Density The relationship between density and form has a different character depending on which side of this relationship is being examined. *Prescribing* density is a situation in which the designer is forced to design to given density conditions so that density is first formulated and form subsequently emerges. This describes the way the density concept has at times been used in practice. Building codes and schemes for the garden city at the beginning of the twentieth century are examples of this. The opposite is true with the use of density when *describing* a specific part of the urban landscape. The form already exists and density is a descriptive outcome. The analysis and diagnosis of the congested city by the *Society for improving the condition of the labouring classes*, discussed in Chapter 2, are examples of such a descriptive use.

When prescribing density the point of departure is specific (density) and the outcome is open (built form). This is less the case if a range of densities, prescribed as a limited space in the Spacematrix (or a limited surface in the Spacemate), is used. The most specific density is characterized by one position in the diagram, but how open is the outcome? This is an important question. How much variation in built form is possible under specific density

1
An urban (or architectural) type is a summary (concept) of urban (or architectural) designs with common characteristics (Jong, T. de and H. Engel, 'Typological Research', in: T.M. de Jong and D.J.M. van der Voordt (eds.), *Ways to Study and Research Urban, Architectural and Technical Design* (Delft: DUP Science, 2002), 103–106, 103). These can be formal or functional: organic form types (tree, flower), geometric form types (pyramid, cube), function type (railway station, shopping centre).

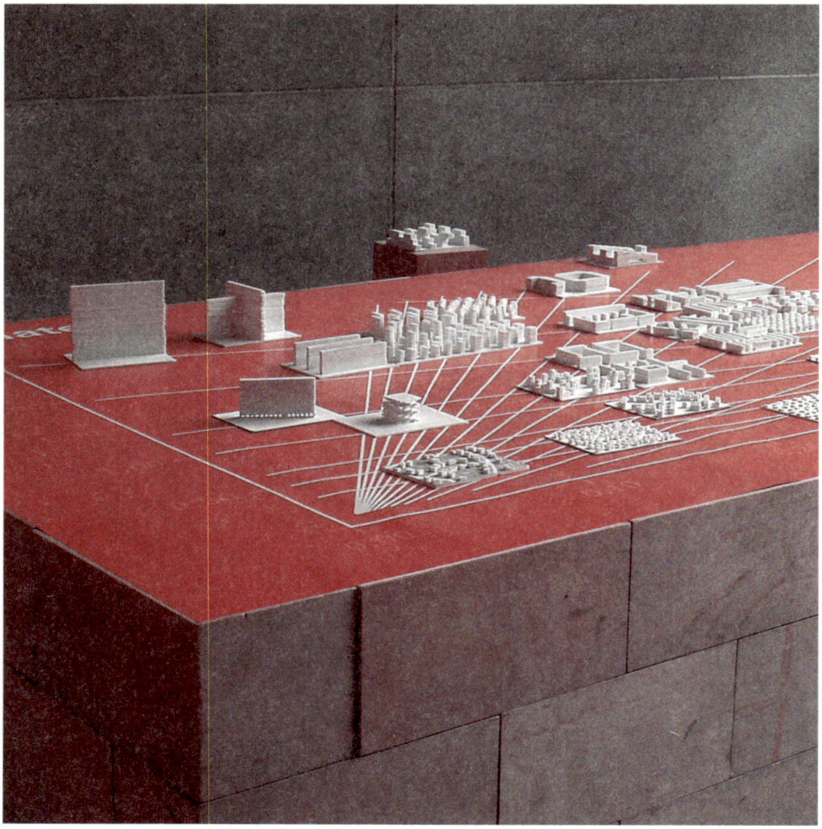

1 Exhibition 'Dwelling on Density', Delft University of Technology, Faculty of Architecture, 2004.

conditions? This of course depends on what is viewed as variation and on the extent to which it is discernible. When each bay window is seen as a variation, an unlimited number of options are present within each density condition. Information that is too detailed distracts from the primal structural properties that are of importance, particularly in the early stages of urban planning. On the other hand, if the resolution is not sharp enough, we risk losing important spatial information and ending up with statistics. However, wrong selections do not exist, and it is merely a question of levels of resolution and their usefulness. If the hypothesis holds, prescribing density in the context of existing constraints imposes sufficient limitations on the resulting composition of urban layouts that fabric types can be differentiated.

When density is applied to describe (map, represent) a part of the urban landscape, we begin with a specific instance of built form (empirical or virtual) to arrive through the use of accepted definitions at an abstract and specific representation. If there is a significant correlation between density and form, then one would expect to find regularities and clusters through which types can be defined. When using the concept of density to describe (part of) the urban landscape one has to remember that density always works with averages. This means that individual variations of the entities that are analysed will be lost when presenting the average. This is less of a problem when the entities are similar. The problem becomes more serious when there is a great variety between them. Any concept describing objects and phenomena around us runs this risk.

A car trip is illustrative of the tension between reality and representation, diversity and average. If the speed of a car trip is recorded one has to choose the relevant time frame. If the journey is not divided into shorter trajectories one ends up with one figure, representing the average speed for the whole trip. On the other end of the representation spectrum, such a detailed account of every change of speed throughout the whole journey is provided that it is merely reconstructed, with all its particular incidents. The key is to define the appropriate level of detail for the analysis that will be applied. In the case of describing density, spread and variation can be described at a variety of scales as was proposed in Chapter 3.

Explorative and Empirical Research

Two research methods have been used in this chapter to investigate the relation between density and urban form and to examine the way results can be prescriptively and descriptively used: explorative and empirical research.

Explorative research is based on deductive reasoning and concerns the geometrical and physical properties of built form and the influences that invented and real world constraints can have on built form. The use of formulas to capture basic geometries not only allows one to make comparisons between different cases, the use of variables also means that the trends are made visible. How does the measurement of network influence the relationship between private and public land? How does concentration of building mass compare to a peripheral distribution? What are the characteristics of such different distributions, under the same density conditions, in terms of building depth, exposure and accessibility? The method resembles the work of Leslie Martin and Lionel March, L.H.J. Angenot and A. Heimans discussed in earlier chapters, and allows great freedom to define, combine and experiment, but is very rigid in its deductive principles of logical reasoning and mathematical precision.

Empirical research can be described as inductive. Here empirical data is used that by definition has been affected by all kinds of real-world constraints. The samples used have specific, historical, geographical, cultural, political and ideological contexts. Changing uses, new standards of acceptance or economic pressure might have led to ex- or intensification. The existence of unique examples is dependent upon there being some interpretative system covering generic concepts. A plethora of individual objects and events constitute the urban realm which is communicated using general concepts. Our empirical research uses typomorphological research undertaken by M.R.G. Conzen and SAR, but places less emphasis on the detail and contingent properties of the urban landscape. We believe that generic knowledge can be found in the empirical evidence and that at times too much emphasis has been placed on details that detract from key issues.

Applying both of these research methods can tell us about the influence of design and planning conventions and the changes that they have gone through. A historical, geographical and cultural interpretation of the empirical material can help to explain what constraints have been important to the structuring of the urban environment, and the changes in their influence over time. Chapter 2 to a large extent illustrates this interpretation of empirical material. Empirical research yields a historical view of individual and collective knowledge accumulated in the urban landscape. Explorative research is able to look beyond the constraints of the present and explore new insights on possible urban forms.

Selection Criteria of Samples

The (empirical) samples used to test the hypothesis have been selected on the basis of representing a broad spectrum of morphological patterns. These have been influenced by a variety of constraints, regulations and preferences from one period to the next (historical spread) and from one country to the other (geographical spread). To limit the number of samples and constraints, we have focused primarily on samples dominated by housing. Three criteria for the selection of samples include:

1. Samples should represent different *morphological patterns*;
2. All *historical periods* should be represented, from medieval to present-day urban environments;
3. Samples should have a certain *geographical and cultural spread*, allowing an investigation into structural similarities and possible differences.

Morphological Spread

To represent a broad range of morphological patterns different building types have to be represented. For this purpose we use the three basic types described by Martin and March: the 'pavilion', the 'street', and the 'court' type.[2] ❷ These are also called *point* (or nucleated) development, *strip* (or linear) development and *block* (or peripheral) development, descriptions that will be used in the following discussion. All three can be found in low-rise, mid-rise and high-rise solutions. This results in a matrix of nine morphological categories.

A wide range of network patterns should also be included. ❸ Here we rely on the work of Manuel de Solà-Morales and Amis Siksna. De Solà-Morales states that the measurements of the urban pattern are decisive for the relationship between general form (street pattern) and built content.[3] Siksna distinguishes three categories of block (or island) size in his study of the robustness of the city layout of North American and Australian city centres.[4] They are small blocks (less than 10,000 m^2), medium sized blocks (between 10,000 and 20,000 m^2) and large blocks (larger than 20,000 m^2). In general, European blocks are smaller and therefore a category of blocks

2
Martin, L., L. March et al., 'Speculations', in: L. Martin and L. March, (eds.), *Urban Space and Structures* (Cambridge: Cambridge University Press, 1972), 28–54, 35–37.

3
Solà-Morales, M. de, 'Towards a Definition: Analysis of Urban Growth in the Nineteenth Century', *Lotus*, 19 June 1978, 28–36.

4
Siksna, A., 'The Effects of Block Size and Form in North American and Australian City Centres', *Urban Morphology* 1 (1997), 19–33, 20.

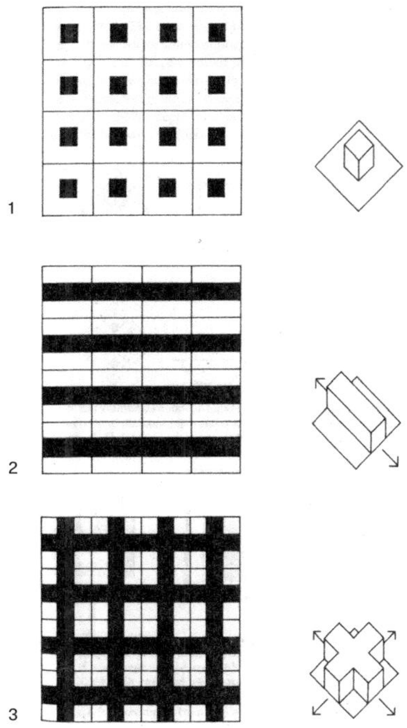

1 'Pavilion' type
2 'Street' type
3 'Court' type

2 'Pavilion', 'street' and 'court' types (Martin and March 1972: 36).

with a size of less than 5,000 m^2 has been added to Siksna's categories to match the European context.

Historical Spread

In Chapter 2, four periods in Dutch history of urban developments were described. The selection of empirical samples is based on the same periods. A subdivision of the third period (1900–1970) has been made to achieve a better representation of this turbulent period, characterized by huge contrasts in doctrines and resulting urban form. The first part covers the period just after the introduction of the *Housing Act* in 1901 and can be characterized as a period in which plans no longer were merely pragmatic land-division plans for the development of the commodity housing. Social, political and aesthetical ideals started to play a greater role. The second part begins after the Second World War with the rebuilding of the Netherlands. It is defined by a state-coordinated realization of the modern ideals expressed in the 1930s by CIAM.

The described periods, covering the time from 1350 to 2000, generally coincide with a cross section of Dutch cities. It includes their first extension areas from the inner city during the seventeenth century, the nineteenth-century expansions and the twentieth-century move to the outskirts. The selection of empirical samples is aimed at having a wide representation of different morphological and network patterns within each historical period, but this was not always possible for the simple reason that not all patterns were present in each period.

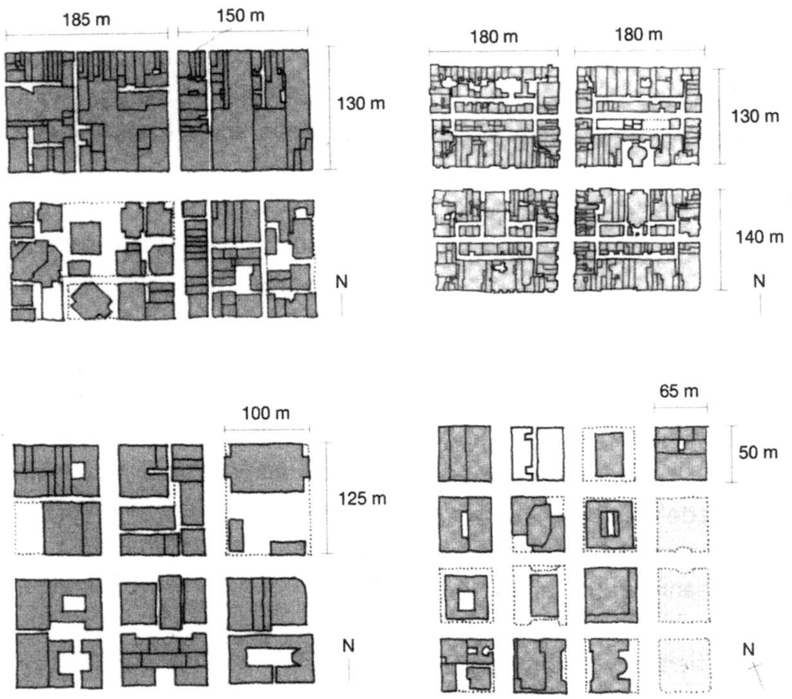

3 Compositional variations of the 'grid' (Marshall 2005: 224).

Geographical and Cultural Spread

To allow us to compare Dutch practice with other geographical and cultural points of reference, we have compared Amsterdam to four other European cities: Berlin in Germany, Barcelona in Spain, Stockholm in Sweden and London in the UK. Furthermore, a comparison with four Asian cities is included to investigate whether the method developed also applies to very different conditions, both culturally and geographically.

The five European capital cities have experienced periods of intensification, city growth and stagnation with rapid expansion starting in the nineteenth century to accommodate population growth and the rural-urban migration that fuelled increasing industrialization. In Berlin, the Greater Berlin Act of 1920 boosted the population by incorporating many hitherto autonomous towns and cities and the city reached almost 4.5 million inhabitants by 1942.[5] Barcelona, on the other hand, did not grow in terms of territory until 1860 when the construction of an expansion plan was initiated. Therefore, at that time, Barcelona had one of the highest population densities in Europe, double that of Amsterdam: 850 inhabitants per hectare in Barcelona compared to 400 inhabitants per hectare in Amsterdam.[6] London showed a continuous growth from the start of the nineteenth century until the Second World War, when London counted 8.6 million residents,[7] while Barcelona counted only 1.8 million inhabitants. Stockholm, where urbanization started later than in the other cities, but continued to grow in terms of population even during the Second World War, had just over 800,000 inhabitants in 1960, comparable to Amsterdam at that time.[8]

5 https://en.wikipedia.org/wiki/Demographics_of_Berlin, accessed November 1, 2020.

6 Busquets, J., *Barcelona, the Urban Evolution of a Compact City* (Rovereto: Nicolodi, 2005), 117.

7 *Vision of Britain through Time*, URL: http://www.visionofbritain.org.uk/unit/10097836/cube/TOT_POP, accessed November 1, 2020.

8 *Befolkningen i Stockholm 1252–2005 (in Swedish). Stockholm Municipality, retrieved from https://en.wikipedia.org/wiki/Stockholm,* accessed November 1, 2020.

During the period of rapid urbanization (1815–1900), the layout of Berlin developed under very liberal planning policies that encouraged land and building speculation. This resulted in notorious housing conditions in the so called *Mietkasernenstadt*, which acquired the dubious reputation of having the worst living conditions in Europe.[9] The same laissez-faire politics was dominant in Amsterdam, but because the characteristics of land and urban layout were to a large extent influenced by natural factors such as existing ditches, rather small and narrow city blocks were the outcome. The city expansion in the same period in Barcelona was again very different. A detailed survey preceded a master plan by engineer Ildefonso Cerdà that consisted of a street layout with large square blocks. Joan Busquets describes in his book *Barcelona, the Urban Evolution of a Compact City* the outstanding nature of this plan by Cerdà and suggests that Cerdà should be included in the list of 'founders' of modern urban planning along with Reinhard Baumeister, Joseph Stübben and Raymond Unwin.[10] In terms of population density, Barcelona's medieval neighbourhoods score highest in the inventory made by Alasdair Rae in 2020 with more than 500 inhabitants per hectare, followed by nineteenth-century neighbourhoods in Stockholm, Amsterdam and Berlin with just over 200 inhabitants per hectare.[11]

9
Taverne, E., *De wortels van de contemporaine stad*, Reader Architectuur- en Stedenbouwgeschiedenis (Groningen: Rijksuniversiteit Groningen, 2000), 39.

10
Busquets, *Barcelona*, op. cit. (note 6), 122–133.

11
https://www.theguardian.com/cities/gallery/2018/mar/22/most-densely-populated- square-kilometres-europe-mapped, accessed November 1, 2020

Intrinsic Properties of the Island

Explorative Research

Prior to the empirical search for regularities and correlations between density and urban form, some questions should be formulated about the range of possible solutions under certain density conditions. How many possible solutions, or actualizations, can be expected under specific density conditions? And if density can be seen as a condition that limits the amount of possible solutions (internal constraint), what other conditions (external constraints) can be named that further diminish the amount of solutions that are probable to be actualized in the real world under certain density conditions?

As mentioned earlier, it is commonly accepted that there is little to no correlation between density and urban form. This presupposes that under a certain density the building mass can take any form: 'Anything goes.' This misconception, in our opinion, is partly caused by the too rough resolution of existing and commonly used density definitions. Using one variable, such as dwellings per hectare or FSI, relies on a far too blunt instrument to make enough sharp differentiations which can be used to construct types or classes. This means that too many examples, or instances, fall under one density value (for example 40 dw/ha), and important differences in properties (such as basic urban form) are drowned. At the other extreme of the spectrum, attempts to capture the complexity of reality that are too detailed run into the opposite problem. The huge respect for difference demands an almost endless amount of properties to be registered. In the end, only very few instances fit a singular compound of descriptions, and the number of classes

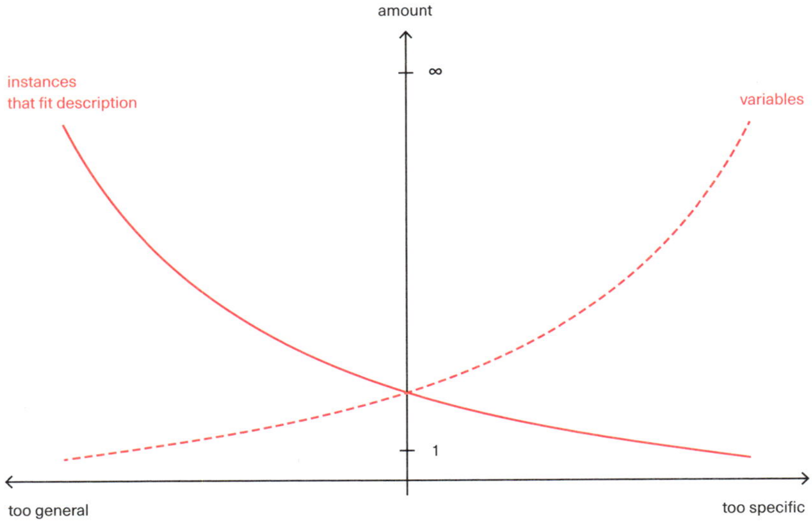

❹ Tension between (too) general and (too) specific.

approaches infinity. Descriptions that are too detailed reproduce a complex reality and leave little space for type constructions and generic conclusions. The balance between the type descriptions and the number of variables is at stake here. ❹ One reason that the Spacematrix method is appropriate for the purpose of differentiating between basic urban forms could be that the quantity of indicators used and their content fits nicely with the quantity of commonly used descriptions of urban landscapes. This speculative assumption would turn into a reasonable explanation if the empirical investigation shows significant correlations between this multivariable density and urban form.

To investigate these conditioning aspects of density on the options for urban form, two experiments were set up. First, a series of design experiments were organized with students from Delft University of Technology, Masters in Architecture and Urbanism.[12] Many models were produced exemplifying various density conditions.[13] Secondly, combinatorics was used to illustrate the deflation of the space of solutions.

12 In collaboration with professor Rudy Uytenhaak (2004).

13 Unfortunately, on 13 May 2008 the models were destroyed during the fire that hit the Faculty of Architecture in Delft.

Design Experiments

The models produced by students during the workshops ranged from transparent (dominated by voids) to compact (dominated by mass), from low-rise to high-rise, and from spacious to dense. Without specifying any additional constraints this resulted in a pure geometrical system of forms in which only mass could be distinguished from open space. However, the constraint of the material and individual preferences in all cases limited the formal solutions.

The students were initially asked to design models with FSI 1.0, resulting in spatial solutions ranging from a concentrated tower of ten storeys to an evenly spread-out mass of one storey. ❺ In other words, the FSI was achieved by working between the extremes of concentrating the building mass or dispersing the same amount of mass. The first strategy resulted in a very low coverage, while in the second no open space remained. In a second step, the students produced models based on a given FSI and GSI, in this case 1.0 and 0.2 respectively. The models demonstrate that plans with the same compactness still show considerable variation in building mass configuration. This is mostly due to the scale of individual buildings. ❻ The building mass becomes dominant when using small dimensions as it is spread over the model, particularly if the GSI increases. ❼ The building mass is concentrated, as is the open space, when smaller building units are combined into bigger blocks.

Even with the shrinking of the bandwidth to a smaller interval (for instance from 'FSI between 0.5 and 1.0' to 'FSI between 0.5 and 0.6'), or to a specific value ('FSI of 0.55') *and* with the addition of more indicators, such as GSI, the possible actualizations of designs still seems infinite. Surely, with a hypersensitivity to differences – every different position of a bay window means a unique actualization, for example – the possibilities are indeed infinite. However, few, many, or no bay windows are not relevant here; such variation does not upset the predefined types, and all fall neatly into a category independently of these – for this purpose – minor differences. Still, even with a rougher typological resolution, a huge amount of possibilities remains. Theoretically, even if 'anything does not go', an infinite amount of solutions can be actualized. However, the size of the 'space of solutions' is further narrowed by what were earlier termed *external* constraints. The reality of measures and real-world constraints cuts away many theoretically possible solutions. Among other things, physical, economic, social and aesthetical requirements limit the possible solutions under a specific density value or bandwidth. One can compare this to the possible solutions for the amount of buttons on a shirt. Everything from one to 100 buttons would work. However, in most cases we find between five and eight buttons on produced and worn shirts. In the same way, theoretically, a closed perimeter block is possible to design, build and inhabit with a very low density if the building depth is 1 m instead of the 10 to 15 m usually encountered at our latitude. However, the extreme costs and the inconvenience of the plan puts an end to the option before it even gets the chance to be formulated. In reality, the existence of such a case is statistically insignificant, as are many other possibilities on the periphery of that which is possible. The reality of spatial requirements (plan organization, access); urban physics (daylight, ventilation, noise); social organization (size of development unit, property structure, regulations); and preferences and acceptance (privacy, view), just to mention a few, quickly shrink the space of solutions.

As the workshop described above progressed, the students were confronted with external constraints such as minimum and maximum building depths, minimum distances between buildings, degrees of variation, etcetera. A total of more than 100 models were developed that demonstrated a

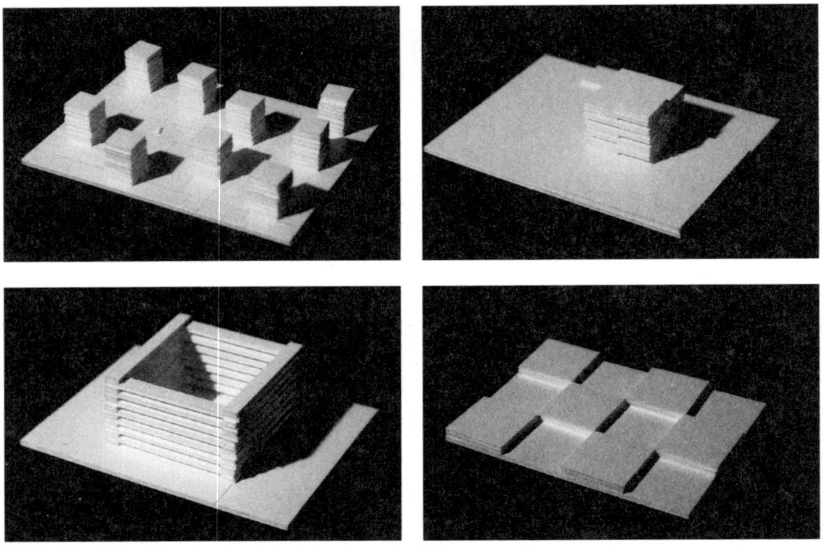

5 Student models with identical FSI of 1.0 (student work MSc3, Delft University of Technology, 2004).

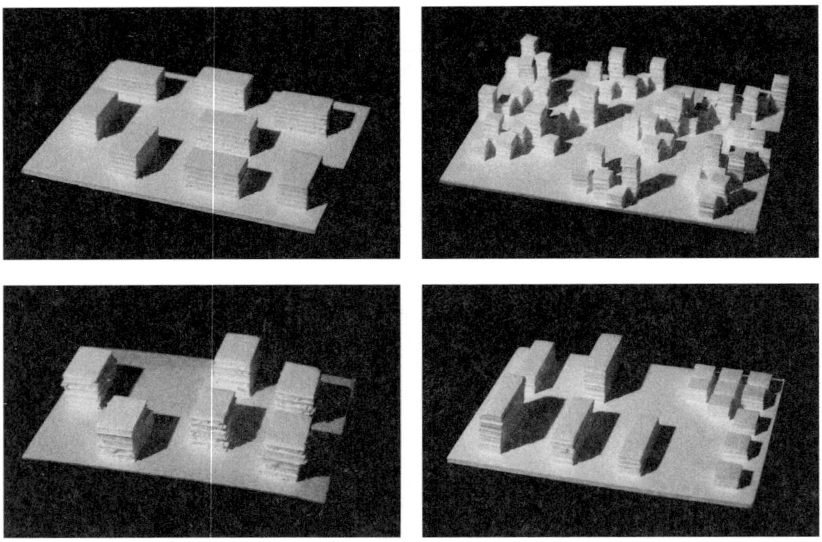

6 Student models with identical FSI of 1.0 and GSI 0.2 (student work MSc3, Delft University of Technology, 2004).

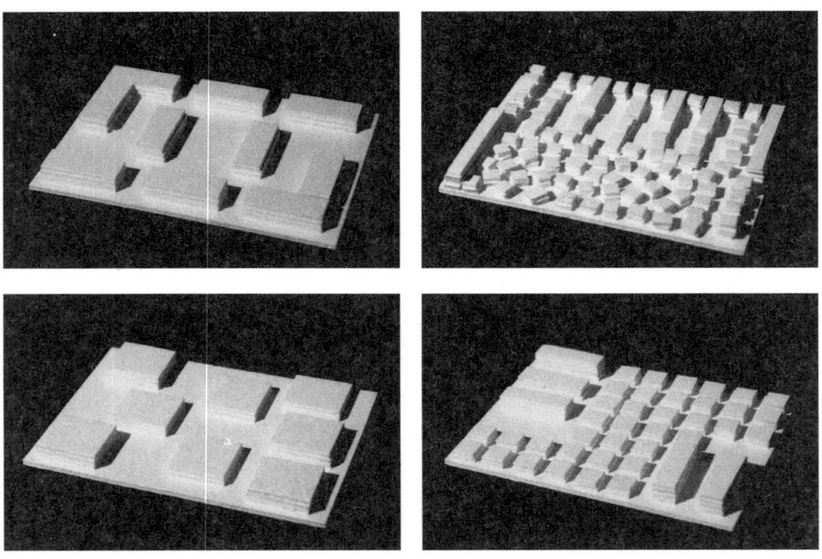

7 Student models with identical FSI of 1.0 and GSI 0.4 (student work MSc3, Delft University of Technology, 2004).

narrowing of (formal) variation as a result of the prescribed constraints. What took place during the workshops could be described as the transition from a situation without limitations to a more detailed set of rules spelling out the requirements. The initial, deliberately prescribed, conditions were formulated in terms of FSI and GSI. These constituted two basic conditions that limit the primary distribution of building mass. In a world where no other guiding principles would be present these conditions seem to be very open, as the models indeed showed. We could then rightly claim that 'almost anything goes'. In the real socio-spatial material world, however, numerous constraints exist. The workshops showed that imposing some simplified versions of these real-world requirements generated solutions that structurally and formally moved closer to each other in the direction of recognizable urban types.

Combinatorics

Variations in GSI can be used to illustrate the tension between the number of solutions and constraints. The variety of solutions with one GSI value (amount of coverage) can be analysed in an abstract and deductive way through combinatorics. Combinatorics is a branch of pure mathematics that studies combinations of objects belonging to a finite set in accordance with certain constraints.[14] It can be used to investigate the number of ways that a specified array of units can be combined. An example of a problem that can be approached by combinatorics is: In how many different combinations can a deck of 52 distinct playing cards be ordered? The answer is 52! (52 factorial), which is equal to about 8.0658×10^{67}.

14
Concise Oxford English Dictionary, Eleventh Edition.

To illustrate a situation with somewhat more limited possibilities, we can use a square cut into nine equal parts. In a grid of nine pixels (3×3), each pixel can be black or white, symbolizing mass or void. The amount of possible configurations can be described as $C(n,p) = n! / (p! \times [n - p]!)$, where n is the number of possible positions (in this case nine) and p the number of black pixels that are to be distributed. In terms of coverage, GSI can be described as p/n. The grid turns from white to black step by step and at every stage all permutations can be drawn and calculated. The level of resolution and precision defines the number of permutations. For example, a fictive building block of 40×40 m, divided into pixels of 20×20 m, 10×10 m or 5×5 m, can have for a coverage of 25 per cent respectively 4, 1,820, and $2{,}75 \times 10^{10}$ possible layouts. This is known as a combinatoric explosion.

When the first pixel is turned black (GSI = $1/9$), nine possibilities exist of which only three are unique. A 'unique permutation' means cases that cannot be achieved through mirroring or rotating one of the other permutations. For C(9,1) this means that there are three unique permutations: the black pixel positioned in the centre, the corner and in the middle of one side. Two black pixels can be arranged in 36 mutations, of which 8 are unique, three pixels in 84 mutations of which 16 are unique, etcetera. In 8, the left

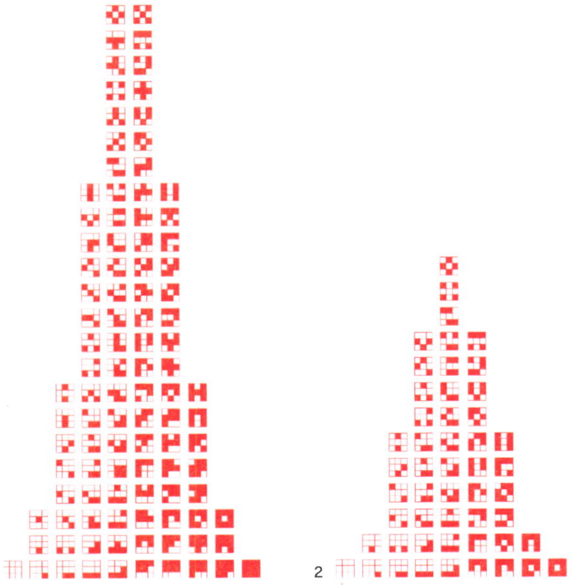

1 without constraints
2 with constraints

(8) Illustration of unique permutations in a grid of three by three pixels.

drawing shows the number of unique permutations for every GSI value (or C(n,p)). Maximum variations occur with a coverage of 4/9 and 5/9.[15]

The number of permutations decreases when two constraints are added: maximum depth of the mass (relates to usability and microclimate) and adjacency to the outer contour of the grid (to ensure accessibility), are added. (8) (9) The number of possibilities decreases even more rapidly when more pixels are filled in. In other words, fewer permutations occur with a higher GSI. This means that without any constraints most permutations have a coverage (GSI) of 0.5. With tighter requirements, however – for instance the requirement that a minimum of three sides are non-built to guarantee privacy, view and daylight – the number of permutations decreases quickly for coverage between 4/9 and 5/9, and is reduced to zero for high coverage.

These experiments show that within the theoretical logic of empty space and mass, most differentiation can be found when 50 per cent of the matrix is white (or void) and the other 50 per cent is black (or mass). Imposed real-world constraints, however, change the trend by decreasing the number of possibilities in general and shift the point for maximum permutations towards layouts with less coverage. Could it be that constraints of the kinds discussed here limit the options to such an extent that we can recognize formal similarities and speak of types? If this is the case the theoretical combinatoric explosion of possibilities might be mitigated by:

1. Intrinsic density conditions (geometrical);
2. External real-world constraints;
3. Our conceptual ability to recognize similarities, ignore differences and define types.

Whether there is enough *significant clustering of formal features* to define types with the use of Spacematrix will be discussed later in this chapter when

15 If we would have used 2 × 2 pixels, 4 × 4, or any even amount, we would have arrived at an optimum where the coverage is 0.5.

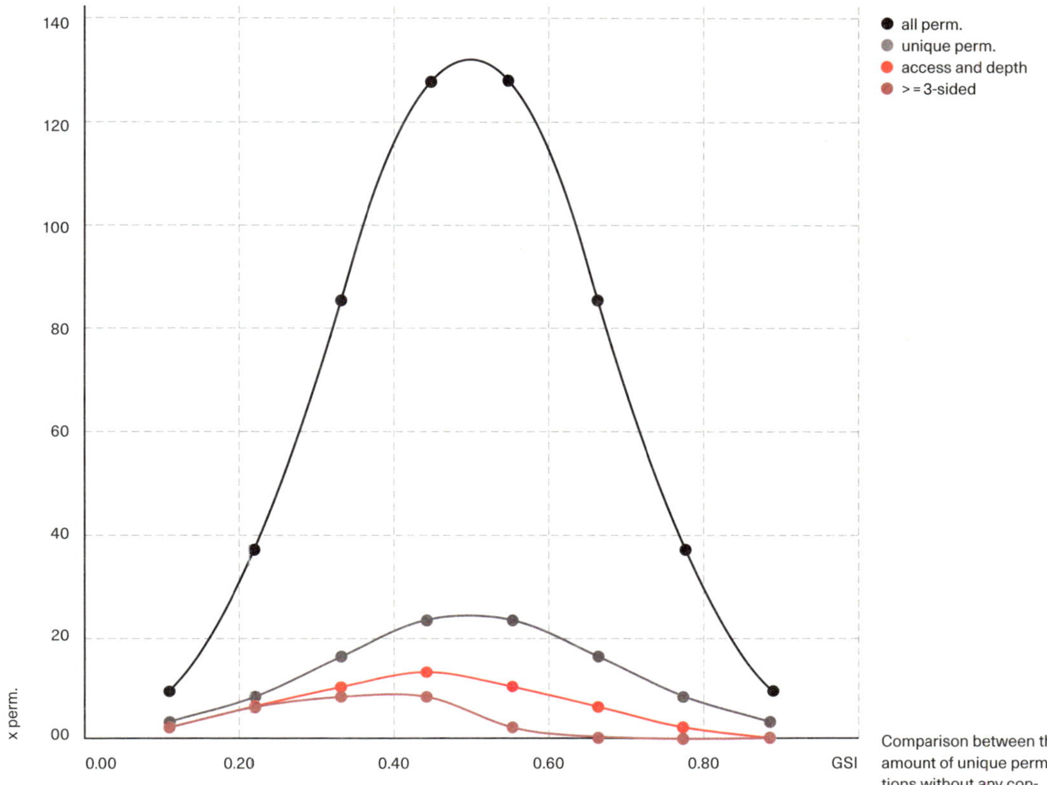

9 Comparison between the amount of unique permutations without any constraints and with constraints.

we analyse the empirical material. But based on the experiments described above, it becomes clear that permutations with higher coverage result in more peripheral dispositions, while in the permutations with more open space other possibilities occur. Varying the composition of the mass when a maximum depth is specified is easier when the coverage is low.

The design experiments and the combinatorial experiments show that reality (models with constraints) is less diverse than the infinite theoretical possibilities of a specific density might suggest. In the following paragraph the empirical material collected in the Netherlands and abroad will be analysed to examine to what extent there is, considering all real-world constraints, a correlation between built form (type) and ranges of density.

Empirical Research

For the classification of the samples, the morphological types as described earlier in this chapter have been used: point (or pavilion), block (or court) and strip development, which can be found in low-rise, mid-rise and high-rise solutions. For the following section, one sample has been chosen as an archetype for each of these nine categories to illustrate the general type 10. The values have in these examples been calculated at the scale of the island.

Wageningen Hoog [NL] Point type low-rise

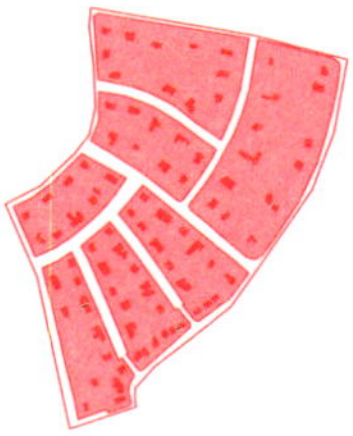

De Berg Zuid [NL] Point type mid-rise

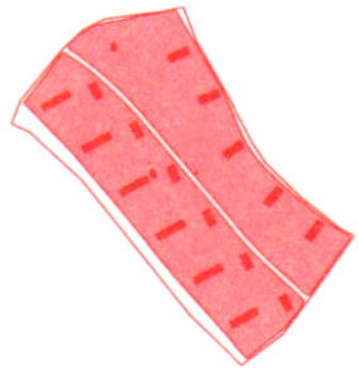

Wilhelminaplein [NL] Point type high-rise

10 Nine archetypical samples (see 11 and 18 for positions in FSI (GSI) (i.e. Spacemate) and N (b)-diagram respectively.

Amsteldorp 1 [NL] Strip type low-rise

Zuidwest Kwadrant 1 [NL] Strip type mid-rise

Langswater [NL] Strip type high-rise

10 Nine archetypical samples (see 11 and 18 for positions in FSI (GSI) (i.e. Spacemate) and N (b) diagram respectively.

Watergraafsmeer 1 [NL] Block type low-rise

De Pijp [NL] Block type mid-rise

Landtong [NL] Block type high-rise

10 Nine archetypical samples (see 11 and 18 for positions in FSI (GSI) (i.e. Spacemate) and N (b)-diagram respectively.

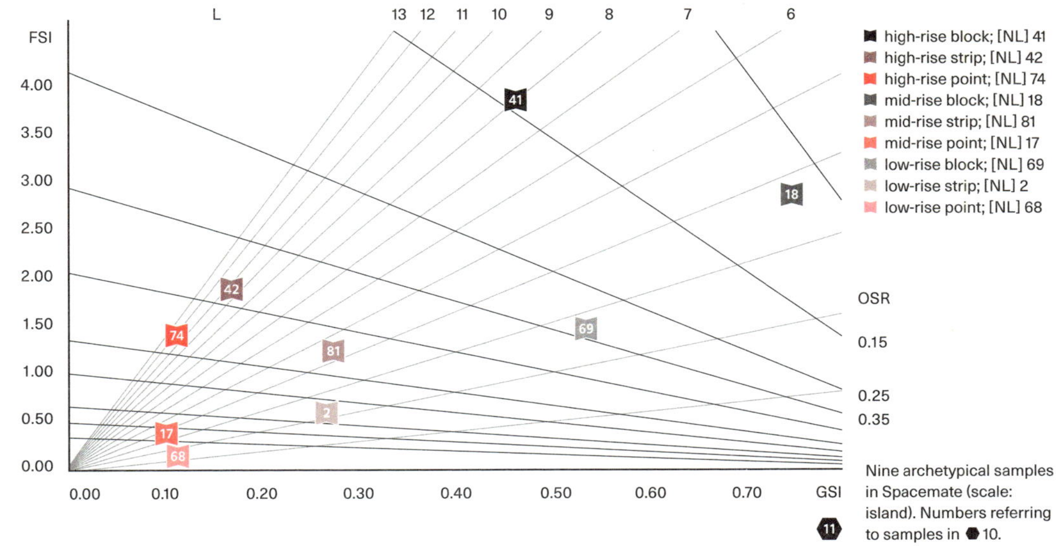

11 Nine archetypical samples in Spacemate (scale: island). Numbers referring to samples in 10.

As can be seen in the Spacemate, each archetype has its own unique position. 11 The low-rise point type is represented by the villas of Wageningen Hoog (68 in 11); De Berg Zuid 17 with mid-rise apartment buildings in green surroundings represents the mid-rise point type; and Wilhelminaplein 74, an area with 12-storey flats, is chosen to represent the high-rise point type. For the strip type, Amsteldorp 1 2, Zuidwest Kwadrant 1 81 and Langswater 42, with building heights of respectively two, five and 11 storeys, have been selected. The (perimeter) block types Watergraafsmeer 69, De Pijp 18 and Landtong 41, with two, five, and eight storeys respectively, have the highest building coverage (GSI). The archetypical samples are shown on the following pages. Interesting to note is that Watergraafsmeer, with the lowest FSI among the block types, is, in terms of FSI, comparable to the mid-rise strip type represented by Zuidwest Kwadrant and the high-rise point type, Koningin Wilhelminahof. In terms of FSI, these samples are similar, but in terms of GSI, building height and OSR, the differences are great. In other words, building types can be distinguished from one another in terms of density, but only when using the multivariable density concept.

In 12 all the Dutch samples have been added to the diagram. Although not all types are equally represented, it is obvious that clusters can be drawn in the diagram 13. Within the low-rise samples, point types such as Wageningen Hoog have a lower GSI and FSI than strip types, such as Amsteldorp, which again have a lower density (GSI and FSI) than the block types. Mid-rise samples show the same logic although in general the density is higher. However, although the differences between the clusters are clear, distinctions between one type and another are sometimes difficult to define. They tend to slowly transcend from one type into another, with all kinds of hybrid forms occurring in between.

Kolenkit (40 in 12 13 14) represents a good example of a hybrid form. Morphologically speaking it can be defined as strip type but in Spacemate

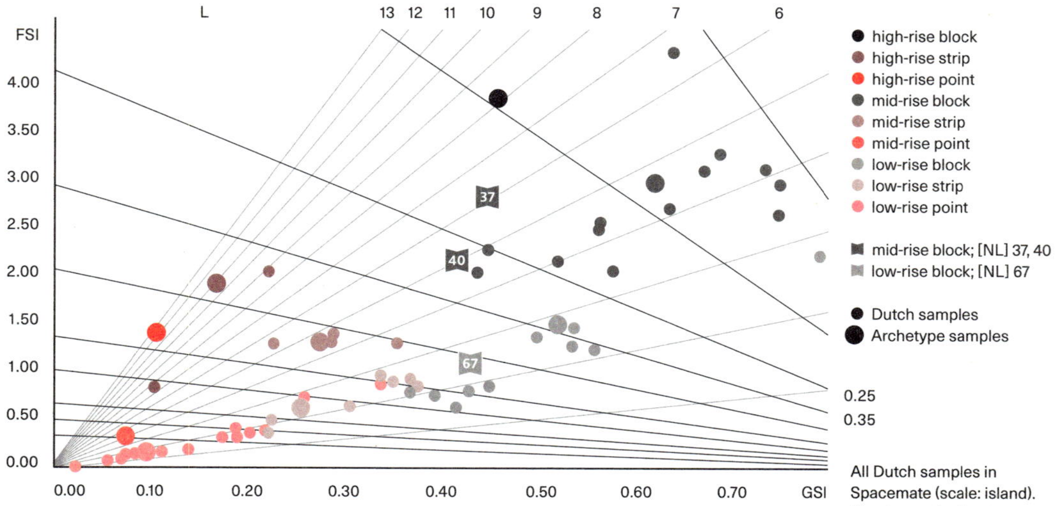

All Dutch samples in Spacemate (scale: island). Numbers referring to samples in 14.

12

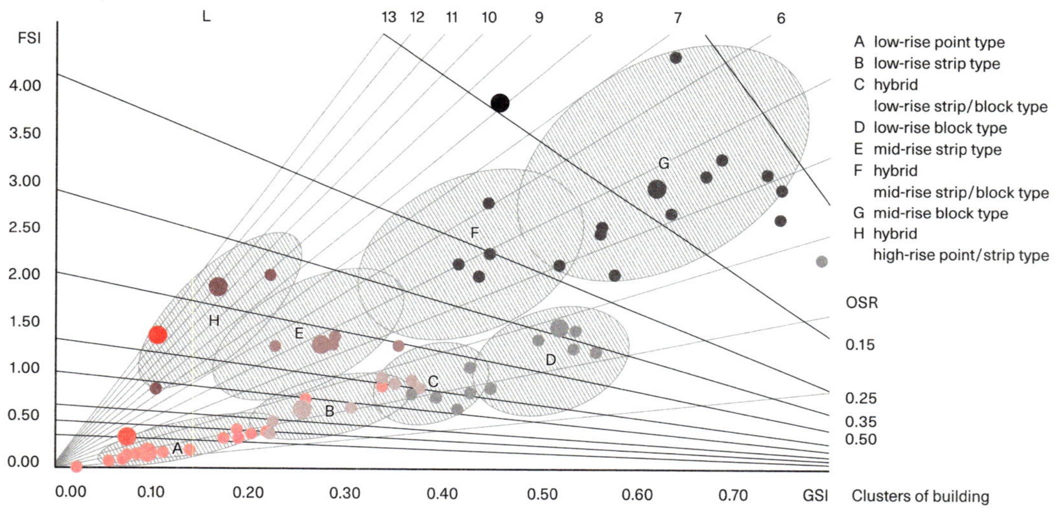

Clusters of building types in Spacemate (scale: island).

13

it is located in close proximity to a cluster of block or court types. Kolenkit is one of the first examples in Amsterdam whereby the closed perimeter block was opened. It was transformed into an open block by having only the short ends removed. Two strips of buildings define one island surrounded by streets. In comparison to other strip types in Osdorp with more space in between, or examples of 'real' strip types with only one building per island, the density of Kolenkit is higher. In other words, Kolenkit is a good example of a hybrid type suspended between the strip and the block type.

Another sample, Java island (37 in 12 13 14), characterized as a block type, has a rather low coverage (GSI) when compared to the other block types. Here, the large size of the inner courts and, therefore, the size of the islands explain the relatively low GSI. It accounts for the deviation from

Kolenkit [NL]

Java island [NL]

Vreewijk [NL]

14 Three examples of 'in-between' types (see ⬢ 12 for position in Spacemate).

the core of the block type cluster. The same can be said about the group of samples situated between the low-rise block type and low-rise strip type. Some samples in this position have transformed from a more strip-like type through intensification of the islands towards a block type. Others have deliberately been designed as a semi-block type with parts of the perimeter of the block left open (Vreewijk 67 in 12 13 14).

Based on the empirical material we can conclude that building types on the scale of islands can be clustered in Spacemate. 13 Six of them describe the archetypes low-rise point, strip and block type; mid-rise strip and block type and high-rise strip type. In addition we found samples positioned close to the borders of these clusters that can be described as 'in-between' types (cluster C, F and H in 13), indicating a hybridization of types as was discussed in the beginning of this chapter. It could, therefore, be worthwhile, and maybe even necessary, to move towards a purely performance-based description of building types. A Spacematrix description could then replace the more conventional, formal types. This would mean that the above described empirical research serves more as a temporary ladder, necessary to make an argument, but which at a certain point is disposed of. Instead of attaching the conventional professional terminology to the suggested clusters, the position(s) – absolute and relative – in itself works as a description that, combined with performance, can be productive and moreover, purged of associative distractions. It is thus possible to imagine a situation where a multivariable density description supplants the limited traditional concepts used to describe the built environment. Whether or not this is desirable is another question. A both/and approach is probably the most realistic: Spacematrix as a spatial DNA, loaded with information about spatial and other associated properties *and* traditional classifications with commonsense connotations. The advantages of a pure density description are also its weakness as the terminology of the professional language game conveys much meaning that is absent in a more technical, instrumental description.

The results of the explorations discussed earlier in this chapter (combinatorics and experiments) match the outcome of the empirical analysis. The expectations created by deductive and geometrical exercises did not suddenly become invalidated by totally unexplained clustering (or lack of it) in the empirical data. In fact the opposite is the case. To date, the multivariable density seems to be highly suited to account for structural differences in urban form. The concept is not too statistical and general, or too detailed and specific. We can conclude that analysis using multivariable density works at the level of the island in conveying structural similarities of building types.

These findings were systematically linked to the earlier work by Martin and March in a paper by Philip Steadman, where he brings together the Spacematrix with Martin and March's work in a comparative exploration.[16] Martin and March described the 'built potential' (FSI) of different built forms in relation to the number of storeys while keeping the depth of the building and the cut-off angle[17] between opposing façades constant. For linear built

16
Steadman, P., 'Density and built form: integrating «Spacemate» with the work of Martin and March', *Environment and Planning B: Planning and Design*, 40 (2013), 341–358.

17
The cut-off angle is the angle between the ground and a line joining the base of one façade to the roofline of the façade opposite. As the cut-off angle is made smaller, the built forms are pushed further apart.

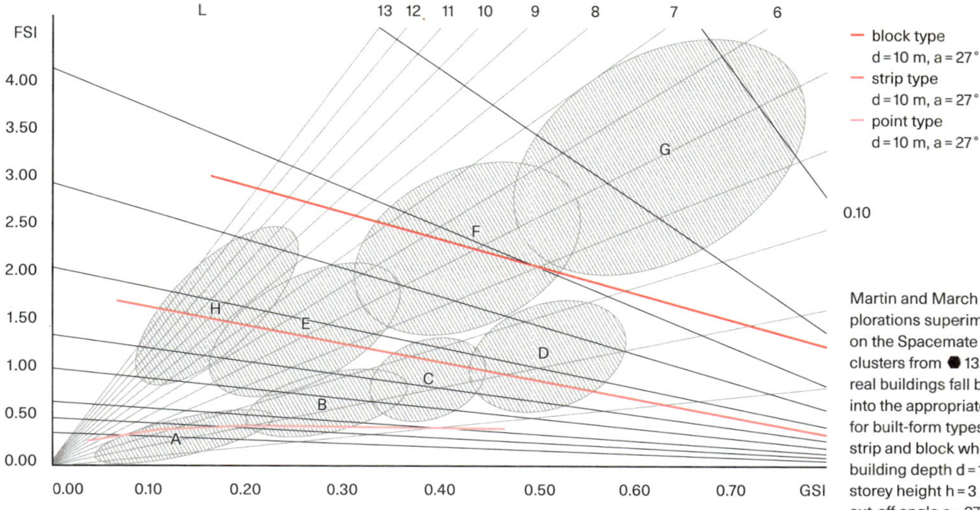

15 Martin and March explorations superimposed on the Spacemate and clusters from 13. The real buildings fall broadly into the appropriate bands for built-form types point, strip and block where building depth d = 10 m, storey height h = 3 m, and cut-off angle a = 27° (Steadman 2013: 353).

forms (strip type) and block types, FSI reaches a maximum, beyond which the density does not rise further despite the increase in the number of storeys (see 4 in Chapter 1). In the case of pavilions (point type), FSI reaches a maximum and then *declines* as more storeys are added.[18] Steadman uses this approach, but plots these results in the Spacemate, including the clustering of types, and shows how the three built forms – points, strips and blocks – describe three curves that change position depending on the set values for the depth of the building and the cut-off angle. 15 This exercise highlights the intrinsic logic of built form where the court type shows a higher built potential (FSI) than, for instance, the point type, partly due to the real-world constraints, in this case limited to two variables, building depth and cut-off angle, confirmed by the empirical findings presented in this book.

18 Martin, L. and L. March (eds.), *Urban Space and Structures* (Cambridge: Cambridge University Press, 1972), 37.

Intrinsic Properties of the Urban Fabric

After having shown how built form can be accurately clustered into types on the level of the island, we will in this paragraph investigate the properties of the urban fabric which, besides the islands, also includes the street network to access these islands.

Explorative Research

To demonstrate the interrelation between some indicators introduced earlier, six schemes of very different nature can be compared. 16 The first two schemes (1 and 4) represent a small mesh size of 50 m (N = 0.04), the second two (2 and 5) have a mesh of 100 m (N = 0.02), and the last two (3 and 6) a mesh of 200 m (N = 0.01). In combination with a street profile width of 5 and 20 m respectively, the sizes of the islands range from 10 to 190 m. The amount of network space, or fabric tare space, is lowest where a very wide mesh size

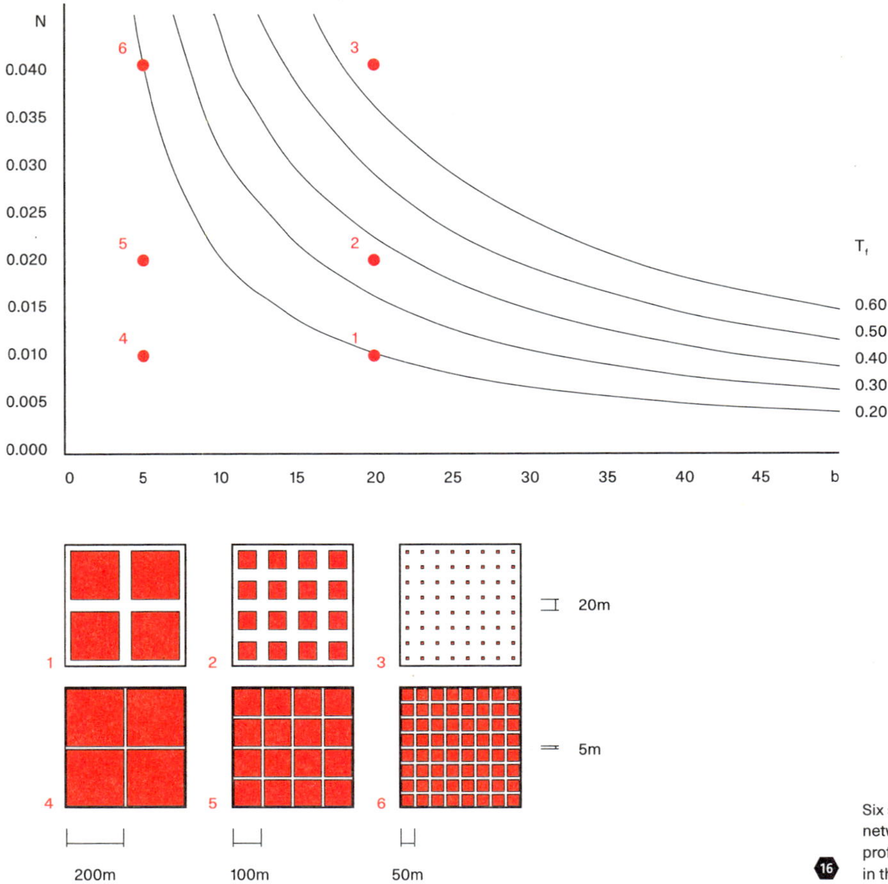

16 Six schemes with varying network density and profile width, positioned in the N (b)-diagram.

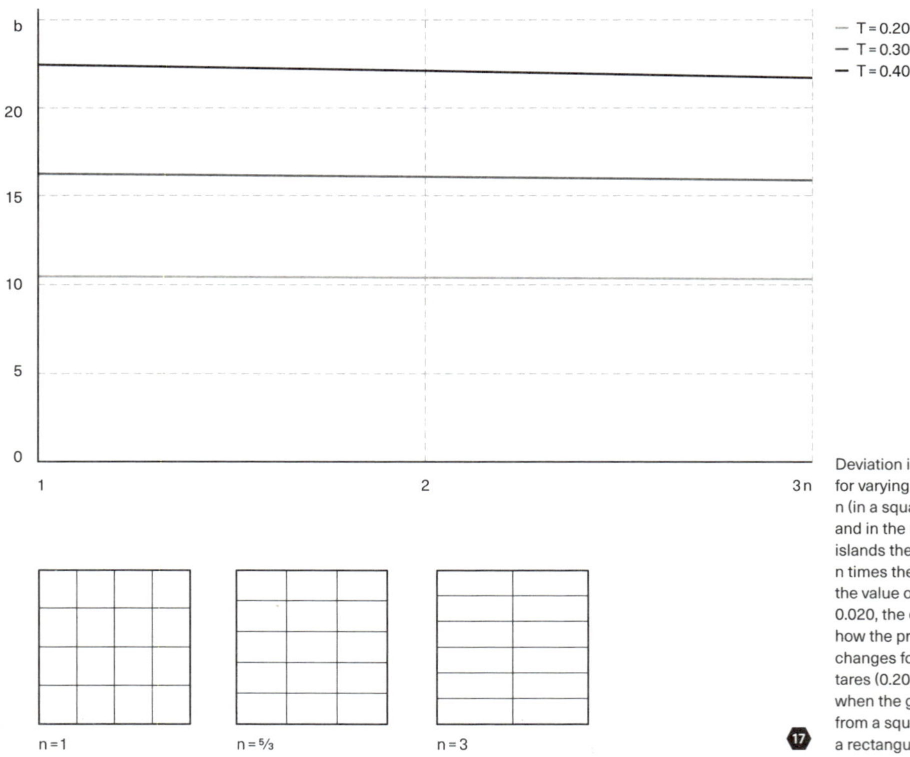

17 Deviation in profile width for varying grid proportions n (in a square mesh n = 1, and in the rectangular islands the longer side is n times the shorter side). If the value of N is set at 0.020, the diagram shows how the profile width changes for three different tares (0.20, 0.30, and 0.40) when the grid transforms from a square (n = 1) to a rectangular one (n = 3).

(large islands) is combined with narrow streets (scheme 3), and highest where a very fine mesh (small islands) and wide streets are present (scheme 4).

N_f, b and T_f are all measurable entities that could quite easily be collected from maps. This, however, demands that there is an existing fabric or a drawn design to study. The relationship between these variables expressed in the formula ⓯ in the previous chapter, and represented in the diagram in ⓰, can help monitor the trade-offs of certain combinations to define some fundamental properties of urban form. Analysing with the use of variables instead of unique examples makes it possible to understand the general trends hidden in the relation between network density, street profile and tare space.

The possible combinations of network density and profile width can be determined in the diagram based on, for instance, the assumption that a minimum of 60 per cent of privately issued land (PIL) is required and that subsequently a maximum of 40 per cent is available for network space.[19] This means that the network density may not be higher than approximately 0.015 when combined with a wide profile of 30 m. For a smaller mesh size than this, but with the same profile width (30 m), the amount of private land quickly falls below 60 per cent. On the other hand, with a narrow street profile, for instance 15 m, the critical level defined as 60 per cent private land will be reached only when the network density becomes higher than 0.030.

19
Of all the Amsterdam samples, three quarters have more than 60 per cent privately issued land, and none less than 50 per cent.

Up to now the grid has been treated as a symmetrical grid where the islands are conceptualized as squares. Although it might be assumed that this offers sufficient accuracy, considerable deviations from real values might make this analysis rather crude. A comparison between the rectangular grid patterns and the square ones used so far in this section may offer some clues about the extent of the deviation. The proportion of the two directions of a grid can be called n. In a square mesh n = 1, and in the rectangular islands the longer side is n times the shorter side. If the formula ⓯ is adapted to this variation in proportions, the deviation of street width can be monitored for different values of n.[20] If the value of N is set at 0.020, the diagram in ⓱ shows how the profile width changes for three different tares (0.20, 0.30, and 0.40) when the grid transforms from a square (n = 1) to a rectangular one (n = 3). The deviation is no more than between 1.4 per cent and 3.4 per cent for n = 3. This can be regarded as negligible for present purposes. Of course, other performances change when squared blocks are transformed into rectangular ones, but the relationship between profile width, tare space and network density remains more or less the same.

20
● $T_f = 1 - [1 - b \times N_f : (n+1)]$ $[1 - n \times b \times N_f : (n+1)]$.
For further details, see ● 19 on page 232.

Empirical Research

To investigate whether regularities can be found within certain network density conditions, the nine archetypical samples as well as all the Dutch samples have been positioned in the N_f(b)-diagram. ⓲ ⓳ The wide representation of network densities (or mesh sizes) can be seen in the spread

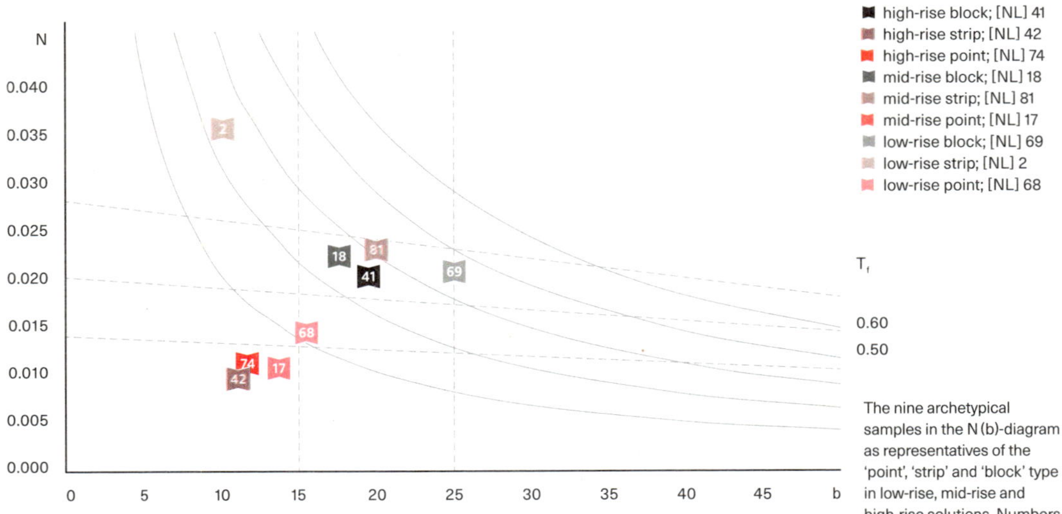

18

The nine archetypical samples in the N (b)-diagram as representatives of the 'point', 'strip' and 'block' type in low-rise, mid-rise and high-rise solutions. Numbers refer to samples in 10.

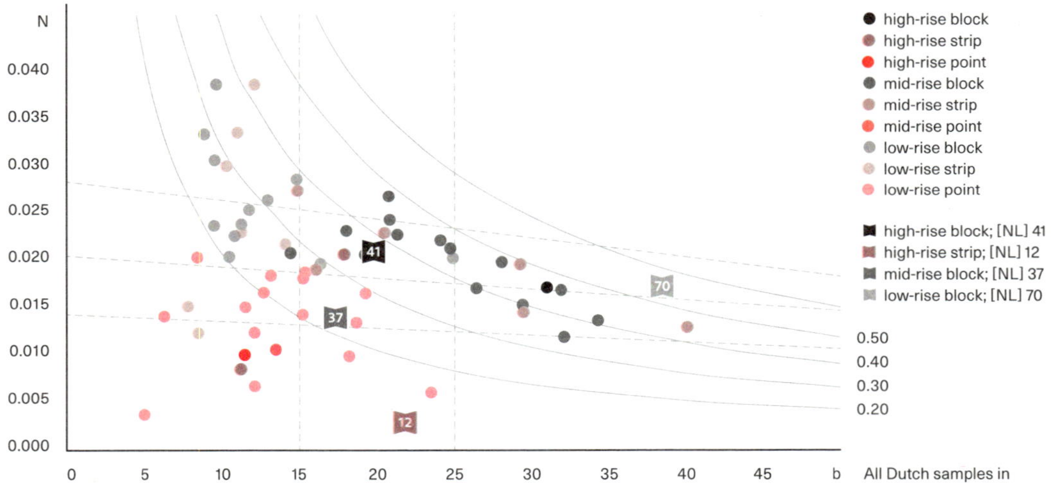

19

All Dutch samples in the N (b)-diagram. Numbers refer to samples in 20.

of the samples along the y-axis ranging between 0.004 and 0.040 or, in terms of meshes, from 50 to 500 m. The most common network densities fall between 0.01 and 0.03, which correspond to a mesh from 65 to 200 m. Based on the block size categories discussed in an earlier paragraph, four zones can be distinguished in the diagram. These can be further divided into three categories of different street widths.

What becomes clearly visible from the diagram with all of the Dutch samples is that the variety in profile widths, represented by the x-axis, is larger when the network density is lower. 19 Therefore, when a fine-meshed urban plan is drawn, narrow streets are apparently needed to ensure enough private land to make the island usable and the plan feasible. We can compare this to the building depth discussed in the previous paragraph. Buildings of

Landtong [NL]

Bijlmer [NL]

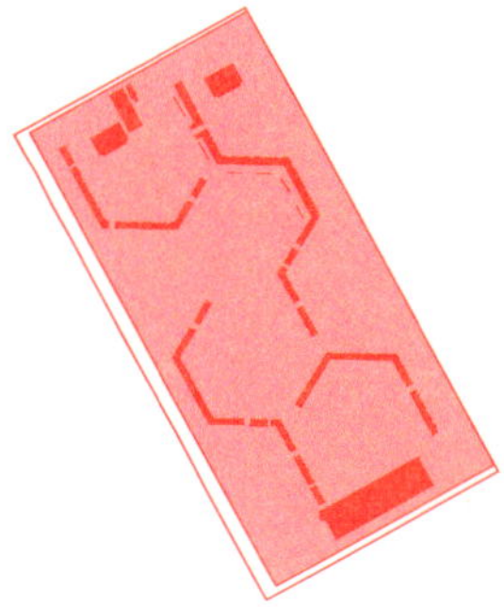

Watergraafsmeer 2 [NL]

Java island [NL]

20 Four samples with different network properties. (see 19 for positions in N(b)-diagram).

5 m deep are theoretically possible but not likely as these are less functional and more costly. Of course, solutions with wider streets are theoretically possible but they are not probable as the practical feasibility diminishes as the size of the islands shrink. With larger mesh sizes the streets can be wider and still have reasonably sized islands.

The samples with the finest grain mostly have narrow streets and the islands contain low-rise buildings. Small- and medium-size islands have larger profile widths, ranging from 5 to 40 m. It can be observed that the samples with narrow streets mostly occur in combination with low-rise building types. Wider streets are often accompanied by higher buildings, especially mid-rise strip and block types.

High-rise types seem to show the least dependency on the size of the islands and the width of the streets. However, when taking a closer look at the samples it becomes clear that some high-rise samples are similar to mid-rise samples in terms of network pattern. These samples, such as Landtong (41 in 19 20) in Rotterdam, have a network density similar to their surroundings and can, from this point of view, be regarded as well-integrated in the urban context. One difference, though, is that instead of four to five storeys, the buildings have more than seven storeys. Samples from downtown New York or Seattle can also be found in these categories. The other high-rise samples with larger-sized network patterns, mostly built in the 1960s, are different. They have their own internal logic in which streets and buildings are disintegrated, in line with ideals of the functionalist city as promoted by CIAM. The Bijlmer (12 in 19 20) in Amsterdam is a good example in the Netherlands of this kind of urban planning.

Some of the samples seem to contradict the conclusions described above. Watergraafsmeer 2 (70 in 19 20) in Amsterdam, for example, is the only low-rise block type with relatively wide streets. One reason might be that this area was realized in a period (the 1930s) when public space was regarded as extremely important. Most low-rise samples, however, do not have such a large amount of tare space, probably due to economic constraints. The amount of network tare space per square metre of gross floor space (network ratio, or ΔOSR; we will return to this indicator in the next chapter) in Watergraafsmeer is extremely high and, therefore, quite costly. Another example is Java Island (37 in 19 20), a mid-rise block type that, in comparison to the other samples within this category, has a rather low network density. Large islands in combination with relatively narrow streets are uncommon in the Netherlands, but, as we will discuss later, more common abroad. It is furthermore interesting to note that in the case of the Dutch samples, building types with higher built densities (mid-rise strip and block types) have more tare space (network) than building types with lower built densities (low-rise point, strip and block types). The higher built density is compensated for by a larger amount of public space.

Based on these findings one can conclude that by defining the density of the network (N), several different building types are still possible.

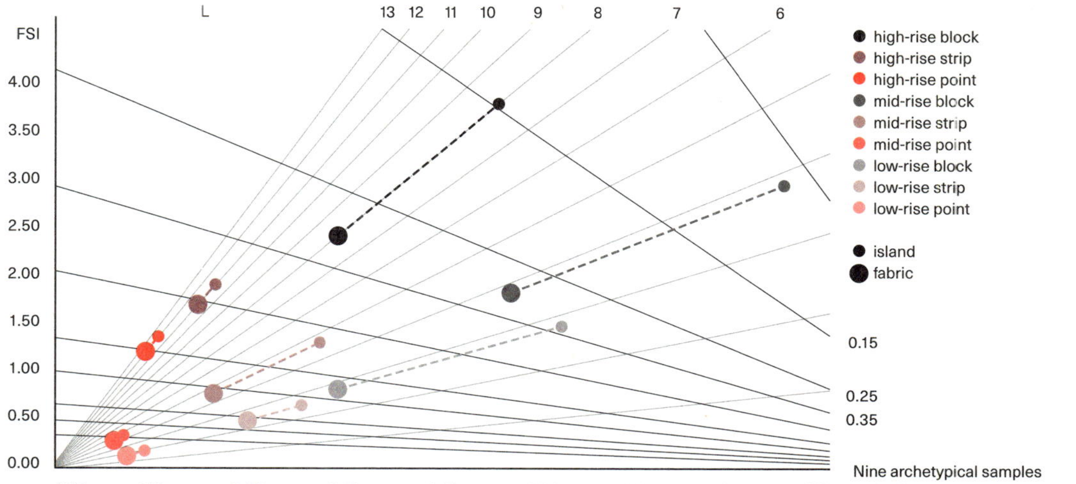

21 Nine archetypical samples in the Spacemate diagram on the scale of the island and the fabric.

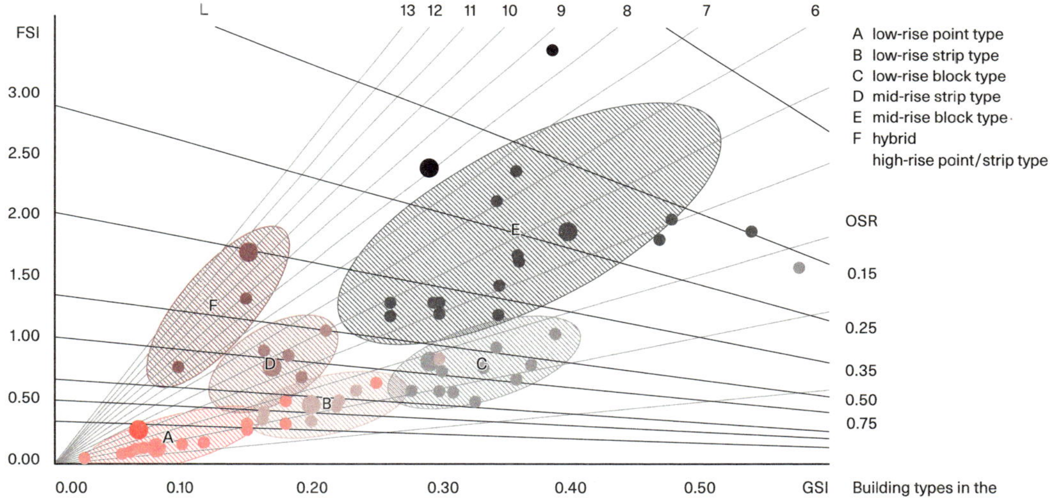

22 Building types in the Spacemate diagram on the scale of the fabric.

However, we also see thathigher N is often combined with low-rise types, but this is not always the case. Furthermore, by combining building and network densities, the performance of an area, in terms of daylight access, public parking, urbanity, privacy and crowdedness changes radically and as such the combination of the two, building and network density, convey more about the performance of an urban fabric than when they are merely treated in isolation.

Urban Fabric Types

An urban fabric type can be viewed as consisting of a specific combination of, on the one hand, a network type (defined by N, b, and T) which

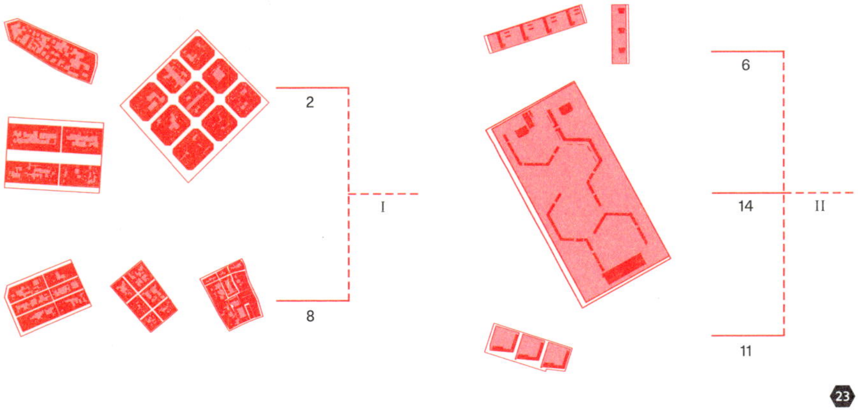

23 Result of the hierarchical clustering for two building types. Mid-rise block (I) and high-rise building types (II) are each divided in two sub-groups with relatively large block sizes (and thus low N) and small blocks (high N) respectively (Berghauser Pont and Olsson 2017).

describes the basic layout of the ground plan and the accompanying series of islands, and on the other hand the building type (defined by FSI, GSI, OSR and L), which describes the infill of the islands.

The amount of network needed to access the islands is incorporated in the density figures on the scale of the urban fabric. The difference between island and fabric density is an indicator of the amount of network space (T_f) needed to access the islands. In order to grasp the consequences of adding network to the islands, the nine archetypes that were discussed earlier are positioned again in the Spacemate, but this time adding the density calculations on the level of the fabric. 21 The GSI and FSI values on the scale of the fabric are all lower than on the scale of the island because of the added tare space. But the different building types still retain unique positions in the diagram, and, when all other Dutch samples are included, the clusters can again be discerned to represent the different building types. 22

The scale of the network, however, is not represented through the amount of network tare space. This can only be grasped using N. Two Amsterdam examples with identical built densities and the same network tare space illustrate this. The Grachtengordel is composed of large islands (N = 0.012) and wide street profiles, while De Pijp, which has the same built density, has small islands (N = 0.023) and narrow streets. Based on one building type, in this case the block type, we can thus arrive at different urban fabric types, because of the variations in network density. The position in the three-dimensional Spacematrix model is therefore different. In a paper presented at the International Seminar on Urban Form (ISUF) in 2017,[21] clustering analysis was used to develop urban fabric types that are hard to recognize without such advanced statistical methods. We used hierarchical clustering where clusters are defined based on the distance between the data points. The core idea is to cluster objects, in this case urban fabrics, that are more related to nearby objects, in terms of data, than to objects farther away.[22]

The result of the hierarchical clustering is presented in 23, showing the grouping of the samples in clusters that show variety in both building type and block size (or network density, N).

21
Berghauser Pont, M. and J. Olsson, 'Typology based on three variables central to Spacematrix using cluster analysis', *ISUF 2017 XXIV international conference: City and territory in the globalization age*, Seville (2017).

22
Wilmink, F.W. and H.T. Uytterschaut, 'Cluster analysis, history, theory and applications', in G. N. van Vark and W. W. Howells (eds.), *Multivariate Statistical Methods in Physical Anthropology* (D. Reidel Publishing Company, 1984), 135–175.

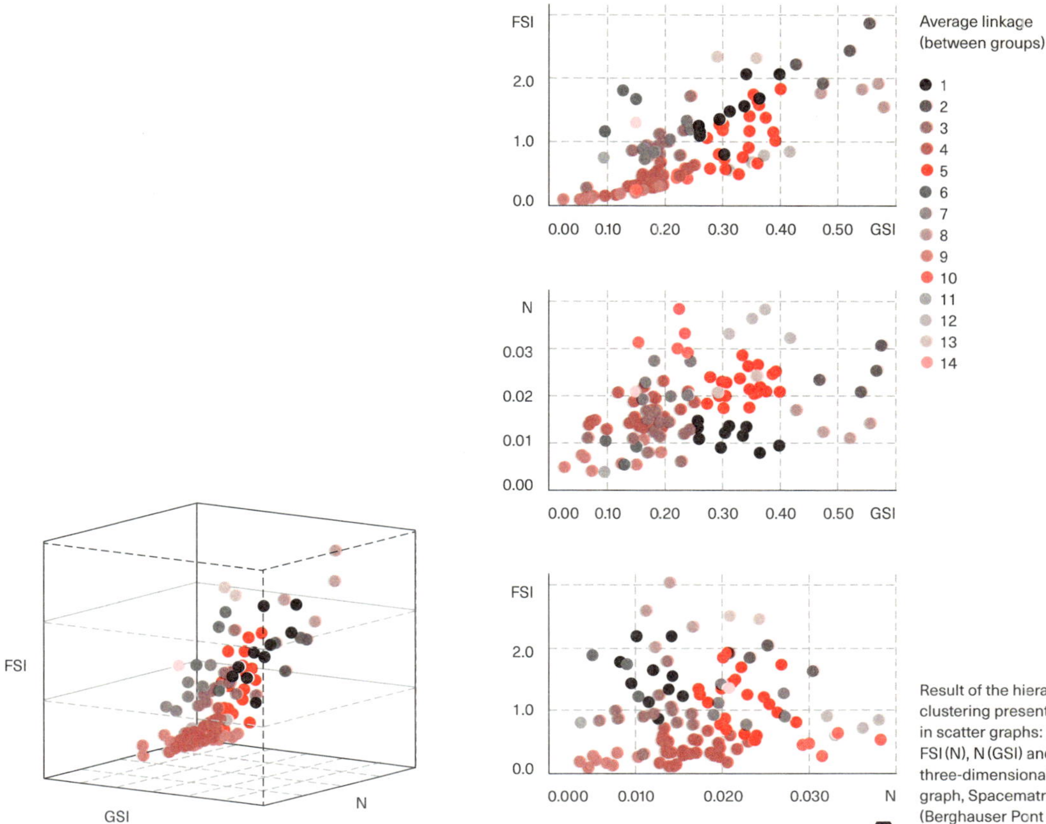

24 Result of the hierarchical clustering presented in scatter graphs: FSI (GSI), FSI (N), N (GSI) and the three-dimensional scatter graph, Spacematrix (Berghauser Pont and Olsson 2017).

The scatter graphs in 24 show the clustering results in the three-dimensional Spacematrix and the three planes of this graph: FSI (GSI), N (GSI) and FSI (N) respectively. In the FSI (GSI) scatter graph the method successfully distinguishes the mid-rise block types (cluster 2 and 8, depicted in orange and red) and high-rise types (cluster 6, 11 and 14, depicted in green). In the N (GSI) scatter graph, we can see that they end up in different clusters because of the differentiation in network density. The two types do not differ when it comes to their GSI values, but differ greatly when it comes to N. Three other clusters (9, 10 and 12, depicted in blue) are worth mentioning. These all belong to the low-rise cluster but differ greatly when it comes to their network density (N) or, in other words, the grain of the urban fabric. Cluster 9 has very large islands of 240 m^2 while cluster 10 and 12 have islands of only 60 m^2. Despite the similarities in L, GSI and FSI, they differ in N and therefore form a separate cluster.

Comparative Research

In order to investigate how generic the findings are that we have presented so far, we compare the results for Amsterdam in the Netherlands with Berlin in Germany, Barcelona in Spain, London in the UK and Stockholm in

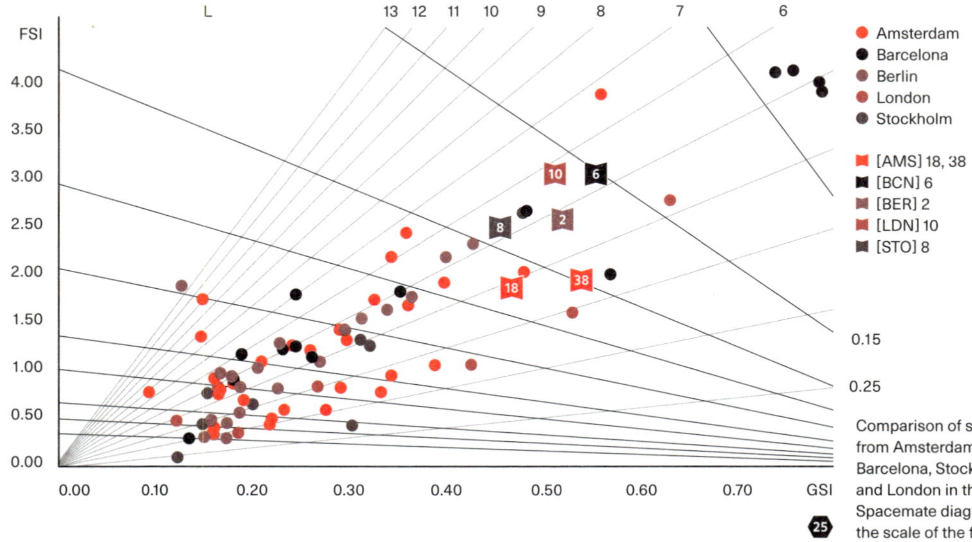

Comparison of samples from Amsterdam, Berlin, Barcelona, Stockholm and London in the Spacemate diagram on the scale of the fabric.

Sweden. Furthermore, changes in density through history have been investigated to sketch the influence of state interventions (building ordinances, standards, etcetera) and changing ideologies (Garden City Movement, CIAM, etcetera). In addition, a comparison with Asian samples allows us to investigate whether the Spacematrix is also valid for situations with much higher densities, such as the samples from four Asian cities – Kuwait, Abu Dhabi, Singapore and Hong Kong – studied by the London School of Economics and Political Science (LSE).[23]

23
LSE Cities, *Resource Urbanisms. Asia's divergent city models of Kuwait, Abu Dhabi, Singapore and Hong Kong* (London School of Economics and Political Science, 2017).

Amsterdam, Berlin, Barcelona, Stockholm and London

When comparing the samples from Berlin and Barcelona with those from Amsterdam, one can initially conclude that the clustering of building types remains valid. A closer look at the areas developed between the seventeenth and the beginning of the twentieth century – a period in which the midrise block type was predominant – shows that the Cerdà grid in Barcelona, Eixample, (6 in 25 26) has the highest intensity ($FSI_f = 2.89$), followed by Soho 10 in London ($FSI_f = 2.67$), Södermalm 8 in Stockholm ($FSI_f = 2.57$) and Chamissoplatz 2 in Berlin ($FSI_f = 2.24$). Samples from Amsterdam have lower building intensities in general, such as the Jordaan 38 ($FSI_f = 1.84$). An exception is the recently developed area Westerdok 72, with a much higher FSI than anything developed earlier ($FSI_f = 3.76$). In the five cities the coverage of the block type is similar, between 0.4 and 0.6. The reason for the difference in built density can thus be found in the height of the buildings and the amount of street network needed to access the buildings. Berlin's Mietkasernenstadt is often described as representing some of the worst housing conditions in Europe. Based on the density figures we can conclude that the reasons for this cannot be found in the physical structure of the Mietkasernen. More probably, as was the case in the Jordaan in Amsterdam, simply too many people lived in too little space.

Furthermore, the urban layout of Berlin, compared to that of Amsterdam, in general shows larger islands. ㉗ All samples from Berlin have network densities of less than 0.020 with a mesh size larger than 100 m. The majority of these samples have a street profile width of 15 to 25 m. The samples are, therefore, all concentrated in two clusters in the N (b) diagram. As a result, all samples have less tare space than the Dutch samples. Although it might seem difficult to intensify such large islands as the access to the buildings becomes problematic (large depth of islands), some of the Berlin samples have different kinds of alleys that enable access to the interior of the islands. The islands are in other words subdivided into smaller sub-islands. This is especially the case in the areas with the highest built intensities. Hackesche Höfe (4 in ㉗ ㉘), for example, has a network density of 0.011 (which is comparable to the Grachtengordel 28) and a street width of 13 m (comparable to that of the Jordaan 38). A closer examination of the island shows that it has numerous entrances to the buildings in the interior of the island, and four

㉖ Street view of six mid-rise block type samples from Amsterdam [AMS], Berlin [BER], Barcelona [BCN], Stockholm [STO] and London [LDN] (see ■ 25 for positions in Spacemate).

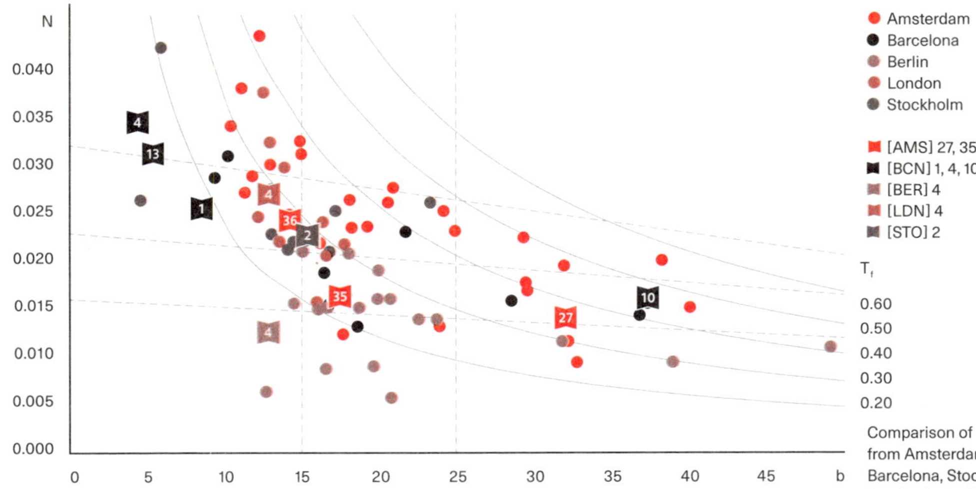

27 Comparison of samples from Amsterdam, Berlin, Barcelona, Stockholm and London in the N(b) diagram on the scale of the fabric.

pedestrian routes crossing it. This kind of subdivision is described by Siksna in his comparison between American and Australian city centres.[24] He concludes that the larger blocks (islands) have in the course of history been eroded and split up into smaller units, while the smaller blocks remained intact. The same conclusion can be reached about Berlin, although in this case many blocks of this kind were originally designed with passages.

24 Siksna, 'The Effects', op. cit. (note 4).

In 'economic' terms the Berlin samples with less street and more floor space can be described as being more optimized than the Dutch samples. But there are other factors that have contributed to the differences found. The existing pattern of canals and ditches in the Netherlands needed to manage water was often used as a basis for urban development. This water system often had a rather fine mesh size from the outset.

Java island (35 in 27 28) represents one of the recent examples from Amsterdam that has similar large measures (N and b) to those frequently found in Berlin. The conditions of the site, being an island with a depth of 130 m, also affected this development. It was difficult to project two blocks within the depth of 130 m. Therefore, larger blocks were designed with extra buildings in the interior to arrive at a higher density. Other recent examples with large blocks are Funen and GWL where, as in Berlin, the buildings are accessed from within these larger blocks.

Most of the samples from Barcelona and Stockholm, except for the medieval ones, also show lower network densities than the older Dutch samples. As a consequence, the mesh size in general is larger. However, the spread in street profiles is much larger in Barcelona, ranging from Barceloneta (1 in 27 28) with less than 9 m to Mar Bella 10 with 40-m-wide streets. The fine-grained samples in Barcelona, all with narrow streets, are found in the oldest parts of the city such as Raval 13. Such fine-grained urban layouts are present in London too, such as in Soho 4, whose history also goes back to the Middle Ages, but is now a major entertainment district.

28 Street view of ten mid-rise block type samples from Amsterdam [AMS], Berlin [BER], Barcelona [BCN], Stockholm [STO] and London [LDN] (see 27 for positions in the N(b) diagram).

Hackesche Höfe [BER] N_f 0.011 and b 12 m

Grachtengordel [AMS] N_f 0.012 and b 32 m

Jordaan [AMS] N_f 0.021 and b 14 m

Java island [AMS] N_f 0.014 and b 17 m

Barceloneta [BCN] N_f 0.070 and b 8 m

Mar Bella [BCN] N_f 0.014 and b 37 m

Raval [BCN] N_f 0.027 and b 6 m

Ciutat Vella [BCN] N_f 0.030 and b 5 m

Södermalm [STO] N_f 0.018 and b 17 m

Soho [LDN] N_f 0.033 and b 13 m

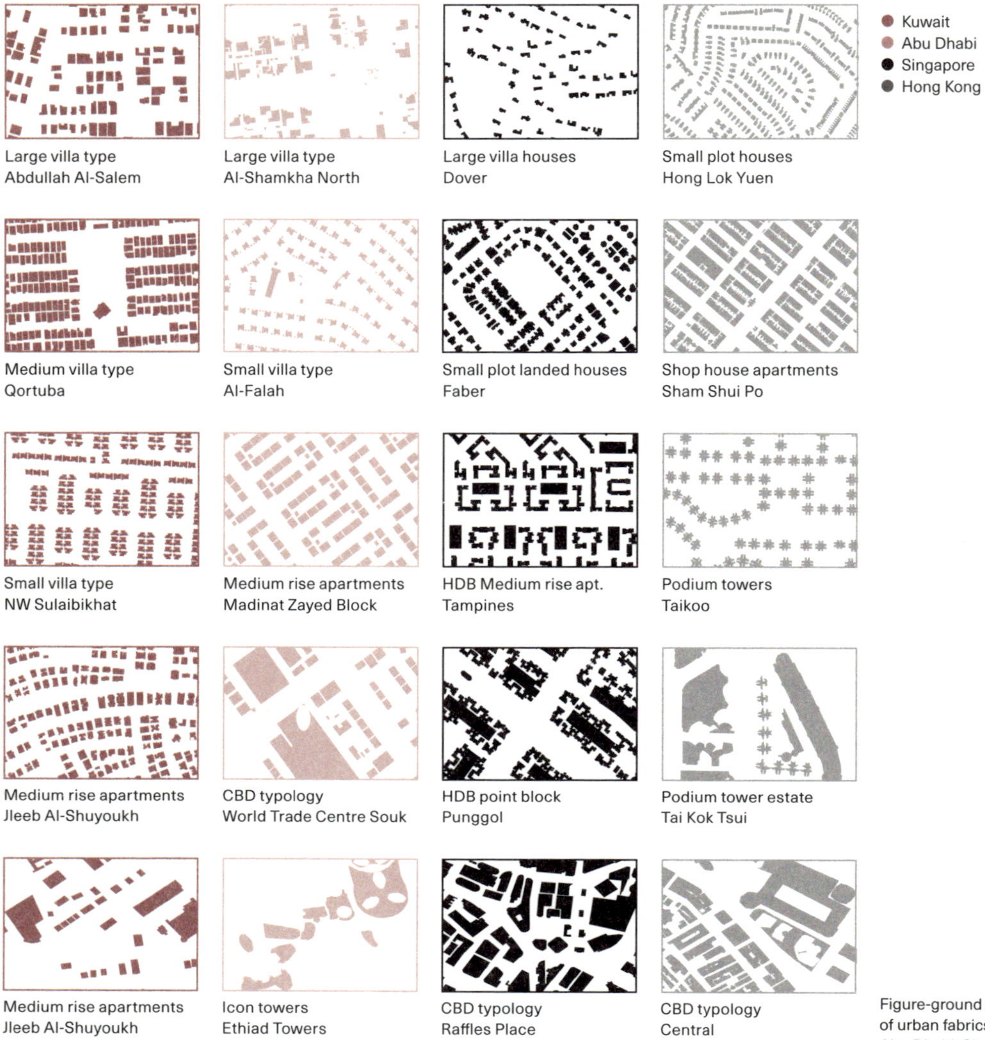

29 Figure-ground maps of urban fabrics in Kuwait, Abu Dhabi, Singapore and Hong Kong (LSE Cities 2017: 54).

Kuwait, Abu Dhabi, Singapore and Hong Kong[25]

A comparison of the European samples with neighbourhoods in the Gulf (Kuwait and Abu Dhabi) and East Asia (Hong Kong and Singapore), is of interest to test the hypothesis that cities from Asia that are assumed to be much denser than their European counterparts also fit into the Spacematrix. Most of the samples fit the clusters defined earlier and prove that types found in Europe can also be found in the Far East. 29 30 It is interesting that a sample from London (Canary Wharf 3 4) with the highest FSI and GSI values in our database, is found more often in Asia. We found yet another cluster with less extreme FSI and GSI values, but still much higher than what is common in Europe, except for one example in Amsterdam, Westerdok 72. These two new clusters could be called 'high rise spacious block' and 'high rise compact block', respectively. These findings can only

25 LSE Cities, 'Resource Urbanisms', op. cit. (note 24), page 53–54. It should be notes that we recalculated the FSI and GSI values based on the demarcation of the area following the rules as defined in Chapter 3.

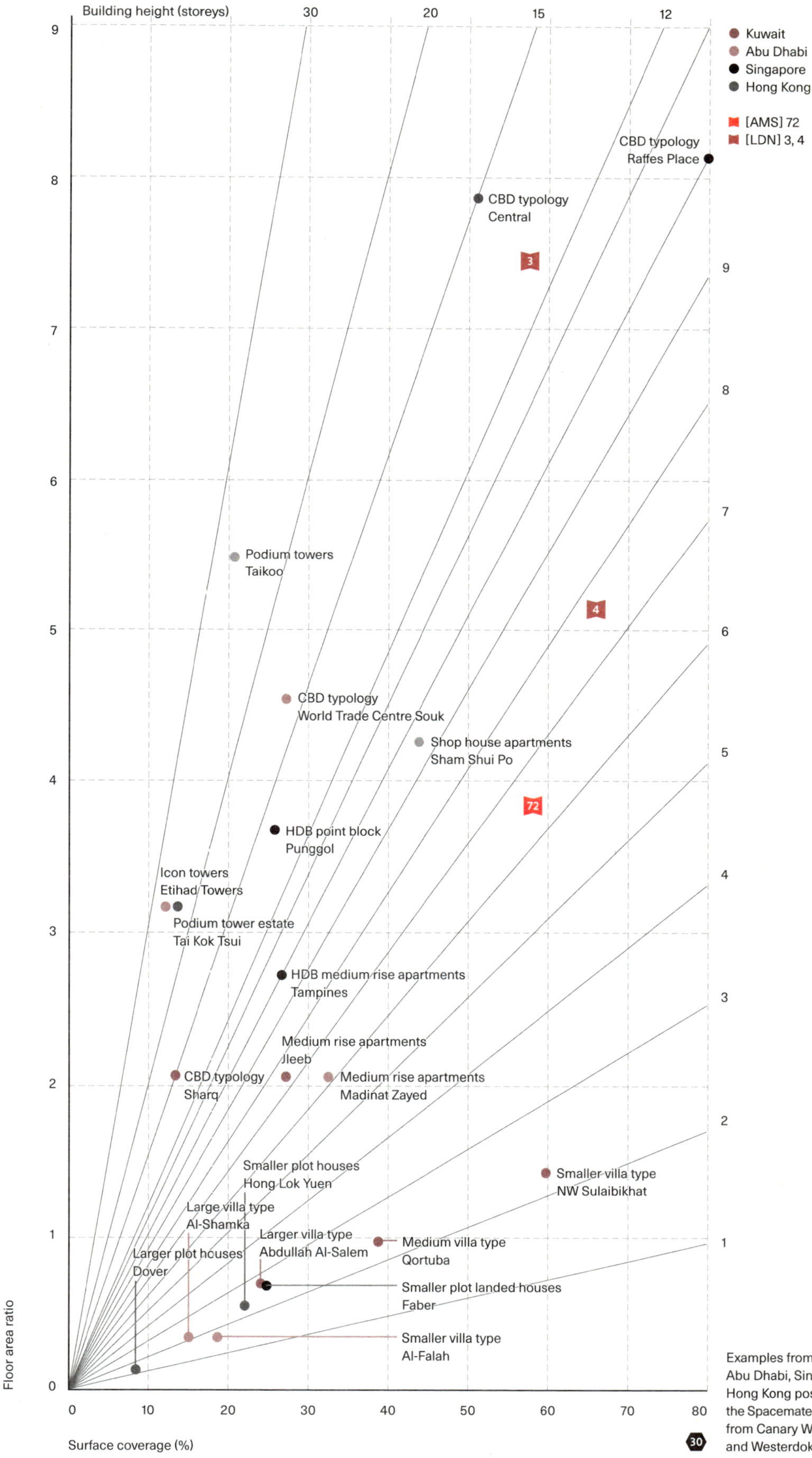

Examples from Kuwait, Abu Dhabi, Singapore and Hong Kong positioned in the Spacemate and samples from Canary Wharf [LDN] and Westerdok [AMS].

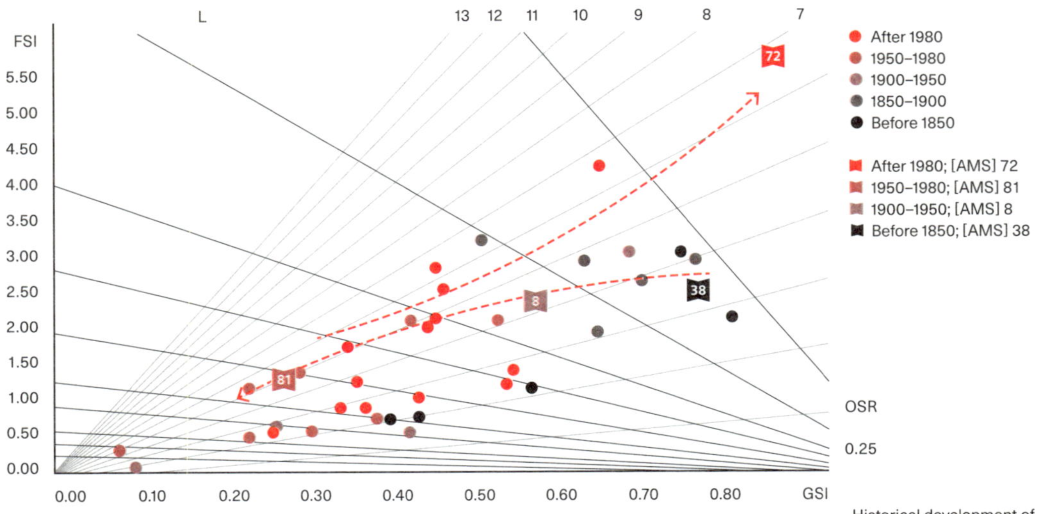

31 Historical development of Amsterdam (scale island).

partly confirm the hypothesis that higher densities are found in Asia; a more correct formulation would be that these higher densities are found more often in Asia.

The Historical Development of Amsterdam

The initial transition from liberal-competitive capitalism to state-managed capitalism at the turn of the twentieth century brought with it a greater emphasis on public space. This may be one of the reasons that during the latter period the amount of tare space shows a relative increase, mainly caused by wider streets. Although it is often presumed that the modernist plans of the 1950s and 1960s contain large amounts of green space, this is not to be found in the amount of network space on the scale of the urban fabric. However, on the lower scale of the island and the higher scale of the district, the amount of tare space is significantly higher during this period. This is found both in terms of green semi-public space within the islands and large parks in and between fabrics. The period from 1950 to 1970 shows a larger spread, with more extremes in network (tare) space. This might be a result of a greater variation in building types in the developments taking place in this period, ranging from fabrics with high-rise apartments to low-rise row housing developments.

One can conclude that despite the different circumstances under which urban plans were designed and realized, the three main characteristics of the urban ground plan, network density, street profile and network (tare) space, do not show a significant change of trend.

Coverage on the scale of the islands, however, shows an immense variation throughout history. Until recently, GSI decreased at a somewhat constant pace from a coverage of more than 75 per cent in the seventeenth century to 60 per cent around 1900 and to less than 30 per cent during

Berlage Plan Zuid 1 [AMS] $FSI_i = 2.41$

Jordaan [AMS] $FSI_i = 2.54$

Westerdok [AMS] $FSI_i = 5.63$

Zuidwest Kwadrant 1 [AMS] $FSI_i = 1.28$

the modern extensions of the 1960s. 31 Put another way, in this historical sequence we can identify a slow transition from compact to more spacious building layouts.

The reasons for this development are numerous and complex and have partly been discussed in Chapter 2. Until 1900 urban developments were driven mostly by pragmatic technical and economic forces, resulting in maximized floor space on the one hand, and, on the other, no more open space than absolutely necessary, mostly in the form of infrastructure. The growth of the population, combined with the absence of building regulations and the difficulties in controlling (illegal) constructions, made expansions of houses, small industries and other buildings in the courtyards a fact. This can be seen very clearly in the Jordaan. (38 in 31 32) Towards the end of the nineteenth century, the practice of city development was reformed. Public space became more important and through the Housing Act (1901) higher standards in terms of daylight access, fresh air and open space were (theoretically) assured. The results only gradually showed up in practice. Berlage Plan Zuid 1 8, designed by Berlage and seen as one of the first examples of large-scale publicly generated housing in the Netherlands, shows a decrease in coverage, both at the level of the island and of the fabric.

The increase in public space (wider streets), larger green inner courts and stricter regulations for buildings resulted in a decrease in GSI. The developments after the Second World War, designed and built based on the CIAM doctrines of living and working in green and spacious environments, resulted in a further decline of the GSI. Compared to the Jordaan, the coverage in Zuidwest Kwadrant 1 81 (constructed in the 1960s) was less than a

32 Street view of four mid-rise block type samples from Amsterdam [AMS] (see 31 for positions in Spacemate).

third (0.29 compared to 0.75 on the scale of the island). Since the 1970s, however, this trend has turned. Economic pressure and a preference for more 'lively' urban environments have led to a decrease in the amount of green open space and a rise in building coverage. Still, due to other constraints, such as the demands of modern traffic (influencing street widths and necessary parking space), and acceptable standards for privacy and light access, coverage does not achieve the levels of the nineteenth century and earlier periods.

The development of the building intensity (FSI) through history shows roughly the same trend as the coverage (GSI). However, due to the differences in building height, there is a wider spread of building intensity within each historical period. Any clear trend for decreasing intensities, such as can be found for coverage, is therefore not evident when intensity is examined in isolation. When looking at the position of each sample in the Spacemate, however, a decrease of built intensity before the 1970s can be spotted for both the low-rise and the mid-rise types. Based on these findings one can conclude that the densities of low-rise and mid-rise types, in the Netherlands at least, have decreased both in terms of intensity as well as in terms of coverage. Only the recent examples have higher values, perhaps in response to functionalist doctrines being put aside for ideas on urbanity, and necessitated by a larger demand for economic efficiency and believe that higher densities contribute to sustainable urban development. The most extreme example is Westerdok 72, an area located near Amsterdam Central Station that can be described as a combination of the mid-rise block typology and the high-rise point typology. The density is the highest in Amsterdam ($FSI_f = 3.76$ and $FSI_i = 5.63$) and surpasses the medieval samples from Barcelona and also most of the samples from the Asian cities discussed earlier.

Scale and Abstraction

So far, the scale levels of the island and fabric have been studied and the correlation between density and urban form investigated. This has led to clusterings of building and urban fabric types. The higher aggregations (district, city and region) and the lower components (lot, building and cell) are outside the scope of this research. We can, however, speculate as to which approaches could be used to expand the current research strategy into other levels of scale. On the scales of district, city and region other types could be researched and defined. For these levels of scale, the notions of built form and urban form lose some of their relevance. Density variables become very statistical as much diversity is shred in the averages at those scales. This, however, means little since the properties on those scales that are relevant to study have more to do with general intensities (built and network) and the distribution of tare (parks, agrarian land, nature, water, etcetera). Thus, the nature of tare, and the spread (variation) and properties of the components

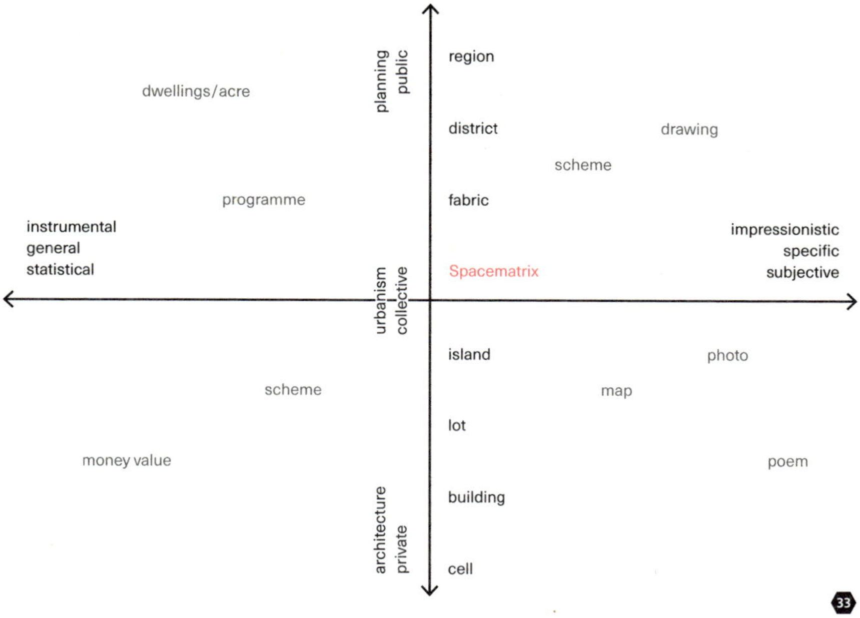

33 Resolution of Spacematrix.

(for example fabrics, network) are probably the most important aspects that should be researched.

The 'spatial DNA', represented through the Spacematrix, connects all the levels of scale and conveys different information: absolute (the position of an island), relative (comparison to other islands constituting a fabric, district, etcetera), contextual (the fabric of which the island is a component) and composite (the components – lots and buildings – that make up the island). This 'Great Chain of Building' of the urban landscape through the scales can be reconnected to the earlier discussion on *resolution*. The horizontal axis in the diagram on page 114 4 can be combined with a vertical scale axis. The result can be viewed in 33. Along the horizontal axis, different representations (or descriptions) of the urban landscape can be arranged. The extremes of specific and general can then be substituted for by a series running from the subjective, for instance artistic expression, via a photo, through detailed and then more reduced maps, passing the Spacematrix representation, then through abstract schemes, and finally ending in statistics and pure numbers. The other axis moves from the smallest component to the larger aggregations. Earlier we maintained that the multivariable density method that has been constructed in this research has the proper resolution to differentiate between building and urban fabric types. The scale levels that have been investigated and show a significant correlation are island and fabric. The higher and lower levels of scale can be assumed to become either too blurred by statistical averages (district, city, region) or to be too specific to be relevant to an understanding of urban structural properties. Thus, the fit between resolution and scale can then be said to be at its greatest in the intersection where multivariable density and the scales of island and fabric intersect.

The matrix in ❸❸ can be further interpreted by assigning different attributes to the axes. The horizontal axis can be said to span the *statistical* and the *subjective*. The abstract left pole has an instrumental character, while the opposite pole leans towards impressionism and solipsism. The position of the Spacematrix representation somewhere in between has a *dialectic* quality; abstract and instrumental, but still deciphering specific spatial properties. Many morphologic analyses can be said to take place somewhere between this middle position and the right end of the horizontal axis, with the position varying depending on whether detailed or more abstract cartographic representations are used. The other axis, the scale hierarchy, coincides well with existing discipline demarcations: the lowest ones being the terrain of architecture; the middle level urbanism, constituting the framework for the first; and the higher scales constituting the field of planning. These levels combine well with the adjectives private (architecture), civic (urbanism) and collective (planning). Summarizing, one could propose that the multivariable density method that has been constructed here combines different dialectic positions; between too big and too small; between collective and private; between too general and too specific; and between planning and architecture. In other words, succinctly describing the dialectic character of urbanism.

Nevertheless, even if the above points to a central role of urbanism, the ideal approach includes, one would assume, an awareness of the totality along both axes, and requires a jumping, iterative way of working with different scales, resolutions and representations. To travel all these positions, one does need to be familiar with the many specific components, methods and techniques needed to assemble an integrated whole. Spacematrix should be one solid piece of ground in this complex matter.

THE PERFORMANCE OF DENSITY

Every density, high or low, has its advantages and disadvantages, depending on the context (place and time) in which it is assessed. Attempts to describe the 'best densities' or the 'good city' have a long history, but all tend towards highly prescriptive recommendations based on the subjective leanings of individual authors in specific contexts.[1] To be able to link negative or positive consequences to urban density we use the arguments of Kevin Lynch in his book *Good City Form*.[2] His arguments rely on the identification of measurable performance dimensions upon which a normative theory of appropriate densities can be built.

These performances are in most cases closely linked to constraints and requirements applied in the real world to secure certain qualities in our cities. At a meeting in Paris in 1905, the causes of health problems, such as cholera outbursts in the city, were discussed. Overcrowding and insufficient daylight in the bedrooms were identified as contributing factors.[3] As a result of these discussions, rules were defined throughout Europe that made street width and building height interdependent. They came to have a great impact on the resulting urban densities and the city development in general as these rules were enshrined by laws. Jonathan Barnett explains how in New York zoning laws, mainly aimed at controlling more abstract considerations of public health and awelfare, unintentionally came to determine the basic design framework of the American city.[4] Rules stipulated the distance that high-rise building had to be set back to permit sunlight to fall on the streets and sidewalks and allow light and air into the interiors of the buildings. These rules were implemented, however, with little attention being paid to their design implications, although the impact on built form and densities was great. These are examples of how constraints imposed in a wider context came to affect the built environment. Later, regulations implemented to influence the development of cities also prescribed densities more directly such as Raymond Unwin's call for maximum density of 12 dwellings to the acre (as part of the Garden City Movement), and the minimal requirement for spaciousness as proposed by Anton Hoenig.

The shifting attitudes towards urban density and its associated qualities not only show ideological changes, but are also very much related to the whole development of the city and the material wealth of its inhabitants.

1
Larice, M. and E. Macdonald (eds.), *The Urban Design Reader* (Oxon: Routledge, 2007), 109.

2
Lynch, K., A Theory of Good City Form (Cambridge, MA: MIT Press, 1981).

3
Rådberg, J., Doktrin och täthet i svenskt stadsbyggande 1875–1975 (Stockholm: Statens råd för byggnadsforskning, 1988).

4
Barnett, J., An Introduction to Urban Design (New York: Harper and Row, 1982).

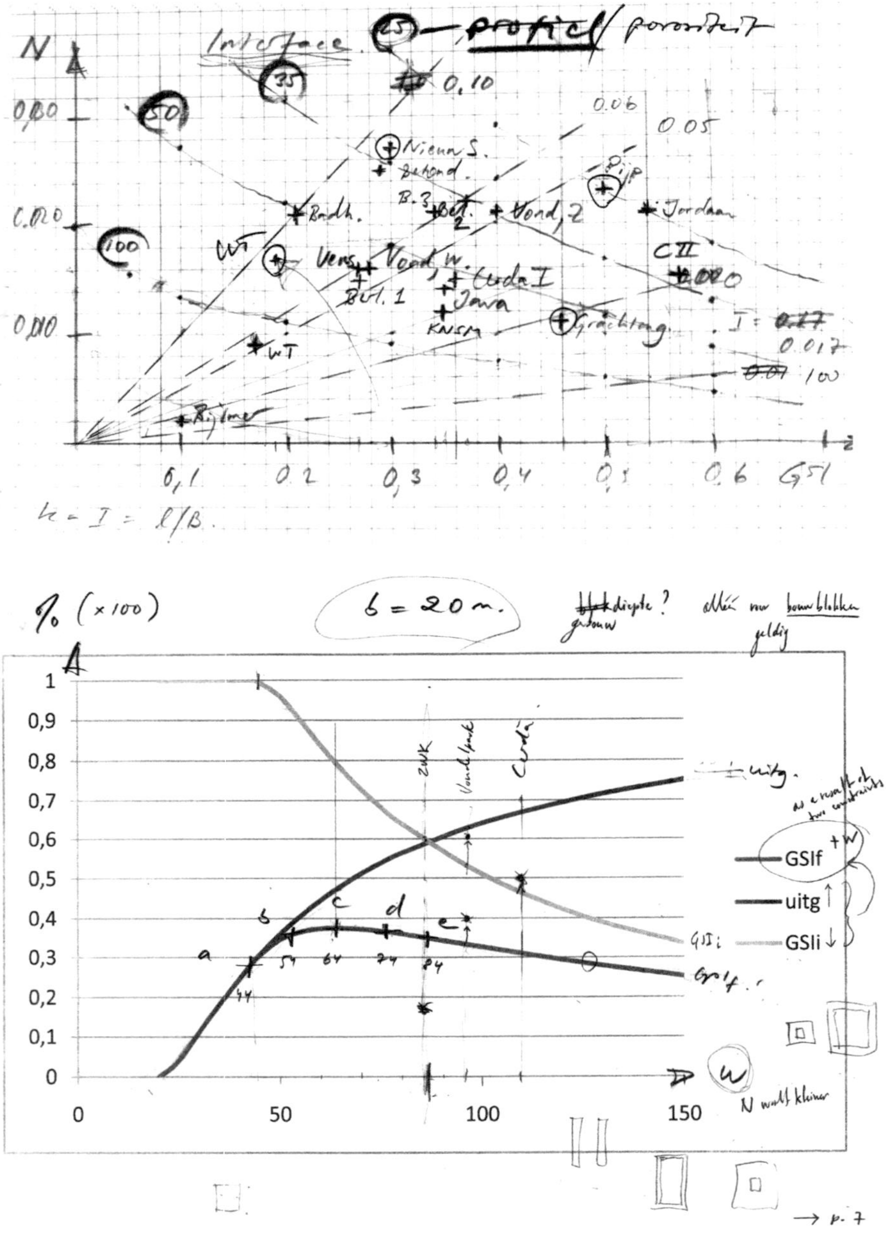

1 Pursuing performances.

Poor people concentrated in inadequate houses that offer poor shelter and damp interiors, situated in narrow alleys with hardly any sanitation whatsoever in congested conditions, with rudimentary or no public services, whether it be in Amsterdam a century ago, or in Bangalore today, can hardly be described other than as inhumane. In contrast, well-educated twenty-first-century knowledge workers shopping and wining and dining next to well-designed public spaces, between high-standard offices and apartment buildings, occupying a similar density, is seen as constituting a 'vibrant urbanity'.

Clearly, the level of material wealth and the availability of technical facilities that can take the edge off of physical inconveniences (electricity, water, sewer, air conditioning, insulation, etcetera) influence the ability to cope with high densities, both historically and at present.

It is therefore necessary to define the relationship between density and performance, and the evaluation of these performances, in any discussion of 'appropriate' densities. This will enable us to understand how constraints influence city development. Performances can further produce important information about problems and possibilities to be expected under different density conditions. 'Problems' and 'possibilities' are of course formulated at a specific moment in time and space and the same performance (daylight access, for example) can be judged as inadequate (too hot) or more than adequate (plenty of daylight), depending on historical and geographical context. What we want to emphasize in what follows is the relative objectivity of performances and the contextuality of the judgement hereof. This is in line with the earlier discussion on the Spacematrix method as a universal interpretative and representative structure, filled with contingent content that is being contextually interpreted and acted on. Performances can be viewed as serving as extensions of the objective character of density into the physical realm of the urban landscape, to suspend the rhetoric, interests and preferences of accompanying judgements.

Let us return for a moment to the terms used by Ernest Alexander, mentioned at the beginning of Chapter 3.[5] Alexander distinguishes between physical density and perceived density. The same physical density can be perceived and evaluated in very different ways, by different people, in different cultures and locations, under different circumstances. We believe a flaw in this approach is that it moves too quickly from the physical to the subjective. Although Alexander makes clear that the perceived reaction is influenced not only by 'individual cognitive factors' but also by external 'sociocultural factors', a focus on the individual experience of density is at the centre of his analysis. We would prefer to linger a little longer on the physical by further investigating separate properties – which we also could refer to as performances – of the built environment in relation to density. The most fundamental sub-properties that have been discussed so far include the amount of built programme (intensity, or FSI), the primary distribution of this programme (coverage, height and spaciousness; or GSI, L and OSR) and the composition and measures of the urban ground plan (N_f, b, and T_f).

5 Alexander, E.R., 'Density Measures: A Review and Analysis', Journal of Architectural and Planning Research 10 (3) 1993, 181–202.

Using performances in this way we can engage with aspects of density without having to use qualifications such as 'too high' or 'too low'. This would enable professionals to better ground their decisions and the trade-offs made between performances. It is important to notice, however, that even if we might aim for neutral performance outcomes, the trade-offs taking place between them are, of course, highly value based. For instance, a choice for more programme at the cost of daylight comes after weighing the pros and cons, perhaps through valuing daylight access higher than built intensity.

We can now compare the series defined by Alexander (A) with the one suggested by us (B):

A. Physical Density – Perceived Density

B. Physical Density – Performances – Standards – Evaluation (Perceived Density)

In B, standards and evaluation represent the two moments when contextual values enter the equation. The standards are of a more collective character (regulations, the urban practice, group of professionals, etcetera), the evaluation is the judgement based on both performance and standards. If A is a good characterization of the personal reaction to built density (good, bad, fear, pleasure, indifference), then B could be viewed as a scheme for the professional engagement with density during analysis and design. It is important to bear in mind that the properties of density have an objective character (for example, one metre of street to every metre of floor space), performances register variable trends, standards (contextually grounded in collective values) supply those variables with a temporarily fixed value (for example the amount of daylight prescribed by a norm), and, finally, the judgement of those performances and the trade-offs between them is made by a professional with knowledge of standards, practical experience and personal preferences.

An interesting question concerning performances is how they were judged and evaluated in the past in comparison to present judgements. In terms of evaluation many would agree to describe the transformation of De Pijp in Amsterdam that took place during the last century as one going from negative overcrowding in 1899 to a situation today of urbanity, with its positive connotations. At the same time, the once much appreciated peace and quiet in the Western Garden Cities of Amsterdam is today viewed as boring 'undercrowding',[6] not in tune with a consumer society where intensity (turnover), commercial interface and thresholds for services are considered to be of the utmost importance.

6 Lozano, E., 'Density in Communities, or the Most Important Factor in Building Urbanity', in: Larice and Macdonald, The Urban, op. cit. (note 1), 312–327, 320–321.

When designing cities we often use existing built environments as a reference. Some qualities appeal to commissioners, consumers and designers while others do not. To also work with and think about the urban landscape in terms of performance can help to avoid inappropriate use of these references. When striving for a vibrant urbanity, the values might to some be obvious (high densities, good accessibility, a mix of functions), but one must also remember that the original physical makeup of an area might not be acceptable today. For example, narrow streets might be incompatible with present norms of accessibility. Such conflicting aspirations might become more explicit through critically working with density and performances.

A quick analysis of constraints and bottlenecks in contemporary practice – which is by no means exhaustive – can provide an overview of relevant performances. Many constraints come from the field of urban physics, some of which have been imposed through building legislation. Examples of such issues are daylight access, sunlight, air pollution and wind. Energy consumption is another performance in this series that is – due to peak oil, climate change and CO_2 reduction targets – increasingly urgent. Performances that are relevant to the urban practice as they determine the feasibility of projects to a large extent are parking, the ratio between public and private land, and commercial exposure. Performances that deal more with the perception of an area include urbanity, privacy and walkability.

In the following, we will explore the relation between density and performance in two ways. First, by means of a systematic review including more than 300 scientific papers on density and its performance.[7] Because few studies use the multivariable approach to density as proposed in Spacematrix, we will highlight the specific density variable used to arrive at the conclusion on performance. In many cases, this is the population density, with a distinction sometimes made between residential and working population. The second approach to exploring the relation between density and performance is deductive and explorative, we will investigate five performances in relation to density as defined by Spacematrix: parking, daylight access, exposure to noise pollution, air quality and urbanity. It should be noted that in both cases, the focus is on the *conditional* character of density for the performance of the urban landscape. In some cases this conditionality is rather direct and obvious (for example user intensity), in other cases more concealed (daylight access), sometimes controversial and tainted by vested interests (happiness), and in some others probably not even worth the effort to pursue (infertility). The amount of daylight, for instance, is straightforward. Even if weather, pollution and interior decoration affect the final daylight penetration in a dwelling, the urban layout plays an important role in conditioning the access of daylight. In many other cases, density might participate as a minor condition in a complex set of physical, social and psychological factors, which can only be investigated through empirical studies that then highlight correlations between density and outcomes such as crime rates or urban stress. Such empirical studies should ideally be replicated by various researches in more than one geographical context to arrive at robust conclusions that do not highlight the specificity of a location, but the generic trend between density and performance. In medical studies, it is common for statistical analyses that combine the results of multiple scientific studies to be used to arrive at effective and safe treatments. In urban planning, this could in similar ways lead to defining design principles with which to obtain more sustainable solutions that are proven to be successful.

7 Berghauser Pont, M. Y., P. G. Berg, P. A. Haupt, A. Heyman, 'A systematic review of the scientifically demonstrated effects of densification', IOP Conf. Ser.: Earth Environ. Sci. 588 052031 (2020).

Systematic Review of Density Performance

A systematic review is used to collect an evidence base that covers, as broadly as possible, the empirically proven links between density and environmental, social and economic performances. The evidence was restricted

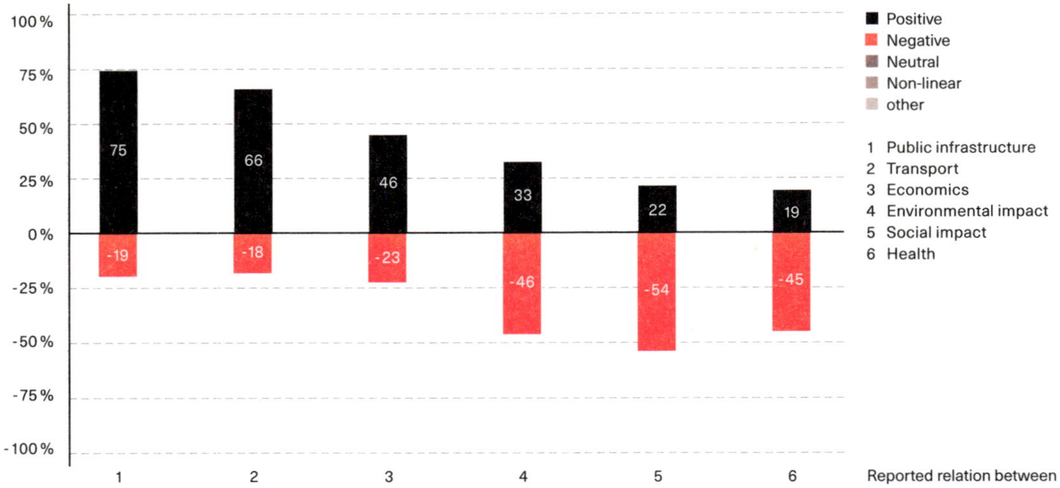

2 Reported relation between density and sustainable urban development.

to empirical studies published in peer-reviewed journals to guarantee scientific rigor. There were no geographical restrictions imposed in the search for articles, nor any time limit.

The objective of the review is to evaluate the effectiveness of higher density (as means) to arrive at more sustainable urban development (the goal). The reported outcomes are categorized in terms of their contribution to sustainable urban development. In most cases, this is rather straightforward, such as preserving limited resources – a fundamental sustainability principle, while this is more challenging in other areas such as economics.[8]

In short, the process of the analysis consisted of three steps: first, a search for articles according to an a priori search strategy;[9] second, the filtering out of obviously irrelevant ones using clearly defined inclusion and exclusion criteria;[10] and thirdly, the reviewing of the final sample by reading the full papers, following a predefined recording method. Based on the inclusion and exclusion criteria, the selection of articles was reduced from 1,208 to 330 papers from which another 101 papers, which did not fulfil all criteria, were excluded in the third step. The results presented below are therefore based on a sample of 229 scientific papers of which 29 per cent are from North America, 31 per cent from Asia and 22 per cent from Europe. The other continents each represent less than 5 per cent of the sample, but more often even less than 1 per cent.

Half of the studies reported a positive relation between density and sustainable urban development, but one third of the studies also show a negative one. Densification thus has both advantages and disadvantages. When looking at the various outcome categories separately, we get a clearer picture of what these advantages and disadvantages are (2). Studies related to public infrastructure, transport and economics more often report positive correlations with density, while ecological, social and health effects of higher densities are for the most part negative. In the following, we will

8
An interpretation has been made on basis of contemporary mainstream discourse on sustainability.

9
The following keywords were used: *TS* = (dens*) *and TS* = (urban *or* city *or* cities) *and TS* = (empiric*) refined further through *Document Type* = (article) *and Languages* = (English). We added another set of keywords to make sure that we include environmental studies that often use the term urban gradient instead of density. These search terms were *TS* = ("urban gradient" *or* "urban rural gradient" *or* "urban to rural gradient") *and TS* = (empiric*). This resulted in a total amount of 1208 papers.

10
We used three criteria: topic, type of study and outcome. See for details: Berghauser Pont et. al. 'A systematic review', op. cit. (note 7).

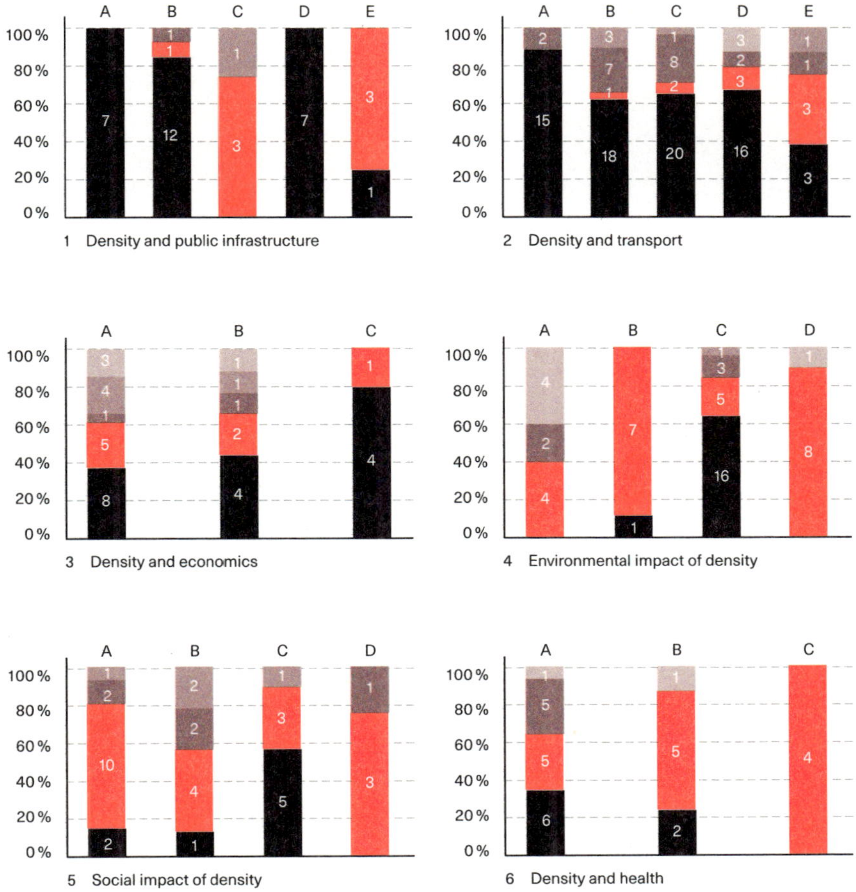

1
A Technical
B Energy efficiency
C Water management
D Service
E Recreation

2
A Public transport
B Pedestrian and bicycle
C Private motorized
D Travel behaviour
E Traffic safety

3
A Productivity
B Property value
C Public finances

4
A Biodiversity
B Ecological conditions
C Macro-climate
D Micro-climate

5
A Well-being
B Social interaction
C Social equity
D Crime

6
A Physical health
B Air quality health impact
C Psychological health

Reported relation between density and sustainable urban development where the six main categories shown in ⬢2 are divided in sub-categories.

⬢3

discuss these outcomes in more detail, dividing the main categories in various subcategories, to better understand the mechanisms that lie behind these diverging results ⬢3.

Density and Public Infrastructure

Public infrastructure includes topics ranging from technical infrastructure such as roads and sewers, energy efficiency of these infrastructures and surface water management, to availability and accessibility of services including recreational infrastructures. Energy efficiency covers both transport-related energy consumption and energy efficiency of various kinds of infrastructures, but mainly in regard to buildings.

In general, the results reveal that higher density provides advantages from a sustainability perspective for technical infrastructures, energy efficiency and service provision. The studies show consensus that higher density contributes positively to these performances. However, higher densities do not create optimal conditions for surface water management and are a threat to the provision and quality of recreational (green) areas. In the case of water management, the lack of pervious surfaces is the main obstacle – which is mainly conditioned by GSI and not so much high FSI. It is also worth noting that a lower provision of green areas does not necessarily mean that residents *perceive* a lower access to green areas.

Technical Infrastructure

There is consensus on the benefits of higher density for technical infrastructure, both in terms of investment costs, operational costs and efficiency. Water service utilities with more customers were able to maintain a higher level of efficiency,[11] similar results are reported for road infrastructure[12] and annual operational costs for energy and water infrastructure are lower.[13]

Energy Efficiency

Higher population density is associated with a lower amount of electricity used for cooling and heating.[14] For instance, energy efficiency increases by approximately 12 per cent when the density in a municipal population doubles.[15] A negative impact of density on energy use is only reported in one study.[16] This is, however, a very limited study comparing only two residences in Chicago where the downtown high-rise used twice as much energy (around 225 GJ/person/year) compared with Oak Park low-rise residences.[17]

Six studies report explicitly on energy consumption related to transport. The results confirm the seminal publication by Newman and Kenworthy,[18] which showed a strong correlation between population density and energy consumption related to transport.[19] But the importance of higher density is not the whole story, because, as one study highlights, the socioeconomic status of the residents is as much an explanation for low energy consumption as is higher population density.[20]

Surface Water Management

Despite the relatively small number of studies, there is clear consensus on the negative impact of higher density on surface water management. The correlation coefficients between the intensity of developed land (GSI) or higher impervious surfaces and the amount of surface

11
Ananda, Jayanath. 'Evaluating the Performance of Urban Water Utilities: Robust Nonparametric Approach'. Journal of Water Resources Planning and Management 140, no. 9 (2014): 04014021.

12
Schiller, Georg. 'Urban Infrastructure: Challenges for Resource Efficiency in the Building Stock'. Building Research and Information 35, no. 4 (2007): 399–411

13
Du, Peng, Antony Wood, and Brent Stephens. 'Empirical Operational Energy Analysis of Downtown High-Rise vs. Suburban Low-Rise Lifestyles: A Chicago Case Study'. Energies 9, no. 6 (2016): 445; Persson, Urban, and Sven Werner. 'Heat Distribution and the Future Competitiveness of District Heating'. Applied Energy 88, no. 3 (2011): 568–76; Pflieger, Geraldine, and Florian Ecoffey. 'The Cost of Urban Sprawl and Its Potential Redistributive Effects: An Empirical Cost Assessment for Water Services in Lausanne (Switzerland)'. Environment and Planning A 43, no. 4 (2011): 850–65.

14
Ko, Yekang, and John D. Radke. 'The Effect of Urban Form and Residential Cooling Energy Use in Sacramento, California'. Environment and Planning B-Planning & Design 41, no. 4 (2014): 573–93; Mashhoodi, Bardia. 'Spatial Dynamics of Household Energy Consumption and Local Drivers in Randstad, Netherlands'. Applied Geography 91 (February 2018): 123–30; Norman, J., H. L. MacLean, and C. A. Kennedy. 'Comparing High and Low Residential Density: Life-Cycle Analysis of Energy Use and Greenhouse Gas Emissions'. Journal of Urban Planning and Development-Asce 132, no. 1 (2006): 10–21; Otsuka, Akihiro, and Mika Goto. 'Estimation and Determinants of Energy Efficiency in Japanese Regional Economies'. Regional Science Policy and Practice 7, no. 2 (2015): 89–101; Rode, Philipp, Christian Keim, Guido Robazza, Pablo Viejo, and James Schofield. 'Cities and Energy: Urban Morphology and Residential Heat-Energy Demand' Environment and Planning B-Planning & Design 41, no. 1 (2014): 138–62; Wang, Lei, Ruyin Long, and Hong Chen. 'Study of Urban Energy Perfomance Assessment and Its Influencing Factors Based on Improved Stochastic Frontier Analysis: A Case Study of Provincial Capitals in China'. Sustainability 9, no. 7 (2017): 1110.

15
Morikawa, Masayuki. 'Population Density and Efficiency in Energy Consumption: An Empirical Analysis of Service Establishments'. Energy Economics 34, no. 5 (2012): 1617–22.

16
Du et. al., 'Empirical Operational', op. cit. (note 13),

17
Ibid.

18
Newman, P. and J. Kenworthy, *Sustainability and Cities: Overcoming Automobile Dependence* (Chicago: University of Chicago Press, 1999).

19
Banister, D., S. Watson, and C. Wood. 'Sustainable Cities: Transport, Energy, and Urban Form'. Environment and Planning B-Planning & Design 24, no. 1 (1997): 125–43; Du et. al., 'Empirical Operational', op. cit. (note 13); Marique, Anne-Francoise, Sebastien Dujardin, Jacques Teller, and Sigrid Reiter. 'Urban Sprawl, Commuting and Travel Energy Consumption'. Proceedings of the Institution of Civil Engineers-Energy 166, no. 1 (2013): 29–41.

20
Modarres, Ali. 'Commuting and Energy Consumption: Toward an Equitable Transportation Policy'. Journal of Transport Geography 33 (2013): 240–49.

runoff are significantly positive.[21] A study from Seoul, South Korea, reports that a 1 per cent increase in GSI can result in approximately $682,300 in flood losses when all else is held constant.[22]

Despite this general trend, the same study in Seoul indicates that high-density solutions can be planned to reduce flood damage by using proper land use management techniques and choosing the correct locations for such developments, avoiding flood-prone areas.

21
Kim, H. W., M.-H. Li, J.-H. Kim, and F. Jaber. "Examining the Impact of Suburbanization on Surface Runoff Using the SWAT." International Journal of Environmental Research 10, no. 3 (2016): 379–90; Li, Baojie, Dongxiang Chen, Shaohua Wu, Shenglu Zhou, Teng Wang, and Hao Chen. 'Spatio-Temporal Assessment of Urbanization Impacts on Ecosystem Services: Case Study of Nanjing City, China'. Ecological Indicators 71 (2016): 416–27; Trudeau, M. P., and Murray Richardson. 'Empirical Assessment of Effects of Urbanization on Event Flow Hydrology in Watersheds of Canada's Great Lakes-St Lawrence Basin'. Journal of Hydrology 541 (2016): 1456–74.

22
Lee, Yoonjeong, and Samuel D. Brody. 'Examining the Impact of Land Use on Flood Losses in Seoul, Korea'. Land Use Policy 70 (2018): 500–509.

Service Infrastructure

Higher density neighbourhoods have better accessibility to public and commercial services,[23] people use services more frequently[24] and the services provided are more diverse.[25] This is important not only from an economic perspective, but especially because having accessible key services in the neighbourhood is important for vulnerable groups.[26]

Interestingly, one study reports that built coverage (GSI) tends to exert greater influence on urban vitality than built intensity (FSI), other things being equal.[27] This might be explained by the relatively larger interface between public space and built façade when the GSI is higher.

23
Dave, Seema. 'Neighbourhood Density and Social Sustainability in Cities of Developing Countries'. Sustainable Development 19, no. 3 (2011): 189–205; Lin, Jen-Jia, and An-Tsei Yang. 'Does the Compact-City Paradigm Foster Sustainability? An Empirical Study in Taiwan'. Environment and Planning B-Planning & Design 33, no. 3 (2006): 365–80.

24
Dempsey, N., C. Brown, and G. Bramley. 'The Key to Sustainable Urban Development in UK Cities? The Influence of Density on Social Sustainability'. Progress in Planning 77 (2012): 89–141.

25
Adolphson, Marcus. "Kernel Densities and Mixed Functionality in a Multicentred Urban Region." Environment and Planning B-Planning & Design 37, no. 3 (2010): 550–66; Schiff, Nathan. 'Cities and Product Variety: Evidence from Restaurants'. Journal of Economic Geography 15, no. 6 (2015): 1085–1123.

26
Dempsey et.al., 'The Key to Sustainable', op. cit. (note 24).

27
Ye, Yu, Dong Li, and Xingjian Liu. 'How Block Density and Typology Affect Urban Vitality: An Exploratory Analysis in Shenzhen, China'. Urban Geography 39, no. 4 (2018): 631–52.

Recreational Infrastructure

The findings in relation to recreational infrastructure show an opposite trend: the higher the residential density is, the lower the overall provision of public and green space is.[28] However, despite this difference in the availability of public and green space, a study in the UK reports that the use of, and perceived access to, public open spaces is relatively high across the different densities.[29] At the same time, residents in higher-density neighbourhoods reported that they were less satisfied with the quality of their local parks and green spaces than residents in lower-density areas.

Further, besides the availability and use of, access to and satisfaction with green areas, a study from North American reports that the willingness to vote in open-space referenda is increasing.[30] This indicates that people care more about open spaces when population densities are higher.

28
Li et.al., 'Spatio-Temporal Assessment', op. cit. (note 21); Lin et.al., 'Does the Compact-City', op. cit. (note 23).

29
Dempsey et.al., 'The Key to Sustainable', op. cit. (note 24).

30
Kline, J. 'Public Demand for Preserving Local Open Space'. Society & Natural Resources 19, no. 7 (2006): 645–59.

Density and Transport

The category transport is studied most frequently, representing more than one third of the articles in the article sample. Three different modalities are distinguished: public transport, active modes of transport such as walking and bicycling, and private motorized transport (the car). The fourth subcategory relates to travel behaviour, including trip distance and choice of modality, and the last covers traffic safety.[31]

Studies on public transport and active modes of transport are equally spread across Europe, North America and Asia, but for the studies on private motorized transport, a large majority of studies are from North America, while only six are from Asia and three studies cover Europe.

There is strong consensus across the studies that higher densities contribute to an increase in the use of public transport and active modes of transport, while they reduce car ownership and vehicle miles travelled by car. The results also highlight some details that are important. First, commuting trips are more strongly related to density than recreational trips. Second, car trips are more dependent on high density at destination, while walking and bicycling is more strongly affected by high density at the location where the trip starts, at home (origin). Third, there seems to be a density threshold above which the positive effect of higher density on reduced car trips and increased walking and bicycling starts to diminish.

The strong consensus among papers on the relation between density and different modes of transport is not found in studies on traffic safety.

Public Transport

Most of the 17 studies on the relation between density and the use of public transport report a positive trend. Thus, denser cities are associated with higher per capita ridership.[32] Most studies investigate commuting and only one reported on weekend ridership where no significant relation with density was found.[33] Of the studies on commuting, various studies report that job density has a stronger correlation with ridership than residential density.[34] That the beneficial effect of employment concentration on public transport is reached at the expense of less walking and bicycling and might thus not lead to less private motorized traffic is noteworthy.[35] Thus, the

31
Emissions and energy consumption related to transport are not reported here but can instead be found in the category ecology (macro-climate) and infrastructure (energy efficiency) respectively.

32
Houston, Douglas, Marlon G. Boarnet, Gavin Ferguson, and Steven Spears. 'Can Compact Rail Transit Corridors Transform the Automobile City? Planning for More Sustainable Travel in Los Angeles'. Urban Studies 52, no. 5 (2015): 938–59;
Renne, John L., Shima Hamidi, and Reid Ewing. 'Transit Commuting, the Network Accessibility Effect, and the Built Environment in Station Areas across the United States'. Research in Transportation Economics 60 (2016): 35–43;
Sung, Hyungun, Keechoo Choi, Sugie Lee, and SangHyun Cheon. 'Exploring the Impacts of Land Use by Service Coverage and Station-Level Accessibility on Rail Transit Ridership'. Journal of Transport Geography 36 (2014): 134–40.

33
Lin, Jen-Jia, and An-Tsei Yang. 'Structural Analysis of How Urban Form Impacts Travel Demand: Evidence from Taipei'. Urban Studies 46, no. 9 (2009): 1951–67.

34
Ingvardson, Jesper Blafoss, and Otto Anker Nielsen. 'How Urban Density, Network Topology and Socio-Economy Influence Public Transport Ridership: Empirical Evidence from 48 European Metropolitan Areas'. Journal of Transport Geography 72 (2018): 50–63;
Pan, Haixiao, Jing Li, Qing Shen, and Cheng Shi. 'What Determines Rail Transit Passenger Volume? Implications for Transit Oriented Development Planning'. Transportation Research Part D-Transport and Environment 57 (2017): 52–63.

35
Coevering, Paul van de, and Tim Schwanen. 'Re-Evaluating the Impact of Urban Form on Travel Patterns in Europe and North-America'. Transport Policy 13, no. 3 (2006): 229–39.

strong correlation found between density and the use of public transport is true for commuting, – where job density is found to be more important than residential density–, but the results for weekend trips are still inconclusive.

Walking and Bicycling

The majority of the 29 studies on the relation between density and active modes of transport report a positive relation with both walking[36] and bike ridership.[37] Some studies distinguish density at the location where the trip starts (origin) and ends (destination) concluding that the residential density is the important variable at the origin, while the working population is more important at the destination.[38] Another study demonstrates that the working population density mainly reduces car use, while the general building density and mixed land use encourage walking.[39] Further, a denser population might result in more walking, but not necessarily more biking activity.[40]

Besides the large number of studies that report a positive relation between density and active modes of transport, seven studies also found it to be insignificant.[41] In other words, they conclude that there is no empirically proven effect of density on walking or bicycling. Reasons for this might be that in the studies that show a positive trend, recreational walking was not included and when this is included, density seems to play a far less important role.[42] The same difference between commuting and recreational travel was found for public transport as was discussed above and is confirmed by a study on recreational bike ridership.[43]

A non-linear relation between density and walking is also reported once.[44] This study indicates that the odds of taking walking trips increase as the residential density increases, but once the density exceeds a certain level (in this study, between 10,000 and 15,000 persons / km^2), this effect declines. Also, for biking a non-linear relation is reported with an optimum in the middle ranges and a lower likelihood of frequent bicycling in the most rural category and the high-density urban category.[45]

Motorised Private Transport

Most of the studies (20 out of 31) report a negative correlation between density and motorized private transport, meaning that car usage decreases when density

36
Ewing, Reid, Amir Hajrasouliha, Kathryn M. Neckerman, Marnie Purciel-Hill, and William Greene. 'Streetscape Features Related to Pedestrian Activity'. Journal of Planning Education and Research 36, no. 1 (2016): 5–15; Houston et.al., 'Can Compact Rail Transit', op. cit. (note 32); Kim, Dohyung, Jiyoung Park, and Andy Hong. 'The Role of Destination's Built Environment on Nonmotorized Travel Behavior: A Case of Long Beach, California'. Journal of Planning Education and Research 38, no. 2 (2018): 152–66; Kim, Saehoon, Sungjin Park, and Jae Seung Lee. 'Meso- or Micro-Scale? Environmental Factors Influencing Pedestrian Satisfaction'. Transportation Research Part D-Transport and Environment 30 (2014): 10–20; Lamiquiz, Patxi J., and Jorge Lopez-Dominguez. 'Effects of Built Environment on Walking at the Neighbourhood Scale. A New Role for Street Networks by Modelling Their Configurational Accessibility?' Transportation Research Part A-Policy and Practice 74 (2015): 148–63; Sung, Hyungun, and Sugie Lee. 'Residential Built Environment and Walking Activity: Empirical Evidence of Jane Jacobs' Urban Vitality'. Transportation Research Part D-Transport and Environment 41 (2015): 318–29; Tian, Guang, and Reid Ewing. 'A Walk Trip Generation Model for Portland, OR'. Transportation Research Part D-Transport and Environment 52 (2017): 340–53.

37
El-Assi, Wafic, Mohamed Salah Mahmoud, and Khandker Nurul Habib. 'Effects of Built Environment and Weather on Bike Sharing Demand: A Station Level Analysis of Commercial Bike Sharing in Toronto'. Transportation 44, no. 3 (2017): 589–613; Coevering and Schwanen, 'Re-Evaluating the Impact', op. cit. (note 35); Zhao, Chunli, Thomas Alexander Sick Nielsen, Anton Stahl Olafsson, Trine Agervig Carstensen, and Xiaoying Meng. 'Urban Form, Demographic and Socio-Economic Correlates of Walking, Cycling, and e-Biking: Evidence from Eight Neighborhoods in Beijing'. Transport Policy 64 (2018): 102–12; Coevering and Schwanen, 'Re-Evaluating the Impact', op. cit. (note 35); Zhao et.al., 'Urban Form, Demographic', op. cit. (note 37).

38
Oliva, Ignacio, Patricia Galilea, and Ricardo Hurtubia. 'Identifying Cycling-Inducing Neighborhoods: A Latent Class Approach'. International Journal of Sustainable Transportation 12, no. 10 (2018): 701–13.

39
Lin, Jen-Jia, and Hsiao-Te Chang. 'Built Environment Effects on Children's School Travel in Taipai: Independence and Travel Mode'. Urban Studies 47, no. 4 (2010): 867–89.

40
Tabeshian, Maryam, and Lina Kattan. 'Modeling Nonmotorized Travel Demand at Intersections in Calgary, Canada Use of Traffic Counts and Geographic Information System Data'. Transportation Research Record, no. 2430 (2014): 38–46.

41
El-Assi et.al., 'Effects of Built Environment', op. cit. (note 37); Sehatzadeh, Bahareh, Robert B. Noland, and Marc D. Weiner. 'Walking Frequency, Cars, Dogs, and the Built Environment'. Transportation Research Part A-Policy and Practice 45, no. 8 (2011): 741–54.

42
Lu, Yi, Long Chen, Yiyang Yang, and Zhonghua Gou. 'The Association of Built Environment and Physical Activity in Older Adults: Using a Citywide Public Housing Scheme to Reduce Residential Self-Selection Bias'. International Journal of Environmental Research and Public Health 15, no. 9 (2018): 1973.

increases, and thus show that higher densities support sustainable urban development.

The studies indicate that higher densities lowered the odds of motorized solo-commuting.[46] Higher density at the trip destination is frequently mentioned as the most important variable,[47] while the density at the home location (origin) is in some cases shown not to be significant at all.[48] It is, however, also outlined that higher population density at home decreases the likelihood of owning more cars[49] and significantly influences non-work-related trips.[50]

As was previous discussed in relation to walking and bicycling, private vehicle trips have also been shown to relate to density in a non-linear manner. Residents living in the lowest density areas were 3.38 times more likely to take private vehicle trips, but this gradually decreases to become insignificant beyond a threshold of around 20,000 inh/km^2.[51]

Travel Behaviour

Average trip distances and commuting duration are lower for residents living in high-density areas than for those living in low-density areas.[52] One study reveals that this is mainly the case when economic density increases,[53] while the same study could not report significant correlations between commuting distance and residential density. Another study reports a negative correlation between density and commuting duration.[54] The reason for these contracting findings might be explained by two opposite effects that, depending on the strongest, results in a positive or negative effect. On the one hand, spatial proximity to amenities reduces travel time, but on the other, congestion following from density increases travel time. When the latter is stronger, this results in a negative correlation between density and travel time.

Further, higher population density is associated with a lower share of trips by automobile and a higher share of walking, cycling and using public transport,[55] confirming what has been discussed before. Also, it is again reported that substantial correlations only are found for functional trips or commuting and not for leisure trips.[56] Cultural differences between mode choices are also highlighted,[57] even after controlling for dissimilarities in socioeconomic factors and land use. For instance, Germans are more likely to walk, cycle and use

43
Sun, Yeran, Yunyan Du, Yu Wang, and Liyuan Zhuang. 'Examining Associations of Environmental Characteristics with Recreational Cycling Behaviour by Street-Level Strava Data'. International Journal of Environmental Research and Public Health 14, no. 6 (2017): 644.

44
Eom, Hyun-Joo, and Gi-Hyoug Cho. 'Exploring Thresholds of Built Environment Characteristics for Walkable Communities: Empirical Evidence from the Seoul Metropolitan Area'. Transportation Research Part D-Transport and Environment 40 (2015): 76–86.

45
McAndrews, Carolyn, Kenta Okuyama, and Jill S. Litt. 'The Reach of Bicycling in Rural, Small, and Low-Density Places'. Transportation Research Record, no. 2662 (2017): 134–42.

46
Coevering and Schwanen, 'Re-Evaluating the Impact', op. cit. (note 35); Zhang, Wenjia, and Ming Zhang. 'Short- and Long-Term Effects of Land Use on Reducing Personal Vehicle Miles of Travel Longitudinal Multilevel Analysis in Austin, Texas'. Transportation Research Record, no. 2500 (2015): 102–9.

47
Cervero, R. 'Built Environments and Mode Choice: Toward a Normative Framework'. Transportation Research Part D-Transport and Environment 7, no. 4 (2002): 265–84;
Lee, Jae-Su, Jin Nam, and Sam-Su Lee. 'Built Environment Impacts on Individual Mode Choice: An Empirical Study of the Houston-Galveston Metropolitan Area'. International Journal of Sustainable Transportation 8, no. 6 (2014): 447–70;
Houston et.al., 'Can Compact Rail', op. cit. (note 32);
Lin and Chang, 'Built Environment Effects', op. cit. (note 39).

48
Ding, Chuan, Yaoyu Lin, and Chao Liu. 'Exploring the Influence of Built Environment on Tour-Based Commuter Mode Choice: A Cross-Classified Multilevel Modeling Approach'. Transportation Research Part D-Transport and Environment 32 (2014): 230–38;
Ding, Chuan, Yaowu Wang, Binglei Xie, and Chao Liu. 'Understanding the Role of Built Environment in Reducing Vehicle Miles Traveled Accounting for Spatial Heterogeneity'. Sustainability 6, no. 2 (2014): 589–601;
Li, Shengxiao, and Pengjun Zhao. 'Exploring Car Ownership and Car Use in Neighborhoods near Metro Stations in Beijing: Does the Neighborhood Built Environment Matter?' Transportation Research Part D-Transport and Environment 56 (2017): 1–17.

49
Chen, Cynthia, Hongmian Gong, and Robert Paaswell. 'Role of the Built Environment on Mode Choice Decisions: Additional Evidence on the Impact of Density'. Transportation 35, no. 3 (2008): 285–99;
Karathodorou, Niovi, Daniel J. Graham, and Robert B. Noland. 'Estimating the Effect of Urban Density on Fuel Demand'. Energy Economics 32, no. 1 (2010): 86–92;
Salon, Deborah. 'Neighborhoods, Cars, and Commuting in New York City: A Discrete Choice Approach'. Transportation Research Part A-Policy and Practice 43, no. 2 (2009): 180–96;
Xiao, Zuopeng, Qian Liu, and James Wang. 'How Do the Effects of Local Built Environment on Household Vehicle Kilometers Traveled Vary across Urban Structural Zones?' International Journal of Sustainable Transportation 12, no. 9 (2018): 637–47.

50
Lee et.al., 'Built Envi ronment Impacts', op. cit. (note 47);

public transport than Americans, even if the Germans live in lower-density areas that the Americans.

Traffic Safety

The combined results of eight studies on the relation between density and traffic safety are inconclusive, with half of the studies reporting a negative and the other half a positive impact. Three studies report that urban density has a statistically significant direct effect on traffic safety, that is, fewer accidents and traffic fatalities.[58] However, two other papers report the opposite and show that an increase in population density yields an increase in traffic accidents.[59] In a systematic review on multifunctional streets, a similar discrepancy was highlighted, where they argued that the number of crashes indeed increased, but their severity and number of fatalities decreased in more central location because of the lower vehicular speed.[60]

Density and Economics

Studies on economics are primarily about the agglomeration effects of densification, such as higher productivity, employment rates, profits or number of entrepreneurs, companies and innovations (60 per cent of the papers on economics), followed by the relation between density and property values (25 per cent) and public finances (15 per cent).

There is strong consensus on the positive role of density on productivity and innovation, but a few studies also emphasize that densities that are too high can shift the ratio between agglomeration benefits and diseconomies related to traffic congestion and / or environmental pollution. Furthermore, agglomeration benefits can result in reduced interest to invest in training and innovation, as well as diminish start-up activity.

Property value is positively affected by density although it is also pointed out that proximity to parks, lakes and open spaces are beneficial. This might explain the non-linear relation reported in one study, in which density is perceived as a disamenity beyond a certain threshold level.

There is consensus on the benefits of higher density for public finances, while the extra costs for public safety should not be ignored.

51
Eom et.al., 'Exploring Thresholds', op. cit. (note 44).

52
Akar, Gulsah, Na Chen, and Steven I. Gordon. "Influence of Neighborhood Types on Trip Distances: Spatial Error Models for Central Ohio." International Journal of Sustainable Transportation 10, no. 3 (2016): 284–93; Ralph, Kelcie, Carole Turley Voulgaris, Brian D. Taylor, Evelyn Blumenberg, and Anne E. Brown. 'Millennials, Built Form, and Travel Insights from a Nationwide Typology of US Neighborhoods'. Journal of Transport Geography 57 (2016): 218–26.

53
Engelfriet, Lara, and Eric Koomen. 'The Impact of Urban Form on Commuting in Large Chinese Cities'. Transportation 45, no. 5 (2018): 1269–95.

54
Raux, Charles, Tai-Yu Ma, Iragael Joly, Vincent Kaufmann, Eric Cornelis, and Nicolas Ovtracht. 'Travel and Activity Time Allocation: An Empirical Comparison between Eight Cities in Europe'. Transport Policy 18, no. 2 (2011): 401–12.

55
Lavery, T. A., A. Paez, and P. S. Kanaroglou. 'Driving out of Choices: An Investigation of Transport Modality in a University Sample'. Transportation Research Part A-Policy and Practice 57 (2013): 37–46; Mendiola, Lorea, Pilar Gonzalez, and Angel Cebollada. 'The Link between Urban Development and the Modal Split in Commuting: The Case of Biscay'. Journal of Transport Geography 37 (2014): 1–9; Ming, Z. 'Travel Choice with No Alternative – Can Land Use Reduce Automobile Dependence?' Journal of Planning Education and Research 25, no. 3 (2006): 311–26; Zhang, M. 'The Role of Land Use in Travel Mode Choice – Evidence from Boston and Hong Kong'. Journal of the American Planning Association 70, no. 3 (2004): 344–60.

56
Forsyth, Ann, J. Michael Oakes, Kathryn H. Schmitz, and Mary Hearst. 'Does Residential Density Increase Walking and Other Physical Activity?' Urban Studies 44, no. 4 (2007): 679–97; Ramezani, Samira, Barbara Pizzo, and Elizabeth Deakin. 'An Integrated Assessment of Factors Affecting Modal Choice: Towards a Better Understanding of the Causal Effects of Built Environment'. Transportation 45, no. 5 (2018): 1351–87.

57
Buehler, Ralph. 'Determinants of Transport Mode Choice: A Comparison of Germany and the USA'. Journal of Transport Geography 19, no. 4 (2011): 644–57.

58
Chen, Peng, and Jiangping Zhou. 'Effects of the Built Environment on Automobile-Involved Pedestrian Crash Frequency and Risk'. Journal of Transport & Health 3, no. 4 (2016): 448–56; Dumbaugh, Eric, and Robert Rae. 'Safe Urban Form: Revisiting the Relationship Between Community Design and Traffic Safety'. Journal of the American Planning Association 75, no. 3 (2009): 309–29; Najaf, Pooya, Jean-Claude Thill, Wenjia Zhang, and Milton Greg Fields. 'City-Level Urban Form and Traffic Safety: A Structural Equation Modeling Analysis of Direct and Indirect Effects'. Journal of Transport Geography 69 (2018): 257–70.

59
Gladhill, Kristie, and Christopher M. Monsere. 'Exploring Traffic Safety and Urban Form in Portland, Oregon'. Transportation Research Record, no. 2318 (2012): 63–74; Iwata, Kazuyuki, and Shunsuke Managi. 'Can Land Use Regulations and Taxes Help Mitigate Vehicular CO_2 Emissions? An Empirical Study of Japanese Cities'. Urban Policy and Research 34, no. 4 (2016): 356–72.

Productivity, Innovation and Density

Most of the studies report a positive contribution of higher density on economic productivity, but it should also be noted that five studies report negative effects and four a non-linear relation. The positive effect of higher density relates to an increase in productivity as a result of agglomeration effect or economy of scale.[61] This is not equal across all markets as some studies point out.[62] For instance, the positive effects for the creative, knowledge-based service industries are considerably larger than those for the manufacturing and retail industries.

When looking at the training skills and training investments[63] as well as entrepreneurship and start-up activity,[64] the relation with density is the opposite. In other words, higher density reduced training investments and lowered the number of start-ups. This might be explained by the fact that higher density increases wages and turnover, which in turn discourages training[65] and the need for specialization.[66] The higher start-up activity in relation to lower density might be explained by the necessity to start your own company in less dense areas with fewer job opportunities.

A non-linear relation between employment density and innovation output is reported as well, with output changing from positive to negative as density increased.[67] This is also found for positive agglomeration effects that were proven to be valid up to a population density of approximately 4,000 persons per square mile (10,000 persons/km^2), after which negative congestion effects become dominant.[68]

Density and Property Value

Both land prices and real estate values increase for higher-density properties or in higher-density neighbourhoods.[69] This indicates a willingness to pay a higher price for projects of greater density. One study reported a non-linear relation, where residential density is perceived as a disamenity beyond a certain threshold, although this effect is indicated to be small.[70] It is also reported that proximity to parks, lakes and open spaces are important for sales prices and that open space amenities are valued higher in dense neighbourhoods where undeveloped land is relatively scarce[71] and can even turn into a negative effect.[72] It should be noted, however, that both of these

60 Stavroulaki, I, M. Berghauser Pont, 'A systematic review of the scientific literature on the theme of multifunctional streets', *IOP Conf. Ser.: Earth Environ. Sci.* 588 (2020), 052046.

61 Ciccone, A. 'Agglomeration Effects in Europe'. European Economic Review 46, no. 2 (2002): 213–27; Fallah, Belal N., Mark D. Partridge, and M. Rose Olfert. 'Urban Sprawl and Productivity: Evidence from US Metropolitan Areas'. Papers in Regional Science 90, no. 3 (August 2011): 451–72; Jennen, Maarten, and Patrick Verwijmeren. 'Agglomeration Effects and Financial Performance'. Urban Studies 47, no. 12 (2010): 2683–2703. Lin and Yang, 'Does the Compact-City', op. cit. (note 23); Zhao, Hong. 'Executive Labor Market Segmentation: How Local Market Density Affects Incentives and Performance'. Journal of Corporate Finance 50 (2018): 1–21.

62 Abel, Jaison R., Ishita Dey, and Todd M. Gabe. 'Productivity and the density of human capital*' Journal of Regional Science 52, no. 4 (2012): 562–86; Cruz, Sara Santos, and Aurora A. C. Teixeira. 'The Neglected Heterogeneity of Spatial Agglomeration and Co-Location Patterns of Creative Employment: Evidence from Portugal'. Annals of Regional Science 54, no. 1 (2015): 143–77; Morikawa, Masayuki. 'Economies of Density and Productivity in Service Industries: An Analysis'. Review of Economics and Statistics 93, no. 1 (2011): 179–92.

63 Brunello, Giorgio, and Maria De Paola. 'Training and Economic Density: Some Evidence Form Italian Provinces'. Labour Economics 15, no. 1 (2008): 118–40.

64 Di Addario, Sabrina, and Daniela Vuri. 'Entrepreneurship and Market Size. The Case of Young College Graduates in Italy'. Labour Economics 17, no. 5 (2010): 848–58; Hans, Lianne, and Sierdjan Koster. 'Urbanization and Start-up Rates in Different Geographies: Belgium, the Netherlands, and Sweden'. Small Business Economics 51, no. 4 (2018): 1033–54.

65 Brunello and De Paola, 'Training and Economic Density', op. cit. (note 63).

66 Caragliu, Andrea, Laura de Dominicis, and Henri L. F. de Groot. 'Both Marshall and Jacobs Were Right!' Economic Geography 92, no. 1 (2016): 87–111.

67 Ke, Shanzi, and Yufeng Yu. 'The Pathways from Industrial Agglomeration to TFP Growth – the Experience of Chinese Cities for 2001–2010'. Journal of the Asia Pacific Economy 19, no. 2 (2014): 310–32.

68 Sedgley, Norman, and Bruce Elmslie. 'Do We Still Need Cities? Evidence on Rates of Innovation from Count Data Models of Metropolitan Statistical Area Patents'. American Journal of Economics and Sociology 70, no. 1 (2011): 86–108; Zheng, X. P. 'Measuring Optimal Population Distribution by Agglomeration Economies and Diseconomies: A Case Study of Tokyo'. Urban Studies 35, no. 1 (1998): 95–112.

studies are based on single-family homes only, with relative low densities. Such low densities, it is further shown, are associated with faster relative growth of property value than the growth recorded in areas of higher density.[73]

Density and Public Finances

The per capita costs of providing public services such as roadways, other transportation, sewers, trash collection, housing and community development, parks, education and libraries decreases as density increases.[74] However, higher density is also associated with higher costs for public safety such as costs related to traffic accidents and an increase in crime.[75] As a result, reduced expenditures for public services as highlighted above may be offset by increased expenditures on public safety.

Environmental Impact of Density

Within the category *environmental impact*, we distinguish effects of density related to biodiversity and ecological conditions as well as climate change effects and micro-climate impacts. Biodiversity focuses mainly on topics related to species diversity, ecological conditions relate to ecosystems and their stability over time, climate change effects cover mainly greenhouse gas emissions and micro-climate is primarily about urban heat island effects.

Overall, the impact of a higher density on the environment is negative, except for the positive effects related to climate change as a result of reduced greenhouse gas emissions, often related to reduced car mobility. It should be noted however, that even though per capita emissions go down, absolute emissions increase in urban areas, which contributes to negative health effects, something we will discuss later. Furthermore, most studies excluded air traffic when reporting on greenhouse gas emissions. When including these emissions, the overall levels of per capita greenhouse gas emissions go up with increasing densities.

There is consensus about the negative impact of higher density on heat stress, that is, higher surface temperatures in cities (urban heat island effect). Vegetation and impervious surfaces are pointed out as the key variables where more hard surfaces and high GSI increase surface temperatures. However, it is hard to distinguish

69
Ding, C. R. 'Urban Spatial Development in the Land Policy Reform Era: Evidence from Beijing'. Urban Studies 41, no. 10 (2004): 1889–1907;
Liu, Lu, and Paul M. Jakus. 'Hedonic Valuation in an Urban High-Rise Housing Market'. Canadian Journal of Agricultural Economics-Revue Canadienne D Agroeconomie 63, no. 2 (2015): 259–7;
Nase, Ilir, Jim Berry, and Alastair Adair. 'Impact of Quality-Led Design on Real Estate Value: A Spatiotemporal Analysis of City Centre Apartments'. Journal of Property Research 33, no. 4 (2016): 309–31.

70
Nilsson, Pia. 'Are Valuations of Place-Based Amenities Driven by Scale?' Housing Studies 32, no. 4 (2017): 449–69

71
Asabere, Paul K. 'The Value of Homes in Cluster Development Residential Districts: The Relative Significance of the Permanent Open Spaces Associated with Clusters'. Journal of Real Estate Finance and Economics 48, no. 2 (2014): 244–55;
Nilsson, 'Are Valuations', op. cit. (note 70).

72
Asabere, 'The Value of Homes', op. cit. (note 71).

73
Byrne, Paul F. 'Determinants of Property Value Growth for Tax Increment Financing Districts'. Economic Development Quarterly 20, no. 4 (2006): 317–29.

74
Carruthers, J. I., and G. F. Ulfarsson. 'Urban Sprawl and the Cost of Public Services'. Environment and Planning B-Planning & Design 30, no. 4 (July 2003): 503–22;
Cubukcu, K. Mert. 'Examining the Cost Structure of Urban Bus Transit Industry: Does Urban Geography Help?' Journal of Transport Geography 16, no. 4 (2008): 278–91;
Edwards, Mary M., and Yu Xiao. 'Annexation, Local Government Spending, and the Complicating Role of Density'. Urban Affairs Review 45, no. 2 (2009): 147–65;
Hortas-Rico, Miriam, and Albert Sole-Olle. 'Does Urban Sprawl Increase the Costs of Providing Local Public Services? Evidence from Spanish Municipalities'. Urban Studies 47, no. 7 (2010): 1513–40

75
Iwata and Managi, 'Can Land Use Regulations', op. cit. (note 59).

their role independently from population density and FSI. Thus, the form of densification might be crucial to mitigate higher surface temperatures.

Similarly, there is consensus about the negative impact of higher density on overall ecological conditions and biodiversity, although this is not true for all species. Urbanization as such has a negative effect on biodiversity, but differences between the kind of urbanization (in high or low densities) can be minor. However, the loss of genetic diversity and population size over time is alarming because it underlines the vulnerability of biodiversity in the long term.

Density and Biodiversity

None of the 11 studies that investigate the relation between density and biodiversity report a positive correlation, but some are inconclusive. There is thus consensus about the negative impact of higher densities on biodiversity. Moreover, it is reported that genetic diversity and population size decreases over time in high-density areas.[76] In studies that report a negative impact of density on biodiversity, the forwarded reason is lower habitat suitability in urban areas compared with rural areas,[77] including a lower richness and abundance of forest species.[78]

An exception is found for 'urban adapters', species that thrive in urbanized areas[79] and small isolated rare plants that were not declining in denser areas. Rather, they appeared to be performing as well in urban settings as in rural ones.[80]

One study worth mentioning reported that the plant and wildlife species composition of clustered housing developments is more like that of dispersed housing developments than that of undeveloped areas.[81] In other words, there is a difference between developed and undeveloped land, but not so much between more or less densely developed land.

Density and Ecological Conditions

Six out of seven papers report declining ecological conditions as a result of higher densities. Housing density correlates highly with higher shares of aggregated impervious surfaces that, in turn, have a negative impact on overall environmental conditions.[82] This is confirmed for streams[83] and natural water in general,[84] as well as for the increased levels of dissolved inorganic nitrogen fluxes.[85]

One study confirming that this negative impact of higher density on environmental pollution also shows the positive effect of concentrated development.[86] This suggests that by improving the quality of and form taken by urbanization, we can achieve more sustainable solutions.

Density and Climate Change

Most of the papers on climate change study the relation between density and greenhouse gas (GHG) emissions. Only one study reports on the relation

76
Rochat, E., S. Manel, M. Deschamps-Cottin, I. Widmer, and S. Joost. 'Persistence of Butterfly Populations in Fragmented Habitats along Urban Density Gradients: Motility Helps'. Heredity 119, no. 5 (2017): 328–38.

77
Li et.al., 'Spatio-Temporal Assessment', op. cit. (note 21).

78
Villasenor, Nelida R., Don A. Driscoll, Martin A. H. Escobar, Philip Gibbons, and David B. Lindenmayer. 'Urbanization Impacts on Mammals across Urban-Forest Edges and a Predictive Model of Edge Effects'. Plos One 9, no. 5 (2014): e97036

79
Ibid

80
Lawson, Dawn M., Cerina K. Lamar, and Mark W. Schwartz. 'Quantifying Plant Population Persistence in Human-Dominated Landscapes'. Conservation Biology 22, no. 4 (2008): 922–28.

81
Lenth, Buffy A., Richard L. Knight, and Wendell C. Gilgert. 'Conservation Value of Clustered Housing Developments'. Conservation Biology 20, no. 5 (2006): 1445–56.

82
Shaker, Richard Ross. 'The Well-Being of Nations: An Empirical Assessment of Sustainable Urbanization for Europe'. International Journal of Sustainable Development and World Ecology 22, no. 5 (2015): 375–87.

83
Alberti, Marina, Derek Booth, Kristina Hill, Bekkah Coburn, Christina Avolio, Stefan Coe, and Daniele Spirandelli. 'The Impact of Urban Patterns on Aquatic Ecosystems: An Empirical Analysis in Puget Lowland Sub-Basins'. Landscape and Urban Planning 80, no. 4 (2007): 345–61.

between density and carbon sequestration, the opposite process of capturing and storing atmospheric carbon dioxide.[87] Within the large group of studies on GHG emissions, two groups can be distinguished where the first investigates GHG emissions by transport (16 studies) and the other group reports on other sources of GHG emissions (8 studies), mainly related to cooling and heating.

There is strong consensus that residents living in communities with higher density emit less GHG emissions from trips, confirming the results discussed above on transport.[88] This is especially found true for passenger vehicle emissions, while for truck-related emissions the results are inconclusive.[89] Besides density, it should be noted that land use characteristics also play an important role. For instance, for non-work trips, higher retail density or mixed land use patterns are found important.[90] The role of working population density, however, is inconclusive; some report that for work trips, in line with the results discussed before, higher job density contributes to lower emission levels,[91] but this effect was not confirmed in a study that controlled for distance to work,[92] while several studies reported a positive effect of higher residential densities.[93] However, the elasticities are small. For instance, a 10 per cent increase in density resulted in a less than 5 per cent reduction in emissions.[94] On the other hand, densities vary a lot in cities and it is shown, for instance, that CO_2 reduction associated with average density (1,250 addresses/km^2) and high density (twice as high; more than 2,500 addresses/km^2) can differ by 30 per cent, which is substantial.[95]

It is important to emphasize that only one paper reports higher overall emissions for metropolitan dwellers, which is explained by the significantly higher emissions from air travel, a factor ignored by all other studies.[96] This highlights the need to look at all transport emissions and should be read as a strong call for more research that includes air travel.

The studies on other types of GHG emissions primarily report that neighbourhoods with higher building density use less energy for cooling and heating.[97] The elasticities for heating and cooling related emissions are similar to transport as reported above; when the density of living increases by 10 per cent, urban carbon emissions decrease by less than 5 per cent.[98]

Despite the reduction of transport- and building-related emissions, a positive relationship is reported

84
Bressler, David W., Michael J. Paul, Alison H. Purcell, Michael T. Barbour, Ed T. Rankin, and Vincent H. Resh. 'Assesment Tools For Urban Catchments: Developing Stressor Gradients'. Journal of the American Water Resources Association 45, no. 2 (2009): 291–305.

85
Lee, T.-Y., Y.-T. Shih, J.-C. Huang, S.-J. Kao, F.-K. Shiah, and K.-K. Liu. 'Speciation and Dynamics of Dissolved Inorganic Nitrogen Export in the Danshui River, Taiwan'. Biogeosciences 11, no. 19 (2014): 5307–21

86
Liu, Qianqian, Shaojian Wang, Wenzhong Zhang, and Jiaming Li. 'Income Distribution and Environmental Quality in China: A Spatial Econometric Perspective'. Journal of Cleaner Production 205 (2018): 14–26.

87
Li et.al., 'Spatio-Temporal Assessment', op. cit. (note 21).

88
Cao, Xiaoshu, and Wenyue Yang. 'Examining the Effects of the Built Environment and Residential Self-Selection on Commuting Trips and the Related CO_2 Emissions: An Empirical Study in Guangzhou, China'. Transportation Research Part D-Transport and Environment 52 (2017): 480–94; Song, Siqi, Mi Diao, and Chen-Chieh Feng. 'Individual Transport Emissions and the Built Environment: A Structural Equation Modelling Approach'. Transportation Research Part A-Policy and Practice 92 (2016): 206–19; Travisi, Chiara M., Roberto Camagni, and Peter Nijkamp. 'Impacts of Urban Sprawl and Commuting: A Modelling Study for Italy'. Journal of Transport Geography 18, no. 3 (2010): 382–92; Wang, Mingshu, Marguerite Madden, and Xingjian Liu. 'Exploring the Relationship between Urban Forms and CO_2 Emissions in 104 Chinese Cities'. Journal of Urban Planning and Development 143, no. 4 (2017): 04017014.

89
Iwata and Managi, 'Can Land Use Regulations', op. cit. (note 59); Gan, Mi, Xiaobo Liu, Si Chen, Ying Yan, and Dandan Li. 'The Identification of Truck-Related Greenhouse Gas Emissions and Critical Impact Factors in an Urban Logistics Network'. Journal of Cleaner Production 178 (2018): 561–71

90
Jing, Li, Lo Kevin, Zhang Pingyu, and Guo Meng. 'Relationship between Built Environment, Socio-Economic Factors and Carbon Emissions from Shopping Trip in Shenyang City, China'. Chinese Geographical Science 27, no. 5 (2017): 722–34; Ma, Jing, Zhilin Liu, and Yanwei Chai. 'The Impact of Urban Form on CO_2 Emission from Work and Non-Work Trips: The Case of Beijing, China'. Habitat International 47 (2015): 1–10.

91
Ma et.al., 'The Impact of Urban Form', op. cit. (note 90).

92
Barla, Philippe, Luis F. Miranda-Moreno, Nikolas Savard-Duquet, Marius Theriault, and Martin Lee-Gosselin. 'Diaggregated Empirical Analysis of Determinant of Urban Travel Greenhouse Gas Emissions'. Transportation Research Record, no. 2156 (2010): 160–69.

93
Cao and Yang, 'Examining the Effects', op. cit. (note 88); Ma et.al., 'The Impact of Urban Form', op. cit. (note 90).

between population density and overall emission levels.[99] Thus, despite the reduction *per capita*, the *overall* levels increase in more urban areas, simply because more people live in these areas. This does not, however, mean that if the same population would live in lower densities, emissions would lessen, on the contrary. It does mean, however, that health effects in denser areas can be high, despite the reduced emissions per capita. Finally, carbon sequestration that could help to reduce the overall CO_2 levels was shown to be lowest in developed urban areas and highest in rural areas.[100] In other words, denser areas have less capacity to mitigate the higher emissions.

Density and Micro-Climate

Most papers on micro-climate investigate the urban heat island effect, measured as increased land surface temperature, and report consensus that the more built up the urban area is, the higher its temperature.[101] Besides higher impervious fraction and greater population density, lower tree canopy cover is also considered to be an explanatory variable.[102] An increase in urban vegetation is also shown to lead to the reduction in the number of hot days or the severity of these hot days.[103] The role of vegetation is thus important and because of the collinearity between these two variables, it is often difficult to determine whether cooling effects are caused by lower density or higher green cover.[104] This also indicates that higher density could be mitigated by more urban greening.

Only one paper reports on outdoor ventilation potential, important for human thermal comfort, building cooling, energy saving and pollutant dispersion.[105] This study displays a strong and significant negative correlation between density and wind measured at the pedestrian level.

Social Impact of Density

To discuss the social impact of higher density, we distinguish well-being, social interaction, social equity and crime. The subcategory well-being or quality of life focuses on the individual, while the subcategory social interaction concerns the meeting and interaction between individuals.

94
Zahabi, Seyed Amir H., Luis Miranda-Moreno, Zachary Patterson, and Philippe Barla. 'Impacts of Built Environment and Emerging Green Technologies on Daily Transportation Greenhouse Gas Emissions in Quebec Cities: A Disaggregate Modeling Approach'. Transportation 44, no. 1 (2017): 159–80.

95
Grazi, Fabio, Jeroen C. J. M. van den Bergh, and Jos N. van Ommeren. 'An Empirical Analysis of Urban Form, Transport, and Global Warming'. *Energy Journal* 29, no. 4 (2008): 97–122.

96
Ottelin, Juudit, Jukka Heinonen, and Seppo Junnila. 'Greenhouse Gas Emissions from Flying Can Offset the Gain from Reduced Driving in Dense Urban Areas'. Journal of Transport Geography 41 (2014): 1–9.

97
Norman et.al., 'Comparing High', op. cit. (note 14); Qin, Bo, and Sun Sheng Han. 'Planning Parameters and Household Carbon Emission: Evidence from High- and Low-Carbon Neighborhoods in Beijing'. Habitat International 37 (2013): 52–60; Son, Cheol Hee, Jong In Baek, and Yong Un Ban. 'Structural Impact Relationships Between Urban Development Intensity Characteristics and Carbon Dioxide Emissions in Korea'. Sustainability 10, no. 6 (2018): 1838.

98
Yi, Yanchun, Sisi Ma, Weijun Guan, and Ke Li. 'An Empirical Study on the Relationship between Urban Spatial Form and CO_2 in Chinese Cities'. Sustainability 9, no. 4 (2017): 672.

99
Wang, Yongming, Dianting Wu, Meixia Wang, Li Zhou, and Jianjun Ding. 'Density, Distance, and Division: Rural Poverty in a Developing-Country Context'. Growth and Change 49, no. 3 (2018): 473–89; Zhou, Chunshan, and Shaojian Wang. 'Examining the Determinants and the Spatial Nexus of City-Level CO_2 Emissions in China: A Dynamic Spatial Panel Analysis of China's Cities'. Journal of Cleaner Production 171 (2018): 917–26.

100
Li et.al., 'Spatio-Temporal Assessment', op. cit. (note 21).

101
Balazs, Bernadett, Janos Unger, Tamas Gal, Zoltan Suemeghy, Janos Geiger, and Sandor Szegedi. 'Simulation of the Mean Ur ban Heat Island Using 2D Surface Parameters: Empirical Modelling, Verification and Extension'. Meteorological Applications 16, no. 3 (2009): 275–87; Christen, A., and R. Vogt. 'Energy and Radiation Balance of a Central European City'. International Journal of Climatology 24, no. 11 (2004): 1395–1421; Kamruzzaman, Md, Kaveh Deilami, and Tan Yigitcanlar. 'Investigating the Urban Heat Island Effect of Transit Oriented Development in Brisbane'. Journal of Transport Geography 66 (2018): 116–24; Kuang, Wenhui, Yinyin Dou, Chi Zhang, Wenfeng Chi, Ailin Liu, Yue Liu, Renhua Zhang, and Jiyuan Liu. 'Quantifying the Heat Flux Regulation of Metropolitan Land Use/Land Cover Components by Coupling Remote Sensing Modeling with in Situ Measurement'. Journal of Geophysical Research-Atmospheres 120, no. 1 (2015): 113–30; Yang, Feng, Feng Qian, and Stephen S. Y. Lau. 'Urban Form and Density as Indicators for Summertime Outdoor Ventilation Potential: A Case Study on High-Rise Housing in Shanghai'. Building and Environment 70 (2013): 122–37.

The social impact of densification is primarily negative apart from social equity, with half of the papers reporting a positive relation. For the other three categories, the studies report a negative relation with density in almost half or more than half of the investigations. There are strong indications that the relation is not linear though, meaning that density has a negative but diminishing (that is, nonlinear) effect on well-being and that medium densities are optimal for social interaction.

The impact of density on social equity highlights housing affordability, poverty and inequality as negative, while the fewer positive results relate to reduced polarization. In combination with reduced affordability, this might actually not be as positive as it sounds. Furthermore, density has a predominantly negative impact on crime measured both in terms of crime rates and feeling safe.

Density and Well-being

More than half of the studies report a negative impact of density on well-being, while only 12 per cent report a positive effect. In two papers the findings of a study on self-estimated life satisfaction report non-significant results, which means that the role density plays could not be statistically proven.[106] In most cases, the negative well-being effects are based on studies using quality-of-life indicators,[107] but in some cases more specific indices are used such as children's stress[108] and nuisance.[109] The quality-of-life indicators often include multiple dimensions,[110] but in the end they all come down to the question: How satisfied are you with your life?

One paper reports that results on pride and attachment, stability, safety and home satisfaction display a non-linear relationship with density.[111] The findings suggest that there is a kind of 'density divide' at around 100 to 140 dwellings per hectare after which the declining trend flattens.

Density and Social Interaction

One might expect a positive density effect given that people living in proximity could find interaction easier. However, the results of the review do not confirm this and density has been shown to affect social interaction negatively in almost half of the studies. For instance, how often a person talks with or visits immediate neighbours

102
Trlica, A., L. R. Hutyra, C. L. Schaaf, A. Erb, and J. A. Wang. 'Albedo, Land Cover, and Daytime Surface Temperature Variation Across an Urbanized Landscape'. Earths Future 5, no. 11 (2017): 1084–1101; Zhao, Hongbo, Hao Zhang, Changhong Miao, Xinyue Ye, and Min Min. 'Linking Heat Source-Sink Landscape Patterns with Analysis of Urban Heat Islands: Study on the Fast-Growing Zhengzhou City in Central China'. Remote Sensing 10, no. 8 (2018): 1268.

103
Chen, Dong, Marcus Thatcher, Xiaoming Wang, Guy Barnett, Anthony Kachenko, and Robert Prince. 'Summer Cooling Potential of Urban Vegetation – a Modeling Study for Melbourne, Australia'. Aims Environmental Science 2, no. 3 (2015): 648–67; Zhao et.al., 'Linking Heat Source-Sink', op. cit. (note 102).

104
Yang, Feng, Stephen S. Y. Lau, and Feng Qian. 'Urban Design to Lower Summertime Outdoor Temperatures An Empirical Study on High-Rise Housing in Shanghai'. Building and Environment 46, no. 3 (2011): 769–85.

105
Yang et.al., 'Urban Form and Density', op. cit. (note 101).

106
Arundel, Rowan, and Richard Ronald. 'The Role of Urban Form in Sustainability of Community: The Case of Amsterdam'. Environment and Planning B-Urban Analytics and City Science 44, no. 1 (2017): 33–53; Brown, Zachary S., Walid Oueslati, and Jerome Silva. 'Links between Urban Structure and Life Satisfaction in a Cross-Section of OECD Metro Areas'. Ecological Economics 129 (2016): 112–21.

107
Baldassare, M., and G. Wilson. 'More Trouble In Paradise – Urbanization And The Decline In Suburban Quality-Of-Life Ratings'. Urban Affairs Review 30, no. 5 (1995): 690–708; Fassio, Omar, Chiara Rollero, and Norma De Piccoli. 'Health, Quality of Life and Population Density: A Preliminary Study on "Contextualized" Quality of Life'. Social Indicators Research 110, no. 2 (2013): 479–88; Kytta, Marketta, Maarit Kahila, and Anna Broberg. 'Perceived Environmental Quality as an Input to Urban Infill Policy-Making'. Urban Design International 16, no. 1 (2011): 19–35; Okulicz-Kozaryn, Adam, and Joan Maya Mazelis. 'Urbanism and Happiness: A Test of Wirth's Theory of Urban Life'. Urban Studies 55, no. 2 (2018): 349–64; Shaker et.al., 'The Well-Being of Nations', op. cit. (note 82).

108
Schwirian, KP, AL Nelson, and PM Schwirian. 'Modeling Urbanism – Economic, Social and Environmental-Stress in Cities'. Social Indicators Research 35, no. 2 (1995): 201–23.

109
Cao, Xinyu. 'How Does Neighborhood Design Affect Life Satisfaction? Evidence from Twin Cities'. Travel Behaviour and Society 5 (2016): 68–76.

110
Fassio et.al., 'Health, Quality of Life', op. cit. (note 107).

111
Bramley, Glen, Nicola Dempsey, Sinead Power, Caroline Brown, and David Watkins. 'Social Sustainability and Urban Form: Evidence from Five British Cities'. Environment and Planning A 41, no. 9 (2009): 2125–42.

tends to be lower, not higher, in high-density areas.[112] Furthermore, density is not positively associated with 'community', including perceptions of safety, social interaction and stability.[113] There is only one paper that contradicts these findings and reports that compactness and density is found to have statistically significant direct positive effects on opportunities to meet new people, the number of close relationships and frequency of socializing.[114] Two papers present inconclusive findings on the link between density and social interaction.[115]

In line with the results for well-being, we found proof that the relation between density and social interaction is not linear. Two papers report a non-linear relationship between density and social interaction. For instance, social interaction and group participation tend to improve as density increases up to a medium level, and then fall off at higher levels.[116] Another paper focusing on social interactions in public outdoor spaces reported a higher number of face-to-face social interactions in urban areas and in rural areas, and lower percentages of respondents living in suburban areas.[117] In other words, medium densities seem to perform worse than both low and high ones.

Density and Social Equity

The results of the studies related to social equity are hard to interpret. Although more than half of the papers indicated a positive association with density, even these findings are at times contradicting. The first positive effect reported is that higher densities correlate negatively with price polarization.[118] In other words, in cities of higher density, a smaller disparity between housing unit prices in the centre and the suburbs was found. However, another study reports that housing affordability decreases when density increases.[119] It might thus be that housing prices increase in general in denser cities, which reduces affordability without affecting polarization.

Furthermore, it is shown that higher incomes grow more quickly in denser cities, suggesting a disproportionate agglomeration of incomes in the highest income categories.[120] Another study partly confirms this, but displays that the relationship between density and income segregation follows a quadratic function, first rising, then falling, as densities increase.[121] In other words,

112
Brueckner, Jan K., and Ann G. Largey. 'Social Interaction and Urban Sprawl'. Journal of Urban Economics 64, no. 1 (2008): 18–34; Jun, Hee-Jung, and Misun Hur. 'The Relationship between Walkability and Neighborhood Social Environment: The Importance of Physical and Perceived Walkability'. Applied Geography 62 (2015): 115–24; Nguyen, Doan. 'Evidence of the Impacts of Urban Sprawl on Social Capital'. Environment and Planning B-Planning & Design 37, no. 4 (2010): 610–27.

113
Dempsey et.al., 'The Key to Sustainable', op. cit. (note 24).

114
Mouratidis, Kostas. 'Built Environment and Social Well-Being: How Does Urban Form Affect Social Life and Personal Relationships?' Cities 74 (2018): 7–20.

115
Dave, 'Neighbourhood Density', op. cit. (note 23); Freeman, L. 'The Effects of Sprawl on Neighborhood Social Ties – An Explanatory Analysis'. Journal of the American Planning Association 67, no. 1 (2001): 69–77.

116
Bramley et.al., 'Social Sustainability', op. cit. (note 111).

117
Berg, Pauline van den, Astrid Kemperman, and Harry Timmermans. 'Social Interaction Location Choice: A Latent Class Modeling Approach'. Annals of the Association of American Geographers 104, no. 5 (2014): 959–72.

118
Antoniucci, Valentina, and Giuliano Marella. 'Is Social Polarization Related to Urban Density? Evidence from the Italian Housing Market'. Landscape and Urban Planning 177 (2018): 340–49.

119
Lin et.al., 'Does the Compact-City', op. cit. (note 23).

120
Sarkar, Somwrita, Peter Phibbs, Roderick Simpson, and Sachin Wasnik. 'The Scaling of Income Distribution in Australia: Possible Relationships between Urban Allometry, City Size, and Economic Inequality'. Environment and Planning B-Urban Analytics and City Science 45, no. 4 (2018): 603–22.

segregation is low in low-density regions, highest for moderately dense regions, and somewhat less high in high density regions. Income segregation increased most in regions whose density did not change and less in regions whose density either grew or fell markedly. These findings reinforce the notion that density has competing and contradictory effects on income segregation.[122] In relation to this, low-income households in denser areas are more likely to experience fuel poverty, that is, spending 10 per cent or more of the household income on energy.[123] This reflects the more vulnerable position of low-income households in higher-density environments, which was confirmed by another study where the most important predictor of social equity is the proportion of social housing. It seems that this offers the opportunity to ameliorate some of the negative effects that the market would otherwise deliver to low-income groups in denser cities.

Besides these predominantly negative outcomes in relation to affordability and income segregation, some positive effects are reported as well. First, higher density is found to result in more equal access to services in general,[124] and in the case of schools it is even shown that the distance to a school is inversely correlated with a student's achievements.[125] As distance tends to increase in areas of lower densities, density can thus indirectly be associated positively with student achievements.

121
Pendall, R., and J. I. Carruthers. 'Does Density Exacerbate Income Segregation? Evidence from US Metropolitan Areas, 1980 to 2000'. Housing Policy Debate 14, no. 4 (2003): 541–89.

122
Ibid.

123
Poruschi, Lavinia, and Christopher L. Ambrey. 'Densification, What Does It Mean for Fuel Poverty and Energy Justice? An Empirical Analysis'. Energy Policy 117 (2018): 208–17.

124
Bramley et.al., 'Social Sustainability', op. cit. (note 111).

125
Talen, E. 'School, Community, and Spatial Equity: An Empirical Investigation of Access to Elementary Schools in West Virginia'. Annals of the Association of American Geographers 91, no. 3 (2001): 465–86.

Density and Crime

The relation between crime and density exhibits a negative trend, with an increase in population density yielding an increase in crime.[126] However, the negative relationship is only significant if the neighbourhood or dwelling is *perceived* as crowded with people, but not when density is measured.[127] Because of the low number of papers in this category, we have to be cautious about these results. Furthermore, all results are based on Asian studies only, which makes it hard to say whether these findings are true in non-Asian contexts as well.

126
Dave, 'Neighbourhood Density', op. cit. (note 23); Iwata and Managi, 'Can Land Use Regulations', op. cit. (note 59); Lin and Yang, 'Does the Compact-City', op. cit. (note 23).

127
Dave, 'Neighbourhood Density', op. cit. (note 23).

Density and Health

Studies on the health impact of density are divided into effects on physical health, air-quality related health and psychological health. The health impact of densification is primarily negative, except for its contribution to more physical activity and reduction of obesity. We can thus conclude that higher density has a positive impact on health when it comes to activating the population to walk more, which, in turn, reduces body mass index (BMI) and obesity-related health problems. Also, it is stressed that this is not due to density alone but relates to a higher mixing of functions that support walking.

Health problems related to air pollution increase when density increases in line with the earlier discussion on GHG emissions. The studies also highlight the importance of large green areas surrounding the cities to mitigate air pollution.

Psychological health is also negatively affected by higher density and the role of compactness or lack of open space is shown to play an important role in this.

Density and Physical Health

The studies on the effects of density on physical health can be subdivided into studies related to obesity and physical activity on the one hand, and other physical health issues such as loss of fertility, lung cancer and heat vulnerability on the other. The studies that report a positive impact of higher density are almost all related to the first group, in which increased density is associated with lower rates of automobile use and higher rates of walking, which in turn is associated with a lower BMI.[128] Only in one study was the result found to be statistically insignificant.[129] It is shown that individuals who move to denser neighbourhoods lose weight and the greater the change in density the greater the weight loss.[130] In line with earlier findings, it is merely functional walking that is affected by density and not recreational walking, where the importance of mixed land uses is emphasized to promote all walking, in addition to high density.[131]

Negative impact of density on physical health is reported in four studies that indicate increased heat vulnerability,[132] a higher death rate in relation to epidemics,[133] lower fertility rates[134] and a higher risk for lung cancer.[135] However, in relation to the latter, another study reported that density had no impact.[136] This study investigated many external factors, establishing that it is traffic and not density that plays a significant role in predicting lung cancer incidence. Higher external traffic volume presents a significant association with higher occurrences of lung cancer, while building density was not found significant. Thus, higher densities in combination with lower motorized traffic volumes might not have a negative impact on lung cancer.

In relation to heat vulnerability, it is interesting to point out that both high-rise areas as well as low-rise but dense (compact) areas suffered many heat-related health problems.[137]

128
Frank, Lawrence D., Michael J. Greenwald, Steve Winkelman, James Chapman, and Sarah Kavage. 'Carbonless Footprints: Promoting Health and Climate Stabilization through Active Transportation'. Preventive Medicine 50 (2010): S99–105; Pendola, Rocco, and Sheldon Gen. 'BMI, Auto Use, and the Urban Environment in San Francisco'. Health & Place 13, no. 2 (2007): 551–56; Yamada, Ikuho, Barbara B. Brown, Ken R. Smith, Cathleen D. Zick, Lori Kowaleski-Jones, and Jessie X. Fan. 'Mixed Land Use and Obesity: An Empirical Comparison of Alternative Land Use Measures and Geographic Scales'. Professional Geographer 64, no. 2 (2012): 157–77.

129
Hess, Daniel Baldwin, and Jessica Kozlowski Russell. 'Influence of Built Environment and Transportation Access on Body Mass Index of Older Adults: Survey Results from Erie County, New York'. Transport Policy 20 (2012): 130–39.

130
Plantinga, Andrew J., and Stephanie Bernell. 'The Association between Urban Sprawl and Obesity: Is It a Two-Way Street?' Journal of Regional Science 47, no. 5 (2007): 857–79.

131
Chaix, Basile, Dustin Duncan, Julie Vallee, Anne Vernez-Moudon, Tarik Benmarhnia, and Yan Kestens. 'The "Residential" Effect Fallacy in Neighborhood and Health Studies Formal Definition, Empirical Identification, and Correction'. Epidemiology 28, no. 6 (2017): 789–97; Forsyth et.al., 'Does Residential Density', op. cit. (note 56); Frank, L. D., M. A. Andresen, and T. L. Schmid. 'Obesity Relationships with Community Design, Physical Activity, and Time Spent in Cars'. American Journal of Preventive Medicine 27, no. 2 (2004): 87–96.

132
Kim, Saehoon, and Youngryel Ryu. 'Describing the Spatial Patterns of Heat Vulnerability from Urban Design Perspectives'. International Journal of Sustainable Development and World Ecology 22, no. 3 (2015): 189–200.

133
Li, Ruiqi, Peter Richmond, and Bertrand M. Roehner. 'Effect of Population Density on Epidemics'. Physica A-Statistical Mechanics and Its Applications 510 (2018): 713–24.

134
Sato, Yasuhiro. 'Economic Geography, Fertility and Migration'. Journal of Urban Economics 61, no. 2 (2007): 372–87.

135
Xu, Wangyue, Xiaojing Zhao, and Lan Wang. 'Impact of Built Environment on Respiratory Health: An Empirical Study'. Nano Life 8, no. 2 (June 2018): UNSP 1840001.

136
Wang, Lan, Xiaojing Zhao, Wangyue Xu, Jian Tang, and Xiji Jiang. 'Correlation Analysis of Lung Cancer and Urban Spatial Factor: Based on Survey in Shanghai'. Journal of Thoracic Disease 8, no. 9 (2016): 2626–37.

137
Kim and Ryu, 'Describing the Spatial', op. cit. (note 132).

Density and Air Quality

Eight studies report on the relation between density and air quality with contradictory findings. Three studies report a negative correlation between density and pollutants; the higher the population density, the higher the air pollution regarding NO_2, CO_2 and PM2.5 particle concentration.[138] Also, population-weighted exposures were higher in compact regions than in sprawing regions for both particulate matter and for ozone.[139] However, another study indicated that an increase in population density is associated with a significant decrease in the concentration of pollutants, but emphasized that this might be explained by the amount of green areas also present.[140] This is confirmed in another study, in which results vary across the region. Some urban zones exert a significant influence on air quality due to congestion, but in other zones opposite results occur because of availability of public transport and large green areas surrounding the cities.[141]

Density and Psychological Health

There is strong consensus on the reported negative impact of density on psychological health. Hence, high-density neighbourhoods have more people with stress-related health problems or depression.[142] Noteworthy is the variation in the role of two density measures in one study where the first describes the intensity of the building bulk using floor area ratio (floor space index, FSI) and the second described building coverage ratio (ground space index, GSI).[143] Contrary to the author's assumption, the results disclose that using FSI in the statistical model decreases the correlation compared with using GSI. This means that the compactness of the built fabric or the lack of open space plays an important role, while FSI and building heights play a relatively small role in explaining perceived urban stress.

Spacematrix-Derived Performance Indicators

In the overview of density performance based on empirical studies presented above, few of the studies discuss density using the multiple variables that we propose in this book. In most cases, density is expressed as population density. In some cases, a distinction is made between residential and working population density, which has provided a better understanding of their distinct roles in both the choice between different modes of transport and the explanation of commuting trips and recreational trips.

Some studies do use the measures FSI and GSI, but very few combine them and very few can therefore translate their results into morphological terms. Four findings we presented above are worth repeating though, as for these the link with Spacemate can be made and, thus, the relation with urban form and building type. First, it is shown that built coverage (GSI) tends to exert greater influence on urban vitality than built intensity (FSI), other things

138
Choi, Kwangyul. 'The Influence of the Built Environment on Household Vehicle Travel by the Urban Typology in Calgary, Canada'. Cities 75 (2018): 101–10; Clark, Lara P., Dylan B. Millet, and Julian D. Marshall. 'Air Quality and Urban Form in US Urban Areas: Evidence from Regulatory Monitors'. Environmental Science & Technology 45, no. 16 (2011): 7028–35; Li et.al., 'Spatio-Temporal Assessment', op. cit. (note 21).

139
Schweitzer, Lisa, and Jiangping Zhou. 'Neighborhood Air Quality, Respiratory Health, and Vulnerable Populations in Compact and Sprawled Regions'. Journal of the American Planning Association 76, no. 3 (2010): 363–71.

140
Choi, 'The Influence', op. cit. (note 138); Yuan, Man, Yan Song, and Liang Guo. 'Exploring Determinants of Urban Form in China through an Empirical Study among 115 Cities'. Sustainability 10, no. 10 (2018): 3648.

141
Mou, Yanchuan, Yan Song, Qing Xu, Qingsong He, and Ang Hu. 'Influence of Urban-Growth Pattern on Air Quality in China: A Study of 338 Cities'. International Journal of Environmental Research and Public Health 15, no. 9 (2018): 1805.

142
Chen, Juan, Shuo Chen, and Pierre F. Landry. 'Urbanization and Mental Health in China: Linking the 2010 Population Census with a Cross-Sectional Survey'. International Journal of Environmental Research and Public Health 12, no. 8 (2015): 9012–24; Dave, 'Neighbourhood Density', op. cit. (note 23); Fassio et.al., 'Health, Quality of Life', op. cit. (note 107).

being equal.[144] In terms of Spacemate, this means the solutions that occupy the upper right corner of the diagram ❹. Second, in the case of water management, the lack of pervious surfaces, directly related to the GSI, is the main obstacle and not so much a high FSI.[145] Third, in relation to heat vulnerability, both high-rise areas and low-rise compact areas suffered from many heat-related health problems.[146] In the Spacemate, these two typologies occupy the upper left corner as well as the lower right corner, leaving room for many typologies and densities that are less affected by heat stress. Fourth, stress was reported to increase more due to a high GSI than to a high FSI.

The above shows how we can define areas within the Spacemate that are empirically proven to correlate with certain outcomes. Besides this empirical approach, we can also derive deductively how variables in Spacemate might contribute to certain performances. In Chapter 3 a distinction was made between the variables used to measure density (base land area, network length, gross floor area and built area), the basic density indicators (FSI, GSI and N), and indicators that can be derived from these, such as OSR, L, w and b. The most basic properties of a built environment can be said to already be present in these variables. On many occasions, such basic data as the amount of programme and the use of the ground surface can add to the understanding of an area in a first survey. Through their simplicity, however, they add little to the understanding of a professional familiar with a specific situation. The basic density indices have the ability to convey more than the rather obvious. Building intensity and compactness of an area can be achieved through the density variables and, in combination, a Spacemate description of probable types can be made. The third group, the derived indicators, can be considered as the most basic performance indicators that have the ability to add information to these descriptions, not by adding new variables, but through combining and extracting from the predefined ones.

The very first derived indicator, introduced on page 97, is a description of a property of the built environment, namely its height (L = FSI / GSI). It is an abstract description as it represents an average of a chosen selection and has no intention to be specific to any individual building. As a matter of fact, this indicative property of average descriptions is present on any level of scale. Even for an individual building, a description such as 'six floors' usually fails to respect partial basements, setbacks and accents. Still, we keep using it because of its pragmatic ability to focus on the main issue, temporarily ignoring specificities. This drowning of the particular in the tide of an averaging description is not – as we have earlier emphasized – a specific characteristic of the use of density, but of every representation (drawing, language, and so forth). The indicators derived through density must thus be treated as abstract approximations and used with the knowledge of its indicative and not literal character. Those derived indicators are valuable in comparisons and for gauging trends, not as descriptions of individual components.

143
Knoell, Martin, Katrin Neuheuser, Thomas Cleff, and Annette Rudolph-Cleff. 'A Tool to Predict Perceived Urban Stress in Open Public Spaces'. Environment and Planning B-Urban Analytics and City Science 45, no. 4 (2018): 797–813.

144
Ye et.al., 'How Block Density', op. cit. (note 27).

145
Kim et.al., 'Examining the Impact', op. cit. (note 21); Li et.al., 'Spatio-Temporal Assessment', op. cit. (note 21); Trudeau and Richardson, 'Empirical Assessment', op. cit. (note 21).

146
Kim and Ryu, 'Describing the Spatial Patterns', op. cit. (note 132).

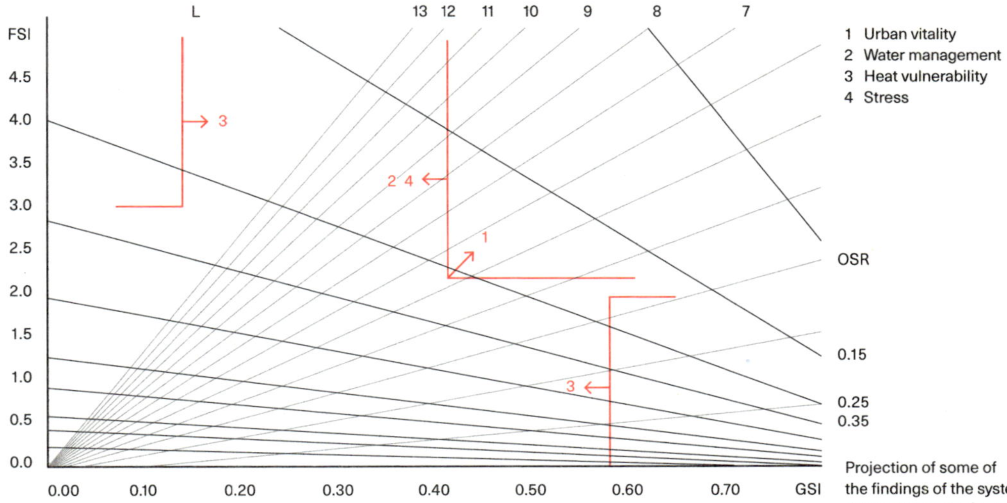

4 Projection of some of the findings of the systematic review in the Spacemate diagram.

Next to the very basic notion of building height introduced in the previous chapter, indicators that depict spaciousness (OSR), and differences between levels of scale (T, or tare) were introduced. Also, two indicators of measurement were suggested that produce an abstract representation of street mesh size (w) and street profile width (b) of a fabric. Other combinations and performances can through creativity and investigation be derived or constructed with the use of the basic density indices FSI, GSI and N.

We will explore five performances: parking, daylight access, noise pollution, air quality and urbanity. This approach could also be extended and applied to many other performances. In all cases, the investigation into the relation between density and performance should always focus on the *conditional* character of density for the performance of the urban landscape. In some cases this conditionality is rather direct and obvious (for example user intensity) and in other cases more concealed (daylight access), but still linked to the physical laws of urban form. Even if weather, pollution and interior decoration affect daylight penetration in dwellings, the urban layout plays an important role in conditioning it.

It is important to emphasize here that the calculations and examples that follow are only intended to identify such conditionalities and uncover trends, and should not be interpreted as directly applicable values. Every concrete situation necessitates a tailor-made approach to take complexity into account. Nevertheless, the formulas and values can be used to support explorative design processes.

Parking

In the current practice of urban planning, parking is often one of the critical bottlenecks. Friction between parking, property and profit is present early in the design process. The point at which it is feasible to opt for a

Zuidwest Kwadrant 3 [NL] $N_f = 0.023$

Zuidwest Kwadrant 2 [NL] $N_f = 0.015$

Parksiedlung Spruch [GER] $N_f = 0.006$

5 Three samples with the same FSI (0.75), but different network density (N) that illustrate the difference in parking performance.

built parking solution instead of public parking on the street is very important as the costs for built parking solutions are generally high and profits are rather low. Furthermore, the potential to create high-quality public pedestrian space in a dense urban setting is dependent on the number of cars on the streets, both moving and parked. Alexander defines a threshold density of 75 parking places per hectare, which means that about 10 per cent of the land is consumed by parking.[147] The basic question posed here is in what way the conditions created by the urban layout (network density and street width) and the amount of building bulk (FSI) determine the parking performance on public streets and on private islands.

147
Alexander, 'Density Measures', op. cit. (note 5), 121.

An initial rough estimate of the parking performance of an area can be undertaken if we relate total programme (FSI_f) to the amount of network (N_f). The first, programme, generates a need for parking, while the second, network, can accommodate all or a part of this need. Three examples are used to help explain the logic of this relation. (5) All three areas have the same FSI on the scale of the fabric but have been realized within different network layouts. In the first example much of the network is used to access the buildings. In the second example, less network is available, and the last example has only a quarter of the amount of network of the first one.

The general parking performance under different density conditions can thus be described in terms of the capacity of the network to accommodate parked cars. This Parking Performance Index (PPI) can be defined as the amount of the parking capacity of the network that is needed for parking:

(20) PPI = Parking need / Parking capacity

A PPI larger than 1.0 means that the capacity is insufficient and a PPI less than 1.0 that the need can be accommodated for by the network. In what follows we will define the two components, capacity and need, more precisely to arrive at a variable description of the parking performance that can be used to assess plans and reveal trends.

Capacity of the Network

First, the capacity of the network has to be determined. Depending on the length and the width of the network, a certain number of cars can, in theory, be parked in this network. The logic of this relationship is rather simple: a fabric with the network density N_f has a certain street length with the average width, b, that can accommodate the parking need generated by the floor space, F, of the same area, A. Two issues are of importance for the capacity of the network: the number of crossings and the possible parking layouts. A specific area has a certain amount of network, described by its network density, N_f. The higher the network density, the more street length is present in that area. Not all of this network, however, can be used for parking. For every crossing the potential parking length is reduced. The resulting density of the network with a potential for parking, N_p, can be described as follows:

21 $$N_p = l_p / A_f$$

l_p = network with parking potential (m)

N_p can be expressed in terms of network density and profile width, tare and privately issued land (PIL), as follows (see pages 231–233 for details):

22 $$N_p = N_f(1 - b \times N_f / 2)$$

23 $$N_p = N_f \times \sqrt{(1 - T_f)}$$

24 $$N_p = N_f \times \sqrt{(PIL)}$$

The capacity of the remaining network to accommodate parked cars depends furthermore on the chosen parking solution. For instance, a layout where cars are parked on one side along the street can accommodate 0.2 cars per metre of network.[148] We can call this the minimum option. The maximum option consists of cars parked on both sides of the street, perpendicular to the street. This results in a maximum capacity of 0.8 cars per metre of network.[149] This varying form factor, r_p, determines the parking capacity on the micro scale. It must of course be chosen bearing the total street width, b, in mind. A maximum solution with double perpendicular parking lots demands a profile width of at least 20.4 m.[150] On the other hand, with only one line of parked cars along the street, the total width might be as little as 12.6 m. The threshold values for r_p used here come from the Stichting Architectuur Research.[151] 6

Parking layout:

- One sided, adjacent
  $r_p = 0.2$ parking lots/m (b > 12.60m)
- Two sided, adjacent
  $r_p = 0.4$ parking lots/m (b > 14.40m)
- One sided, perpendicular
  $r_p = 0.4$ parking lots/m (b > 15.60m)
- Two sided, one adjacent, one perpendicular
  $r_p = 0.6$ parking lots/m (b > 17.40m)
- Two sided, perpendicular
  $r_p = 0.8$ parking lots/m (b > 20.40m)

148
Parking space 2.5 × 5 m, i.e. one parking space in 5 m / 1 / 5 = 0.2 / m.

149
Parking space 2.5 × 5 m, i.e. two parking spaces in 2.5 m / 2.5 / 2 = 0.8 / m.

150
For this example, the profile studies by Stichting Architectuur Research have been used. See Stichting Architectuur Research, Deciding on Density: An Investigation into High Density Allotments with a View to the Waldeck Area, The Hague (Eindhoven, 1977).

151
Ibid., 50.

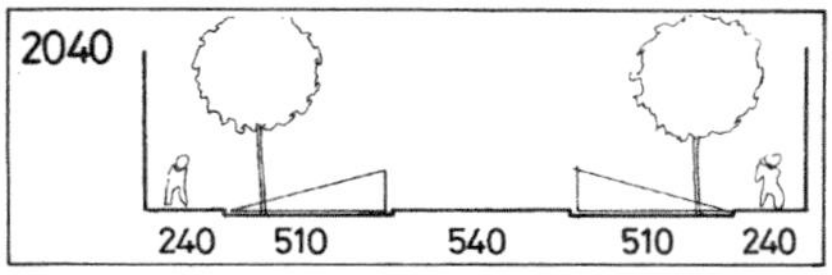

Two-sided parking, perpendicular
r_p = 0.8 parking lots/m (b > 20.40m)

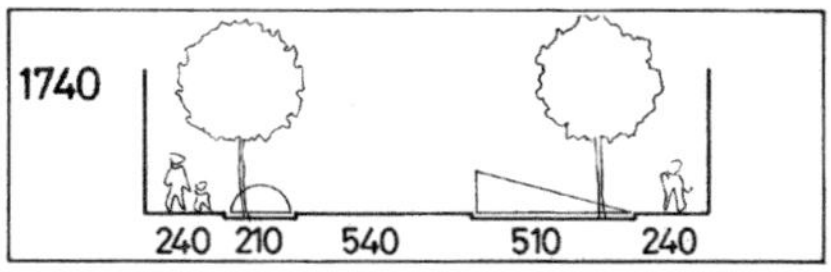

Two-sided parking, adjacent and perpendicular
r_p = 0.6 parking lots/m (b > 17.40m)

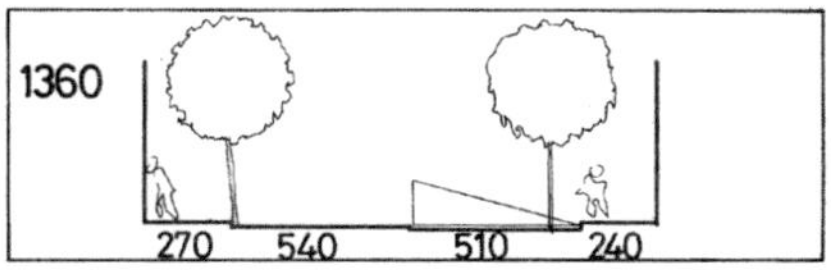

One-sided parking, perpendicular
r_p = 0.4 parking lots/m (b > 15.60m)

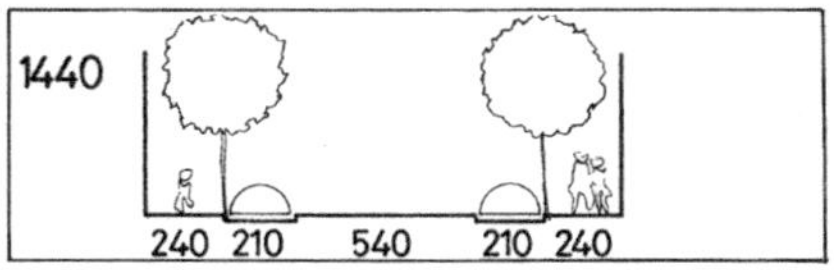

Two-sided parking, adjacent
r_p = 0.4 parking lots/m (b > 14.40m)

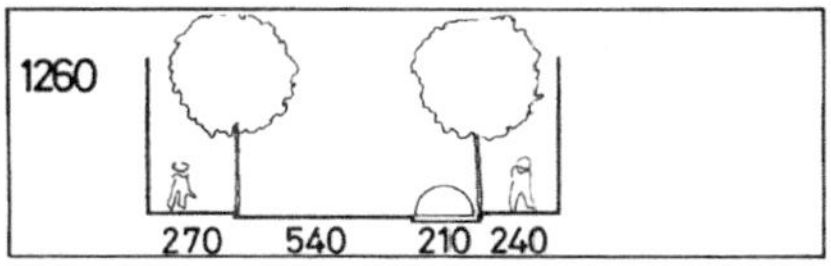

One-sided parking, adjacent
r_p = 0.2 parking lots/m (b > 12.60m)

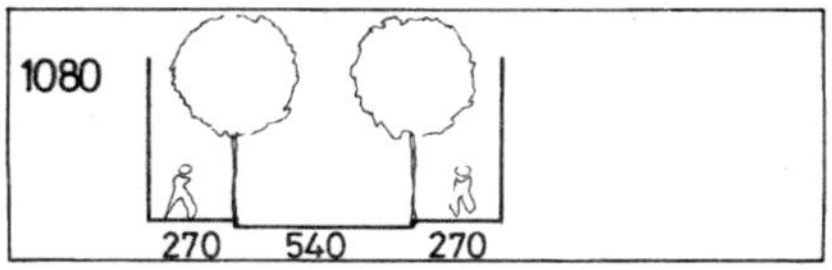

No parking

6 Threshold values for different r_p values; based on starting points defined by SAR in Deciding on Density (SAR 1977: 50).

The capacity of the public network to accommodate parked vehicles, expressed as the potential amount of parking lots per m² of a plan area (/m²) can now be described as:

25 $$\text{Parking capacity (per m}^2) = r_p \times N_f \times \sqrt{(1 - T_f)}$$

or

26 $$\text{Parking capacity (per hectare)} = 10{,}000 \times r_p \times N_f \times \sqrt{(1 - T_f)}$$

Parking Need

The other part necessary to indicate the parking performance of an area is the parking need generated by the traffic. Part of this is generated by external traffic (visitors, for instance) but most of the need will be generated by homes and work places in the area (except for areas dominated by shopping centres, cultural centres or other large attractors). In other words, the parking need is largely generated by the floor area, which can be expressed in terms of FSI. For housing the required parking can either be related to the number of dwellings or to the amount of floor area. In the last case this is mostly expressed as the number of parking places per 100 m² of floor area. For offices and other work places norms are often used that relate the required parking to floor area.

In its simplest form the parking need of a plan area can be expressed as follows:

(27) $$\text{Parking need} = FSI_f \times n_p / 100$$

n_p = the number of parking spaces needed for every 100 m^2 of floor area.

In most cases the total programme of a fabric, FSI_f, is composed of different functions (houses, work places, services, etcetera). Different parking norms can be defined for every separate programme and different values can even be defined for different types of housing. In the event of a programmatic spread (functional mix) we can define the needed parking as follows:

(28) $$\text{Parking need} = FSI_f \times (x_a \times n_{pa} + \ldots + x_z \times n_{pz}) / 10{,}000$$

x_a = the percentage of programme a;
n_{pa} = the number of parking spaces needed for every 100 m^2 of floor space with programme a.[152]

152 Example of parking norms used by Goudappel-Coffeng for a project in Hoorn in 2008: 1.6 parking spaces per dwelling (including visitors), 4 parking spaces per 100 m² of shop space, 2 parking spaces per 100 m² of office space.

Parking Performance Index

The thresholds where public parking will become problematic or, more importantly, when built parking solutions will be necessary, can be derived from the combination of need and capacity. We can now return to (20) and compose the Parking Performance Index, PPI, by inserting (23) and (27) in (20):

(29) $$PPI = (FSI_f \times n_p) / [100 \times r_p \times N_f \times \sqrt{(1 - T_f)}]$$

Values of PPI lower than 1.0 mean that the network can accommodate the generated parking need with the chosen parking solution. If the PPI exceeds 1.0 this means that the capacity of the network is too low or that the required number of parking spaces is too high (too many cars for too few parking lots). The value of the index also gives an idea of how dominant parking will be in the street. For instance, a PPI of 0.6 means that there is an overcapacity and only 60 per cent of the network will be needed for parking in the chosen layout. In the case that the PPI exceeds 1.0 we can choose to either change the norm; create more capacity by adding more network; add parking on the island (surface or underground); choose another parking layout (perpendicular instead of parallel, for instance); or decrease the built programme. A combination of all these measures could also be applied.

The maximum programme that can be realized in an area before built parking will be necessary is:

(30) $$FSI_{max} = 100 \times PPI \times r_p \times N \times \sqrt{(1 - T_f)} / n_p$$

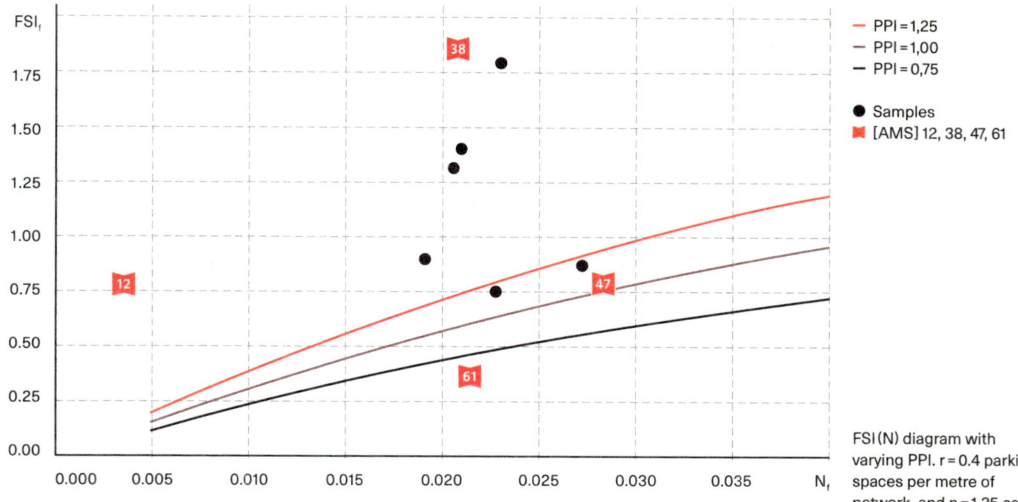

7 FSI (N) diagram with varying PPI. r = 0.4 parking spaces per metre of network, and n = 1.25 car per 100 m^2 of floor space.

In this case the value of n_p has to be adapted to the theoretical street width, b. The choice for a value for PPI determines the acceptable amount of parked cars in the street space.

An indication of the performance concerning surface parking can be derived through positioning some of the empirical samples in a FSI (N) diagram. 7 shows a situation where a parking capacity of 0.4 parking spaces per metre of network and 1.25 cars per 100 m^2 of floor space has been handled to construct thresholds for a specific parking layout (r_n = 0.4; n_p = 1.25). Only those samples with a theoretical street width of around 15 m have been used. Samples located under the black line (PPI = 0.75) have little problem solving all the parking along the network. Between this line and the next continuous line (PPI = 1), more than 75 per cent of the streets are taken up by parking and the car thus dominates public space. A position above this line implies that there is too much programme and/or too little network realized to solve the parking in the network. In such cases the excess need can be accommodated by parking on private land (surface or underground), or by accepting a less generous parking norm (a lower value for n_p). However, if the performance is satisfactory, meaning that PPI < 1, views can still vary as to whether this is acceptable or not. Some might find it too crowded with cars; others could claim that the norm is too low and would prefer at least 2 cars per 100 m^2 of floor space instead of 1.25.

In the example described above the chosen parking layout was two-sided parallel parking (or one-sided perpendicular) with r_p = 0.4. 8 shows the maximum FSI for different parking layouts and PPI = 1.0. A higher network density, or smaller islands, allows for a higher FSI. The slightly curved lines of the figure are due to an increased number of crossings as the network density increases. The three examples used in the beginning of this paragraph are positioned in the diagram to illustrate the relation between FSI and N, and parking performance. From the graph it is obvious that in

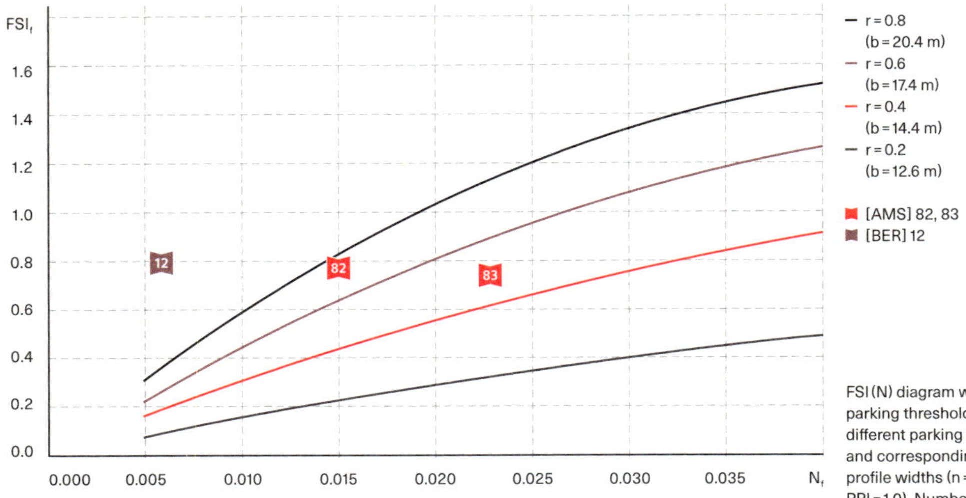

8

FSI (N) diagram with parking thresholds for different parking layouts and corresponding profile widths (n = 1.25; PPI = 1.0). Numbers refer to samples in 5.

the first sample, Zuidwest Kwadrant 3 (83 in 8), all parking can easily be solved on the streets and that the second, Zuidwest Kwadrant 2 82, needs the entire street capacity for parking (two-sided, perpendicular). The last sample, Parksiedlung Spruch 12, cannot solve the parking need in the public street, and a large underground parking garage has been constructed to accommodate the cars. The diagram is here used to evaluate three built environments, but could also be used to guide the design process. Based on, for instance, a given programme (FSI_f) street profile, and the goal to accommodate all the required parking space on the streets, the most efficient network density can be derived from the diagram.

Thresholds of Parking

The thresholds of surface parking are important, particularly for low-rise developments as built parking solutions are mostly unfeasible here. As shown above, the capacity of the network to accommodate the parking need generated by the dwellings depends on the network density and the width of the street profile that determines the possible parking layout options. There are many variables that are interdependent of each other and that together determine the parking performance. To better understand the relationship between these variables another trend can be gauged with the help of the earlier used N (b)-diagram. In the diagram in 9 the gradient is drawn of the maximum FSI that can be realized if the entire capacity of the network is used (PPI = 1). The diagram conveys the situation of one-sided parking, adjacent to the street ($r_p = 0.2$ and thus starting at a street width of 12.6 m). The maximum FSI for other parking solutions can be derived using the formula 30. The diagram in 10 shows how the continuously increasing profile width brings with it a sudden jump in capacity when enough measure (street width) allows for a parking layout with larger capacity (r_p increases from 0.2 to 0.4, from 0.4 to 0.6, etcetera).[153]

153 Next to the capacity of the streets, the islands can also offer additional parking space within the non-built parts of the island or with built parking garages. The extra parking needed in the case that the PPI for the fabric exceeds 1.0 (= shortage) can be expressed as $PPI_p = 20 \times [FSI_f \times n_p / 100 - r_p \times N \times \sqrt{(1 - T_f)}] / (1 - T_f)$, where PPI_p = the percentage of the privately available land (uitgeefbaar) needed for parking.

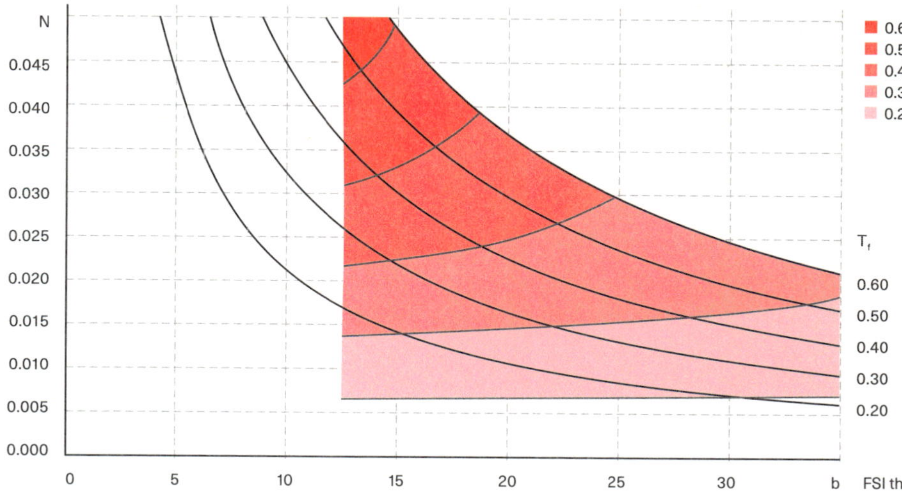

9 FSI threshold values for $r_p = 0.2$ (one sided, adjacent parking, b > 12.6 m) (PPI = 1).

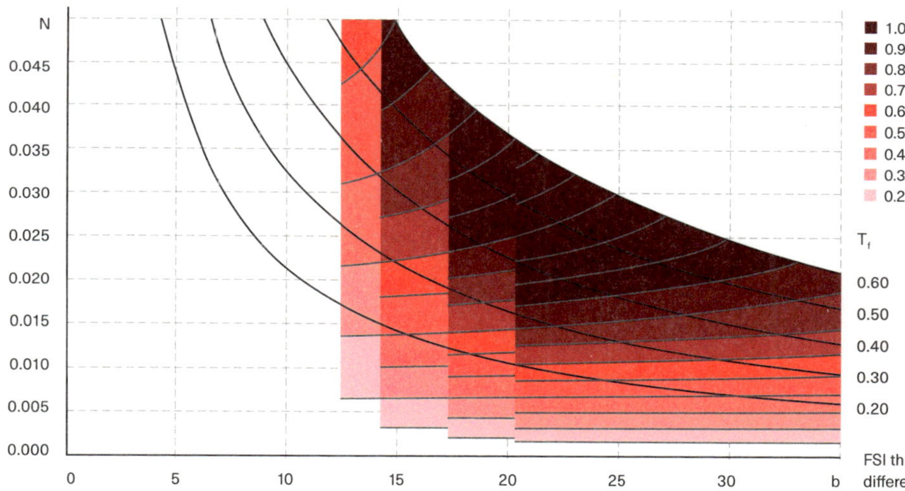

10 FSI threshold values for different r_p values (from 0.2 to 0.4, from 0.4 to 0.6, etc.) (PPI = 1).

Daylight[154]

This section serves to unravel some of the conditional aspects of density on the daylight performance of the urban fabric. In what follows, we will conclude that OSR plays a very central role herein. The uncovered correlation between OSR and daylight performance can be seen as rehabilitating this indicator of spaciousness and, with hindsight, credit Hoenig for his aspiration to create a qualitative spatial indicator. The daylight performance, this section will show, can be integrated with the Spacemate, making it possible to gauge this performance in the interior, the exterior and for different floor levels of a section.

Daylight and solar radiation have a great impact on the climate in the city, both in the interior of buildings and in public space. Furthermore, the

154 Parts of this paragraph use results from a research project on which the chairs of architecture, urbanism and building technology have been cooperating (financed by Verrijking door Samenwerking at Delft University of Technology, 2004). The project is described in Haupt, P. and M. van Esch, 'Daylight and Urban Density', in: H. Bekkering et al. (eds.), The Architectural Annual 2005–2006, Delft University of Technology (Rotterdam: 010 Publishers, 2007), 86–91.

potential to create high-quality interiors in a dense urban situation is dependent on the amount of daylight that is allowed to penetrate the interiors of the buildings. With enough artificial light, anything goes, but if daylight is considered essential to human well-being and an important ingredient for high spatial qualities and energy saving, the daylight intensity of the exterior and interior of the urban fabric has a strong influence on the limits of density and building types. The basic question posed in this section is to what degree the conditions created by the amount of *programme* (FSI) and *primary distribution* – coverage (GSI) and building height (L) – determine the daylight performance in the urban exterior and the architectural interior. If this is substantial, how great is the influence of *secondary distribution* – in this case building depth – compared to these basic conditions? This part of the research employs both deduction and data from DIALux[155] simulations. The focus here is on indirect daylight and not on solar radiation and shading.

155
DIALux was originally a simulation program for artificial light, but since 2007 daylight simulation has been added (see www.dialux.com).

Daylight performance is, on the one hand, a result of a series of reductions of daylight access and on the other, an increase of light through reflections. The reduction of daylight in the interior can be described as a situation in which the sky is gradually obstructed by the ceiling, neighbouring buildings, the partitioning walls of the interior, and finally by the façade covering the interior. The daylight performance of the exterior (street, courtyard) is primarily influenced by the street (or courtyard) profile properties, defined as the distance between buildings and the height of those buildings. The loss of daylight can in both cases partly be compensated by reflections through the texture and colour of interior and exterior surfaces (ground, walls and façades).

The most basic situation in the section was examined to illustrate how the daylight performance of the exterior and the interior of buildings differs in situations with varying FSI and GSI. It represents only a partial description of the urban fabric but it does have the advantage of providing a manageable amount of information and variables. The conclusions on the performance of the sections should not be extrapolated into general conclusions on urban fabrics, but they certainly do indicate trends and can be used as a guide for further investigation of urban fabrics in all its dimensions.

Any Light versus No Light

In its most simplistic form, the daylight performance can be described as the percentage of the total floor area that is exposed to the sky and thus lit. Daylight performance in general can be described by the Daylight Performance Index, DPI_n. The notation n indicates the value of the Daylight Factor (daglichtfactor), DF, which expresses the quotient between the light intensity (lux) at a certain point and the light intensity in a non-obstructed situation in 'the open field'. In an open field, no obstructions are present and DF is 100. In a compact alley DF might decrease to 30, and at a point a couple of metres behind the façade, this value might be reduced to 3. This means that the intensity of the daylight in the alley of this example is 30 per cent of the intensity that we could measure – and experience – in an open, non-obstructed field. In the interior this is further reduced to just 3 per cent of the open-field situation.

DPI_0 describes the daylight performance by comparing areas with a Daylight Factor of any value above zero with all of the available floor area. DPI_0 thus only makes a distinction between areas exposed to daylight ($DF > 0$) and dark (non-exposed) areas ($DF = 0$). A DPI_0 of 100 (or more) means that all of the floor area is exposed to some amount of daylight.

For a section without interior walls and with no reflection (which we can call the urban casco), the consequences for the daylight performance on the ground floor, the floor level with the least daylight, have been examined using a series of variations. ⓫ In the first series (A), the amount of programme is changed while the ground coverage remains constant. This means that the GSI has been kept constant as FSI and L vary. The second series (B) describes different primary distributions. In this case, the amount of programme, or FSI, remains the same, and the ground coverage and height differ.

The results for the different scenarios have been arrived at through simulations with DIALux and with calculations. ⓬ shows that the performance is proportionally inverted to the FSI, or the amount of programme. More programme means less daylight on the ground floor. This conclusion could in most cases be made based on individual experience, but the non-linear character of the trend is difficult to unravel purely by intuition and practical experience. The rate of decrease is high when the FSI is low and slows down when the FSI becomes higher.

This demonstrates the relationship of daylight performance to the amount of programme, but how does the primary distribution of this programme influence the daylight performance? If a comparison is made between situations with the same FSI (amount of programme), but with differing GSI (coverage), the trend is also one of decline. A distribution with high buildings and low GSI has a better performance than low buildings with less distance between each building, and thus a high GSI, although they both accommodate the same amount of programme (FSI).

The formula for the geometry of the section that combines these trends can be expressed as follows:[156]

㉛ $$DPI_0 = 200(1 - GSI) / (FSI - GSI)$$

This formula shows that for the section, the percentage of floor surface exposed to *any* daylight (DPI_0) can be described purely with density variables. The diagrams in ⓬ show the correlation between theory (formula 31) and computer simulations with DIALux.

Two other series of transformation, regarding the distribution of building mass with a constant Spacemate density, have been studied to understand the influence of the secondary distribution on daylight performance. If a

156 For an extensive argumentation of the construction of the formulae, see pages 231–233.

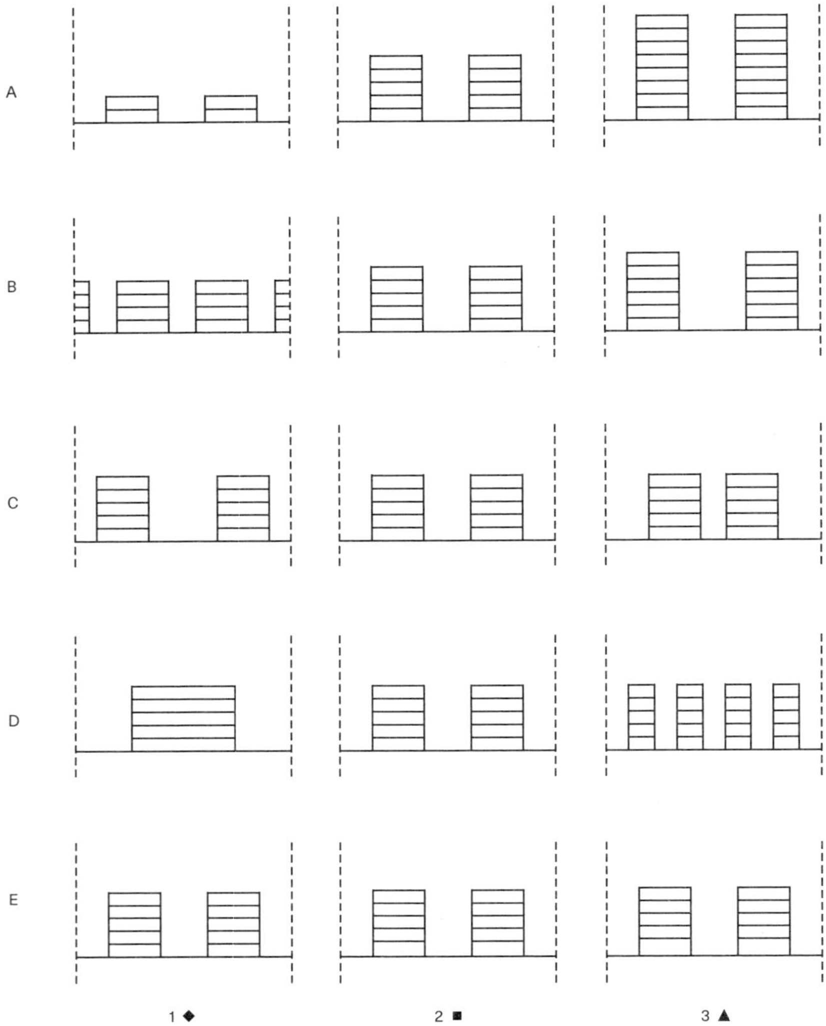

A GSI constant, FSI variable
B FSI constant, GSI variable
C GSI and FSI constant, position variable
D GSI and FSI constant, building depth variable
E GSI and FSI constant, height of ground floor variable

11 Series of transformations.

situation with a constant distance between buildings is compared to a situation where the street width differs from the size of the courtyards, it appears that the daylight performance remains constant. (Series C in 11, and left diagram in 13) Also when deep buildings, placed at great distance from each other, are compared to slender buildings close to each other, no difference in performance occurs. (Series D in 11) This further confirms the conclusion that daylight performance to a large extent is conditioned by density, that is, FSI and GSI.

Finally, the influence of the floor height has been investigated. The above formula 31 can be transformed into:

32 $$DPI_0 = 200 \times h_n(1 / GSI - 1) / H$$

h_n = the floor height on the nth floor (m);
H = the remaining building height above the nth floor (m).

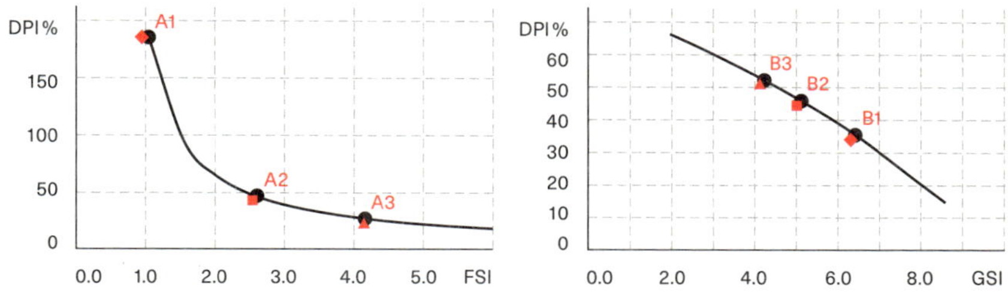

12 Results of calculations and simulations for series A (left) and B (right).

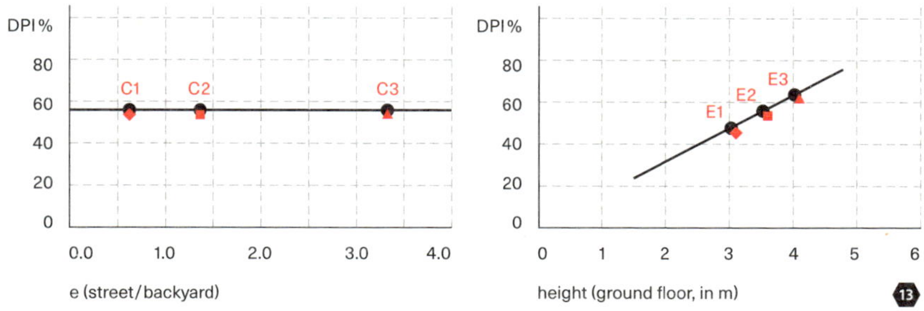

13 Series of calculations and simulations for series C (left) and E (right).

Here we can see that the daylight performance is directly proportional to the height of the floor considered. This is also confirmed by DIALux simulations. (Series E in 11, and right diagram in 13)

Real Levels of Daylight

Up to now the position of zero lux (or DF = 0) in the interior has been used to trace density trends. This, of course, is not very relevant to the real situation where sufficient levels of daylight for different activities are used. For instance, DF = 0.5 can at the latitude of the Netherlands be considered enough for a human being to be able to orientate in a room, DF = 2.5 is required to read and do paperwork, and, if this is done during the whole day, DF = 5 is preferable.[157] It should be noted, however, that the absolute values of the intensity greatly varies during the day, and are dependent on the season and geographical position. A Daylight Factor of 60 at a specific position, on the other hand, means that the daylight intensity at this position will always be 60 per cent of the open field intensity: 60 per cent of the low intensity on a clouded and grey afternoon, but likewise 60 per cent of the intensity on a clear summer noon. The Daylight Factor thus describes a property of a building and its environment itself, no matter if it is the sun or the moon that is shining (or not).

Besides these objections with respect to the performance of the interior, the intensity in the exterior (streets and courtyards) also needs to be scrutinized based on real values and levels of acceptance. An exterior with no light, DF = 0, does not exist (otherwise it would by definition not be an exterior), but still, there are of course variations in the intensity of the daylight at the exterior.

157 NEN 12464–1:2002 Light and lighting – Lighting of work places – Part 1: Indoor work places (NEN 2003). For office work 500 lux is recommended and for most home activities between 200 and 300 lux is recommended. The DF thresholds are based on a conservative estimation of an intensity of 10.000 lux in the open field through which we arrive at a Daylight Factor of 5 for office work and 2.5 for home activities.

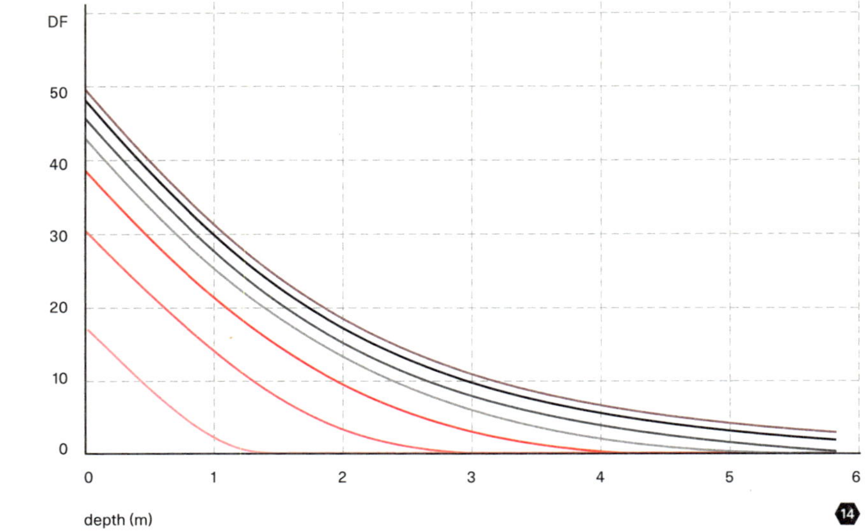

Simulations of the different intensities at the interior with different degrees of obstruction (street width).

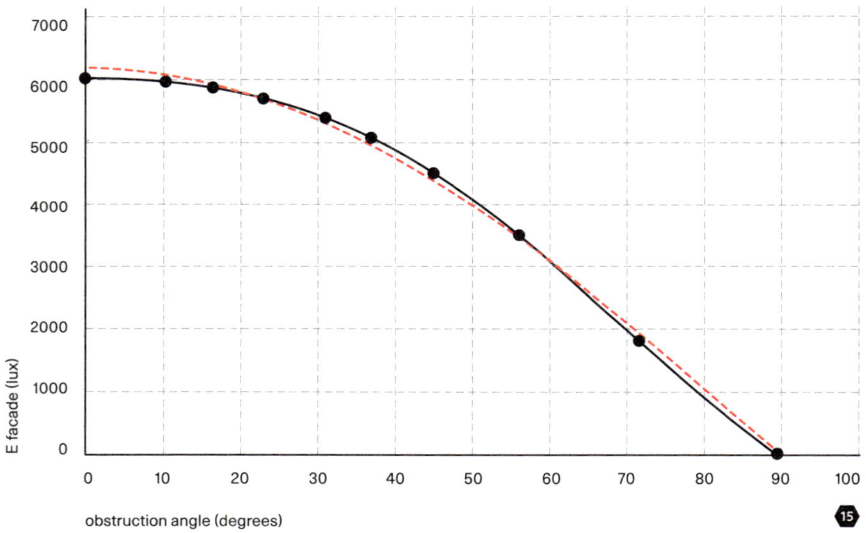

The trend at the façade can quite accurately be described by a cosine function.

To expand the discussion to real levels of daylight, we start by looking at the distribution of daylight in the interior. (14) shows the different intensities in the interior with different degrees of obstruction. In the diagram, the distance of an obstructing object varies between 5 and 80 m. If the different intensities at the façade are related to the angle of obstruction, a diagram as shown in (15) can be constructed. This shows a trend that quite accurately can be described by a cosine function. At the façade, with no external obstruction, the intensity is half of the intensity in the open field, or, DF = 50. (16) This means that the intensity at the façade as a function of the angle of obstruction, $DF_f(\alpha_f)$, can be described as follows:

(33) $$DF_f = 50 \times \cos \alpha_f$$

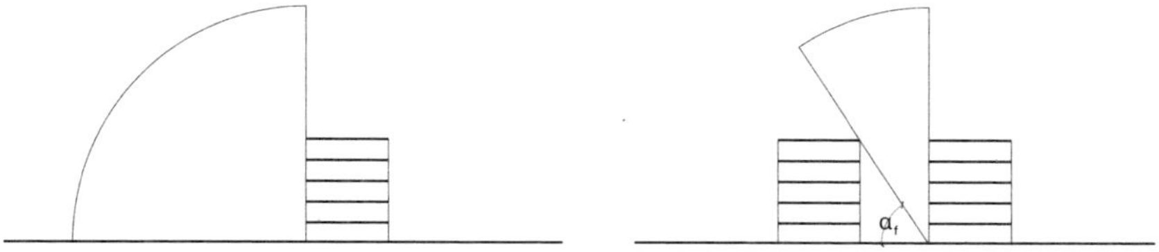

16 Contribution of the sky to the intensity at the façade without (left) and with (right) external obstruction.

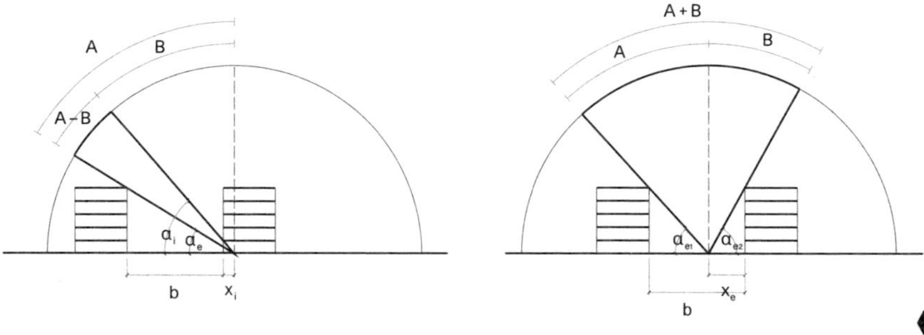

17 Contribution of the sky to the intensity in the interior, A − B (left); and exterior, A + B (right).

To be able to describe the intensity at any other position than the façade, we must take into account both the *internal angle of obstruction* (α_i) and the *external angle of obstruction* (α_e). The gap between these two, the *daylight angle,* determines the intensity at a random point in the interior.

It can be shown, by using 33 that the Daylight Factor, DF_i, at a point in the interior of the building at a distance x_i from the façade can be determined by $DF_i = 50 \times (\cos\alpha_e - \cos\alpha_i)$, where α_e is the external angle, and α_i the internal angle of obstruction. For the exterior, the formula changes into $DF_e = 50 \times (\cos\alpha_{e1} + \cos\alpha_{e2})$, where α_{e1} and α_{e2} are the two exterior angles of obstruction.

The daylight factor at the distance x from the façade for interior (DF_i) and exterior (DF_e) thus becomes:

34 $$DF_i = 50 \times (\cos\alpha_e - \cos\alpha_i)$$

35 $$DF_e = 50 \times (\cos\alpha_{e1} + \cos\alpha_{e2})$$

The different angles can be derived through the geometry of the section 17:

$$\tan\alpha_e = L \times h / (b + x_i)$$

$$\tan\alpha_i = h / x_i$$

$$\tan\alpha_{e1} = L \times h / (b - x_e)$$

$$\tan\alpha_{e2} = L \times h / x_e$$

It now becomes possible to continuously describe the daylight factor at every position through the section:

36 $$DF_i = 50 \times \{\cos[\arctan(L \times h / (b + x_i))] - \cos[\arctan(h / x_i)]\}$$

37 $$DF_e = 50 \times \{\cos[\arctan(L \times h / (b - x_e))] + \cos[\arctan(L \times h / x_e)]\}$$

L = number of floors;
h = average floor height (m);
b = profile width (m);
x_i = distance from façade, interior (m);
x_e = distance from façade, exterior (m).

Based on these formulae the Daylight Factor has been calculated for three sections in which the street width and GSI remain constant ($b = 12$ m, and GSI = 0.5), but the programme – and thus building height – vary: FSI = 1.0 and $L = 2$; FSI = 1.5 and $L = 3$; and FSI = 3.0 and $L = 6$. The Daylight Factor through the section is represented in 18.

For the series A to D that were described earlier, the trends for real values can now be studied, both for the interior and the exterior. Diagrams in 19 show that the decrease of the Daylight Factor on the exterior follows the same trend as the interior, both in its dependency on the FSI and the GSI. In addition to this, the real values for the interior can be compared to the simulated and theoretical result for DPI_0 that were shown in 12. They are, as could be expected, lower, but follow the same trends. 20

This continuous description of the light intensity for the exterior and the interior shows how daylight performances of built space can be described. Depending on the programmatic requirements one can for an interior define the required minimum Daylight Factor for an activity or programme, and the desired amount of surface with that minimum Daylight Factor in relation to all built surface. In housing, for example, one could define the required Daylight Factor for served areas (e.g. living room, kitchen) as at least 2.5, and attempt to have a minimum of 60 per cent of the floor area at such levels. This means that $DPI_{2.5}$ should be larger than 60. The remaining 40 per cent would then be suitable for circulation, service spaces, storage, and so forth.

With the use of practical levels of daylight intensity the building depth becomes essential to the practical performance of the interior, whereas this is of no relevance to the theoretical approach of zero lux (DPI_0). In an unobstructed situation the theoretical DPI_0 will always be 100 per cent, whatever depth the building might have. However, when we gauge practical values, such as $DF > 5$, there are limitations. This can be explained by the above formula 36 and is also easy to confirm with simulations. For a floor height of 3 m this means that a Daylight Factor larger than 5 can never be reached at

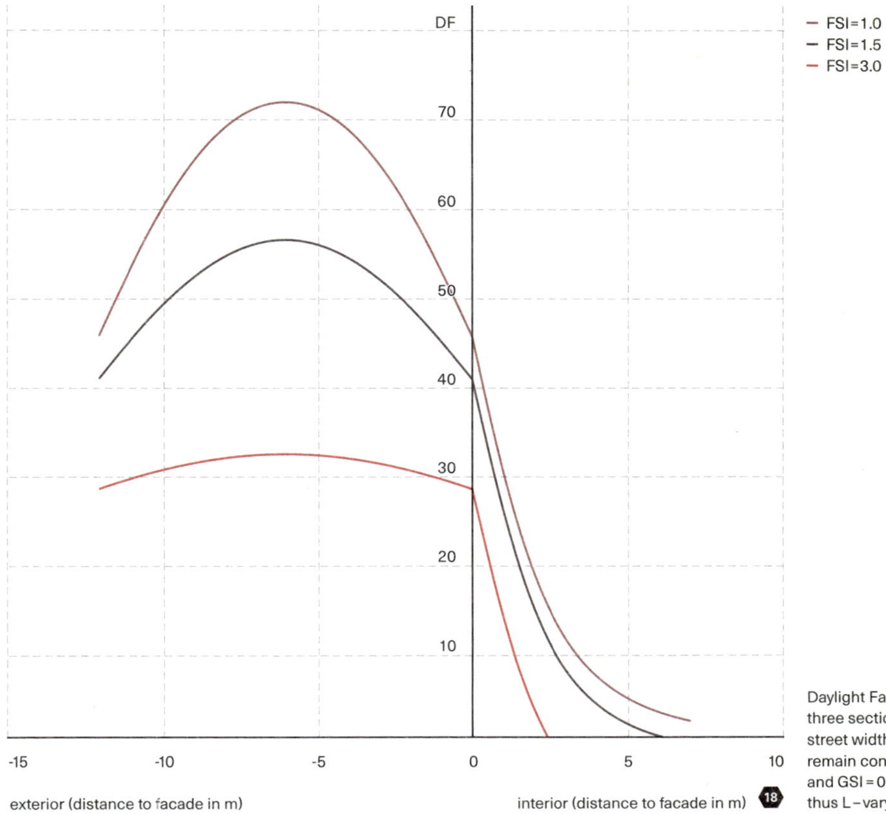

18

Daylight Factor (DF) for three sections in which the street width and GSI remain constant (b = 12 m and GSI = 0.5), but FSI – and thus L – vary.

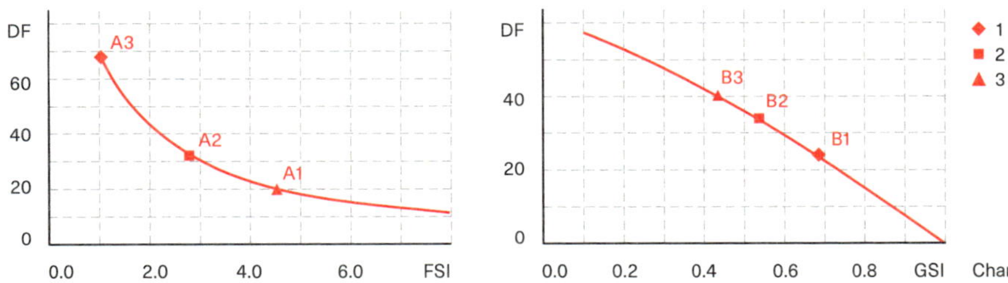

19

Changes in Daylight Factor in the exterior for series A (left) and B (right) in 11.

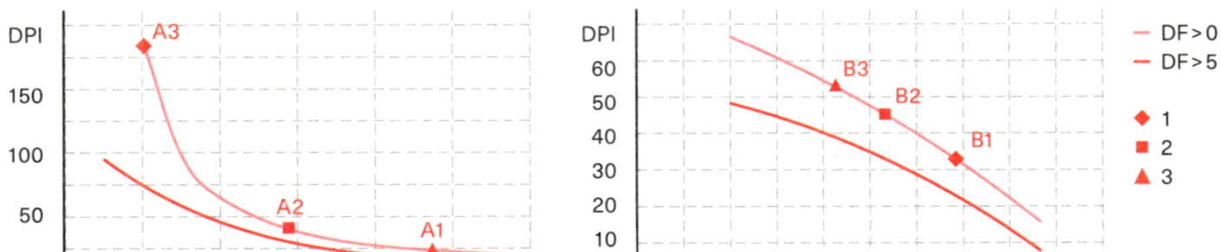

Practical values (DF > 5) in the interior for series A (left) and B (right) in 11.

20

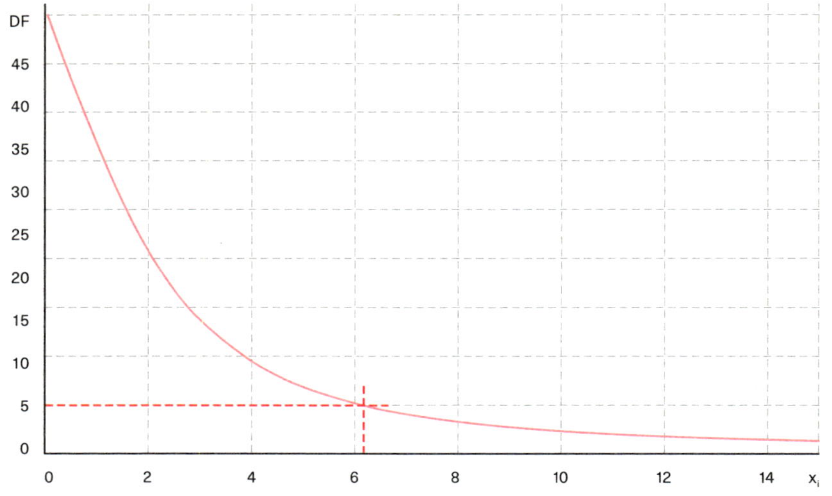

21

Situation with no external obstruction. A Daylight Factor larger than 5 can never be reached at a greater distance than 6 m from the facade (h = 3 m).

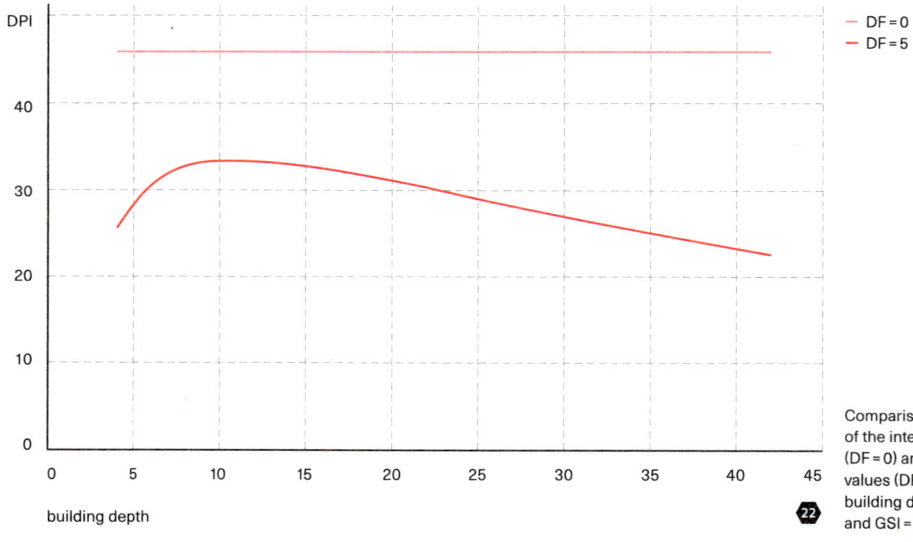

22

Comparison of DPI of the interior in theory (DF = 0) and for real values (DF > 5) for different building depths (FSI = 2.6, and GSI = 0.5).

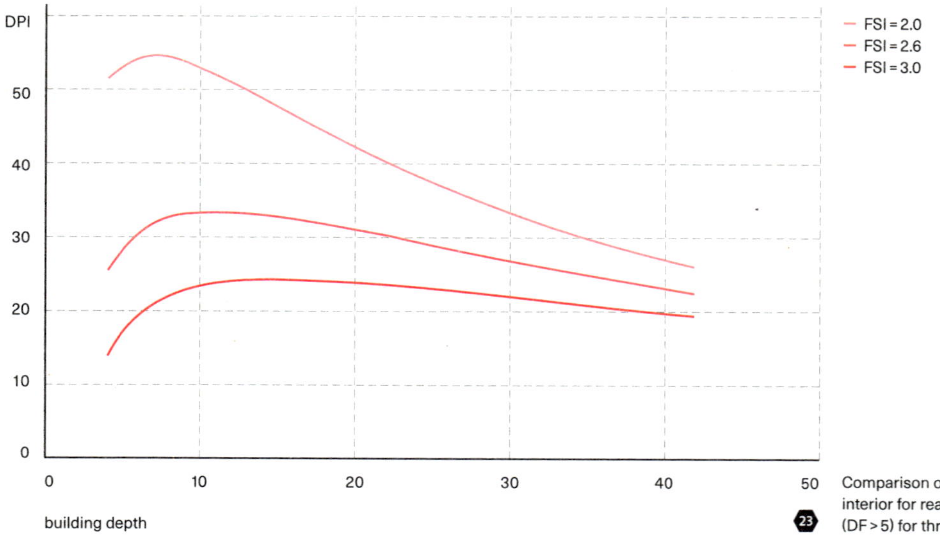

23

Comparison of DPI of the interior for real values (DF > 5) for three densities.

a distance greater than 6 m from the façade, even with no external obstruction whatsoever. ㉑ This applies, as in previous examples, to situations with an open façade, no partition walls and zero reflection.

In the earlier series D, where the building depth varied with constant FSI and GSI ⑪, the daylight performance (DPI_0) was constant, independent of the building depth. When the series is studied for real values, however, the values are not only lower, but also vary. ㉒ Here one can identify a clear optimum for the performance at a certain building depth. In the case of series D (FSI = 2.6; GSI = 0.5), the maximum performance of the interior takes place in buildings with a depth of approximately 10 m.

For other densities, the peak performance takes place at different building depths. A lower density has its optimum with less deep buildings, in this case 7 m, and for a higher density the maximum performance is achieved with rather deep buildings of around 15 m. However, the same daylight performance can be reached with deeper buildings of lower density.

When it comes to the trade-offs between building depth and the width of the open space (courtyards and streets), one can conclude that with one and the same density the daylight performance of the exterior increases when building mass is concentrated: thicker buildings mean wider open space, and thus a smaller angle of obstruction and more daylight in the exterior (GSI and FSI constant). At the same time, increasing the building depth beyond the peak, as shown in ㉓, results in a reduced performance of the interior.

Daylight Performance Index

So far we have investigated the dependence of the daylight performance (in interior and exterior) on the different density indicators. As those indicators (GSI, FSI) are the same ones that constitute the core of the Spacematrix method, it could be revealing to represent the daylight trends in one of its projections, the Spacemate. The series of transformation that were described earlier (A1 to A3, and B1 to B3 in ⑪) can be positioned in the Spacemate diagram. By using the formula ㉛ $DPI_0 = 200 \times (1 - GSI) / (FSI - GSI)$ gradients can be added which describe the daylight performance of the interior for each specific density condition. ㉔

The DPI_0 gradients are comparable to the Open Space Ratio gradients as can be seen when comparing the above formula to formula ⑤ $OSR = (1 - GSI) / FSI$ derived in Chapter 3. The only difference between OSR and DPI_0 is that for calculating the daylight performance, the floor area on the ground level is subtracted from the total amount of building bulk. This means that daylight performance on the ground floor can be described as the OSR of the floors above.

So far, only the daylight performance on the ground floor has been examined. By using the Spacemate diagram the daylight performance of all floors above the ground floor can easily be assessed. ㉕ shows the position

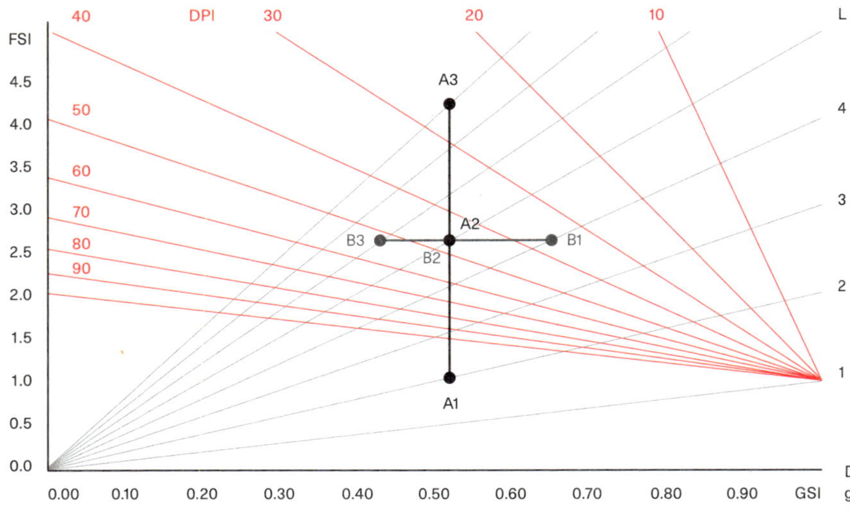

24 DPI in the interior as gradients in Spacemate (series A and B in 11).

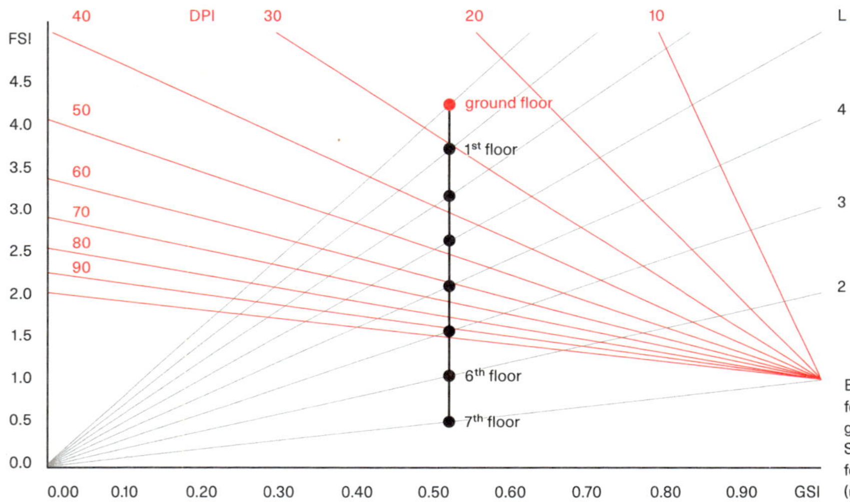

25 Example of the way DPI for each storey can be gauged based on a given Spacemate position; for ground floor, DPI = 26 (upper red circle in diagram); 1st floor, DPI = 31; 2nd floor, DPI = 37, etc.

of section A3 11 in the Spacemate. For the ground floor the daylight performance can be read directly from the diagram ($DPI_0 = 26$). For each storey above the ground floor the performance can be reached by subtracting the lower storeys. In the diagram this means to move down step by step, from layer to layer, until the last gradient of one storey is reached. In the example the daylight performance of the top two floors, the sixth and seventh floors, are more than 100 per cent.

24 25 show the gradients for the DPI using the zero lux (or $DF > 0$) demarcation of 'dark' and 'light' areas. To describe the performance for real values in the section that has been investigated in this paragraph, two more factors that complicate the performance of the exterior and interior must be taken into account. These are the Daylight Factor values and the depth

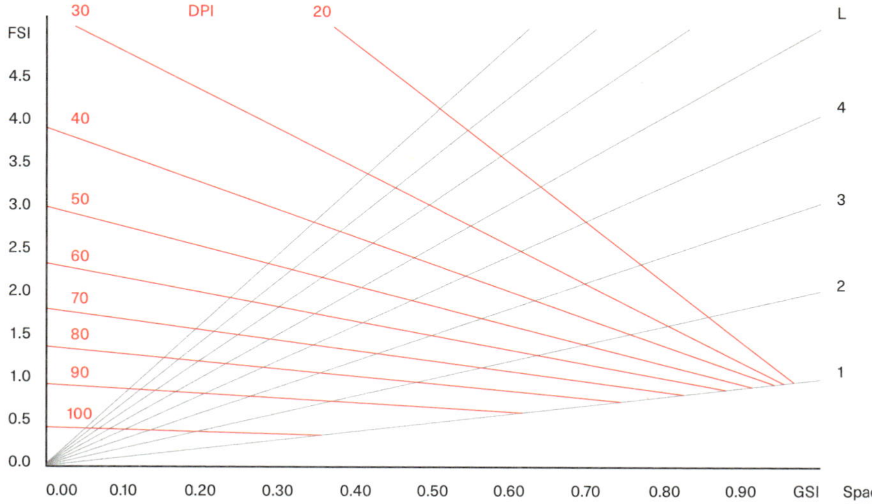

26 Spacemate with gradients DPI in the interior (DF > 5; d = 12 m, h = 3 m).

of the buildings. However, even when these factors are taken into consideration, the trend of the gradient does not change. 26 The spread of its absolute values change only when a different daylight factor is used as a standard or another building depth is applied.

Finally, the performance of the exterior in relation to density can be represented with the use of Spacemate. In the middle of a street or courtyard, the two angles in 35 have the same value. This means that the formula for the performance in the middle of the open space, can be described as:

38 $$DF_e = 100 \times \cos \alpha_e$$

The external obstruction angle in the middle of the open space can be arrived at through:

39 $$\tan \alpha_e = 2 \times h / (d \times OSR)$$

38 then becomes:

40 $$DF_e = 100 \times \cos\{\arctan[(2 \times h / (d \times OSR)]\}$$

h = floor height;
d = building depth.

The formula shows that for a constant floor height and building depth, the performance of the exterior space depends only on the OSR. This means that also for the exterior, a performance gradient can be constructed in

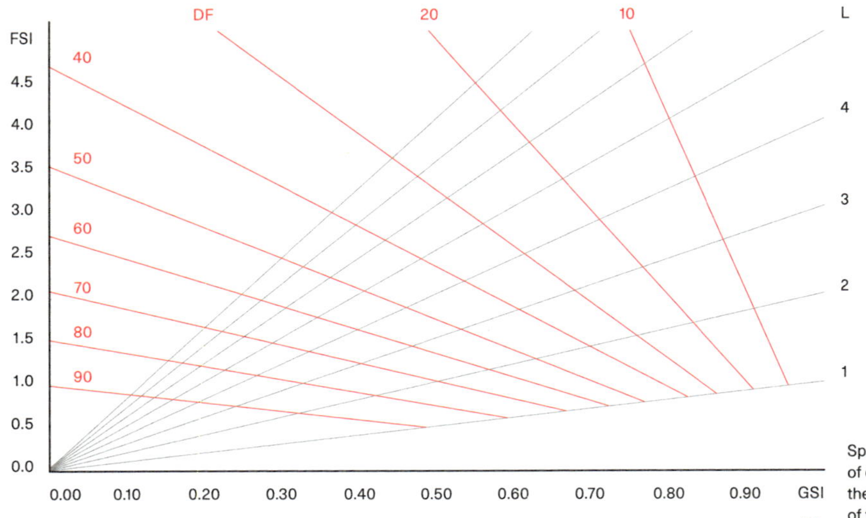

27

Spacemate with gradients of daylight factor (DF) in the exterior, in the middle of the open space (d = 12 m, h = 3 m).

Spacemate. 27 shows such a gradient for buildings with a depth of 12 m and a floor height of 3 m.

Daylight and Spaciousness

The above investigation shows a basic relation between density and daylight performance of the section. This is the case both for the interior and the exterior. However, the trends only become comprehensible if a multivariable model of density is applied. Sure, intuition, experience and even calculations lead us to conclude that more programme means less daylight, high buildings obstruct more than low ones, and that more compact layouts are less daylight intense than spacious ones. But only when these are combined do the general trends become visible. The analyses and representations in Spacemate show an intimate relation between daylight performance and OSR. This might in retrospective shed some light on the centrality of the concept of spaciousness (Weitraumigkeit) introduced by Hoenig in the 1920s and restore some of its aspirations as an indicator of quality of the urban fabric.

The gradients of daylight performance in Spacemate also demonstrate that for one and the same amount of programme (FSI), a high and spacious layout will perform better than a lower and more compact one, both in the interior and the exterior. Thus if the performance of daylight in the built interior and exterior is seen as an important part of the overall quality of the built environment (biological and psychological well-being, energy saving, etcetera), and if we regard intensive land use as a necessity in a world of limited space and resources, then we have to conclude that high and spacious fabrics score better than low and compact ones. On the other hand, high-rise developments are often critiqued for a lack of human scale of buildings and open spaces. Some might therefore end up promoting the compact historical city of the nineteenth and beginning of the twentieth centuries as an attractive alternative to the spacious post-war urban expansions that are too high and the compact suburban developments of more recent years that are too low. This does not change the fact that even such a familiar city form should be scrutinized and constantly investigated to be further understood, optimized and judged. Not least in matters concerning daylight performance.

Air and Noise Pollution[158]

According to the World Health Organization, the top two causes of disease are air pollution and environmental noise.[159] Numerous studies, both international and Swedish, have shown that air pollution, especially particles, contributes to long-term morbidity and mortality from cardiovascular and respiratory diseases.[160] Concerning noise, there is significant and increasing evidence for serious health effects due to long-term exposure to high-level traffic noise in dwellings, including annoyance, sleep disturbance and ischaemic heart disease.[161] Future plans to reduce both air and noise pollution are considered insufficient, whereby additional measures are needed of which one can be found in the form and placement of buildings in relation to roads. A simplified example is a courtyard with an opening towards a busy street that facilitates ventilation of the street space and thereby improves the air quality in the street.[162] Such openings may, however, prevent an effective reduction of noise levels in the courtyard.[163] This so-called 'quiet side concept' is something urban densification projects rely on to a large extent, allowing higher noise levels towards the noisy street if a quiet (or muted) side to each apartment is guaranteed.[164]

To test the relation between the Spacemate variables and noise and air pollution, first, six theoretical urban models (cases) are used (28). Second, simulation software is used to calculate the levels of noise exposure and air pollution in space. Third, the relation between urban form and noise exposure and air pollution is studied using mean values of exposure for the yard (private land) and sidewalks surrounding the street-block (public land) separately. To study the effects of building types on the distribution of noise exposure and air pollution,

158
Part of this text is earlier published at the ISUF conference, Nicosia, 2019.

159
(WHO 2018, 2019).

160
Brook et al. 2012; Zang et al. 2014; Fridell et al. 2014).

161
Basner et al. 2013; Munzel et al. 2014

162
Haeger-Eugensson et al. 2013

163
e.g. Hornikx et al. 2011

164
e.g. City of Gothenburg 2016

Case 1

FSI	GSI	OSR	L
1.82	0.36	0.35	5.0

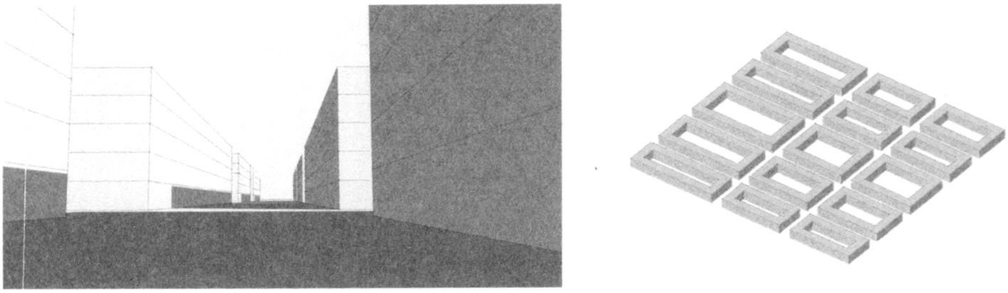

Case 2

FSI	GSI	OSR	L
1.82	0.33	0.37	5.6

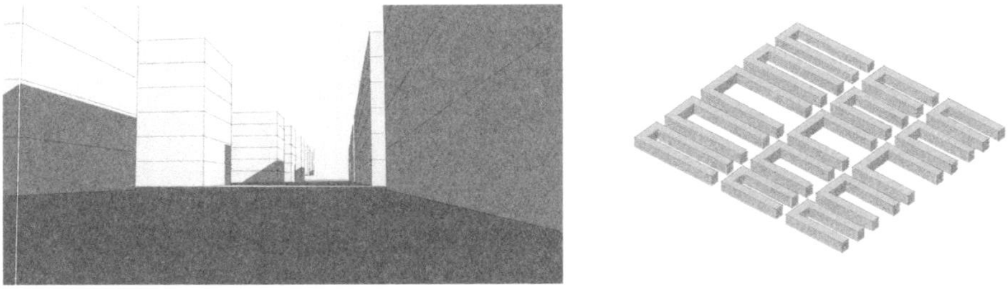

Case 3

FSI	GSI	OSR	L
1.82	0.29	0.39	6.4

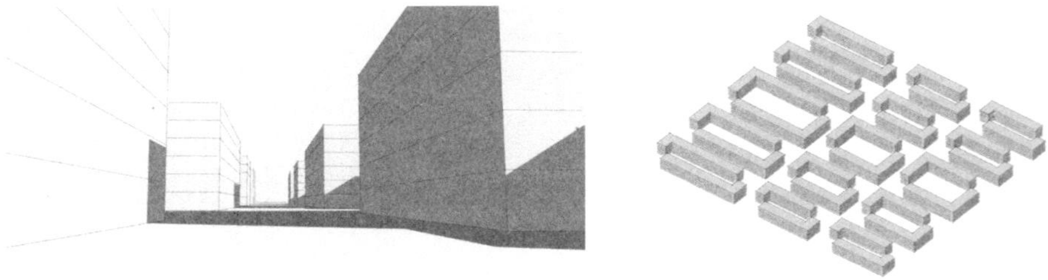

Case 4

FSI	GSI	OSR	L
1.82	0.29	0.39	6.4

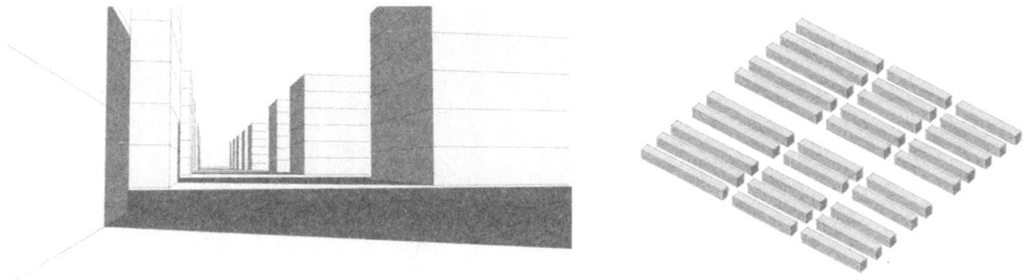

Case 5

FSI	GSI	OSR	L
1.82	0.20	0.44	9.1

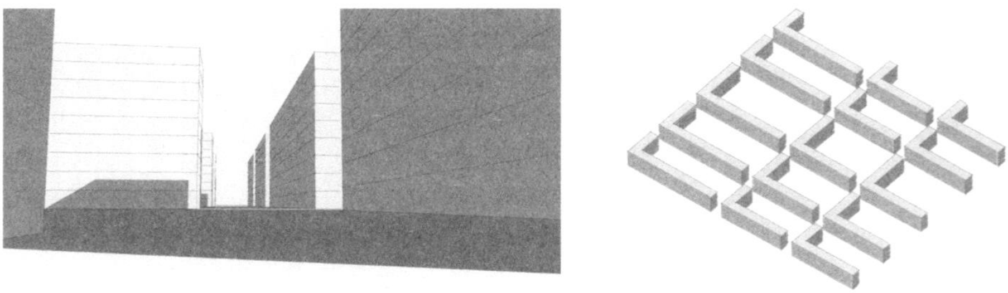

Case 6

FSI	GSI	OSR	L
1.82	0.13	0.48	14.0

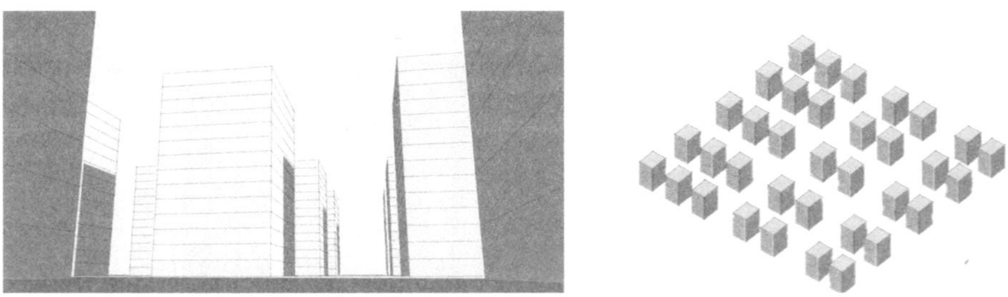

29 The exposure values are taken from the shaded block in the middle of the area studied.

the six models were situated in an unbuilt area in central Gothenburg. The location is necessary to have a constant, but realistic background level of noise exposure and air pollution, where we then place the six cases to study the isolated effect of changes in building type and density.

Modeling Noise Exposure

Concerning the acoustic modelling of urban form, most aspects can be considered using available noise-mapping software, including the background noise levels from a larger area. However, since these methods are not applicable to closed courtyards,[165] an extension is applied using results from the Qside project.[166] A commercial software[167] is used following a prediction model[168] that considers 27 frequency components of the sound, five reflections and neutral weather conditions. The traffic flow on each of the local roads is 1,500 vehicles/24 h (average for one year), consisting of 95 per cent light, 2.5 pre cent medium heavy and 2.5 per cent heavy vehicles, driving 50 km/h.

165 Kropp et al. 2004

166 Estevez Mauritz et al. 2014

167 Soundplan, version 8.0

168 Nord2000 Road

To compare the effects of the different morphological types, mean and highest values of noise exposure (in dBA) are used as well as the standard deviation within the area. The values are taken from the street-block in the middle of the area studied 29 to avoid disturbance from the context and to ensure the isolation of the impact of the building type only on noise level distributions.

For noise exposure, the results show that the mean values are relatively stable in the sidewalk area, while they increase in the yards, from 45 dB in case 1 (perimeter block type) to almost 55 dB in case 6 (point building type) 30 31. The highest values in the yards reach almost 60 dB in case 6. The values in the sidewalk and yard areas vary, depending on the morphological

28 Six theoretical urban models (cases) to test the relation between the Spacemate variables and noise and air pollution.

Case 1

FSI	GSI	OSR	L
1.82	0.36	0.35	5.0

Case 2

FSI	GSI	OSR	L
1.82	0.33	0.37	5.6

Case 3

FSI	GSI	OSR	L
1.82	0.29	0.39	6.4

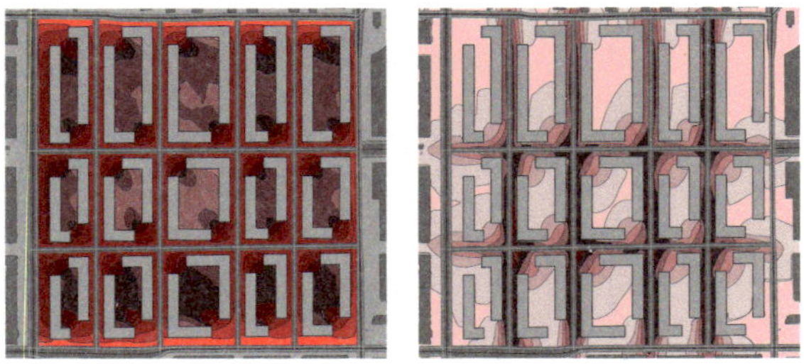

Case 4

FSI	GSI	OSR	L
1.82	0.29	0.39	6.4

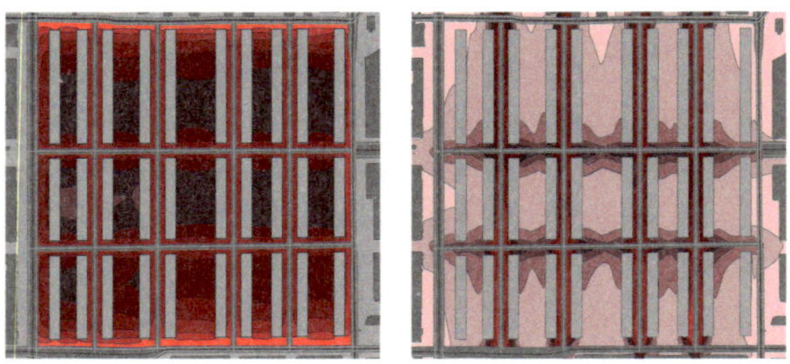

Case 5

FSI	GSI	OSR	L
1.82	0.20	0.44	9.1

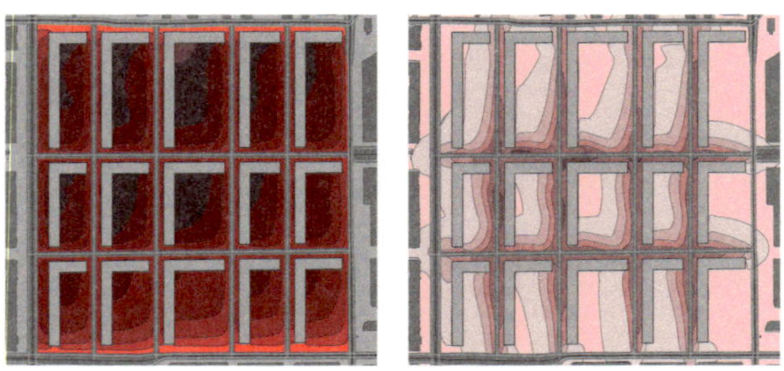

Case 6

FSI	GSI	OSR	L
1.82	0.13	0.48	14.0

— Road
Building

Left: Noise level LAeq (24 h in dB)

- <= 40
- <= 43
- <= 46
- <= 49
- <= 52
- <= 55
- <= 58
- <= 61
- <= 64
- <= 67
- <= 70
- > 70

Right: Concentration NO_x (in ug / m^3)

- <= 5
- <= 10
- <= 15
- <= 20
- <= 25
- <= 30
- <= 35
- <= 40
- <= 45
- > 45

30 Distribution of noise exposure (dB) and air pollutants (NO_x).

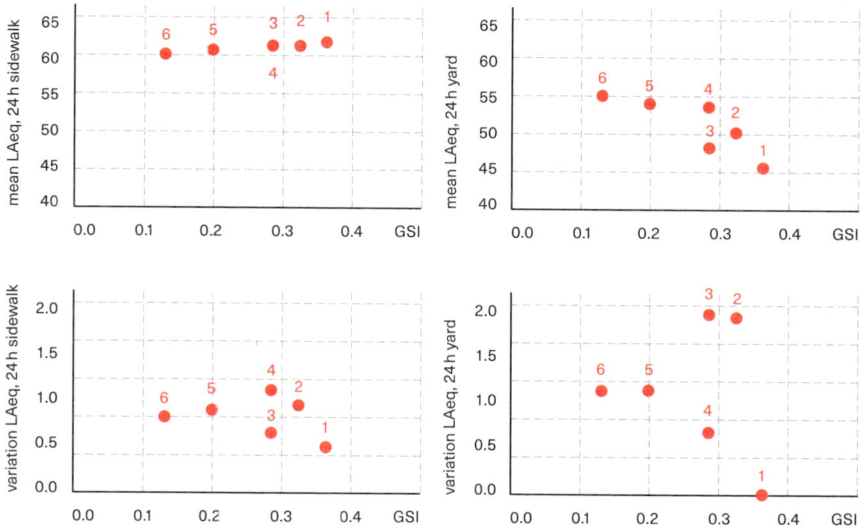

31 Levels of noise exposure (dB) in relation to building type and density (GSI values) with results on sidewalks (left) and yards (right).

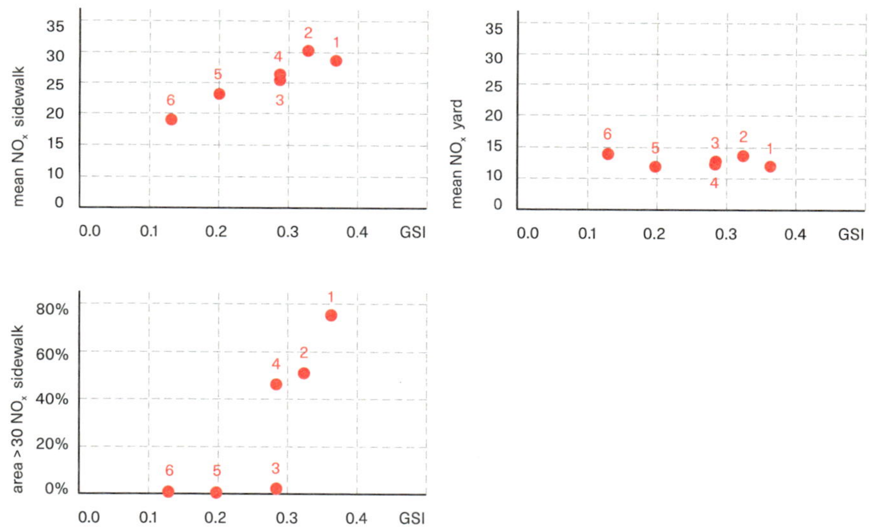

32 Levels of air pollutants (NO_x) in relation to building type and density (GSI values) with results on sidewalks (left) and yards (right).

type, especially in the yards. Most variation in the yard is found in type 2 (U-block) and 3 (open corners), while type 1 (block) and 4 (strip) show the least variation. Low mean noise exposure in type 1 is thus constant for the whole yard, while in type 2 and 3 we find areas with low, but also relatively high exposure. The yard in type 4 has less variation, but in general a higher exposure. Summarizing, the sidewalks are equally exposed to noise, independent of the morphological type, while the yards in the block type (case 1) perform much better than the strip (4), L-block (5) and point type (6). The half open block types (cases 3 and 4) have lower mean exposure with relatively high variations. Typically, the open corners are more exposed to noise than the enclosed parts of the yard.

Modeling Air Pollution

For studying the effect on air quality of different morphological types, we use, for local modelling, the CFD-model (MISKAM).[169] The meteorological input is based on results from urban scale modelling (TAPM meteorological dynamic model),[170] including the six morphological types that create a modified wind field. To compare the effects of the different morphological types, mean values of air pollution are used (NOx values per unit area) as well as maps showing the distribution of the air pollutants in space.

For air pollution, the results show that the mean concentration of nitrogen oxides are relatively stable in the yard area, while they increase on the sidewalks, from a yearly mean concentration of nitrogen oxides of 5 in case 6 (point type) to almost 30 in case 1 (block type) and 2 (U-block type) 30 32. Furthermore, a high percentage of the sidewalks in cases 1, 2 and 4 have a concentration of more than 30, while case 3 (open corners) stays below this threshold, despite similar mean levels.

169 Haeger-Eugensson et al. 2013

170 Chen et al

Exposures to Noise and Air Pollution

Interestingly, the results of noise exposure and air pollutants show opposing results. Types that reduce noise exposure in the yards, increase air pollution on the sidewalks and vice versa, types that reduce concentration of nitrogen oxides on the sidewalk, increase noise exposure in the yards. This is most apparent for the block type (case 1) with 'quiet yards, but polluted streets', but also for the strip and point types (case 5 and 6) with 'noisy yards, but less polluted streets'. The other three types show a more complex trade-off between noise exposure and air pollution: U-block type (2), open corner block type (3) and L-block type (4). From an air pollution perspective, the open corner block type (3) performs better than the other two, because it has a more even distribution of pollutants on the sidewalks, while the others have similar mean values, but higher values on half of the sidewalk area. From the noise exposure perspective, the U-block type (2) and open corner block type (3) perform equally well with lower mean values and a high variation, meaning that the yards have, besides noisy areas, also more quiet parts. Thus, type 3 stands out positively in both perspectives, albeit not best from one perspective alone.

Speculations on 'Urbanity'

Since the 1980s, 'urbanity' has achieved a central position in discussions on the city, mostly as a concept with rather positive connotations. 'Overcrowding' and 'urbanity' might be regarded as two different interpretations of similarly intense situations, the choice between the two terms depending on how the quality of life taking place in an area is judged: *overcrowding* can be used to describe collectives of people in the ghettos a century ago or the cramped settlements in developing countries today, whereas *urbanity* might be more suitable to large gatherings of people, composed of emancipated individuals, consuming and interacting on terraces, around museums and along shopping streets. Urbanity has in its present use a positive connotation while overcrowding is mostly associated with the negative connotations of combining physical concentration and social misery.

Eduardo Lozano describes urbanity as the potential for inhabitants and institutions in a town or city to interact.[171] This potential is partly created by density and, in turn, encourages higher density, according to Lonzano. Diversity, complexity, identity and flexibility are terms that are often associated with urbanity. The concept is frequently used to describe a human condition of plurality, difference, interaction and communication.[172] Although all kinds of social and spatial factors are involved in producing diversity, a dense concentration of people is, according to both Jane Jacobs and Lozano, one of the prerequisites for a flourishing and diverse city: 'The other factors that influence how much diversity is generated, and where, will have nothing much to influence if enough people are not there.'[173]

The term 'urbane' has its origin in the Latin dichotomy of *urbanus* versus *ruralis*.[174] To be urbane is to be equipped with courtesy, refinement, politeness and civility. *Urbanus* was the domain of the civilized citizen of the Roman city, in contrast to *ruralis*, the uncontrolled areas of the barbarian and uncivilized rural masses, alternatively the tranquil backwardness of the countryside. In many ways urbanity still has connotations of a smooth and literate style, free of barbarism and other inappropriate behaviour. Richard Sommers remarks that a concept such as urbanity also often works as an attractive front, shielding much of the blunt commercial and exclusive character of urban developments.[175] A high concentration of purchasing power thus seems to be stimulating to urbanity, while a high concentration of poverty tends to be deemed as dull, overcrowded and a suitable opportunity for regeneration. The urbanity that is striven for in present policies can from such a perspective be criticized for being largely covert gentrification, revitalizing not so much the chances of ordinary citizens, but describing a win-win situation for the city elites (developers, politicians and the creative and middle and upper classes):

171
Lozano, 'Density in Communities', op. cit. (note 6).

172
Hajer, M., De stad als publiek domein (Amsterdam: Wiardi Beckman Stichting, 1989);
Heeling, J., H. Meyer and J. Westrik, Het ontwerp van de stadsplattegrond (Amsterdam: SUN, 2002);
Jacobs, J., The Death and Life of Great American Cities (New York: Random House, 1992), originally published in 1961;
Meyer, H., F. de Josselin de Jong and M.J. Hoekstra (eds.), Het ontwerp van de openbare ruimte (Amsterdam: SUN, 2006), 9–30;
Urhahn, G.B. and M. Bobic, Strategie voor stedelijkheid (Bussum: Uitgeverij THOTH, 1996);
Wouden, R. van der (ed.) De stad op straat: De openbare ruimte in perspectief (The Hague: Sociaal en Cultureel Planbureau, 1999);
Zijderveld, A.C., Steden zonder stedelijkheid: Cultuurhistorische verkenning van een beleidsprobleem (Deventer: van Loghum Slaterus, 1983).

173
Jacobs, J., The Death, op. cit. (note 20), 205.

174
Thesaurus: urbane; 'The sophisticated manners of a true cosmopolite.' Refinement, assurance, wide social experience, charm, good taste, tact and propriety, etcetera.

175
Sommer, R.M., 'Beyond Centers, "fabrics," and the Culture of Congestion: Urban Design as a Metropolitan Enterprise', Harvard Design Magazine fall 2006/winter 2007, 50–59, 50.

> The good city is primarily associated with the ability of its physical spaces to support a rich and intricate visuality that promotes what is, in practice, the pleasures of the yuppie lifestyle and its programme of shopping and dining, of fitness, of stylishness and mobility, and of a certain level of associative urban connoisseurship.[176]

176
Sorkin, M., 'The End(s) of Urban Design', Harvard Design Magazine fall 2006/ winter 2007, 5–18, 12.

Present enthusiasm for urbanity and the dynamics and vitality of city life is not a neutral phenomenon, but carries ideological bias. Next to the affirmative stance towards the accelerating intensity of urban life, there exists also a critical and sometimes dystopian intellectual tradition. To the first, the modern urban condition equals opportunity and expansion, to the second it leads to alienation and loss of personal and cultural identity. Terms such as alienation, loss of the Self, and chaos are associated with this line of thought on the effect of the modern city on human experience. Writers such as Charles Baudelaire, Walter Benjamin and Knut Hamsun point to the destabilizing effects on humans of the dynamics and speed of the rapidly modernizing city.

José Lluís Sert and Lewis Mumford and, more recently Mike Davis and Michael Sorkin, are examples of intellectuals that have all taken a critical stance on (aspects of) modernity, capitalism and the impact of the city on human life. Mumford favours a decentralized regionalism against the 'The Myth of Megalopolis'.[177] In a spirit resembling the scepticism towards industrialization and mass production of William Morris and the Arts and Crafts movement in England – but perhaps more misanthropic and less romantic – Mumford grieves the loss of humanism through modern history. He views urban history through the 'oft-repeated urban cycle of growth, expansion, and disintegration', and warns that the modern megalopolises face the same destiny as antique Rome. Davis's recent neo-Marxist criticism of the urban condition attacks the 'dynamic, ever-growing social inequality, [which] is the very engine of the contemporary [neoliberal] economy'. In the book with the apocalyptic title *Evil Paradises: Dreamworlds of Neoliberalism*, Davis describes how 'the spatial logic of neoliberalism (cum plutonomy) revives the most extreme colonial patterns of residential segregation and zoned consumption'.[178] In a global perspective, 'the bright archipelagos of utopian luxury and "supreme lifestyles" are mere parasites on a "planet of slums"'. This reads like a twenty-first-century global version of Engels' book on Manchester: *The Conditions of the Working Class in England in 1844*.

177
Mumford, L., The City in History: Its Origins, Its Transformations, and Its Prospects (New York: Harcourt, Brace and World, 1961).

178
Davis, M. and D.B. Monk (eds.), Evil Paradises: Dreamworlds of Neoliberalism (New York: The New Press, 2007).

In contrast to these sceptics, Jacobs can be seen as central to the rehabilitation of the city and its dynamic potential against both modernists (Le Corbusier, et al.) and regionalists such as Mumford. Present day examples of affirmative attitudes to urban economic and psychosocial dynamics can be found in Richard Florida's emphasis on the relationship between the urban, a creative class and economic competitiveness, and Peter Hall's book

Cities in Civilization in which the golden ages of civilization through history are recorded and related to the culturally and economically innovative and productive climate of interactive city life.[179]

The wide range of analyses and judgements on the urban condition and its positive and negative connotations, where in the examples mentioned here 'modernity is either embraced with blind and uncritical enthusiasm or otherwise condemned with a neo-Olympian remoteness and contempt',[180] shows that it is not easy to distil a consensus from the existing views of what can be understood by 'urbanity'. Furthermore, even the intrinsic relationships to physical conditions have at times also been questioned. Melvin Webber describes urbanity as mainly being dependent on openness and accessibility.[181] These are aspects that do not necessarily have to be conditioned by the physical givens of the built environment. With modern communication technologies, an urbanity defined in this way can be sustained that is not dependent on the physical contacts between people, according to Webber. The research group OSA (*Onderzoeksgroep Stedenbouw en Architectuur*) at the University of Leuven in Belgium adds 'network urbanity' to the discussion. This is an urbanity which has no relationship to the old, dense city and develops on the urban fringe.[182]

It can be concluded from this that the notion of urbanity is a very elastic one. We do not here want to take a stance on any correct definition or suggest a new one, but prefer to delineate the notion of urbanity into separate sub-properties, focusing on the physical-spatial properties of the built environment. We suggest that physical factors such as interface (the relationship between buildings and network), building surface (coverage), grain (or block) size, profile width and tare space (proportion of private and public space) can be viewed as elements contributing to a description and understanding of the concept of urbanity. In this paragraph we will, therefore, discuss the performance of some of these properties in relation to density. If such properties are seen as being central to the definition of urbanity, then the outcome might help to judge the degree of urbanity in an area. If this is not the case, if for example the more traditional definition of urbanity as physically conditioned is deemed irrelevant, then these performances can still convey specific characteristics of the built landscape without explicitly being labelled conditions for urbanity. Depending on the view taken on urbanity, one is free to incorporate the performances of the sub-properties as a description of a situation as being more or less urbane, or just leave them as descriptions among others, but not necessarily essential to the chosen notion of urbanity. Below we will discuss the sub-properties user intensity, catchment and network and connectivity ratio. This series of sub-properties is certainly not exhaustive, and, as was the case for parking and daylight access, the analyses constitute starting points for further investigation rather than presenting absolute values of performances.

179
Florida, R., Cities and the Creative Class (New York: Routledge, 2005); Hall, P., Cities in Civilization (London: Phoenix, 1999).

180
Berman, M., All That Is Solid Melts into Air: The Experience of Modernity (New York: Penguin Books, 1988, first published in the USA by Simon & Schuster in 1982), 24.

181
Webber, M., 'The Urban Place and the Non-Place Urban Realm', in: M. Webber et al., Explorations in Urban Structure (Philadelphia: University of Pennsylvania, 1964).

182
Stonor, T., Digital urbanism: The role of technology in the future of our cities (2014), https://www.academyofurbanism.org.uk/digital-urbanism-the-role-of-technology-in-the-future-of-our-cities/ (accessed 4 November 2020).

User Intensity

Lozano describes the relationship between density, user intensity and urbanity in North American cities as based on the concept of viable thresholds:

> At certain densities (thresholds), the number of people within a given area is sufficient to generate the interactions needed to make certain urban functions or activities viable. Clearly, the greater the number and variety of urban activities, the richer the life of a community; thus, urbanity is based on density.[183]

Following this line of thought, Amsterdam in 1880 can be described as being much more urbane than it is today. In 1880 the average population density in Amsterdam was almost 600 inhabitants per hectare. Today, the city is nine times less intensely inhabited; the population density was 64 inhabitants per hectare in 2000.

Lozano describes a series of density thresholds as being critical to different levels of urbanity (or lack of it). The distinctions made are based on housing density[184] and are very much related to development types commonly found in the USA. According to Lozano, the first threshold can be found at 20 dwellings per hectare (40 inhabitants per hectare) 'since below that level it is difficult to provide community facilities in close proximity to the dwellings'.[185] The urban fabrics are dominated by detached houses and semi-detached two-family houses and can be positioned in Spacemate ($FSI_f = 0.3$; $GSI_f = 0.15$).[186] ❸❸ The next threshold is found starting at 130 dwellings per hectare (260 inhabitants per hectare or $FSI_f = 2.0$). Above this level, according to Lozano, 'there can be a wide variety of facilities and activities easily accessible to each dwelling'.[187] Jacobs argues that an even higher density is necessary if we are to speak of urbanity.[188] The bandwidth described by Jacobs starts at 175 dwellings per hectare (350 inhabitants per hectare or FSI 2.2) and has a maximum of 350 dwellings per hectare (700 inhabitants per hectare or FSI 4.4). Higher intensities, according to Jacobs, lead to standardization and, therefore, to an absence of diversity. Lozano, in a similar way, highlights different complications and less positive performances when densities become very high. Urbanity is certainly present, but in Lozano's opinion issues such as parking, congestion, lack of open space and privacy make it a very unattractive form of urbanity.

Discussing user density, one also needs to take into account the split between residential and non-residential users, as well as the composition of the latter. Workplaces, tourists and visitors of different kinds of amenities; all contribute differently to the user intensity of network and other public spaces. A one-sided focus on residential users overlooks a great deal of important activity that further increases user intensity.

Potential user intensity is dependent on internal and external factors. One internal factor is the one sketched so far; the potential for a presence

183 Lozano, 'Density in Communities', op. cit. (note 6), 316.

184 Lozano uses dwelling units per acre (1 acre = 0.404 hectare).

185 Lozano, 'Density in Communities', op. cit. (note 6), 317.

186 Based on the following assumptions: an occupancy rate of 2.0 (similar to the situation in Amsterdam in 2000); the gross floor area of a dwelling is 150 m^2; and the network tare space is 30 per cent.

187 Lozano, 'Density in Communities', op. cit. (note 6), 317.

188 Jacobs, J., The Death, op. cit. (note 20).

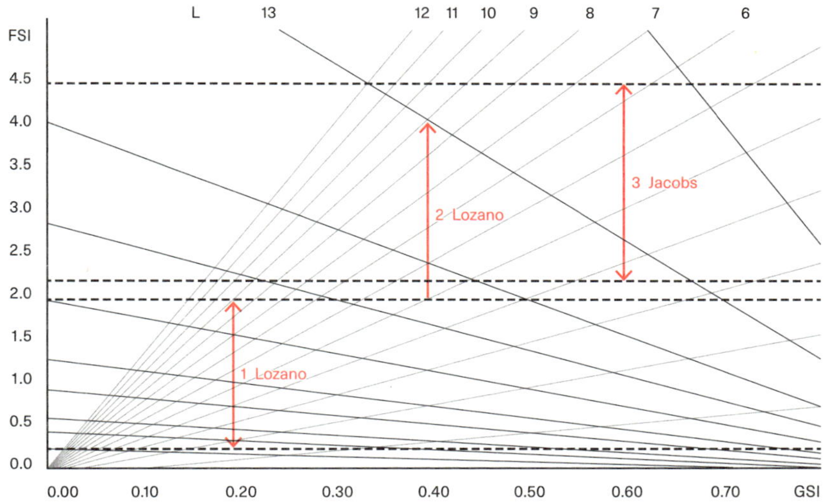

1 thresholds for community facilities (Lozano 1990)
2 thresholds for a wide variety of activities (Lozano 1990)
3 thresholds for urbanity and diversity (Jacobs 1961)

33 Spacemate with thresholds for urbanity as expressed by Lozano and Jacobs (scale: fabric).

of plenty of people in an area, generated by the floor space present in that area. The second, the external factor, depends on the modes of transport and the accessibility for those different modes in an area. Inner-city shops do not only rely on clients who live within walking distance. Even if an area has a relative high density, it will probably not generate enough consumers locally to support a large and diverse mix of retail outlets. A large portion of consumers come to those shops over long distances, all using different modes of transport. Therefore, the potential in this case consists of an internal component generated by the area itself and an external component. In many cases amenities rely almost entirely on external users. Malls and hospitals on the fringe, and a restaurant with a good reputation in an 'off' location are examples of attractors that have virtually no local user component. Necessity and choice, in combination with good transport (private car or public transport), draw visitors from a large catchment area. Matters such as centrality, transportation techniques, real estate economics, historically grown concentrations, transport pricing, and so forth all affect this external component. Berghauser Pont et al.[189] found a significant correlation between characteristics of the urban environment, more specifically built density and street centrality, and the number of people on the street based on a full day pedestrian count survey in several neighbourhoods in London, Amsterdam and Stockholm. They demonstrate that built density explains the intensity of pedestrian flow, while variations in street centrality, or relative position in the system as whole, explain the distribution of this intensity within each area.

189 REF 2019

Density and Catchment

Preindustrial, dense city settlements provided (and still do) a relatively large catchment area, even when most movements were made on foot.

Much of the general decline in density discussed in Chapter 2 has been possible because of developments in transport techniques. The sprawling suburbs of North America are impossible to imagine without the private car. But in relation to density and catchment area, what do these historical changes look like?

A half-hour trip by foot, bike or by car approximately covers an area of 20, 175 and 700 km^2 respectively.[190] For equal densities one could roughly state that the car has increased the potential for employment, commercial spending and social contact by more than 35 times compared to the most ancient transport method and four times compared to the bike. However, if a high-density city layout (the inner city of Amsterdam, for instance, with an FSI of 2.0) with walking and biking as dominant modalities is compared to a layout with low densities relying mainly on transport by car (for instance Phoenix, Arizona, FSI 0.1), and the catchment is expressed in floor area and not in ground surface only, then the advantage of potential interaction for the car decreases to a factor of almost two compared to walking. In such a comparison the bike in Amsterdam performs better than the car in Phoenix: five times as much floor space is within the reach of the biker compared to the motorist. If the sizes of dwellings are considered – larger suburban villa's in Phoenix (175 m^2) versus smaller apartments in Amsterdam (75 m^2) – the walker in Amsterdam performs slightly better than the motorist in Phoenix (1.3 times more dwellings can be reached on foot). By bike, almost 12 times more addresses can be reached than by car in this example.

190 Based on a half-hour trip with an average walking speed of 5 km/h, biking speed of 15 km/h, and driving speed of 30 km/h.

If public transport options such as tram, bus and metro are considered, the car's reach remains larger. Public transport covers areas between 150 and 400 km^2, compared to 700 km^2 for the car.[191] If a comparison is made between the two city layouts used above (FSI 2.0 based on public transport and FSI 0.1 relying on the car), however, then the picture looks different. In terms of potential floor area that can be reached, public transport scores between four (tram and bus) and twelve (metro) times better than the private car.

191 Again, based on a half-hour trip with an average speed for bus and tram of 20 km/h, metro 35 km/h and car 30 km/h. Although the speed of tram, bus and metro is similar to the car, the catchment for public transport is lower due to the fact that a part of the travel time is spent walking to and from the stops, 12 minutes walking (1 km) in this example. For both car and public transport (tram and bus), the average speed is generally limited by higher densities due to congestion. This is not taken into account here.

As 26 on page 62 illustrated, there seems to be an inverted relation between transport energy consumption and built density. Focusing on another aspect of transport, CO_2 emission, we find even larger differences between the sprawl and more dense settlements. The half-hour journey by car produces between 1.8 to 3.8 kg of CO_2, depending on the type of car. The comparable journey by public transport produces between 0.3 and 0.5 kg of CO_2. If these two factors are combined – absolute CO_2 production and the amount of floor area that potentially can be reached in the two examples – the efficiency can be calculated. The car can potentially reach 20 to 40 m^2 of floor area for every mg of CO_2 that is produced, while public transport brings an individual the choice of 800 to 1,600 m^2 of floor area for the same mg of CO_2. In a situation with better filled busses than the present averages, the difference becomes even more remarkable: 20 to 40 m^2 of floor area compared to 3,400 m^2 of floor area per mg of CO_2 (factor 85 to 170).

34 Three modalities compared in terms of space consumption.

Low-density, car-dependent layouts provide less choice (less potential floor area, or activity, to interact with), while consuming more energy and producing more CO_2 compared to higher densities with public transport. In addition to the larger efficiency in interaction for public transport in dense settlements, the space consumption of the transportation modalities themselves differ significantly, as 34 illustrates.

Block Size and Walkability

Besides user intensity in general terms, the number of people and vehicles moving and staying in the public streets can also be viewed as elementary to urbanity. This intensity can roughly be captured by the indicator GSI (coverage), as a high coverage within the islands, and thus little open (private) space, forces people into the public streets. The coverage mentioned by Jacobs as successful for generating urbanity range from 60 to 80 per cent of the lots (or islands), leaving the other 20 to 40 per cent non-built as courtyards. This high coverage on the scale of the island, combined with high built intensity (FSI) and little network (tare) space, should then generate a high intensity of movements and interaction between people in the streets.

The basic definition of OSR describes the relationship between gross floor area and all non-built space of the fabric. Often, however, it is of interest to assess the relation between gross floor area and the public portion of the non-built space (in this case the network area). This network ratio, ΔOSR, can be calculated as the difference between the OSR values of the fabric and island:

41 $$\Delta OSR = (A_f - \sum A_i) / F$$

or

42 $$\Delta OSR = OSR_f - OSR_i$$

Examples with a very low network ratio (ΔOSR) and thus a high pressure on the public network are the medieval parts of Barcelona (Gotic, Raval). In these compact areas with narrow alleys, a combination of a high coverage within the islands (90 per cent), little network tare space (less than 20 per cent), and high built intensities (FSI_f of almost 4.0) contribute to a very low network ratio. The lowest network ratio in Amsterdam can be found in the city centre (Jordaan, De Pijp, Grachtengordel), but also areas of more recent date such as Java and KNSM have low rates.

This is one way to indicate the pressure or intensity in the public network generated by the floor area. However, its value is very much dependent on the surface area of the network. Two areas with the same network ratio, such as the Grachtengordel and De Pijp, can have different network densities. The amount of floor area in relation to network length thus differs. This relation, FSI / N, translates into the possibility for public and / or commercial functions to interact with potential users in the street. The number of potential passers-by increases with an increase in programme and a decrease in network density.

If these two indicators are considered in isolation, more programme on larger islands increases the 'pressure' on the public network. However, the exposure or accessibility of the islands contradicts these findings. The potential exposure of private space (islands) in relation to public (network) space depends on the measurements of the islands alone. Large islands have relatively little exposure (or accessibility) as the façade length is limited. This exposure ratio can be formulated as the potential façade length to island area in which the potential façade length is equivalent to the length of the perimeter of the island.

The number of intersections as an indicator for circulation convenience or walkability is considered to be another important factor in relation to urbanity.[192] The (internal) connectivity of a fabric can be said to be conditioned by this factor.[193] In fabrics with more streets and intersections (and thus smaller islands), people have a larger variety of routes to choose from. This stimulates interaction which, as discussed earlier, is seen as one defining characteristic of urbanity. Both island size and the numbers of crossings are related to network density (N). The connectivity ratio, or the amount of crossings per hectare, increases proportionally to the square of the network density:

192
Jacobs, J., The Death, op. cit. (note 20);
Siksna, A., 'The Effects of Block Size and Form in North American and Australian City Centres', Urban Morphology 1 (1997), 19–33.

193
Marshall, S., Streets & Patterns (Oxon: Spon Press, 2005).

43 $$\text{Connectivity Ratio} = N^2 / 4$$

An interesting observation that can be made from the above analysis of the basic geometry of the fabric (and its relation to properties that are often considered to be central to urbanity), is the conflicting nature of the pressure on public space (network ratio), the exposure and (internal) connectivity depending on the amount of crossings. All are regarded as important to urbanity. Intensity is (internally) generated not only by the amount of programme and its primary distribution, but also by the amount of network that has to accommodate the generated movements and its centrality that attracts people from elsewhere to the area. Less network, and thus larger islands, concentrates the movements and thus increases the intensity within the network in terms of network ratio. However, this increase of scale – more programme on larger islands and thus more intensity within the public network – conflict with and are tempered by the architectural organization of the island. The exposure and accessibility of the island and the human scale of a walkable urban fabric put a limit on the simplistic endeavour for more intensity, which to some is supposed to equal urbanity. The tension between these performances produces an outcome that is a compromise, neither too large nor too small.

Performance Based Design

Every performance can be viewed as a descriptive layer that, when combined with others, can be used to clarify different consequences for the quality of urban environments. It is important to emphasize that the performances that have been discussed above define a – mostly maximal – potential. The conditions that are set by density in these cases are primary conditions that limit the performance of a fabric. This in no way indicates that a particular concrete form designed under those conditions automatically performs accordingly. The potential and limits are defined, but in every particular instance this potential can be (more or less) fully actualized or (more or less) 'sabotaged'. However, being a condition does indicate that limits are set on that which is possible. For example, in the case of daylight access, an open façade makes maximum use of the daylight potential, a glass curtain wall will decrease the performance a little due to pragmatic reasons, while a totally closed façade can be said to 'sabotage' the existing potential.

As discussed earlier, performance can be defined as a combination of objective properties defined by density and contextual standards. In the case of daylight access the standards will differ due to, for instance, geographical location. In Sweden the urge to maximize daylight access (light and passive solar energy) is larger than in Spain (heat). For parking, the standards are very dependent on political restrictions and market demands.

Urban form can be considered as one of the performances. Here we have added, besides all the empirically studied effects of density, parking, daylight, noise and air pollution and 'urbanity'. All performances are negotiable and can be used to identify conflicting programmes and necessary trade-offs. And by so doing the design task can be formulated with greater precision. Difficulties or inconsistencies can be spotted at an early stage in the design process. Designers who engage with the built environment on this basis would have more space and time for a more detached analysis of the properties of density, instead of making instant quick leaps to normative judgments that rely on intuitive conclusions and personal experience. Sometimes quick judgements can get in the way of experimentation and innovation. A suspension of judgement can be achieved by engaging with density and performance in an iterative fashion.

To work with performances in this way could strengthen the role of the urban professionals earlier in the design process and in relation to other disciplines such as engineers, economists and planners. As described in Chapters 1 and 2, this becomes more important in the process of negotiation between private and public actors engaged in the earliest phases of designing and planning the city. Urban density and performance could help urban professionals to reclaim technical, economic and demographic issues that have fallen, or are in danger of falling, outside the urban discipline.

6

QUALITIES OF DENSITY

This book started off with a critical examination of the history of existing concepts of density and different measuring methods. As shown in Chapters 2 and 3, density was already present in early twentieth-century city building, and was used both to diagnose an ailing city and to prescribe solutions to the problems. Density was often used as part of the ideological agenda of urban professionals, ranging from Raymond Unwin, Reinhard Baumeister and the Garden City Movement at the beginning of the twentieth century, striving for a more healthy and social city, through to the modernist planners of CIAM and their preference for high-rise developments in a green and functionally organized city, via Jane Jacobs's advocacy for a compact city of medium height in the 1960s, to the late twentieth-century pursuit of urbanity and 'parallel revaluating of the [dense] city as the site of desirable middle-class lifestyles'.[1] All are examples of very different doctrines, relying on different applications of density to make their argument. These doctrinal shifts can be charted in the Spacemate. ❶

Serving as one of the instruments of modernist planning, density has lost much of its shine since the 1970s. At the same time, rather simplistic density measurements have continued to be used to formulate policies, plan ambitions and draw up contracts. Both these facts have been to the detriment of the notion: on the one hand, there is an association with the missionary zeal of a technocratic functionalism, and on the other, a lack of precision in its pragmatic use in current practice.

The development of the *Spacematrix method* to measure density and identify a series of associated properties is the main result of our research. We have redefined density as a multivariable and multi-scalar phenomenon to counter the existing Babel-like confusion in the terminology currently being used by those working in the urban field. Furthermore, through the use of this multivariable and multi-scalar approach, density can be related to urban form and other performances as has been shown in Chapters 4 and 5. This makes it possible to reposition the concept of density in the field of urban design and research. From an instrument to prescribe the programme of a given area, density can become a tool to guide both quantitative and qualitative ambitions in the urban planning and design process.

1
Sorkin, M., 'The End(s) of Urban Design', *Harvard Design Magazine* fall 2006/ winter 2007, 5–18, 10.

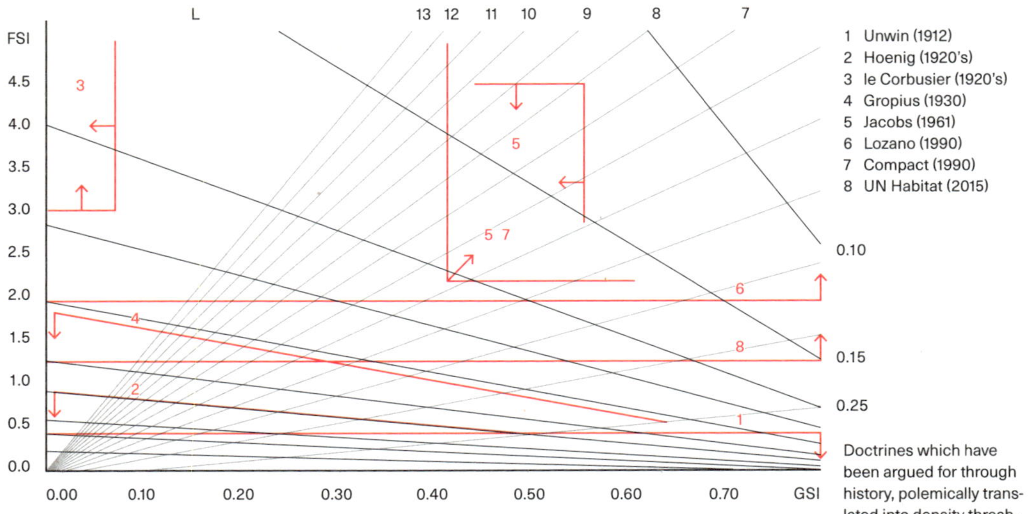

Doctrines which have been argued for through history, polemically translated into density thresholds in the Spacemate.

The addition of the review of over 300 studies on densities effects contributes to a better understanding of density trade-offs. The strong dichotomy between, on the one hand, the primarily positive effects of density on resource efficiency (mainly related to different kind of infrastructure), transport and economics and, on the other, the mostly negative environmental and social effects (from well-being to health) is striking. This formulates a challenging task for urban planners, who have to balance these two spheres (the system and the lifeworld), while at the same time acknowledging the need for some form of densification to handle current urbanization rates.

A Multivariable and Multi-Scalar Definition of Density

Instead of expressing density through the number of dwellings per hectare, which is still dominant in practice and research, we have demonstrated that density should be treated as a *multivariable* phenomenon. The difference between high, spacious and compact, low developments with one and the same building bulk can only be made when density is viewed as a *composite of indicators*. Furthermore, we have argued for the integration of network density within the multivariable definition of density. This is, as far as we are aware, a unique addition to density research. By adding network density, an indicative size of the mesh of the urban fabric, its islands and street profile can be integrated in the definition of density. The combination of indicators proved to be adequate in defining fabric types and their performance in terms of parking, daylight, connectivity, exposure, etcetera.

In addition to being defined as a multivariable phenomenon, density should also be approached as a *multi-scalar* phenomenon. Knowledge of how density behaves through the scales generates important information about the distribution of built and open spaces. Adding a large park or a piece of large-scale infrastructure on the scale of a district reduces the density within that district, or, when this is unfeasible, necessitates compensation through higher densities on the lower scales. On the other hand, small-scale decisions and developments add up and result in a compound spatial claim on the scale of a city and region. Architecture and urban design on the micro scale must thus be related to urban space consumption and the associated spatial, environmental, economic and social consequences on the macro scale. And vice versa.

The creation of consensus concerning the Spacematrix method could ensure a certain objectivity that can dispel much of the confusion and subjectivity that surrounds the current application of density. Our research provides urbanists, be they researchers or planners and designers, with the definition of scales, the way boundaries on each level of scale are drawn and a method to calculate and compare different densities. Most important here is that the different stakeholders use the same set of definitions, such as published in the Dutch standard for measuring urban density that was, based on the methods of this book, published in 2013 (NEN 9300).[2]

The last couple of years, the use of the Spacemate by a wide range of practitioners and researchers in urban planning and design has increased significantly. Some of the results have been added to this book, such as the densities of Asian urban fabrics that were first published in a report by the London School of Economics (LSE Cities). They also made use of the Spacematrix method in their Energy Report, which is worth mentioning here.[3] Furthermore, various doctoral theses have been published that build on the work presented in this book, including Eva Minoura's thesis *Uncommon Ground*,[4] in which the use of courtyards is studied in relation to density and territoriality, and Evgeniya Bobkova's thesis *Towards a Theory of Natural Occupation*, where in line with the typologies for buildings, a typology for plot structures is developed.[5]

Performance-Based Descriptions

The empirical samples that have been analysed in this research show that fabric types cluster in different positions in the Spacemate diagram ❷. These types do not have rigid borders, but slowly transform from one density position to another. What is most important to understand is that the conditions set by density very much influence the performance of a built environment. We suggest that performance-based descriptions of fabrics could become more important than the traditional image- or activity-based descriptions. Instead of naming low-rise block types or high-rise strip types, the fabric type could be described and prescribed solely by its Spacematrix density and the performance characteristics embedded in this density. The results of our research can hereby also be of great value to more traditional typomorphological research, as it relates urban form to density and performances other than form.

2 https://infostore.saiglobal.com/en-us/standards/nen-9300-2013-815919_saig_nen_nen_1948783/

3 LSE Cities, *Resource Urbanisms. Asia's divergent city models of Kuwait, Abu Dhabi, Singapore and Hong Kong* (London School of Economics and Political Science, 2017); LSE Cities, *Cities and Energy. Urban Morphology and Heat Energy Demand* (London School of Economics and Political Science, 2014).

4 Minoura, E., *Uncommon Ground: Urban Form and Social Territory*, PhD thesis KTH (2016).

5 Bobkova, E., *Towards a theory of natural occupation: developing theoretical, methodological and empirical support for the relation between plot systems and urban processes*, PhD thesis Chalmers (2019).

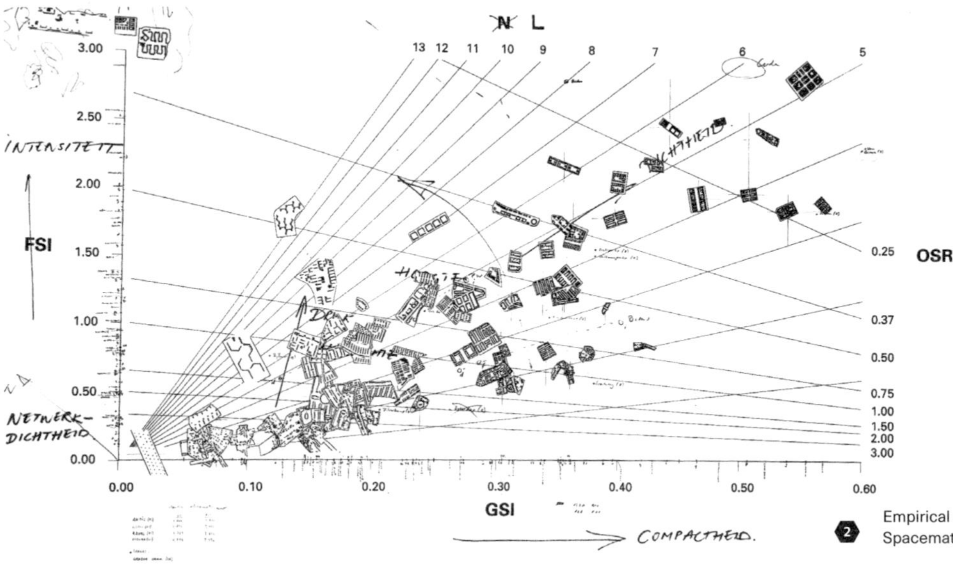

2 Empirical samples in the Spacemate.

In Chapter 5, we discussed such performances, based on a systematic review using more than 300 empirical studies as well as through various deductive explorations, studying parking, daylight access, noise and air pollution and urbanity. While the review sheds light on the real-life effects of density recorded through empirical investigation, the explorations highlight the physical laws of urban form in relation to, for instance, daylight access or noise exposure. Many more performances of urban fabrics could, and in our opinion should be researched and related to density in the same manner, contributing to a better underpinning of urban plans and designs. Instead of creating images, urban professionals will then be more involved with defining the conditions under which specific qualities (positive and negative) are most likely to be realized. This is especially the case for higher densities. In the light of the problems of increased urban space consumption and urbanization, intensification will frequently become unavoidable. Understanding the capacity of space and the effects that density has on the performance and quality of the built landscape then becomes even more important.

We recommend that a distinction be made between *hard* and *soft* performances. Hard performances are more closely related to the geometry and the physics of the built environment and can be approached quantitatively through explorative research. Examples of such hard performances include parking and daylight access, which have been treated in Chapter 5, but also aspects such as traffic capacity, energy use, wind, noise and air quality. Examples of soft performances are urbanity, traffic behaviour and stress. This category of performances has both hard and soft ingredients. They are in many ways conditioned by the density and geometry of the built environment (distance, potential user intensity in open space, etcetera), but can only realistically be calibrated if collective and individual valuation are taken into account. In addition to explorative research, the correlation between soft performances and built density must be explored through more qualitative surveys as were discussed in Chapter 5 as part of the systematic review.

Based on the same review, we found gaps in the knowledge of some topics, three of the most important ones which we want to highlight. First, there is a need to study transport including air traffic, as this is mostly neglected in the vast number of transport-related studies. This is troublesome because results that include air traffic show opposite findings from those that exclude it. Second, leisure trips should be studied more because current studies are inconclusive in this respect, while we know very well how density effects commuting trips. Third, more studies are needed that investigate density and open (green) space simultaneously, because the balance between the two is shown to be important to mitigate negative environmental and health effects and make cities more climate proof in terms of water management and urban heat islands. There might even be links between these three mechanisms, where a scarcity of green in cities and a lack of accessible green nearby lies behind an increase of longer trips by air and shorter trips by car to reach more distant alternatives.

Sustainable Densities

As shown in Chapter 2 with the example of Amsterdam, there has been an exponential increase in per capita urban space consumption since the end of the nineteenth century. The causes and effects of this 'demo-spatial' development are the subject of intense debate among academics and experts. However, there seems to be a general consensus that sprawling cities, private mobility and high levels of energy consumption go hand in hand. Car mobility makes suburbia possible, and suburbia demands private mobility. Decreasing densities further contribute to car dependency, CO production and climate change. Certainly, high-density alternatives to sprawling cities do not provide an instant solution to the problems of energy consumption and CO_2 production caused by car mobility, but they are prerequisites for other policies to combat climate change such as fiscal incentives, carbon rationing, investments in public transport, and so forth. These will be largely incompatible with low densities. The idea to densify our cities is more and more regarded as the key solution to arrive at a more sustainable city form, and since the 1990s it has been the main planning strategy. As was discussed in Chapter 2, this has resulted in an increase of density in Amsterdam of 17 per cent between 2000 and 2020. Thus, after an annual growth of the urban footprint of almost 2 per cent over the last 100 years, the urban footprint has started to decrease. It is argued that densification provides several environmental gains, especially related to the reduction of greenhouse gas emissions, innovation and economic growth. However, as the systematic review in Chapter 5 has shown, the solution of densification is not as simple as it seems, and density trade-offs might be the urban problems of tomorrow. It is important to point out, however, that the aim here is not to discredit densification, but to argue for the necessity of developing cities based on empirically supported knowledge.

On many fronts in society, an awareness of energy efficiency and conservation is manifest. In the area of spatial planning and design, more attention should be given to what could be called space economy. Space should be regarded as a scarce product. Not because it is really scarce in itself – the Netherlands could theoretically house the whole population in densities comparable to Los Angeles without any great spatial problem – but because an increased consumption of it corresponds to a larger consumption of other finite resources, and the increased production of waste and emissions. Studying the capacity of space and exposing the negative impacts of both dispersed and compact settlements can contribute to a larger awareness of the spatial dimension of the present crises.

Viewing urban density as a multivariable and multi-scalar phenomenon can at an early stage in decision making and urban planning contribute to more sustainable ways of city development. Knowledge of the relationship between density, urban space consumption and the environmental consequences of urbanization should be central to both policymaking and the planning and design practice.

The Professional Challenge

Other crucial challenges facing urban professionals have been described in this book. They are very much related to the all-encompassing neoliberalization of society of the last three decades. The privatization of spatial developments has led to a project-based planning approach where earlier public initiation and guidance (more or less centralized and publicly generated) has been scattered into localized particularities. Furthermore, globalization, the associated intensified competition between cities and regions, and the strengthening of an economic growth paradigm have contributed to a continuous increase of urban space consumption. All these processes have conditioned the present practice of city development and very much defined the task of the urban professional. For urbanism, this has meant that all actors are forced to negotiate quantitative goals and qualitative ambitions very early in the process of city development. Furthermore, the dynamics of the market makes programmes accidental and necessitates an open-ended and flexible planning and design process. The same market dynamics also fosters the use of imagery to attract investments, businesses, skilled employees, tourists, etcetera, and as such promotes a scattered project-based approach where 'seduction and inspiration' are prime effects, resulting in a kind of inverted blueprint planning. The end goal in such a situation is no longer a programme, but an image.

Both economic stagnation and environmental deprivation on a global scale at the beginning of the twenty-first century will have their repercussions on the nature of urban landscapes, existing as well as new ones. The trickledown effects of these developments will most certainly also be visible in spatial matters. As the state has regained some of its influence in the wake of current crises, the knowledge and instruments necessary to translate political goals into spatial results should become very important. This might result in a stronger emphasis on regulations and guidelines. To formulate such guidelines, the performance of different urban environments on many fronts – spatial, environmental, economic – will become central to decision making.

In this book a method has been presented that neither focuses specifically on the image nor on the programme for the city. The Spacematrix method provides urban professionals with an instrument that can simultaneously address quantity and quality, content and image, flexibility and precision. It can be used to make pre-designs in which the main programmatic and spatial qualities are described. Based on these, the feasibility of the project and other performances can be estimated. At the same time, the method allows for enough flexibility to incorporate changes during the process of realization.

An important contribution could be made to the national planning reports or structural visions on lower scale levels. The *Structuurvisie Randstad 2040* states the ambition to realize 500,000 new homes in the Randstad, of which 40 per cent should be realized within existing cities. If the other 60 per cent (300,000 dwellings) were to be realized in suburban areas dominated by detached housing types ($FSI_f = 0.5$), almost two times the area of Amsterdam would be required.[6] If this spatial claim is judged to be too large, and the addition has to take place on only half of this area (thus the size of Amsterdam), then density has to increase, be it on the scale of the fabric (requiring other fabric types) or the district and city (less green, working areas, etcetera). The Spacematrix method could be effective in understanding the relationship between such national plans mainly concerned with programme, the need for certain types of living environments and their effects in terms of space consumption, as well as social, economic and environmental performance. Changes in the demands for one of these components will affect all the others. Evaluating the result could lead to changes in other components, which will then again affect the parts and the whole. Such an iterative approach should profit from a simultaneous understanding of the quantitative and qualitative consequences on different levels of scale, and thus make better underpinned decisions possible. That this is needed, was proven by a review of 59 comprehensive plans in Sweden, where frequently used motives for densification were often deemed more positive for sustainable urban development than can be scientifically supported, especially in relation to social impacts.[7]

Furthermore, truly flexible plans could be made using the Spacematrix method. Neither the image nor the programme is predetermined through the method, but density and performances are conditions under

6
Based on 150 m^2 of floor space per dwelling, an FSI_f of 0.50, and needed tare space between fabrics and urbanized land comparable to the Amsterdam case (50 per cent).

7
Haupt P A, M Y Berghauser Pont, V Alstäde, P G Berg, 'A systematic review of motives for densification in Swedish planning practice', *IOP Conf. Ser.: Earth Environ. Sci.* 588 (2020), 052030.

Building types for the entire metropolitan area Amsterdam using the measure accessible density and Spacemate clusters.

which the plan can be developed further by individuals, either in a competitive, self-organizing process, or by urban professionals in a more publicly guided process. Such a performance-based design is regarded by many as the new way to make urban plans, leaving blueprint planning – both image and programme driven – behind.

The Science of Urban Density

Density has the capacity to facilitate the communication between many different disciplines. Architecture, urban planning, traffic engineering, building physics, environmental sciences, social sciences, ecology, geography and economics; to those, density can act as a catalyst for a truly interdisciplinary branch of research: the science of urban density. We see three important fields of research for the future.

First, the exploration of the relation between density and its performances should be continued and deepened, whereby three important research questions in need of further study are identified: first, do people living in higher density travel more by plane and how does density affect leisure trips – two topics often ignored despite the vast number of transport-related studies. The second question is broader and more challenging, but crucial for the development of sustainable dense cities: can the combination of density and open (green) space contribute to mitigating the proven negative environmental and health effects of densification and make cities more climate proof in terms of water management and urban heat islands? Thirdly, the relation between density and performance should be studied with more precision by addressing density as a multivariable and multi-scalar phenomenon, but also by acknowledging the possibility of non-linear relationships.

Second, research into the relation between the multivariable approach to density to characterize a specific *place*, and analyses to understand the spatial interrelatedness of streets in a city, *location*, would enhance two fields of research that are currently often separate. In the past ten years, important steps have been taken by the research group SMoG at Chalmers University of Technology Sweden, led by Meta Berghauser Pont and Lars Marcus.[8] They have shown the importance of both built density as developed within the Spacematrix framework and street centrality as developed within the Space Syntax framework. This integrated approach makes it possible to upscale density analysis to entire cities by measuring *accessible* density ❸,[9] and has been shown successful in explaining pedestrian flows, intensities and their fluctuations during the day.[10] Besides the need for further integral studies of this kind, we especially see a need to transfer this knowledge into design-decision support tools to evaluate the effectiveness of design proposals. Examples of such tools are the Place Syntax Tool (PST), an open-source tool for performing spatial analyses that combines the space syntax description of the urban environment with descriptions of attraction, including accessible density. The tool is currently available as a plugin for QGIS, an open source GIS program.[11] Recently, a more user-friendly frontend has been developed, based on PST, to make such analysis more accessible for GIS illiterates, the Urban Calculator.[12]

Finally, the extension of the approach presented in this book to the scale of the city and the region is of great importance. At these scales, the notion of tare space becomes central. The way the urban fabrics are

8
https://www.smog.chalmers.se/

9
Berghauser Pont, M., and Marcus, L., 'Innovations in measuring density. From area and location density to accessible and perceived density', *Nordic Journal of Architectural Research* (2014).

10
Berghauser Pont, M., G. Stavroulaki, L. Marcus, 'Development of urban types based on network centrality, built density and their impact on pedestrian movement', *Environment and Planning B: Urban analytics and city science* 46:8 (2019): 1549–1564; Stavroulaki, G., D. Bolin, M. Berghauser Pont, L. Marcus, E. Håkansson, 'Statistical modelling and analysis of big data on pedestrian movement', *Proceedings of the 12th Space Syntax Symposium*, JiaoTong University, Beijing, China (2019).

11
https://github.com/SMoG-Chalmers/PST/tags

12
https://www.researchgate.net/publication/338689356_URBAN_CALCULATOR

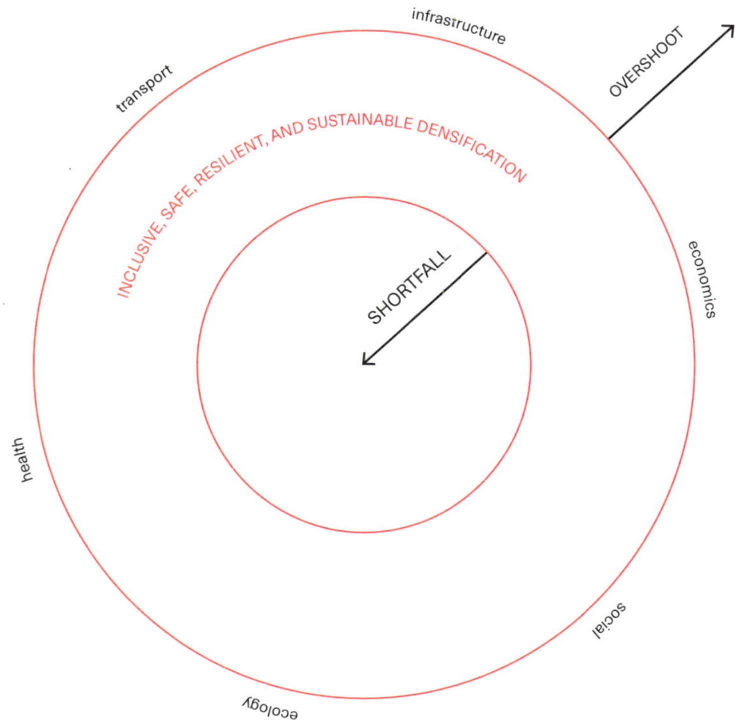

4 'Density Doughnut' that describes the conflicting consequences of densification, inspired by *Doughnut Economics*, a new economic model developed by Kate Raworth.

distributed within a city or region is decisive for the spatial qualities that can be achieved. The focus on the relation between architecture and urbanism, which has been dominant until now, would then shift to urbanism and landscape ecology. These scales are, in the light of the scarcity of land and other finite resources, necessary to address, and could lead to new distribution patterns of tare space within cities and regions. Such an approach would engage with cities as socioecological systems, which presents an alternative research programme on sustainable urban development and offers a far broader conception of urban sustainability than current discourses. It addresses cities on the relevant systems level, where, moreover, social, economic and ecological urban systems are combined. This fits well with *Doughnut Economics*, a new economic model developed by Kate Raworth that describes the social and planetary boundaries within which lies an environmentally safe and socially just space in which humanity can thrive.[13] One can imagine a 'Density Doughnut' 4 that describes the conflicting consequences of densification, visualized by a doughnut of which the inner circle defines minimum densities to ensure that certain sustainability goals are guaranteed, such as access to service and reduction of GHG emissions. The external borders define maximum densities beyond which lie unacceptable consequences for human health, well-being and environmental degradation.[14]

13
Raworth, K., Doughnut Economics: Seven Ways to Think Like a 21st-Century Economist, (*Vermont: White River Junction, 2017*).

14
Berghauser Pont, M., 'Munken som kan rädda vår stad', *Stadsbyggnad* 2 (2019).

LIST OF REFERENCES

Abel, Jaison R., Ishita Dey, and Todd M. Gabe. "Productivity and the Density of Human Capital*." *Journal of Regional Science* 52, no. 4 2012: 562–86.

Abrahamse, J.A., 'De ruimtelijke ontwikkeling van Amsterdam in de zeventiende eeuw en de opkomst van de stedebouw als wetenschap', in: B. Bakker and E. Schmitz eds., *Het aanzien van Amsterdam: Panorama's, plattegronden en profielen uit de Gouden Eeuw* Bussum: Uitgeverij THOTH, 2007, 24–41.

Adolphson, Marcus. "Kernel Densities and Mixed Functionality in a Multicentred Urban Region." *Environment and Planning B-Planning & Design* 37, no. 3 2010: 550–66.

Ahlfeldt, G. and E. Pietrostefani, *Demystifying Compact Urban Growth: Evidence From 300 Studies From Across the World* London and Washington: Coalition for Urban Transitions, 2017.

Akar, Gulsah, Na Chen, and Steven I. Gordon. "Influence of Neighborhood Types on Trip Distances: Spatial Error Models for Central Ohio." *International Journal of Sustainable Transportation* 10, no. 3 2016: 284–93.

Alberti, Marina, Derek Booth, Kristina Hill, Bekkah Coburn, Christina Avolio, Stefan Coe, and Daniele Spirandelli. 'The Impact of Urban Patterns on Aquatic Ecosystems: An Empirical Analysis in Puget Lowland Sub-Basins'. *Landscape and Urban Planning* 80, no. 4 2007: 345–61.

Alexander, C., et al., *A Pattern Language: Towns, Buildings, Construction* New York: Oxford University Press, 1977.

Alexander, E.R., 'Density Measures: A Review and Analysis', *Journal of Architectural and Planning Research* 10 3 1993, 181–202.

Ananda, Jayanath. 'Evaluating the Performance of Urban Water Utilities: Robust Nonparametric Approach'. *Journal of Water Resources Planning and Management* 140, no. 9 2014: 04014021.

Angel, S., J. Parent, D.L. Civco, A.M. Blei, *Making Room for a planet of Cities*, Lincoln Institute of Land Policy, 2011.

Angenot, L.H.J., *Verhandelingen over het vraagstuk van de dichtheid van bebouwing* Alphen aan den Rijn: N. Samsom NV, 1954.

Anonymous, 'Nota tegen rommelig bouwen', *NRC Handelsblad* 28 June 2008.

ANP, 'CDA wil 5 miljoen extra parkeerplaatsen', *de Volkskrant* 1 July 2008.

Ashworth, G.J. and H. Voogd, 'Public Sector Market Planning: An Approach to Urban Revitalisation', paper presented at the conference *European Cities: Growth and Decline* The Hague, April 1992.

Antoniucci, Valentina, and Giuliano Marella. 'Is Social Polarization Related to Urban Density? Evidence from the Italian Housing Market'. *Landscape and Urban Planning* 177 2018: 340–49.

Arundel, Rowan, and Richard Ronald. 'The Role of Urban Form in Sustainability of Community: The Case of Amsterdam'. *Environment and Planning B-Urban Analytics and City Science* 44, no. 1 2017: 33–53

Asabere, Paul K. 'The Value of Homes in Cluster Development Residential Districts: The Relative Significance of the Permanent Open Spaces Associated with Clusters'. *Journal of Real Estate Finance and Economics* 48, no. 2 2014: 244–55.

Bach, B., et al., *Urban Design and Traffic; A Selection from Bach's Toolbox/Stedebouw en verkeer; een selectie uit de gereedschapskist van Bach* Ede: Crow, 2006.

Balazs, Bernadett, Janos Unger, Tamas Gal, Zoltan Suemeghy, Janos Geiger, and Sandor Szegedi. 'Simulation of the Mean Urban Heat Island Using 2D Surface Parameters: Empirical Modelling, Verification and Extension'. *Meteorological Applications* 16, no. 3 2009: 275–87.

Baldassare, M., and G. Wilson. 'More Trouble in Paradise – Urbanization and the Decline in Suburban Quality-of-Life Ratings'. *Urban Affairs Review* 30, no. 5 1995: 690–708.

Banister, D., S. Watson, and C. Wood. 'Sustainable Cities: Transport, Energy, and Urban Form'. *Environment and Planning B-Planning & Design* 24, no. 1 1997: 125–43.

Barla, Philippe, Luis F. Miranda-Moreno, Nikolas Savard-Duquet, Marius Theriault, and Martin Lee-Gosselin. 'Diaggregated Empirical Analysis of Determinant of Urban Travel Greenhouse Gas Emissions'. *Transportation Research Record*, no. 2156 2010: 160–69.

Barnett, J., 'Omaha by Design – All of It: New Prospects in Urban Planning and Design', *Harvard Design Magazine* Spring/Summer 2005, 44–49.

Barnett, J., *An Introduction to Urban Design* New York: Harper and Row, 1982.

Barré, F., 'The Desire for Urbanity', *Architectural Design* 11/12 1980, 4–7.

Berg, Pauline van den, Astrid Kemperman, and Harry Timmermans. 'Social Interaction Location Choice: A Latent Class Modeling Approach'. *Annals of the Association of American Geographers* 104, no. 5 2014: 959–72.

Berghauser Pont, M. Y., P. G. Berg, P. A. Haupt, A. Heyman, 'A systematic review of the scientifically demonstrated effects of densification', *IOP Conf. Ser.: Earth Environ. Sci.* 588 052031 2020.

Berghauser Pont, M., G. Stavroulaki, L. Marcus, 'Development of urban types based on network centrality, built density and their impact on pedestrian movement', *Environment and Planning B: Urban analytics and city science* 46:8 2019: 1549–1564.

Berghauser Pont, M., 'Munken som kan rädda vår stad', *Stadsbyggnad* 2 2019.

Berghauser Pont, M. and J. Olsson, 'Typology based on three variables central to Spacematrix using cluster analysis', *ISUF 2017 XXIV international conference: City and territory in the globalization age*, Seville 2017.

Berghauser Pont, M., and Marcus, L., 'Innovations in measuring density. From area and location density to accessible and perceived density', *Nordic Journal of Architectural Research* 2014.

Berghauser Pont, M. And P. Haupt, *Spacemate: The Spatial Logic of Urban Density* Delft: DUP Science, 2004.

Berman, M., *All That Is Solid Melts into Air: The Experience of Modernity* New York: Penguin Books, 1988, first published in the USA by Simon & Schuster in 1982.

Bik, M. and D. Linders, *Factsheet – prognose: Bevolkingsontwikkeling Rotterdam 2003–2017* Rotterdam: Centrum voor Onderzoek en Statistiek, 2003.

Bobkova, E., *Towards a theory of natural occupation: developing theoretical, methodological and empirical support for the relation between plot systems and urban processes*, PhD thesis Chalmers 2019.

Bramley, Glen, Nicola Dempsey, Sinead Power, Caroline Brown, and David Watkins. 'Social Sustainability and Urban Form: Evidence from Five British Cities'. *Environment and Planning A* 41, no. 9 2009: 2125–42.

Brenner, N., *New State Spaces: Urban Governance and the Rescaling of Statehood* Oxford: Oxford University Press, 2004.

Brenner, N. and N. Theodore, *Spaces of Neoliberalism: Urban Restructuring in North America and Western Europe* Oxford: Blackwell Publishing, 2002.

Brenner, R., *The Economics of Global Turbulence: The Advanced Capitalist Economies from Long Boom to Long Downturn, 1945–2005* London: Verso, 2006.

Bressler, David W., Michael J. Paul, Alison H. Purcell, Michael T. Barbour, Ed T. Rankin, and Vincent H. Resh. 'Assessment Tools for Urban Catchments: Developing Stressor Gradients'. *Journal of the American Water Resources Association* 45, no. 2 2009: 291–305.

Brown, Zachary S., Walid Oueslati, and Jerome Silva. 'Links between Urban Structure and Life Satisfaction in a Cross-Section of OECD Metro Areas'. *Ecological Economics* 129 2016: 112–21.

Brueckner, Jan K., and Ann G. Largey. 'Social Interaction and Urban Sprawl'. *Journal of Urban Economics* 64, no. 1 2008: 18–34.

Bruegmann, R., *Sprawl: A Compact History* Chicago: University of Chicago Press, 2005.

Brunello, Giorgio, and Maria De Paola. 'Training and Economic Density: Some Evidence Form Italian Provinces'. *Labour Economics* 15, no. 1 2008: 118–40.

Brunner, C., *Densité & forms urbaines dans la métropole marseillaise* Marseilles: Edition Imbernon, 2005.

Buchanan, C.D., *Mixed Blessing: The Motor in Britain* London: Leonard Hill, 1958.

Buehler, Ralph. 'Determinants of Transport Mode Choice: A Comparison of Germany and the USA'. *Journal of Transport Geography* 19, no. 4 2011: 644–57.

Bureau Parkstad, *Een blik vooruit: Vijf jaar vernieuwingsoperaties in Amsterdam Nieuw West: evaluatie en keuzerichtingen* Amsterdam, 2005.

Bureau Parkstad, *Ruimtelijke kwaliteitskader ParkStad: Toetsingskader, instrumentarium en handvat voor ontwerpers*, second concept Amsterdam, May 2001.

Bureau Parkstad, *Richting ParkStad 2015: Ontwikkelingsplan voor de vernieuwing. Samenvatting*, Concept Amsterdam, February 2001.

Bureau Parkstad, *Leefmilieus ParkStad: Bijlage 5 – Richting Parkstad 2015*, Concept Amsterdam, February 2001.

Burg, A.J. van der and B.L. Vink, 'Randstad Holland towards 2040 – Perspectives from National Government', 44th ISOCARP Congress Dalian, China 16–19 September 2008.

Busquets, J., *Barcelona, the Urban Evolution of a Compact City* Rovereto: Nicolodi, 2005.

Buys, L., and E. Miller, 'Residential satisfaction in inner urban higher-density Brisbane, Australia. Role of dwelling design, neighbourhood and neighbours', *Journal of Environmental Planning and Management* 55 2012, 319–338.

Byrne, Paul F. 'Determinants of Property Value Growth for Tax Increment Financing Districts'. *Economic Development Quarterly* 20, no. 4 2006: 317–29.

Calabrese, L.M., *Reweaving UMA: Urbanism, Mobility, Architecture* Rotterdam: Optima Grafische Communicatie, 2004.

Cammen, H. van der, and L. de Klerk, *Ruimtelijke Ordening: Van grachtengordel tot Vinex-wijk* Utrecht: Het Spectrum, 2003.

Campoli, J. and A.S. MacLean, *Visualizing Density* Cambridge, MA: Lincoln Institute of Land Policy, 2007.

Cao, Xiaoshu, and Wenyue Yang. 'Examining the Effects of the Built Environment and Residential Self-Selection on Commuting Trips and the Related CO_2 Emissions: An Empirical Study in Guangzhou, China'. *Transportation Research Part D-Transport and Environment* 52 2017: 480–94.

Cao, Xinyu. 'How Does Neighborhood Design Affect Life Satisfaction? Evidence from Twin Cities'. *Travel Behaviour and Society* 5 2016: 68–76

Carbonell, A. and R. Yaro, 'American Spatial Development and the New Megalopolis', *Land Lines*, 17 2 2005.

Carruthers, J. I., and G. F. Ulfarsson. 'Urban Sprawl and the Cost of Public Services'. *Environment and Planning B-Planning & Design* 30, no. 4 2003: 503–22.

Castex, J., J-C. Depaule and P. Panerai, *De rationele stad: Van bouwblok tot wooneenheid* Amsterdam: SUN, 2003, originally published in 1977 as *Formes urbaines: de l'ilot a la barre.*

CBS, *Historie bouwnijverheid vanaf 1899* The Hague: Statistics Netherlands, 2008.

CBS, *Kerncijfers postcodegebied 2004* The Hague: Statistics Netherlands, 2006.

Cervero, R. 'Built Environments and Mode Choice: Toward a Normative Framework'. *Transportation Research Part D-Transport and Environment* 7, no. 4 2002: 265–84.

CETAT, *Indicateurs morphologiques pour l'amenagement: Analyse de 50 périmetres batis situes sur le canton de Geneve* Geneva: Departement des traveaux publics, 1986.

Chaix, Basile, Dustin Duncan, Julie Vallee, Anne Vernez-Moudon, Tarik Benmarhnia, and Yan Kestens. 'The "Residential" Effect Fallacy in Neighborhood and Health Studies Formal Definition, Empirical Identification, and Correction'. *Epidemiology* 28, no. 6 2017: 789–97.

Chen, Cynthia, Hongmian Gong, and Robert Paaswell. 'Role of the Built Environment on Mode Choice Decisions: Additional Evidence on the Impact of Density'. *Transportation* 35, no. 3 2008: 285–99.

Chen, Dong, Marcus Thatcher, Xiaoming Wang, Guy Barnett, Anthony Kachenko, and Robert Prince. 'Summer Cooling Potential of Urban Vegetation-a Modeling Study for Melbourne, Australia'. *Aims Environmental Science* 2, no. 3 2015: 648–67.

Chen, Juan, Shuo Chen, and Pierre F. Landry. 'Urbanization and Mental Health in China: Linking the 2010 Population Census with a Cross-Sectional Survey'. *International Journal of Environmental Research and Public Health* 12, no. 8 2015: 9012–24.

Chen, Peng, and Jiangping Zhou. 'Effects of the Built Environment on Automobile-Involved Pedestrian Crash Frequency and Risk'. *Journal of Transport & Health* 3, no. 4 2016: 448–56.

Choi, Kwangyul. 'The Influence of the Built Environment on Household Vehicle Travel by the Urban Typology in Calgary, Canada'. *Cities* 75 2018: 101–10.

Christen, A., and R. Vogt. 'Energy and Radiation Balance of a Central European City'. *International Journal of Climatology* 24, no. 11 2004: 1395–1421.

Churchman, A., 'Disentangling the Concept of Density', *Journal of Planning Literature*, 13 4 1999, 389–411.

Ciccone, A. 'Agglomeration Effects in Europe'. *European Economic Review* 46, no. 2 2002: 213–27.

City of New York, *Zoning Handbook* New York, 1990.

Claessens, F. and E. van Velzen, 'De actualiteit van het stedelijk project', *Stedebouw & Ruimtelijke Ordening*, 87 4 2006, 32–37.

Clark, Lara P., Dylan B. Millet, and Julian D. Marshall. 'Air Quality and Urban Form in US Urban Areas: Evidence from Regulatory Monitors'. *Environmental Science & Technology* 45, no. 16 15 2011: 7028–35.

Coevering, Paul van de, and Tim Schwanen. 'Re-Evaluating the Impact of Urban Form on Travel Patterns in Europe and North-America'. *Transport Policy* 13, no. 3 2006: 229–39.

Conzen, M.R.G., *Alnwick, Northumberland: A Study in Town-Plan Analysis,* series: The Institute of British Geographers, publication 27 London: Philip, 1960.

Couch, C., L. Leontidou and G. Petschel-Held, *Urban Sprawl in Europe: Landscapes, Land-Use Change & Policy* Oxford: Blackwell Publishing, 2007.

Crimson, *Too Blessed to Be Depressed: Crimson Architectural Historians 1994–2002* Rotterdam: 010 Publishers, 2002.

Cruz, Sara Santos, and Aurora A. C. Teixeira. 'The Neglected Heterogeneity of Spatial Agglomeration and Co-Location Patterns of Creative Employment: Evidence from Portugal'. *Annals of Regional Science* 54, no. 1 2015: 143–77

Davis, M., *Planet of Slums* London / New York: Verso, 2006.

Davis, M. and D.B. Monk eds., *Evil Paradises: Dreamworlds of Neoliberalism* New York: The New Press, 2007.

Dave, Seema. 'Neighbourhood Density and Social Sustainability in Cities of Developing Countries'. *Sustainable Development* 19, no. 3 2011: 189–205.

Dempsey, N., C. Brown, and G. Bramley. 'The Key to Sustainable Urban Development in UK Cities? The Influence of Density on Social Sustainability'. *Progress in Planning* 77 2012: 89–141.

Di Addario, Sabrina, and Daniela Vuri. 'Entrepreneurship and Market Size. The Case of Young College Graduates in Italy'. *Labour Economics* 17, no. 5 2010: 848–58.

Dijkstra, C., M. Reitsma and A. Rommerts, *Atlas Amsterdam* Bussum: Uitgeverij THOTH, 1999.

Ding, C. R. 'Urban Spatial Development in the Land Policy Reform Era: Evidence from Beijing'. *Urban Studies* 41, no. 10 2004: 1889–1907.

Ding, Chuan, Yaoyu Lin, and Chao Liu. 'Exploring the Influence of Built Environment on Tour-Based Commuter Mode Choice: A Cross-Classified Multilevel Modeling Approach'. *Transportation Research Part D-Transport and Environment* 32 2014: 230–38.

Ding, Chuan, Yaowu Wang, Binglei Xie, and Chao Liu. 'Understanding the Role of Built Environment in Reducing Vehicle Miles Traveled Accounting for Spatial Heterogeneity'. *Sustainability* 6, no. 2 2014: 589–601.

Du, Peng, Antony Wood, and Brent Stephens. 'Empirical Operational Energy Analysis of Downtown High-Rise vs. Suburban Low-Rise Lifestyles: A Chicago Case Study'. *Energies* 9, no. 6 2016: 445.

Duivesteijn, A., *Notie van ruimte: Op weg naar de vijfde nota ruimtelijke ordening*, Parlementaire werkgroep vijfde nota ruimtelijke ordening The Hague: Sdu uitgevers, 2000.

Dumbaugh, Eric, and Robert Rae. 'Safe Urban Form: Revisiting the Relationship Between Community Design and Traffic Safety'. *Journal of the American Planning Association* 75, no. 3 2009: 309–29.

Edwards, Mary M., and Yu Xiao. 'Annexation, Local Government Spending, and the Complicating Role of Density'. *Urban Affairs Review* 45, no. 2 2009: 147–65.

El-Assi, Wafic, Mohamed Salah Mahmoud, and Khandker Nurul Habib. 'Effects of Built Environment and Weather on Bike Sharing Demand: A Station Level Analysis of Commercial Bike Sharing in Toronto'. *Transportation* 44, no. 3 2017: 589–613.

Elliott, D.L., *A Better Way to Zone: Ten Principles to Create More Livable Cities* Washington, DC: Island Press, 2008.

Engel, H., 'Randstad Holland in kaart', in: F. Claessens and H. Engel eds., *OverHolland 2* Amsterdam: SUN, 2005, 22–44.

Engel, H. and E. van Velzen, 'De vorm van de stad: Nederland na 1945', in: E. Taverne and I. Visser eds., *Stedebouw: De geschiedenis van de stad in de Nederlanden van 1500 tot heden* Nijmegen: SUN, 1993, 276–282.

Engelfriet, Lara, and Eric Koomen. 'The Impact of Urban Form on Commuting in Large Chinese Cities'. *Transportation* 45, no. 5 2018: 1269–95.

European Commission, *The Green Paper—A 2030 framework for climate and energy policies* 2013, retrieved October 7, 2017, from https://ec.europa.eu/energy/sites/ener/files/publication/GP_EN_web.pdf.

Ewing, Reid, Amir Hajrasouliha, Kathryn M. Neckerman, Marnie Purciel-Hill, and William Greene. 'Streetscape Features Related to Pedestrian Activity'. *Journal of Planning Education and Research* 36, no. 1 2016: 5–15.

Fallah, Belal N., Mark D. Partridge, and M. Rose Olfert. 'Urban Sprawl and Productivity: Evidence from US Metropolitan Areas'. *Papers in Regional Science* 90, no. 3 2011: 451–72.

Faludi, A. and A. van der Valk, *Rule and Order: Dutch Planning Doctrine in the Twentieth Century* Dordrecht: Kluwer Academic Publishers, 1994.

Fassio, Omar, Chiara Rollero, and Norma De Piccoli. 'Health, Quality of Life and Population Density: A Preliminary Study on "Contextualized" Quality of Life'. *Social Indicators Research* 110, no. 2 2013: 479–88.

Fernandez Per, A., and J. Mozas, *DBOOK: Density, Data, Diagrams, Dwellings* Vitoria-Gasteiz: a+t ediciones, 2007.

Fernandez Per, A., and J. Mozas, *Densidad/Density* Vitoria-Gasteiz: a+t ediciones, 2004.

Floet, W.W. and E. Gramsbergen, *Zakboek voor de woonomgeving* Rotterdam: 010 Publishers, 2001.

Florida, R., *Cities and the Creative Class* New York: Routledge, 2005.

Eom, Hyun-Joo, and Gi-Hyoug Cho. 'Exploring Thresholds of Built Environment Characteristics for Walkable Communities: Empirical Evidence from the Seoul Metropolitan Area'. *Transportation Research Part D-Transport and Environment* 40 2015: 76–86.

Forsyth, Ann, J. Michael Oakes, Kathryn H. Schmitz, and Mary Hearst. 'Does Residential Density Increase Walking and Other Physical Activity?' *Urban Studies* 44, no. 4 2007: 679–97.

Forsyth, A., 'Measuring Density: Working Definitions for Residential Density and Building Density', *Design Brief*, 8 2003, Design Center for American Urban Landscape, University of Minesota.

Frank, L. D., M. A. Andresen, and T. L. Schmid. 'Obesity Relationships with Community Design, Physical Activity, and Time Spent in Cars'. *American Journal of Preventive Medicine* 27, no. 2 2004: 87–96.

Freeman, L. 'The Effects of Sprawl on Neighborhood Social Ties – An Explanatory Analysis'. *Journal of the American Planning Association* 67, no. 1 2001: 69–77.

Gan, Mi, Xiaobo Liu, Si Chen, Ying Yan, and Dandan Li. 'The Identification of Truck-Related Greenhouse Gas Emissions and Critical Impact Factors in an Urban Logistics Network'. *Journal of Cleaner Production* 178 2018: 561–71.

Gao, J., O'Neill, B.C. Mapping global urban land for the 21st century with data-driven simulations and Shared Socioeconomic Pathways. *Nat Commun* 11, 2302 2020.

Gladhill, Kristie, and Christopher M. Monsere. 'Exploring Traffic Safety and Urban Form in Portland, Oregon'. *Transportation Research Record*, no. 2318 2012: 63–74.

Grazi, Fabio, Jeroen C. J. M. van den Bergh, and Jos N. van Ommeren. 'An Empirical Analysis of Urban Form, Transport, and Global Warming'. *Energy Journal* 29, no. 4 2008: 97–122.

Gren, Å, J Colding, M Berghauser Pont and L Marcus, 'How Smart is Smart Growth? Examining the Environmental Validation Behind City Compaction', *Ambio* 48 2018.

Haaland, C. and C. K. van den Bosch, 'Challenges and strategies for urban green-space planning in cities undergoing densification: A review', *Urban Forestry & Urban Greening*, 14:4 2015, 760–71.

Hajer, M., 'Rekenen of tekenen?', *Staatscourant*, 11 October 2000, 3.

Hajer, M., *De stad als publiek domein* Amsterdam: Wiardi Beckman Stichting, 1989.

Hall, P., *Cities in Civilization* London: Phoenix, 1999.

Hall, P., *Cities of Tomorrow* Oxford: Blackwell Publishers, 1996.

Hameleers, M. ed., *Kaarten van Amsterdam 1866–2000* Bussum: Uitgeverij THOTH, 2002.

Hans, Lianne, and Sierdjan Koster. 'Urbanization and Start-up Rates in Different Geographies: Belgium, the Netherlands, and Sweden'. *Small Business Economics* 51, no. 4 2018: 1033–54.

Harvey, D., *A Brief History of Neoliberalism* Oxford: Oxford University Press, 2005.

Harvey, D., 'New Urbanism and the Communitarian Trap', in: W.S. Saunders ed., *Sprawl and Suburbia*, A Harvard Design Magazine Reader Minneapolis: University of Minnesota Press, 2005.

Harvey, D., 'From Managerialism to Entrepreneurialism: The Transformation in Urban Governance in Late Capitalism', *Geografiska Annaler* 71B 1989, 3–17.

Harvey, D., *The Urbanization of Capital* Baltimore: John Hopkins University Press, 1985.

Haupt P A, M Y Berghauser Pont, V Alstäde, P G Berg, 'A systematic review of motives for densification in Swedish planning practice', *IOP Conf. Ser.: Earth Environ. Sci.* 588 2020, 052030.

Haupt, P., 'Adriaan Geuze, Rem Koolhaas och staden som inte längre finns', *Arkitektur*, 1 1996, 68–73.

Haupt, P. and M. van Esch, 'Daylight and Urban Density', in: H. Bekkering et al. eds., *The Architectural Annual 2005–2006*, Delft University of Technology Rotterdam: 010 Publishers, 2007, 86–91.

Heeling, J., H. Meyer and J. Westrik, *Het ontwerp van de stadsplattegrond* Amsterdam: SUN, 2002.

Heimans, A., *Bebouwingsdichtheid en grondgebruik voor de woningbouw in stadsuitbreidingen* The Hague: Ten Hagen, 1965.

Hellinga, H. and P. de Ruijter, *Algemeen Uitbreidingsplan Amsterdam 50 jaar* Amsterdam: Amsterdamse Raad voor de Stedebouw, 1985.

Hereijgers, A. and E. van Velzen, *De naoorlogse stad, een hedendaagse ontwerpopgave* Rotterdam: NAi Publishers, 2001.

Hess, Daniel Baldwin, and Jessica Kozlowski Russell. 'Influence of Built Environment and Transportation Access on Body Mass Index of Older Adults: Survey Results from Erie County, New York'. *Transport Policy* 20 2012: 130–39.

Hillier, B. and Hanson, J., *The social logic of space* Cambridge: Cambridge University Press, 1984.

Hobma, F., De verwevenheid van publiekrechtelijk en privaatrechtelijk handelen. In: I. Bruil et al. eds., *Integrale gebiedsontwikkeling: Het stationsgebied 's-Hertogenbosch* Amsterdam: SUN, 2004, 280–293.
Hobsbawm, E., *The Age of Extremes: 1914–1991* London: Michael Joseph, 1994.
Hobsbawm, E., *The Age of Empire: 1875–1914* London: Weidenfeld and Nicholson, 1987.
Hobsbawm, E., *The Age of Capital: 1848–1875* London: Weidenfeld and Nicholson, 1975.
Hobsbawm, E., *The Age of Revolution: 1789–1848* London: Weidenfeld and Nicholson, 1962.
Hoenig, A., 'Baudichte und Weitraumigkeit', *Baugilde* 10 1928, 713–715.
Hong, Jinhyun, Qing Shen, and Lei Zhang. 'How Do Built-Environment Factors Affect Travel Behavior? A Spatial Analysis at Different Geographic Scales'. *Transportation* 41, no. 3 2014: 419–40.
Hortas-Rico, Miriam, and Albert Sole-Olle. 'Does Urban Sprawl Increase the Costs of Providing Local Public Services? Evidence from Spanish Municipalities'. *Urban Studies* 47, no. 7 2010: 1513–40.
Houston, Douglas, Marlon G. Boarnet, Gavin Ferguson, and Steven Spears. 'Can Compact Rail Transit Corridors Transform the Automobile City? Planning for More Sustainable Travel in Los Angeles'. *Urban Studies* 52, no. 5 2015: 938–59.
Howley, P.. 'Sustainability versus liveability. An exploration of central city housing satisfaction', *International Journal of Housing Policy*, 10 2010, 173–189.
Hulsman, B., 'Die domme steden', *NRC Handelsblad* 28 February / 1 March 2009, 4–5.

Ingvardson, Jesper Blafoss, and Otto Anker Nielsen. 'How Urban Density, Network Topology and Socio-Economy Influence Public Transport Ridership: Empirical Evidence from 48 European Metropolitan Areas'. *Journal of Transport Geography* 72 2018: 50–63.
Iwata, Kazuyuki, and Shunsuke Managi. 'Can Land Use Regulations and Taxes Help Mitigate Vehicular CO_2 Emissions? An Empirical Study of Japanese Cities'. *Urban Policy and Research* 34, no. 4 2016: 356–72.

Jacobs, J., *The Death and Life of Great American Cities* New York: Random House, 1992, originally published in 1961.
Jameson, F., *Postmodernism, or, the Cultural Logic of Late Capitalism* London: Verso, 1991.
Jenks, M., E. Burton and K. Williams eds., *The Compact City: A Sustainable Urban Form?* London: E&FN Spoon, 1996.
Jennen, Maarten, and Patrick Verwijmeren. 'Agglomeration Effects and Financial Performance'. *Urban Studies* 47, no. 12 2010: 2683–2703
Jing, Li, Lo Kevin, Zhang Pingyu, and Guo Meng. 'Relationship between Built Environment, Socio-Economic Factors and Carbon Emissions from Shopping Trip in Shenyang City, China'. *Chinese Geographical Science* 27, no. 5 2017: 722–34.
Jong, T. de, et al., *Sun Wind Water Earth Life and Living: Legends for Design* Delft: Publicatiebureau Bouwkunde, 2004.
Jong, T. de and H. Engel, 'Typological Research', in: T.M. de Jong and D.J.M. van der Voordt eds., *Ways to Study and Research Urban, Architectural and Technical Design* Delft: DUP Science, 2002, 103–106.
Jong, T. de and D.J.M. van der Voordt, 'Criteria for Scientific Study and Design', in: T.M. de Jong and D.J.M. van der Voordt eds., *Ways to Study and Research Urban, Architectural and Technical Design* Delft: DUP Science, 2002, 19–30.
Jong, T. de and D.J.M. van der Voordt eds., *Ways to Study and Research Urban, Architectural and Technical Design* Delft: DUP Science, 2002
Jun, Hee-Jung, and Misun Hur. 'The Relationship between Walkability and Neighborhood Social Environment: The Importance of Physical and Perceived Walkability'. *Applied Geography* 62 2015: 115–24.

Kamruzzaman, Md, Kaveh Deilami, and Tan Yigitcanlar. 'Investigating the Urban Heat Island Effect of Transit Oriented Development in Brisbane'. *Journal of Transport Geography* 66 2018: 116–24
Kann, F. van and W. Leduc, 'Synergy between regional planning and energy as a contribution to a carbon neutral society – energy cascading as a new principle for mixed land-use'. Paper presented at the SCUPAD conference Salzburg, Austria, 2008.
Karathodorou, Niovi, Daniel J. Graham, and Robert B. Noland. 'Estimating the Effect of Urban Density on Fuel Demand'. *Energy Economics* 32, no. 1 2010: 86–92.
Ke, Shanzi, and Yufeng Yu. 'The Pathways from Industrial Agglomeration to TFP Growth – the Experience of Chinese Cities for 2001–2010'. *Journal of the Asia Pacific Economy* 19, no. 2 2014: 310–32.
Kendig, L., *Performance Zoning* Washington, DC: Planners Press, APA, 1980.
Kim, Dohyung, Jiyoung Park, and Andy Hong. 'The Role of Destination's Built Environment on Nonmotorized Travel Behavior: A Case of Long Beach, California'. *Journal of Planning Education and Research* 38, no. 2 2018: 152–66.
Kim, H. W., M.-H. Li, J.-H. Kim, and F. Jaber. "Examining the Impact of Suburbanization on Surface Runoff Using the SWAT." *International Journal of Environmental Research* 10, no. 3 2016: 379–90.
Kim, Saehoon, Sungjin Park, and Jae Seung Lee. 'Meso- or Micro-Scale? Environmental Factors Influencing Pedestrian Satisfaction'. *Transportation Research Part D-Transport and Environment* 30 2014: 10–20
Kim, Saehoon, and Youngryel Ryu. 'Describing the Spatial Patterns of Heat Vulnerability from Urban Design Perspectives'. *International Journal of Sustainable Development and World Ecology* 22, no. 3 2015: 189–200.
Klerk, L. de, *De modernisering van de stad 1850–1914: De opkomst van de planmatige stadsontwikkeling in Nederland* Rotterdam: NAi Publishers, 2008.
Klerk, L. de, *Particuliere plannen: Denkbeelden en initiatieven van de stedelijke elite inzake volkswoningbouw en de stedebouw in Rotterdam, 1860–1950* Rotterdam: NAi Publishers, 1998.
Kline, J. 'Public Demand for Preserving Local Open Space'. *Society & Natural Resources* 19, no. 7 2006: 645–59.
Kloos, M. and D. Wendt, *Formats for Living: Contemporary Floor Plans in Amsterdam* Amsterdam: ARCAM / Architectura & Natura Press, 2000.
Knoell, Martin, Katrin Neuheuser, Thomas Cleff, and Annette Rudolph-Cleff. 'A Tool to Predict Perceived Urban Stress in Open Public Spaces'. *Environment and Planning B-Urban Analytics and City Science* 45, no. 4 2018: 797–813.
Ko, Yekang, and John D. Radke. 'The Effect of Urban Form and Residential Cooling Energy Use in Sacramento, California'. *Environment and Planning B-Planning & Design* 41, no. 4 2014: 573–93.
Koolhaas, R., *S,M,L,XL* Rotterdam: 010 Publishers, 1995.
Koolhaas, R., *Delirious New York* Rotterdam: 010 Publishers, 1994.
Kuang, Wenhui, Yinyin Dou, Chi Zhang, Wenfeng Chi, Ailin Liu, Yue Liu, Renhua Zhang, and Jiyuan Liu. 'Quantifying the Heat Flux Regulation of Metropolitan Land Use / Land Cover Components by Coupling Remote Sensing Modeling with in Situ Measurement'. *Journal of Geophysical Research-Atmospheres* 120, no. 1 2015: 113–30.
Kuenzli, P. and A. Lengkeek, *Urban jazz: Pleidooi voor de zelfgebouwde stad* Rotterdam: 010 Publishers, 2004.
Kunstler, J., 'Review of Sprawl: A Compact History', *Salmagundi* 152 Fall 2006, 175–183.
Kusumo, C., *Railway Stations, Centres and Markets: Change and Stability in Patterns of Urban Centrality* Dissertation Delft University of Technology, 2007.
Kytta, Marketta, Maarit Kahila, and Anna Broberg. 'Perceived Environmental Quality as an Input to Urban Infill Policy-Making'. *Urban Design International* 16, no. 1 2011: 19–35.

Lamiquiz, Patxi J., and Jorge Lopez-Dominguez. 'Effects of Built Environment on Walking at the Neighbourhood Scale. A New Role for Street Networks by Modelling Their Configurational Accessibility?' *Transportation Research Part A-Policy and Practice* 74 2015: 148–63.
Laloli, H.M., 'Beter wonen? Woningmarkt en residentiële segregatie in Amsterdam 1850–1940', in: O.W.A. Boonstra et al. eds., *Twee eeuwen Nederland geteld: Onderzoek met de digitale volks-, beroeps- en woningtellingen 1795–2001* The Hague: DANS and CBS, 2007.
Larice, M. and E. Macdonald eds., *The Urban Design Reader* Oxon: Routledge, 2007.
Lavery, T. A., A. Paez, and P. S. Kanaroglou. 'Driving out of Choices: An Investigation of Transport Modality in a University Sample'. *Transportation Research Part A-Policy and Practice* 57 2013: 37–46.

Lawson, Dawn M., Cerina K. Lamar, and Mark W. Schwartz. 'Quantifying Plant Population Persistence in Human-Dominated Landscapes'. *Conservation Biology* 22, no. 4 2008: 922–28.

Le Corbusier, *Towards a New Architecture* Los Angeles: Getty Research Institute, 2007, originally published in 1923 as *Vers une architecture*.

Lee, Jae-Su, Jin Nam, and Sam-Su Lee. 'Built Environment Impacts on Individual Mode Choice: An Empirical Study of the Houston-Galveston Metropolitan Area'. *International Journal of Sustainable Transportation* 8, no. 6 2014: 447–70

Lee, T.-Y., Y.-T. Shih, J.-C. Huang, S.-J. Kao, F.-K. Shiah, and K.-K. Liu. 'Speciation and Dynamics of Dissolved Inorganic Nitrogen Export in the Danshui River, Taiwan'. *Biogeosciences* 11, no. 19 2014: 5307–21.

Lee, Yoonjeong, and Samuel D. Brody. 'Examining the Impact of Land Use on Flood Losses in Seoul, Korea'. *Land Use Policy* 70 2018: 500–509.

Leeuwen, H. van, 'Geef bouwgrond niet aan speculanten', *NRC Handelsblad* 18 August 2008.

Lengkeek, A., *Stedelijkheid als rendement: Privaat initiatief voor publieke ruimte* Haarlem: Trancity, 2007.

Lenth, Buffy A., Richard L. Knight, and Wendell C. Gilgert. 'Conservation Value of Clustered Housing Developments'. *Conservation Biology* 20, no. 5 2006: 1445–56.

Li, Baojie, Dongxiang Chen, Shaohua Wu, Shenglu Zhou, Teng Wang, and Hao Chen. 'Spatio-Temporal Assessment of Urbanization Impacts on Ecosystem Services: Case Study of Nanjing City, China'. *Ecological Indicators* 71 2016: 416–27.

Li, Ruiqi, Peter Richmond, and Bertrand M. Roehner. 'Effect of Population Density on Epidemics'. *Physica A-Statistical Mechanics and Its Applications* 510 2018: 713–24.

Li, Shengxiao, and Pengjun Zhao. 'Exploring Car Ownership and Car Use in Neighborhoods near Metro Stations in Beijing: Does the Neighborhood Built Environment Matter?' *Transportation Research Part D-Transport and Environment* 56 2017: 1–17.

Lin, Jen-Jia, and Ting-Yu Shin. 'Does Transit-Oriented Development Affect Metro Ridership? Evidence from Taipei, Taiwan'. *Transportation Research Record*, no. 2063 2008: 149–58.

Lin, Jen-Jia, and An-Tsei Yang. 'Structural Analysis of How Urban Form Impacts Travel Demand: Evidence from Taipei'. *Urban Studies* 46, no. 9 2009: 1951–67.

Lin, Jen-Jia, and An-Tsei Yang. 'Does the Compact-City Paradigm Foster Sustainability? An Empirical Study in Taiwan'. *Environment and Planning B-Planning & Design* 33, no. 3 2006: 365–80.

Lin, Jen-Jia, and Hsiao-Te Chang. 'Built Environment Effects on Children's School Travel in Taipai: Independence and Travel Mode'. *Urban Studies* 47, no. 4 2010: 867–89.

Liu, Lu, and Paul M. Jakus. 'Hedonic Valuation in an Urban High-Rise Housing Market'. *Canadian Journal of Agricultural Economics-Revue Canadienne D Agroeconomie* 63, no. 2 2015: 259–73.

Liu, Qianqian, Shaojian Wang, Wenzhong Zhang, and Jiaming Li. 'Income Distribution and Environmental Quality in China: A Spatial Econometric Perspective'. *Journal of Cleaner Production* 205 2018: 14–26.

Loon, P.P. van, E. Heurkens and S. Bronkhorst, *Urban Decision Room: An Urban Management Instrument* Amsterdam: IOS Press, 2008.

Lörzing, H., W. Klemm, M. Van Leeuwen and S. Soekimin, *Vinex! Een morfologische verkenning* Rotterdam: NAi Publishers, 2006.

Lozano, E., 'Density in Communities, or the Most Important Factor in Building Urbanity', in: M. Larice and E. Macdonald eds., *The Urban Design Reader* Oxon: Routledge, 2007, 312–327.

LSE Cities, *Resource Urbanisms. Asia's divergent city models of Kuwait, Abu Dhabi, Singapore and Hong Kong* London School of Economics and Political Science, 2017.

LSE Cities, *Cities and Energy. Urban Morphology and Heat Energy Demand* London School of Economics and Political Science, 2014.

Lu, Yi, Long Chen, Yiyang Yang, and Zhonghua Gou. 'The Association of Built Environment and Physical Activity in Older Adults: Using a Citywide Public Housing Scheme to Reduce Residential Self-Selection Bias'. *International Journal of Environmental Research and Public Health* 15, no. 9 2018: 1973.

Lynch, K., *A Theory of Good City Form* Cambridge, MA: MIT Press, 1981.

MA, *Millennium ecosystem assessment. Ecosystems and human well-being: synthesis* Washington, DC: Island Press, 2005.

Ma, Jing, Zhilin Liu, and Yanwei Chai. 'The Impact of Urban Form on CO_2 Emission from Work and Non-Work Trips: The Case of Beijing, China'. *Habitat International* 47 2015: 1–10.

Maarse, A., 'Wetten en regels', *Rooilijn* 41 3 2008, 155.

Marique, Anne-Francoise, Sebastien Dujardin, Jacques Teller, and Sigrid Reiter. 'Urban Sprawl, Commuting and Travel Energy Consumption'. *Proceedings of the Institution of Civil Engineers-Energy* 166, no. 1 2013: 29–41.

Marshall, S., *Streets & Patterns* Oxon: Spon Press, 2005.

Martin, L. and L. March eds., *Urban Space and Structures* Cambridge: Cambridge University Press, 1972.

Martin, M. and C. Wagenaar, 'Stadsverfraaing en stadsuitbreiding', in: E. Taverne and I. Visser eds., *Stedebouw: De geschiedenis van de stad in de Nederlanden van 1500 tot heden* Nijmegen: SUN, 1993, 124–129.

Mashhoodi, Bardia. 'Spatial Dynamics of Household Energy Consumption and Local Drivers in Randstad, Netherlands'. *Applied Geography* 91 2018: 123–30.

McAndrews, Carolyn, Kenta Okuyama, and Jill S. Litt. 'The Reach of Bicycling in Rural, Small, and Low-Density Places'. *Transportation Research Record*, no. 2662 2017: 134–42.

Meer, A.J. van der, *Gemeentegrenzen Nederland 1795 – heden*, dissertation OTB Research Institute, Delft University of Technology, 2007.

Meijsmans, N., 'The Urban Project on a Regional Scale?', paper presented at the conference *The Urban Project* Delft, the Netherlands 4–7 June 2008.

Mendiola, Lorea, Pilar Gonzalez, and Angel Cebollada. 'The Link between Urban Development and the Modal Split in Commuting: The Case of Biscay'. *Journal of Transport Geography* 37 2014: 1–9.

Metz, T. and M. Pflug, *Atlas van Nederland in 2005: De Nieuwe Kaart* Rotterdam: NAi Publishers, 1997.

Meyer, H. et al., *Ruimtelijke transformaties in kleine nederzettingen: West-Nederland: 1850–2000* Delft: Delft University of Technology, Faculty of Architecture, 2006.

Meyer, H., F. de Josselin de Jong and M.J. Hoekstra eds., *Het ontwerp van de openbare ruimte* Amsterdam: SUN, 2006.

Meyer, H., 'In dienst van de stad onder postmoderne condities / Working for the City under Post-modern Conditions', in: H. Meyer and L. van den Burg eds., *In dienst van de stad / Working for the City* Amsterdam: SUN, 2005, 64–68.

Meyer, H., 'Plan Analysis', in: T.M. de Jong and D.J.M. van der Voordt eds., *Ways to Study and Research Urban, Architectural and Technical Design* Delft: DUP Science, 2002, 125–136.

Meyer, H., *City and Port: Transformation of Port Cities London, Barcelona, New York, Rotterdam* Utrecht: International Books, 1999.

Ming, Z. 'Travel Choice with No Alternative – Can Land Use Reduce Automobile Dependence?' *Journal of Planning Education and Research* 25, no. 3 2006: 311–26.

Minoura, E., *Uncommon Ground: Urban Form and Social Territory*, PhD thesis KTH 2016.

Modarres, Ali. 'Commuting and Energy Consumption: Toward an Equitable Transportation Policy'. *Journal of Transport Geography* 33 2013: 240–49.

Moll, H., 'Vuile teringstad: Vijf eeuwen besmettelijke ziekten in Amsterdam', *NRC Handelsblad* 31 January 2001.

Morikawa, Masayuki. 'Economies of Density and Productivity in Service Industries: An Analysis'. *Review of Economics and Statistics* 93, no. 1 2011: 179–92.

Morikawa, Masayuki. 'Population Density and Efficiency in Energy Consumption: An Empirical Analysis of Service Establishments'. *Energy Economics* 34, no. 5 2012: 1617–22.

Mou, Yanchuan, Yan Song, Qing Xu, Qingsong He, and Ang Hu. 'Influence of Urban-Growth Pattern on Air Quality in China: A Study of 338 Cities'. *International Journal of Environmental Research and Public Health* 15, no. 9 2018: 1805.

Moudon, A.V., 'Getting to Know the Built Landscape: Typomorphology', in: K. Franck and L. Schneekloth eds., *Ordering Space: Types in Architecture and Design* New York: Van Nostrand Reinhold, 1994, 289–311.

Mouratidis, Kostas. 'Built Environment and Social Well-Being: How Does Urban Form Affect Social Life and Personal Relationships?' *Cities* 74 2018: 7–20

Mumford, L., *The City in History: Its Origins, Its Transformations, and Its Prospects* New York: Harcourt, Brace and World, 1961.

Municipality of Almere, *Concept Structuurvisie Almere 2.0* Almere: Municipality of Almere and MVRDV, 2009.
Municipality of Amersfoort, *Amersfoort in cijfers* Amersfoort: Onderzoek en statistiek, 2006.
Municipality of Amsterdam, *Uitwerkingsplan kerngebied Reimerswaalbuurt* Amsterdam: Neighbourhood Council Osdorp/Ymere, 2005.
Municipality of Amsterdam, *Studie hoogbouw in Amsterdam-Noord* Amsterdam: Neighbourhood Council Amsterdam-Noord, R&EB, 2003.
Municipality of Amsterdam, *Structuurplan Amsterdam: Kiezen voor stedelijkheid* Amsterdam: dRO, 2003.
Municipality of Amsterdam, *Meten met twee maten: Referentieplannen bebouwingsintensiteit* Amsterdam: dRO, coördinatieteam Optimalisering Grondgebruik, 2001.
Municipality of Amsterdam, *Midwest: Differentiatie en intensivering in de Westelijke Tuinsteden* Amsterdam: dRO, 1999.
Municipality of Amsterdam, *Algemeen Uitbreidingsplan van Amsterdam AUP: Nota van toelichting* Amsterdam: Stadsdrukkerij Amsterdam, 1934.
Municipality of den Haag, *Haagse referentie projecten: Achtergronddocument: Uitwerking structuurvisie den Haag 2020* The Hague: DSO-ROMZ, 2006.
Municipality of Rotterdam, *Stadsvisie Rotterdam: Spatial Development Strategy 2030* Rotterdam: dS+V, 2007.
Municipality of Rotterdam, *De Rotterdamse woonmilieuprofielen-atlas* Rotterdam: dS+V, afdeling Wonen, 2003.
Municipality of Tilburg, *Ontwikkelingsvisie Piushavengebied* Tilburg, 2002.
Musch, M., 'Polder Ground', *OASE* 52 1999, 16–31.
MVRDV, *Metacity/Datatown* Rotterdam: 010 Publishers, 1999.
MVRDV, *Farmax* Rotterdam: 010 Publishers, 1998.

Najaf, Pooya, Jean-Claude Thill, Wenjia Zhang, and Milton Greg Fields. 'City-Level Urban Form and Traffic Safety: A Structural Equation Modeling Analysis of Direct and Indirect Effects'. *Journal of Transport Geography* 69 2018: 257–70.
Nase, Ilir, Jim Berry, and Alastair Adair. 'Impact of Quality-Led Design on Real Estate Value: A Spatiotemporal Analysis of City Centre Apartments'. *Journal of Property Research* 33, no. 4 2016: 309–31.
Neighbourhood Council Slotervaart, *Stedebouwkundig Plan Sloterweg Zuid West*, Amsterdam, 2006.
NEN, *NEN 2580: Areas and Volumes of Buildings – Terms, Definitions and Methods of Determination* Delft: NEN, 2007.
NEN, *NEN 12464-1:2002: Light and Lighting – Light of Workplaces – Part 1: Indoor Workplaces* Delft: NEN, 2003.
Netherlands Institute for Spatial Research, *Demographic Decline and Spatial Development: Planning for the Consequences of Population Changes, Summary* The Hague, 2006, available online at: http://rpb.ddg5.tamtam.nl/upload/documenten/summary_demographicdecline.pdf accessed 19 November 2008.
Neuman, M., 'The Compact City Fallacy', *Journal of Planning Education and Research* 25 2005, 11–26.
Newman, P. and J. Kenworthy, *Sustainability and Cities: Overcoming Automobile Dependence* Chicago: University of Chicago Press, 1999.
Nguyen, Doan. 'Evidence of the Impacts of Urban Sprawl on Social Capital'. *Environment and Planning B-Planning & Design* 37, no. 4 2010: 610–27.
Nilsson, Pia. 'Are Valuations of Place-Based Amenities Driven by Scale?' *Housing Studies* 32, no. 4 2017: 449–69.
Norman, J., H. L. MacLean, and C. A. Kennedy. 'Comparing High and Low Residential Density: Life-Cycle Analysis of Energy Use and Greenhouse Gas Emissions'. *Journal of Urban Planning and Development-Asce* 132, no. 1 2006: 10–21
Nozzi, D., *Road to Ruin: An Introduction to Sprawl and How to Cure It* Westport: Praeger Publishers, 2003.
Nycolaas, J., *Volkshuisvesting: Een bijdrage tot de geschiedenis van woningbouw en woningbeleid in Nederland, met name sedert 1945* Nijmegen: SUN, 1974.

Okulicz-Kozaryn, Adam, and Joan Maya Mazelis. 'Urbanism and Happiness: A Test of Wirth's Theory of Urban Life'. *Urban Studies* 55, no. 2 2018: 349–64.
Oliva, Ignacio, Patricia Galilea, and Ricardo Hurtubia. 'Identifying Cycling-Inducing Neighborhoods: A Latent Class Approach'. *International Journal of Sustainable Transportation* 12, no. 10 2018: 701–13.
Openshaw, S., P.J.A. Taylor, 'A million or so correlation coefficients: three experiments on the modifiable areal unit problem', *Stat. Appl. Spat. Sci.*, 21 1979, 127–144.
O+S, Statistics available on www.os.amsterdam.nl 2007.
Otsuka, Akihiro, and Mika Goto. 'Estimation and Determinants of Energy Efficiency in Japanese Regional Economies'. *Regional Science Policy and Practice* 7, no. 2 2015: 89–101.
Ottelin, Juudit, Jukka Heinonen, and Seppo Junnila. 'Greenhouse Gas Emissions from Flying Can Offset the Gain from Reduced Driving in Dense Urban Areas'. *Journal of Transport Geography* 41 2014: 1–9.
Ottens, E., 'De aanloop naar de Woningwet: "de holen der mensen…"', in: J. Keesom ed., *Wonen. Woning. Wet. Wij wonen – 100 jaar Woningwet* Amsterdam: Stedelijke Woningdienst Amsterdam, 2000, 9–40.

Pan, Haixiao, Jing Li, Qing Shen, and Cheng Shi. 'What Determines Rail Transit Passenger Volume? Implications for Transit Oriented Development Planning'. *Transportation Research Part D-Transport and Environment* 57 2017: 52–63.
Pendall, R., and J. I. Carruthers. 'Does Density Exacerbate Income Segregation? Evidence from US Metropolitan Areas, 1980 to 2000'. *Housing Policy Debate* 14, no. 4 2003: 541–89.
Pendola, Rocco, and Sheldon Gen. 'BMI, Auto Use, and the Urban Environment in San Francisco'. *Health & Place* 13, no. 2 2007: 551–56.
Persson, Urban, and Sven Werner. 'Heat Distribution and the Future Competitiveness of District Heating'. *Applied Energy* 88, no. 3 2011: 568–76.
Panerai, P., 'De schaal van het bouwblok', in: S. Komossa et al., *Atlas van het Hollandse bouwblok* Bussum: Uitgeverij THOTH, 2002, 11–14.
Peponis, J., S. Bafna and Z. Zhang, 'The connectivity of streets: reach and directional distance', *Environmental and Planning B: Planning and Design*, 35 2018, 881–901.
Permeta architecten, *Task Force Ruimtewinst. Assist Alkmaar: Een groeimodel voor de Waterkwekerij*, in cooperation with Rudy Uytenhaak, commissioned by DHV Ruimte en Mobiliteit, Amsterdam, 2007.
Permeta architecten, 'Verdichtingsstudie groeimodel', *TFR-update* 5, Haarlem: Task Force Ruimtewinst, Provincie Noord-Holland 2007, 8–10.
Permeta architecten, *Project Ondersteboven*, in cooperation with Delft University of Technology, commissioned by VROM/DGR Amsterdam, 2005.
Permeta architecten, *Spacemate – Zuidoostlob: Kwantitatieve analyse van dichtheden en transformaties*, in cooperation with Delft University of Technology, commissioned by dRO Amsterdam, 2004.
Permeta architecten, *FSI-GSI-OSR als instrumentarium voor verdichting en verdunning: Case study Nieuw West*, commissioned by Bureau Parkstad Amsterdam, 2002.
Permeta architecten, *FSI-GSI-OSR: Atlas Westelijke Tuinsteden, instrumentarium voor verdichting en verdunning*, commissioned by Bureau Parkstad Amsterdam, 2001.
Permeta architecten, *FSI-GSI-OSR als instrumentarium voor verdichting en verdunning: Case study Nieuw West*, commissioned by Bureau Parkstad Amsterdam, 2000.
Pflieger, Geraldine, and Florian Ecoffey. 'The Cost of Urban Sprawl and Its Potential Redistributive Effects: An Empirical Cost Assessment for Water Services in Lausanne Switzerland'. *Environment and Planning A* 43, no. 4 2011: 850–65.
Plantinga, Andrew J., and Stephanie Bernell. 'The Association between Urban Sprawl and Obesity: Is It a Two-Way Street?' *Journal of Regional Science* 47, no. 5 2007: 857–79.
Plas, G. van der, 'Amsterdam 1750–1850: van stadsstaat naar hoofdstad', in: E. Taverne and I. Visser eds., *Stedebouw: De geschiedenis van de stad in de Nederlanden van 1500 tot heden* Nijmegen: SUN, 1993, 148–159.
Poruschi, Lavinia, and Christopher L. Ambrey. 'Densification, What Does It Mean for Fuel Poverty and Energy Justice? An Empirical Analysis'. *Energy Policy* 117 2018: 208–17.

Poulantzas, N., *State, Power, Socialism* London: Verso, 2000, originally published in 1978 as *L'Etat, le Pouvoir, le Socialisme*.
Province of North-Holland, *Bouwen voor Waterland 2020* Haarlem, 2004.
Punter, J., 'Design Guidelines in American Cities: Conclusions', in: M. Larice and E. Macdonald eds., *The Urban Design Reader* Oxon: Routledge, 2007, 500–516.

Qin, Bo, and Sun Sheng Han. 'Planning Parameters and Household Carbon Emission: Evidence from High- and Low-Carbon Neighborhoods in Beijing'. *Habitat International* 37 2013: 52–60.

RACM, *Nota Belvedere* The Hague: The National Service for Archaeology, Cultural Landscape and Built Heritage, 1999.
Rådberg, J., *Doktrin och täthet i svenskt stadsbyggande 1875–1975* Stockholm: Statens råd för byggnadsforskning, 1988.
Ralph, Kelcie, Carole Turley Voulgaris, Brian D. Taylor, Evelyn Blumenberg, and Anne E. Brown. 'Millennials, Built Form, and Travel Insights from a Nationwide Typology of US Neighborhoods'. *Journal of Transport Geography* 57 2016: 218–26.
Rapaport, A., 'Toward a Redefinition of Density', *Environment and Behaviour* 7 2 1975, 7–32.
Ramezani, Samira, Barbara Pizzo, and Elizabeth Deakin. 'An Integrated Assessment of Factors Affecting Modal Choice: Towards a Better Understanding of the Causal Effects of Built Environment'. *Transportation* 45, no. 5 2018: 1351–87.
Raux, Charles, Tai-Yu Ma, Iragael Joly, Vincent Kaufmann, Eric Cornelis, and Nicolas Ovtracht. 'Travel and Activity Time Allocation: An Empirical Comparison between Eight Cities in Europe'. *Transport Policy* 18, no. 2 March 2011: 401–12.
Raworth, K., Doughnut Economics: Seven Ways to Think Like a 21st-Century Economist, *Vermont: White River Junction, 2017.*
Rees, W., 'Ecological Footprint and Appreciated Carrying Capacity: What Urban Economics Leave Out', *Environment and Urbanisation* 4 2 1992, 121–130.
Renne, John L., Shima Hamidi, and Reid Ewing. 'Transit Commuting, the Network Accessibility Effect, and the Built Environment in Station Areas across the United States'. *Research in Transportation Economics* 60 2016: 35–43.
Rochat, E., S. Manel, M. Deschamps-Cottin, I. Widmer, and S. Joost. 'Persistence of Butterfly Populations in Fragmented Habitats along Urban Density Gradients: Motility Helps'. *Heredity* 119, no. 5 2017: 328–38.
Rode, Philipp, Christian Keim, Guido Robazza, Pablo Viejo, and James Schofield. 'Cities and Energy: Urban Morphology and Residential Heat-Energy Demand'. *Environment and Planning B-Planning & Design* 41, no. 1 2014: 138–62.
Roding, J., 'Vande oirdeningh der Steden', in: E. Taverne and I. Visser eds., *Stedebouw: De geschiedenis van de stad in de Nederlanden van 1500 tot heden* Nijmegen: SUN, 1993, 51–56.
Rofé, Y., 'Space and Community: The Spatial Foundations of Urban Neighborhoods', *Berkeley Planning Journal* 10 1995, 107–125.
Rosenberg, C.E., *The Cholera Years: The United States in 1832, 1849 and 1866* Chicago: The University of Chicago Press, 1987.
Rowe, C. and F. Koetter, *Collage City* Cambridge, MA: MIT Press, 1978.
Ruijter, P. de, *Voor volkshuisvesting en stedebouw* Utrecht: Matrijs, 1987.
Rutte, R., *A Landscape of Towns: Urbanization in the Netherlands from the 11th to the 19th Centuries* Delft: Delft University of Technology, Faculty of Architecture, 2004.

Salon, Deborah. 'Neighborhoods, Cars, and Commuting in New York City: A Discrete Choice Approach'. *Transportation Research Part A-Policy and Practice* 43, no. 2 2009: 180–96.
Sandercock, L., 'Anatomy of Civic Ambition in Vancouver: Toward Humane Density', in: W.S. Saunders ed., *Urban Planning Today* Minneapolis: University of Minnesota Press, 2006, 48–62.
Sarkar, Somwrita, Peter Phibbs, Roderick Simpson, and Sachin Wasnik. 'The Scaling of Income Distribution in Australia: Possible Relationships between Urban Allometry, City Size, and Economic Inequality'. *Environment and Planning B-Urban Analytics and City Science* 45, no. 4 2018: 603–22.
Sassen, S., 'Too Big to Save: The End of Financial Capitalism'. Available online at HTTP: http://www.opendemocracy.net accessed 24 November 2009.
Sato, Yasuhiro. 'Economic Geography, Fertility and Migration'. *Journal of Urban Economics* 61, no. 2 2007: 372–87
Saunders, W.S., 'Cappuccino Urbanism, and Beyond', *Harvard Design Magazine* fall 2006/winter 2007, 3.
Schiff, Nathan. 'Cities and Product Variety: Evidence from Restaurants'. *Journal of Economic Geography* 15, no. 6 2015: 1085–1123.
Schiller, Georg. 'Urban Infrastructure: Challenges for Resource Efficiency in the Building Stock'. *Building Research and Information* 35, no. 4 2007: 399–411.
Schreuder, A., 'Wat goed in Breda past, past niet overal in de Randstad', *NRC Handelsblad* 13/14 September 2008, 5.
Schuit, J. van der, H. Van Amsterdam, M. Breedijk and A. Hendriks, *Ruimte in cijfers 2006* The Hague: Netherlands Institute for Spatial Research, 2006.
Schweitzer, Lisa, and Jiangping Zhou. 'Neighborhood Air Quality, Respiratory Health, and Vulnerable Populations in Compact and Sprawled Regions'. *Journal of the American Planning Association* 76, no. 3 2010: 363–71.
Schwirian, KP, AL Nelson, and PM Schwirian. 'Modeling Urbanism – Economic, Social and Environmental-Stress in Cities'. *Social Indicators Research* 35, no. 2 1995: 201–23.
Sedgley, Norman, and Bruce Elmslie. 'Do We Still Need Cities? Evidence on Rates of Innovation from Count Data Models of Metropolitan Statistical Area Patents'. *American Journal of Economics and Sociology* 70, no. 1 2011: 86–108.
Sehatzadeh, Bahareh, Robert B. Noland, and Marc D. Weiner. 'Walking Frequency, Cars, Dogs, and the Built Environment'. *Transportation Research Part A-Policy and Practice* 45, no. 8 2011: 741–54.
Segeren, A., *De grondmarkt voor woningbouwlocaties* Rotterdam: NAi Publishers, 2007.
Sennet, R., *The Fall of Public Man* New York: Knopf, 1977.
Sert, J.L., *Can Our Cities Survive? An ABC of Urban Problems, Their Analysis, Their Solutions Based on Proposals Formulated by the CIAM* Boston: Harvard University Press, 1942.
Shaker, Richard Ross. 'The Well-Being of Nations: An Empirical Assessment of Sustainable Urbanization for Europe'. *International Journal of Sustainable Development and World Ecology* 22, no. 5 2015: 375–87.
Siksna, A., 'The Effects of Block Size and Form in North American and Australian City Centres', *Urban Morphology* 1 1997, 19–33.
Sola-Morales, M. de, 'Towards a Definition: Analysis of Urban Growth in the Nineteenth Century', *Lotus*, 19 June 1978, 28–36.
Sommer, R.M., 'Beyond Centers, "fabrics," and the Culture of Congestion: Urban Design as a Metropolitan Enterprise', *Harvard Design Magazine* fall 2006/winter 2007, 50–59.
Son, Cheol Hee, Jong In Baek, and Yong Un Ban. 'Structural Impact Relationships Between Urban Development Intensity Characteristics and Carbon Dioxide Emissions in Korea'. *Sustainability* 10, no. 6 2018: 1838.
Song, Siqi, Mi Diao, and Chen-Chieh Feng. 'Individual Transport Emissions and the Built Environment: A Structural Equation Modelling Approach'. *Transportation Research Part A-Policy and Practice* 92 2016: 206–19.
Sorkin, M., 'The Ends of Urban Design', *Harvard Design Magazine* fall 2006/winter 2007, 5–18.
Sorkin, M. ed., *A Theme Park: The New American City and the End of Public Space* New York: Hill and Wang, 1992.
Steadman, P., 'Density and built form: integrating «Spacemate» with the work of Martin and March', *Environment and Planning B: Planning and Design*, 40 2013, 341–358.
Stichting Architectuur Research, *Deciding on Density: An Investigation into High Density Allotments with a View to the Waldeck Area, The Hague* Eindhoven, 1977.
Stavroulaki, I, M. Berghauser Pont, 'A systematic review of the scientific literature on the theme of multifunctional streets', *IOP Conf. Ser.: Earth Environ. Sci.* 588 2020, 052046.
Stavroulaki, G., D. Bolin, M. Berghauser Pont, L. Marcus, E. Håkansson, 'Statistical modelling and analysis of big data on pedestrian movement', *Proceedings of the 12th Space Syntax Symposium*, JiaoTong University, Beijing, China 2019.
Ståhle, A., *Compact Sprawl: Exploring Public Open Space and Contradictions in Urban Density* Stockholm: KTH, 2008.

Stonor, T., Digital urbanism: The role of technology in the future of our cities (2014), https://www.academyofurbanism.org.uk/digital-urbanism-the-role-of-technology-in-the-future-of-our-cities/ (accessed 4 November 2020).

Sun, Yeran, Yunyan Du, Yu Wang, and Liyuan Zhuang. 'Examining Associations of Environmental Characteristics with Recreational Cycling Behaviour by Street-Level Strava Data'. *International Journal of Environmental Research and Public Health* 14, no. 6 2017: 644.

Sung, Hyungun, Keechoo Choi, Sugie Lee, and SangHyun Cheon. 'Exploring the Impacts of Land Use by Service Coverage and Station-Level Accessibility on Rail Transit Ridership'. *Journal of Transport Geography* 36 2014: 134–40.

Sung, Hyungun, and Sugie Lee. 'Residential Built Environment and Walking Activity: Empirical Evidence of Jane Jacobs' Urban Vitality'. *Transportation Research Part D-Transport and Environment* 41 2015: 318–29.

Tabeshian, Maryam, and Lina Kattan. 'Modeling Nonmotorized Travel Demand at Intersections in Calgary, Canada Use of Traffic Counts and Geographic Information System Data'. *Transportation Research Record*, no. 2430 2014: 38–46.

Talen, E. 'School, Community, and Spatial Equity: An Empirical Investigation of Access to Elementary Schools in West Virginia'. *Annals of the Association of American Geographers* 91, no. 3 2001: 465–86.

Taverne, E., 'Kan de erfgoed de ruimtelijke ordening redden?', in: F. Claessens and H. Engel eds., *OverHolland 2* Amsterdam: SUN, 2005, 107–110.

Taverne, E., *De wortels van de contemporaine stad*, Reader Architectuur- en Stedenbouwgeschiedenis Groningen: Rijksuniversiteit Groningen, 2000.

Terlouw, E., 'A House of One's Own', *OASE* 52 1999, 32–77.

Tian, Guang, and Reid Ewing. 'A Walk Trip Generation Model for Portland, OR'. *Transportation Research Part D-Transport and Environment* 52 2017: 340–53.

Travisi, Chiara M., Roberto Camagni, and Peter Nijkamp. 'Impacts of Urban Sprawl and Commuting: A Modelling Study for Italy'. *Journal of Transport Geography* 18, no. 3 2010: 382–92.

Trlica, A., L. R. Hutyra, C. L. Schaaf, A. Erb, and J. A. Wang. 'Albedo, Land Cover, and Daytime Surface Temperature Variation Across an Urbanized Landscape'. *Earths Future* 5, no. 11 2017: 1084–1101.

Trudeau, M. P., and Murray Richardson. 'Empirical Assessment of Effects of Urbanization on Event Flow Hydrology in Watersheds of Canada's Great Lakes-St Lawrence Basin'. *Journal of Hydrology* 541 2016: 1456–74

Tummers, L.J.M. and J.M. Tummers-Zuurmond, *Het land in de stad: De stedebouw van de grote agglomeratie* Bussum: Uitgeverij THOTH, 1997.

UN, National Statistical Offices/UN/Euromonitor International, 2009.

UN-Habitat, *Leveraging density. Urban patterns for a green economy* Nairobi: UN-Habitat. ISBN 978-92-1-132463-1, 2012 and UN-Habitat. 2015. Available from https://unhabitat.org/a-new-strategy-of-sustainable-neighbourhood-planning-five-principles.

Unwin, R., *Nothing Gained by Overcrowding! How the Garden City Type of Development May Benefit Both Owner and Occupier* Westminster: P.S. King & Son, 1912.

Unwin, R., *Town Planning in Practice* London: T.Fisher Unwin, 1909.

Urban Task Force. *Towards an Urban Renaissance*. Final Report of the Urban Task Force chaired by Lord Rogers London, Urban Task Force, 1999.

Urhahn, G.B. and M. Bobic, *Strategie voor stedelijkheid* Bussum: Uitgeverij THOTH, 1996.

Urhahn, G.B. and M. Bobic, *A Pattern Image* Bussum: Uitgeverij THOTH, 1994.

Urhahn Urban Design, *De woonwijk van de toekomst*, Idea book for the Bouwfonds Award, organized by the NIROV, 2000.

Uytenhaak, R., *Cities Full of Space: Qualities of Density* Rotterdam: 010 Publishers, 2008.

Venema, H., 'Bos en Lommer', in: S. Komossa et al. eds., *Atlas van het Hollandse bouwblok* Bussum: Uitgeverij THOTH, 2002, 112–123.

Villasenor, Nelida R., Don A. Driscoll, Martin A. H. Escobar, Philip Gibbons, and David B. Lindenmayer. 'Urbanization Impacts on Mammals across Urban-Forest Edges and a Predictive Model of Edge Effects'. *Plos One* 9, no. 5 2014: e97036.

VROM, *Structuurvisie Randstad 2040: Naar een duurzame en concurrerende Europese topregio* The Hague: Ministry of Spatial Planning and the Environment, 2008, presented by the Dutch cabinet on 5 September 2008.

VROM, *Standaard vergelijkbare bestemmingsplannen 2006* The Hague: Ministry of Spatial Planning and the Environment, Directoraat-Generaal Ruimte, 2006.

VROM, *Nota ruimte – ruimte voor ontwikkeling* The Hague: Ministry of Spatial Planning and the Environment, 2004.

VROM, *Vijfde nota over de ruimtelijke ordening* The Hague: Ministry of Spatial Planning and the Environment, 2001.

VROM, *Nota wonen: Mensen, wensen, wonen* The Hague: Ministry of Spatial Planning and the Environment, 2000.

VROM, *Vierde nota over de ruimtelijke ordening extra* The Hague: Ministry of Spatial Planning and the Environment, 1994.

VROM, *Vierde nota over de ruimtelijke ordening* The Hague: Ministry of Housing, Physical Planning and the Environment, 1988.

VROM, *Structuurschets stedelijke gebieden* The Hague: Ministry of Housing, Physical Planning and the Environment, 1983.

VROM, *Derde nota over de ruimtelijke ordening* The Hague: Ministry of Housing, Physical Planning and the Environment, 1973–1983.

VROM, *Verstedelijkingsnota* The Hague: Ministry of Housing, Physical Planning and the Environment, 1976.

VROM, *Tweede nota over de ruimtelijke ordening* The Hague: Ministry of Housing, Physical Planning and the Environment, 1966.

VROM, *Wet op de ruimtelijke ordening* The Hague: Ministry of Housing, Physical Planning and the Environment, 1965.

VROM, *Nota inzake de ruimtelijke ordening* The Hague: Ministry of Housing, Physical Planning and the Environment, 1960.

Wagenaar, M., 'Amsterdam 1860–1940: Een bedrijvige stad', in: E. Taverne and I. Visser eds., *Stedebouw: De geschiedenis van de stad in de Nederlanden van 1500 tot heden* Nijmegen: SUN, 1993, 218–234.

Wang, Lan, Xiaojing Zhao, Wangyue Xu, Jian Tang, and Xiji Jiang. 'Correlation Analysis of Lung Cancer and Urban Spatial Factor: Based on Survey in Shanghai'. *Journal of Thoracic Disease* 8, no. 9 2016: 2626–37.

Wang, Lei, Ruyin Long, and Hong Chen. 'Study of Urban Energy Performance Assessment and Its Influencing Factors Based on Improved Stochastic Frontier Analysis: A Case Study of Provincial Capitals in China'. *Sustainability* 9, no. 7 2017: 1110.

Wang, Mingshu, Marguerite Madden, and Xingjian Liu. 'Exploring the Relationship between Urban Forms and CO_2 Emissions in 104 Chinese Cities'. *Journal of Urban Planning and Development* 143, no. 4 2017: 04017014.

Wang, Yongming, Dianting Wu, Meixia Wang, Li Zhou, and Jianjun Ding. 'Density, Distance, and Division: Rural Poverty in a Developing-Country Context'. *Growth and Change* 49, no. 3 2018: 473–89.

Webber, M., 'The Urban Place and the Non-Place Urban Realm', in: M. Webber et al., *Explorations in Urban Structure* Philadelphia: University of Pennsylvania, 1964.

Wigmans, G., 'Maatschappelijke trends en gebiedsontwikkeling: Een probleemschets', in: I. Bruil et al. eds., *Integrale gebiedsontwikkeling: Het stationsgebied 's-Hertogenbosch* Amsterdam: SUN, 2004, 30–49.

Wilmink, F.W. and H.T. Uytterschaut, 'Cluster analysis, history, theory and applications', in G. N. van Vark and W. W. Howells eds., *Multivariate Statistical Methods in Physical Anthropology* D. Reidel Publishing Company, 1984, 135–175.

Wintershoven, L., *Demografisch eeuwboek Amsterdam: Ontwikkelingen tussen 1900 en 2000* Amsterdam: dRO, 2000.

Wouden, R. van der ed. *De stad op straat: De openbare ruimte in perspectief* The Hague: Sociaal en Cultureel Planbureau, 1999.

Wright, F.L., *The Disappearing City* New York: W.F. Payson, 1932.

Xiao, Zuopeng, Qian Liu, and James Wang. 'How Do the Effects of Local Built Environment on Household Vehicle Kilometers Traveled

Vary across Urban Structural Zones?' *International Journal of Sustainable Transportation* 12, no. 9 2018: 637–47.
Xu, Wangyue, Xiaojing Zhao, and Lan Wang. 'Impact of Built Environment on Respiratory Health: An Empirical Study'. *Nano Life* 8, no. 2 2018: UNSP 1840001.

Yamada, Ikuho, Barbara B. Brown, Ken R. Smith, Cathleen D. Zick, Lori Kowaleski-Jones, and Jessie X. Fan. 'Mixed Land Use and Obesity: An Empirical Comparison of Alternative Land Use Measures and Geographic Scales'. *Professional Geographer* 64, no. 2 2012: 157–77.
Yang, Feng, Stephen S. Y. Lau, and Feng Qian. 'Urban Design to Lower Summertime Outdoor Temperatures An Empirical Study on High-Rise Housing in Shanghai'. *Building and Environment* 46, no. 3 2011: 769–85.
Yang, Feng, Feng Qian, and Stephen S. Y. Lau. 'Urban Form and Density as Indicators for Summertime Outdoor Ventilation Potential: A Case Study on High-Rise Housing in Shanghai'. *Building and Environment* 70 2013: 122–37
Ye, Yu, Dong Li, and Xingjian Liu. 'How Block Density and Typology Affect Urban Vitality: An Exploratory Analysis in Shenzhen, China'. *Urban Geography* 39, no. 4 2018: 631–52.
Yi, Yanchun, Sisi Ma, Weijun Guan, and Ke Li. 'An Empirical Study on the Relationship between Urban Spatial Form and CO_2 in Chinese Cities'. *Sustainability* 9, no. 4 2017: 672.
Yoshida, H. and M. Omae, 'An approach for analysis of urban morphology: methods to derive morphological properties of city blocks by using an urban model and their interpretations', *Computers, Environments and Urban Systems*, 29 2005, 223–247.
Yuan, Man, Yan Song, and Liang Guo. 'Exploring Determinants of Urban Form in China through an Empirical Study among 115 Cities'. *Sustainability* 10, no. 10 2018: 3648.

Zahabi, Seyed Amir H., Luis Miranda-Moreno, Zachary Patterson, and Philippe Barla. 'Impacts of Built Environment and Emerging Green Technologies on Daily Transportation Greenhouse Gas Emissions in Quebec Cities: A Disaggregate Modeling Approach'. *Transportation* 44, no. 1 2017: 159–80.
Zhang, M. 'The Role of Land Use in Travel Mode Choice – Evidence from Boston and Hong Kong'. *Journal of the American Planning Association* 70, no. 3 2004: 344–60.
Zhang, Wenjia, and Ming Zhang. 'Short- and Long-Term Effects of Land Use on Reducing Personal Vehicle Miles of Travel Longitudinal Multilevel Analysis in Austin, Texas'. *Transportation Research Record*, no. 2500 2015: 102–9.
Zhao, Chunli, Thomas Alexander Sick Nielsen, Anton Stahl Olafsson, Trine Agervig Carstensen, and Xiaoying Meng. 'Urban Form, Demographic and Socio-Economic Correlates of Walking, Cycling, and e-Biking: Evidence from Eight Neighborhoods in Beijing'. *Transport Policy* 64 2018: 102–12.
Zhao, Hong. 'Executive Labor Market Segmentation: How Local Market Density Affects Incentives and Performance'. *Journal of Corporate Finance* 50 2018: 1–21.
Zhao, Hongbo, Hao Zhang, Changhong Miao, Xinyue Ye, and Min Min. 'Linking Heat Source-Sink Landscape Patterns with Analysis of Urban Heat Islands: Study on the Fast-Growing Zhengzhou City in Central China'. *Remote Sensing* 10, no. 8 2018: 1268.
Zheng, X. P. 'Measuring Optimal Population Distribution by Agglomeration Economies and Diseconomies: A Case Study of Tokyo'. *Urban Studies* 35, no. 1 1998: 95–112.
Zhou, Chunshan, and Shaojian Wang. 'Examining the Determinants and the Spatial Nexus of City-Level CO_2 Emissions in China: A Dynamic Spatial Panel Analysis of China's Cities'. *Journal of Cleaner Production* 171 2018: 917–26
Zijderveld, A.C., *Steden zonder stedelijkheid: Cultuurhistorische verkenning van een beleidsprobleem* Deventer: van Loghum Slaterus, 1983.
Zimmerman, A.L., *Ruimtegebruik in de stedebouw* Amsterdam: Woningstichting Eigen Haard, 2007.

DERIVATION OF FORMULAE

Derivation of ❹

$L = F / B$

$L = (F / A) / (B / A)$

$FSI = F / A$ def ❷

$GSI = B / A$ def ❸

$\mathbf{L = FSI / GSI}$

Derivation of ❺

$FSI = F / A$ def ❷

$F = FSI \times A$

$GSI = B / A$ def ❸

$B = GSI \times A$

$OSR = (A - B) / F$ def

$OSR = (A - A \times GSI) / (A \times FSI)$

$\mathbf{OSR = (1 - GSI) / FSI}$

The construction of OSR gradients in the Spacemate:

$OSR = (1 - GSI) / FSI$

$FSI\,(GSI) = 1 / OSR - GSI / OSR$

$GSI\,(FSI) = 1 - OSR \times FSI$

Intersection with y-axis: $FSI\,(0) = 1 / OSR$

Intersection with x-axis: $GSI\,(0) = 1$

Derivation of ❼ and ❽

$GSI_f = B / A_f$ def ❸

$A_f = B / GSI_f$

$GSI_i = B / \sum A_i$ def ❸

$\sum A_i = B / GSI_i$

$T_f = (A_f - \sum A_i) / A_f$ def ❻

$T_f = 1 - (B / GSI_i) / (B / GSI_f)$

$\mathbf{T_f = 1 - GSI_f / GSI_i}$

❽ is derived in the same way, but B is substituted for by F

Derivation of ⓬ and ⓭

$T_f = 1 - GSI_f / GSI_i$ def ❼

$1 - T_f = GSI_f / GSI_i$

$PIL = 1 - T_f$ def ⓫

$\mathbf{PIL = GSI_f / GSI_i}$

⓭ is derived in the same way, but GSI_f and GSI_i are substituted for by FSI_f and FSI_i

Derivation of ⓮

$N_f = [\sum l_i + (\sum l_e) / 2] / A_f$ def ❶

For a grid with n squares with a mesh-size w:

$[\sum l_i + (\sum l_e) / 2] = 2n \times w$

$A_f = n \times w^2$

$N_f = 2n \times w / (n \times w^2)$

$N_f = 2 / w$

$\mathbf{w = 2 / N_f}$

Derivation of ⑮

$T = (A_f - \sum A_i) / A_f$ def ⑥
$A_f = w^2$
$A_i = (w - b)^2$
$T_f = [w^2 - (w - b)^2] / w^2$
$T_f = 1 - (w - b)^2 / w^2$
$(w - b)^2 / w^2 = 1 - T_f$
$1 - b / w = \sqrt{(1 - T_f)}$
$b = w[1 - \sqrt{(1 - T_f)}]$
$w = 2 / N_f$
$\mathbf{b = 2[1 - \sqrt{(1 - T_f)}] / N_f}$

Derivation of ⑯

$b = 2[1 - \sqrt{(1 - T_f)}] / N_f$ ⑮
$T_f = 1 - GSI_f / GSI_i$
$\mathbf{b = 2[1 - \sqrt{(GSI_f / GSI_i)}] / N_f}$

Derivation of ⑰

$b = 2[1 - \sqrt{(1 - T_f)}] / N_f$ ⑮
$b \times N_f / 2 = 1 - \sqrt{(1 - T_f)}$
$\sqrt{(1 - T_f)} = 1 - b \times N_f / 2$
$1 - T_f = (1 - b \times N_f / 2)^2$
$\mathbf{T_f = 1 - (1 - b \times N_f / 2)^2}$

Derivation of ⑱

$T_f = 1 - (1 - b \times N_f / 2)^2$ ⑰
$1 - T_f = (1 - b \times N_f / 2)^2$
$PIL = 1 - T_f$ def ⑪
$\mathbf{PIL = (1 - b \times N_f / 2)^2}$

Deviation of ⑲

$N_f = [\sum I_i + (\sum I_e) / 2] / A_f$ def ①
$N_f = (w_x + w_y) / (w_x \times w_y)$
$w_x = n \times w_y$
$w_y = (n + 1) / (n \times N_f)$
$T_f = (A_f - \sum A_i) / A_f$ def ⑥
$T_f = 1 - A_i / A_f$
$A_i = (w_x - b)(w_y - b)$
$A_f = w_x \times w_y$
$T_f = 1 - (w_x - b)(w_y - b) / (w_x \times w_y)$
$T_f = 1 - (n \times w_y - b)(w_y - b) / (n \times w_y{}^2)$
$w_y = (n + 1) / (n \times N_f)$
$\mathbf{T_f = 1 - [1 - b \times N_f / (n + 1)][1 - n \times b \times N_f / (n + 1)]}$

From this last, b can be derived through:

$\mathbf{b = (n + 1)^2 / (2n \times N) -}$
$\mathbf{\sqrt{[(n + 1)^4 / (4n^2 \times N^2) - T \times (n + 1)^2 / (n \times N^2)]}}$

Derivation of ㉒

$N_p = I_p / A_f$ def ㉑

$I_p = 4(w - b) / 2$
$N_p = 2(w - b) / w^2$
$w = 2 / N_f$ ⑭
$N_p = 2(2 / N_f - b) / (2 / N_f)^2$
$\mathbf{N_p = N_f(1 - b \times N_f / 2)}$

Derivation of ㉓

$N_p = N_f(1 - b \times N_f / 2)$ ㉒
$b = 2[1 - \sqrt{(1 - T_f)}] / N_f$ ⑮
$b \times N_f / 2 = 1 - \sqrt{(1 - T_f)}$
$N_p = N_f\{1 - [1 - \sqrt{(1 - T_f)}]\}$
$\mathbf{N_p = N_f \times \sqrt{(1 - T_f)}}$

Derivation of ㉔

$PIL = 1 - T_f$ def ⑪
$N_p = N_f \times \sqrt{(1 - T_f)}$ ㉓
$\mathbf{N_p = N_f \times \sqrt{(PIL)}}$

Derivation of (31)

$DPI_0 = x_0 \times 2 \times 100 / d$
$x_0 / h = (l - d + x_0) / (L \times h)$
$x_0 = (l - d) / (L - 1)$
$DPI_0 = (l - d) \times 200 / [d \times (L - 1)]$
$DPI_0 = 200 \times (l / d - 1) / (L - 1)$
$GSI = d / l$
$L = FSI / GSI$ (4)
$DPI_0 = 200 \times (1 / GSI - 1) / (FSI / GSI - 1)$
$DPI_0 = 200 \times GSI(1 / GSI - 1) / (FSI - GSI)$
$\mathbf{DPI_0 = 200 \times (1 - GSI) / (FSI - GSI)}$

Derivation of (32)

$x_0 / h_n = (l - d) / H$
$x_0 = h_n(l - d) / H$
$DPI_0 = x_0 \times 2 \times 100 / d$
$DPI_0 = 200 \times h_n(l - d) / (d \times H)$
$DPI_0 = 200 \times h_n(l / d - 1) / H$
$\mathbf{DPI_0 = 200 \times h_n(1 / GSI - 1) / H}$

Derivation of (38)

$DF_e = 50 \times (\cos\alpha_{e1} + \cos\alpha_{e2})$
$\alpha_{e1} = \alpha_{e2}$
$\cos\alpha_{e1} = \cos\alpha_{e2} = \cos\alpha_e$
$DF_e = 50 \times (\cos\alpha_{e1} + \cos\alpha_{e2})$
$DF_e = 50 \times (\cos\alpha_e + \cos\alpha_e)$
$\mathbf{DF_e = 100 \times \cos\alpha_e}$

Derivation of (39)

$\tan\alpha_e = 2h \times L / (l - d)$
$\tan\alpha_e = 2h \times L / [d(l / d - 1)]$
$\tan\alpha_e = (2h / d)(FSI / GSI) / (1 / GSI - 1)$
$\tan\alpha_e = (2h / d)[FSI / (1 - GSI)]$
$\mathbf{\tan\alpha_e = 2h / (d \times OSR)}$

Derivation of (42)

$OSR_f = (1 - GSI_f) / FSI_f$ (5)
$GSI_f = B / A_f$ def (3)
$FSI_f = F / A_f$ def (2)
$OSR_f = (1 - B / A_f) / (F / A_f)$
$OSR_f = (A_f - B) / F$
$A_f = F \times OSR_f + B$
$OSR_i = (1 - GSI_i) / FSI_i$ (5)
$GSI_i = B / \sum A_i$ def (3)
$FSI_i = F / \sum A_i$ def (2)
$OSR_i = (1 - B / \sum A_i) / (F / \sum A_i)$
$OSR_i = (\sum A_i - B) / F$
$\sum A_i = F \times OSR_i + B$
$\Delta OSR = (A_f - \sum A_i) / F$ def (41)
$\Delta OSR = [(F \times OSR_f + B) - (F \times OSR_i + B)] / F$
$\Delta OSR = (F \times OSR_f + B - F \times OSR_i - B) / F$
$\mathbf{\Delta OSR = OSR_f - OSR_i}$

Derivation of (43)

Connectivity Ratio $= c / A_f$ def

where
c = amount of crossing per hectare

Every square in a grid has 4 corners with each ¼ of a crossing. In a grid of n squares:

$c = n \times 4 \times 1 / 4$
$A_f = n \times w^2$
$w = 2 / N_f$ (11)

Connectivity Ratio $= (n \times 4 \times 1 / 4) / (n \times w^2)$
Connectivity Ratio $= 1 / w^2$
Connectivity Ratio $\mathbf{= N_f^2 / 4}$

SAMPLES FROM THE NETHERLANDS

1 ACHTERBOS
De Ronde Venen

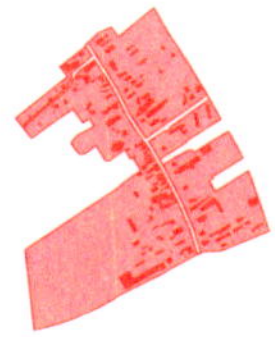

Island				
A	FSI	GSI	OSR	L
15.7 ha	0.21	0.13	4.25	1.60
Fabric				
A	FSI	GSI	OSR	L
16.4 ha	0.20	0.12	4.45	1.60
N	w	b	T	
0.005 /m²	385 m	8 m	4 %	

2 AMSTELDORP 1
Amsterdam

Island				
A	FSI	GSI	OSR	L
2.1 ha	0.88	0.35	0.74	2.50
Fabric				
A	FSI	GSI	OSR	L
3.2 ha	0.59	0.23	1.30	2.50
N	w	b	T	
0.033 /m²	60 m	11 m	33 %	

3 AMSTELDORP 2
Amsterdam

Island				
A	FSI	GSI	OSR	L
3.5 ha	1.33	0.50	0.38	2.66
Fabric				
A	FSI	GSI	OSR	L
5.0 ha	0.92	0.34	0.72	2.66
N	w	b	T	
0.026 /m²	76 m	13 m	31 %	

4

ANLOO
Aa en Hunze

Island				
A	FSI	GSI	OSR	L
15.7 ha	0.18	0.11	4.86	1.62
Fabric				
A	FSI	GSI	OSR	L
18.4 ha	0.16	0.10	5.81	1.62
N	w	b	T	
0.013 /m²	158 m	12 m	15 %	

5

BALLOO
Aa en Hunze

Island				
A	FSI	GSI	OSR	L
22.1 ha	0.09	0.06	10.72	1.51
Fabric				
A	FSI	GSI	OSR	L
24.2 ha	0.08	0.05	11.79	1.51
N	w	b	T	
0.007 /m²	275 m	12 m	9 %	

6

BERGEN 1
Bergen

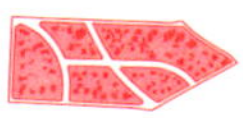

Island				
A	FSI	GSI	OSR	L
5.1 ha	0.37	0.20	2.13	1.84
Fabric				
A	FSI	GSI	OSR	L
6.9 ha	0.27	0.15	3.11	1.84
N	w	b	T	
0.019 /m²	106 m	15 m	27 %	

7

BERGEN 2
Bergen

Island				
A	FSI	GSI	OSR	L
4.0 ha	0.39	0.22	2.03	1.75
Fabric				
A	FSI	GSI	OSR	L
5.0 ha	0.31	0.18	2.68	1.75
N	w	b	T	
0.017 /m²	119 m	13 m	20 %	

8

BERLAGE PLAN ZUID 1
Amsterdam

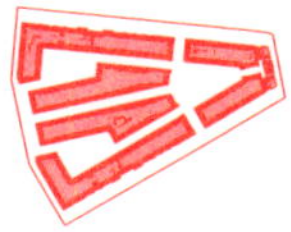

Island				
A	FSI	GSI	OSR	L
7.7 ha	2.41	0.56	0.18	4.27
Fabric				
A	FSI	GSI	OSR	L
14.5 ha	1.28	0.30	0.55	4.27
N	w	b	T	
0.017 /m²	117 m	32 m	47 %	

9

BERLAGE PLAN ZUID 2
Amsterdam

Island				
A	FSI	GSI	OSR	L
5.6 ha	2.99	0.67	0.11	4.44
Fabric				
A	FSI	GSI	OSR	L
10.4 ha	1.61	0.36	0.40	4.44
N	w	b	T	
0.022 /m²	91 m	24 m	46 %	

10

BERLAGE PLAN ZUID 3
Amsterdam

Island				
A	FSI	GSI	OSR	L
4.3 ha	2.33	0.63	0.16	3.71
Fabric				
A	FSI	GSI	OSR	L
7.2 ha	1.39	0.37	0.45	3.71
N	w	b	T	
0.021 /m²	95 m	22 m	41 %	

11

BETONDORP
Amsterdam

Island				
A	FSI	GSI	OSR	L
8.8 ha	0.77	0.37	0.82	2.09
Fabric				
A	FSI	GSI	OSR	L
11.7 ha	0.58	0.28	1.24	2.09
N	w	b	T	
0.024 /m²	84 m	11 m	25 %	

12

BIJLMER OUD
Amsterdam

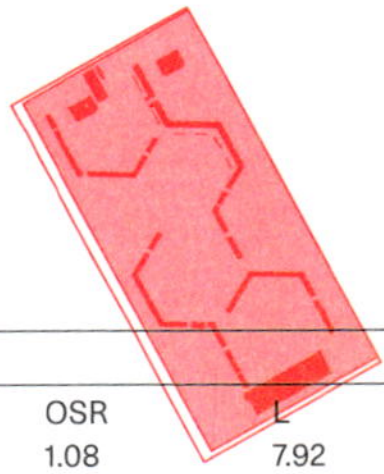

Island				
A	FSI	GSI	OSR	L
30.8 ha	0.83	0.10	1.08	7.92
Fabric				
A	FSI	GSI	OSR	L
33.4 ha	0.76	0.10	1.18	7.92
N	w	b	T	
0.004 /m²	546 m	22 m	8 %	

13

BLOKZIJL
Steenwijk

Island				
A	FSI	GSI	OSR	L
4.1 ha	0.90	0.46	0.60	1.95
Fabric				
A	FSI	GSI	OSR	L
5.4 ha	0.69	0.35	0.94	1.95
N	w	b	T	
0.036 /m²	55 m	7 m	24 %	

14

BORSSELE
Borsele

Island				
A	FSI	GSI	OSR	L
4.7 ha	0.38	0.22	2.03	1.71
Fabric				
A	FSI	GSI	OSR	L
5.3 ha	0.34	0.20	2.37	1.71
N	w	b	T	
0.015 /m²	130 m	8 m	12 %	

15

BUURT NEGEN
Amsterdam

Island				
A	FSI	GSI	OSR	L
2.1 ha	1.35	0.29	0.53	4.71
Fabric				
A	FSI	GSI	OSR	L
3.3 ha	0.86	0.18	0.95	4.71
N	w	b	T	
0.027 /m²	73 m	15 m	37 %	

16

COLIJNSPLAAT
Noord-Beveland

Island				
A	FSI	GSI	OSR	L
3.9 ha	0.74	0.39	0.81	1.89
Fabric				
A	FSI	GSI	OSR	L
5.0 ha	0.58	0.30	1.21	1.89
N	w	b	T	
0.022 /m²	89 m	11 m	23 %	

17

DE BERG ZUID
Amersfoort

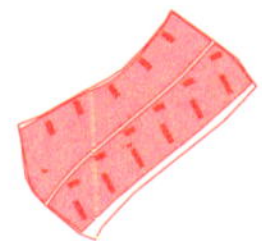

Island				
A	FSI	GSI	OSR	L
9.2 ha	0.33	0.08	2.78	4.34
Fabric				
A	FSI	GSI	OSR	L
10.7 ha	0.28	0.07	3.28	4.34
N	w	b	T	
0.011 /m²	183 m	14 m	14 %	

18

DE PIJP
Amsterdam

Island				
A	FSI	GSI	OSR	L
3.3 ha	2.84	0.75	0.09	3.79
Fabric				
A	FSI	GSI	OSR	L
5.2 ha	1.78	0.47	0.30	3.79
N	w	b	T	
0.023 /m²	87 m	18 m	37 %	

19

DE VESTE
Helmond

Island				
A	FSI	GSI	OSR	L
1.0 ha	1.59	0.53	0.30	3.00
Fabric				
A	FSI	GSI	OSR	L
1.4 ha	1.16	0.39	0.53	3.00
N	w	b	T	
0.025 /m²	81 m	12 m	27 %	

20 DOUVE WEIEN
Heerlen

Island				
A	FSI	GSI	OSR	L
5.2 ha	0.33	0.18	2.53	1.85
Fabric				
A	FSI	GSI	OSR	L
6.2 ha	0.27	0.15	3.16	1.85
N	w	b	T	
0.015 /m^2	131 m	12 m	17 %	

21 DREISCHOR
Schouwen-Duiveland

Island				
A	FSI	GSI	OSR	L
3.9 ha	0.53	0.29	1.33	1.81
Fabric				
A	FSI	GSI	OSR	L
4.8 ha	0.43	0.24	1.77	1.81
N	w	b	T	
0.029 /m^2	69 m	7 m	19 %	

22 DWARSGRACHT
Steenwijkerland

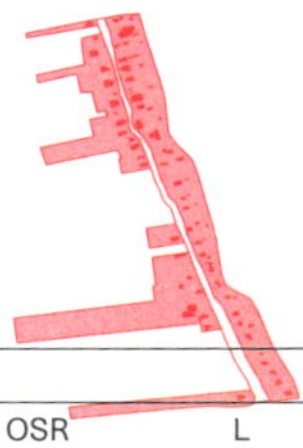

Island				
A	FSI	GSI	OSR	L
11.7 ha	0.13	0.08	7.10	1.70
Fabric				
A	FSI	GSI	OSR	L
12.5 ha	0.12	0.07	7.60	1.70
N	w	b	T	
0.004 /m^2	550 m	17 m	6 %	

23 EMMER-ERFSCHEIDENVEEN
Emmen

Island				
A	FSI	GSI	OSR	L
8.9 ha	0.12	0.07	8.07	1.64
Fabric				
A	FSI	GSI	OSR	L
10.4 ha	0.10	0.06	9.61	1.64
N	w	b	T	
0.007 /m^2	302 m	24 m	15 %	

24

FEYENOORD
Rotterdam

Island				
A	FSI	GSI	OSR	L
2.4 ha	2.07	0.52	0.23	3.98
Fabric				
A	FSI	GSI	OSR	L
4.1 ha	1.19	0.30	0.59	3.98
N	w	b	T	
0.023 /m²	88 m	21 m	42 %	

25

FUNEN
Amsterdam

Island				
A	FSI	GSI	OSR	L
3.9 ha	2.43	0.46	0.22	5.24
Fabric				
A	FSI	GSI	OSR	L
5.5 ha	1.73	0.33	0.39	5.24
N	w	b	T	
0.010 /m²	206 m	32 m	29 %	

26

GEES
Coevorden

Island				
A	FSI	GSI	OSR	L
2.9 ha	0.20	0.14	4.26	1.45
Fabric				
A	FSI	GSI	OSR	L
3.5 ha	0.17	0.12	5.24	1.45
N	w	b	T	
0.020 /m²	98 m	8 m	16 %	

27

GOEDEREEDE
Goedereede

Island				
A	FSI	GSI	OSR	L
2.4 ha	1.04	0.51	0.48	2.06
Fabric				
A	FSI	GSI	OSR	L
2.9 ha	0.86	0.42	0.68	2.06
N	w	b	T	
0.032 /m²	62 m	6 m	17 %	

28

GRACHTENGORDEL
Amsterdam

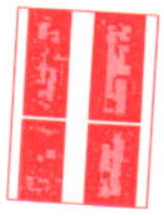

Island				
A	FSI	GSI	OSR	L
7.1 ha	3.00	0.73	0.09	4.08
Fabric				
A	FSI	GSI	OSR	L
11.0 ha	1.94	0.48	0.27	4.08
N	w	b	T	
0.012 /m²	164 m	32 m	35 %	

29

GWL TERREIN
Amsterdam

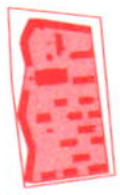

Island				
A	FSI	GSI	OSR	L
4.8 ha	1.70	0.33	0.40	5.16
Fabric				
A	FSI	GSI	OSR	L
6.4 ha	1.28	0.25	0.59	5.16
N	w	b	T	
0.008 /m²	248 m	33 m	25 %	

30

HEEMRAADSSINGEL
Rotterdam

Island				
A	FSI	GSI	OSR	L
6.9 ha	1.98	0.58	0.21	3.42
Fabric				
A	FSI	GSI	OSR	L
11.5 ha	1.18	0.35	0.55	3.42
N	w	b	T	
0.017 /m²	116 m	26 m	40 %	

31

HEVEADORP
Doorwerth

Island				
A	FSI	GSI	OSR	L
10.1 ha	0.44	0.22	1.76	2.04
Fabric				
A	FSI	GSI	OSR	L
12.2 ha	0.37	0.18	2.24	2.04
N	w	b	T	
0.020 /m²	102 m	9 m	18 %	

32

HOLENDRECHT 1
Amsterdam

Island				
A	FSI	GSI	OSR	L
11.8 ha	1.27	0.36	0.51	3.57
Fabric				
A	FSI	GSI	OSR	L
21.9 ha	0.69	1.18	4.45	3.57
N	w	b	T	
0.013 /m²	152 m	40 m	46 %	

33

HOLENDRECHT 2
Amsterdam

Island				
A	FSI	GSI	OSR	L
2.0 ha	0.92	0.37	0.69	2.50
Fabric				
A	FSI	GSI	OSR	L
4.1 ha	0.45	0.18	1.82	2.50
N	w	b	T	
0.019 /m²	103 m	31 m	51 %	

34

HOOG SOEREN
Apeldoorn

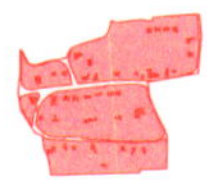

Island				
A	FSI	GSI	OSR	L
7.4 ha	0.14	0.08	6.39	1.88
Fabric				
A	FSI	GSI	OSR	L
8.1 ha	0.13	0.07	7.06	1.88
N	w	b	T	
0.014 /m²	385 m	6 m	9 %	

35

HUISDUINEN
Den Helder

Island				
A	FSI	GSI	OSR	L
1.6 ha	0.33	0.19	2.41	1.75
Fabric				
A	FSI	GSI	OSR	L
2.0 ha	0.27	0.15	3.20	1.75
N	w	b	T	
0.031 /m²	64 m	7 m	21 %	

36

IJLST
Wymbritseradeel

Island

A	FSI	GSI	OSR	L
6.1 ha	0.39	0.23	1.99	1.65

Fabric

A	FSI	GSI	OSR	L
7.5 ha	0.31	0.19	2.59	1.65

N	w	b	T
0.008 /m²	259 m	26 m	19 %

37

JAVA ISLAND
Amsterdam

Island

A	FSI	GSI	OSR	L
4.7 ha	2.72	0.45	0.20	6.08

Fabric

A	FSI	GSI	OSR	L
6.2 ha	2.09	0.34	0.31	6.08

N	w	b	T
0.014 /m²	140 m	17 m	23 %

38

JORDAAN
Amsterdam

Island

A	FSI	GSI	OSR	L
4.7 ha	2.54	0.75	0.10	3.40

Fabric

A	FSI	GSI	OSR	L
6.5 ha	1.84	0.54	0.25	3.40

N	w	b	T
0.021 /m²	96 m	14 m	28 %

39

KNSM ISLAND
Amsterdam

Island

A	FSI	GSI	OSR	L
3.3 ha	4.17	0.64	0.09	6.50

Fabric

A	FSI	GSI	OSR	L
5.8 ha	2.34	0.36	0.27	6.50

N	w	b	T
0.024 /m²	83 m	21 m	44 %

40

KOLENKIT
Amsterdam

Island				
A	FSI	GSI	OSR	L
1.8 ha	2.08	0.42	0.28	5.00
Fabric				
A	FSI	GSI	OSR	L
3.5 ha	1.06	0.21	0.75	5.00
N	w	b	T	
0.020 /m²	102 m	29 m	49 %	

41

LANDTONG
Amsterdam

Island				
A	FSI	GSI	OSR	L
2.8 ha	3.72	0.46	0.15	8.10
Fabric				
A	FSI	GSI	OSR	L
4.5 ha	2.36	0.29	0.30	8.10
N	w	b	T	
0.021 /m²	96 m	20 m	37 %	

42

LANGSWATER
Amsterdam

Island				
A	FSI	GSI	OSR	L
2.9 ha	1.86	0.17	0.45	11.05
Fabric				
A	FSI	GSI	OSR	L
3.2 ha	1.67	0.15	0.51	11.05
N	w	b	T	
0.009 /m²	222 m	11 m	10 %	

43

MOLENAARSGRAAF
Graafstroom

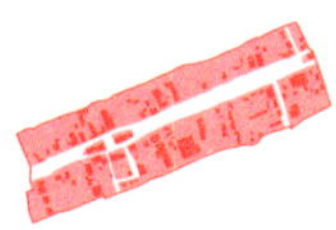

Island				
A	FSI	GSI	OSR	L
9.5 ha	0.30	0.20	2.67	1.54
Fabric				
A	FSI	GSI	OSR	L
11.6 ha	0.25	0.16	3.40	1.54
N	w	b	T	
0.010 /m²	195 m	18 m	18 %	

44

NAGELE
Noordoostpolder

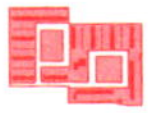

Island				
A	FSI	GSI	OSR	L
3.4 ha	0.37	0.22	2.07	1.68
Fabric				
A	FSI	GSI	OSR	L
4.3 ha	0.30	0.18	2.76	1.68
N	w	b	T	
0.016 /m²	124 m	13 m	20 %	

45

NIEHOVE
Groningen

Island				
A	FSI	GSI	OSR	L
4.7 ha	0.31	0.19	2.61	1.64
Fabric				
A	FSI	GSI	OSR	L
5.7 ha	0.26	0.16	3.30	1.64
N	w	b	T	
0.020 /m²	102 m	9 m	18 %	

46

NIEUWPOORT
Liesveld

Island				
A	FSI	GSI	OSR	L
2.7 ha	0.84	0.45	0.66	1.86
Fabric				
A	FSI	GSI	OSR	L
3.4 ha	0.67	0.36	0.96	1.86
N	w	b	T	
0.020 /m²	98 m	10 m	20 %	

47

NIEUW SLOTEN
Liesveld

Island				
A	FSI	GSI	OSR	L
4.3 ha	1.24	0.54	0.38	2.31
Fabric				
A	FSI	GSI	OSR	L
6.9 ha	0.77	0.33	0.86	2.31
N	w	b	T	
0.028 /m²	70 m	15 m	38 %	

48

NIMRODPARK
Hilversum

Island				
A	FSI	GSI	OSR	L
14.8 ha	0.16	0.08	5.76	1.88
Fabric				
A	FSI	GSI	OSR	L
19.4 ha	0.12	0.06	7.75	1.88
N	w	b	T	
0.014 /m^2	146 m	19 m	24 %	

49

NOLENSSTRAAT
Amsterdam

Island				
A	FSI	GSI	OSR	L
2.8 ha	1.25	0.23	0.62	5.47
Fabric				
A	FSI	GSI	OSR	L
3.9 ha	0.89	0.16	0.94	5.47
N	w	b	T	
0.019 /m^2	105 m	16 m	28 %	

50

NOORDEREILAND
Rotterdam

Island				
A	FSI	GSI	OSR	L
2.7 ha	3.16	0.69	0.10	4.59
Fabric				
A	FSI	GSI	OSR	L
5.2 ha	1.65	0.36	0.39	4.59
N	w	b	T	
0.027 /m^2	75 m	21 m	48 %	

51

NOORDERHOF
Amsterdam

Island				
A	FSI	GSI	OSR	L
2.4 ha	1.42	0.54	0.33	2.65
Fabric				
A	FSI	GSI	OSR	L
3.2 ha	1.03	0.39	0.59	2.65
N	w	b	T	
0.025 /m^2	79 m	12 m	27 %	

52

OUDE BOTERINGE
Groningen

Island				
A	FSI	GSI	OSR	L
3.1 ha	2.13	0.79	0.10	2.70
Fabric				
A	FSI	GSI	OSR	L
4.2 ha	1.56	0.58	0.27	2.70
N	w	b	T	
0.030 /m²	66 m	9 m	27 %	

53

PEPERKLIP
Rotterdam

Island				
A	FSI	GSI	OSR	L
2.6 ha	2.20	0.45	0.25	4.89
Fabric				
A	FSI	GSI	OSR	L
4.5 ha	1.28	0.26	0.58	4.89
N	w	b	T	
0.014 /m²	144 m	34 m	42 %	

54

ROSENGAARDE
Dalfsen

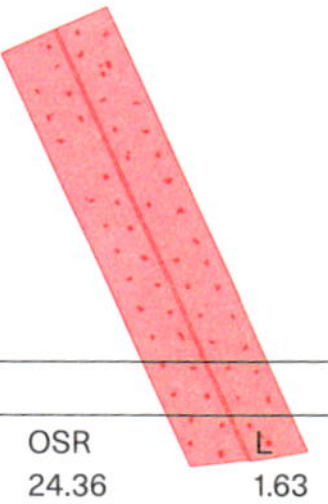

Island				
A	FSI	GSI	OSR	L
21.6 ha	0.04	0.02	24.36	1.63
Fabric				
A	FSI	GSI	OSR	L
22.1 ha	0.04	0.02	24.91	1.63
N	w	b	T	
0.004 /m²	461 m	5 m	2 %	

55

SLOTEN
Gaasterland-Sloten

Island				
A	FSI	GSI	OSR	L
3.6 ha	0.79	0.43	0.73	1.83
Fabric				
A	FSI	GSI	OSR	L
5.0 ha	0.57	0.31	1.20	1.83
N	w	b	T	
0.033 /m²	60 m	9 m	27 %	

56

SLOTERMEERLAAN
Amsterdam

Island				
A	FSI	GSI	OSR	L
2.8 ha	0.85	0.38	0.74	2.24
Fabric				
A	FSI	GSI	OSR	L
4.8 ha	0.50	0.22	1.57	2.24
N	w	b	T	
0.038 /m²	52 m	12 m	41 %	

57

SLOTERMEER NOORD
Amsterdam

Island				
A	FSI	GSI	OSR	L
3.3 ha	0.64	0.31	1.09	2.07
Fabric				
A	FSI	GSI	OSR	L
4.6 ha	0.46	0.22	1.71	2.07
N	w	b	T	
0.030 /m²	67 m	10 m	28 %	

58

STADSTUINEN
Rotterdam

Island				
A	FSI	GSI	OSR	L
5.8 ha	2.46	0.57	0.18	4.35
Fabric				
A	FSI	GSI	OSR	L
11.0 ha	1.28	0.29	0.55	4.35
N	w	b	T	
0.020 /m²	101 m	28 m	48 %	

59

STAPHORST
Staphorst

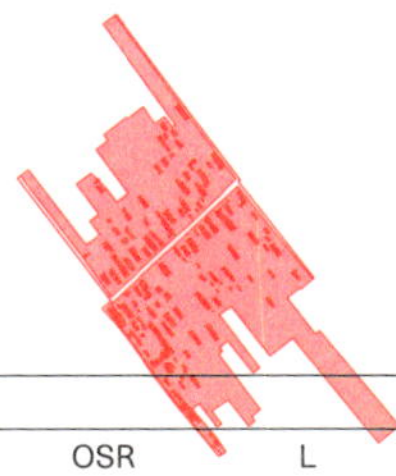

Island				
A	FSI	GSI	OSR	L
19.4 ha	0.22	0.16	3.83	1.39
Fabric				
A	FSI	GSI	OSR	L
20.5 ha	0.21	0.15	4.08	1.39
N	w	b	T	
0.005 /m²	392 m	10 m	5 %	

60

STEVENSWEERT
Maasgouw

Island				
A	FSI	GSI	OSR	L
3.0 ha	1.20	0.56	0.37	2.15
Fabric				
A	FSI	GSI	OSR	L
4.4 ha	0.80	0.37	0.78	2.15
N	w	b	T	
0.038 /m²	53 m	10 m	33 %	

61

TROELSTRALAAN
Amsterdam

Island				
A	FSI	GSI	OSR	L
2.6 ha	0.50	0.23	1.54	2.22
Fabric				
A	FSI	GSI	OSR	L
3.7 ha	0.36	0.16	2.33	2.22
N	w	b	T	
0.022 /m²	92 m	14 m	28 %	

62

VAILLANTLAAN
The Hague

Island				
A	FSI	GSI	OSR	L
1.3 ha	2.60	0.64	0.14	4.10
Fabric				
A	FSI	GSI	OSR	L
2.4 ha	1.42	0.35	0.46	4.10
N	w	b	T	
0.021 /m²	94 m	25 m	46 %	

63

VENSERPOLDER
Amsterdam

Island				
A	FSI	GSI	OSR	L
7.3 ha	1.97	0.44	0.28	4.49
Fabric				
A	FSI	GSI	OSR	L
12.2 ha	1.17	0.26	0.63	4.49
N	w	b	T	
0.016 /m²	129 m	29 m	40 %	

64

VIJFHUIZEN
Haarlemmermeer

Island				
A	FSI	GSI	OSR	L
1.0 ha	0.86	0.34	0.76	2.54
Fabric				
A	FSI	GSI	OSR	L
1.4 ha	0.64	0.25	1.17	2.54
N	w	b	T	
0.018 /m²	109 m	15 m	26 %	

65

VOGELWIJK
The Hague

Island				
A	FSI	GSI	OSR	L
5.3 ha	0.71	0.26	1.05	2.73
Fabric				
A	FSI	GSI	OSR	L
7.5 ha	0.50	0.18	1.64	2.73
N	w	b	T	
0.017 /m²	120 m	19 m	30 %	

66

VONDELPARK
Amsterdam

Island				
A	FSI	GSI	OSR	L
4.5 ha	2.86	0.62	0.13	4.61
Fabric				
A	FSI	GSI	OSR	L
7.0 ha	1.84	0.40	0.33	4.61
N	w	b	T	
0.021 /m²	97 m	19 m	36 %	

67

VREEWIJK
Rotterdam

Island				
A	FSI	GSI	OSR	L
1.7 ha	0.63	0.42	0.93	1.52
Fabric				
A	FSI	GSI	OSR	L
2.1 ha	0.50	0.33	1.35	1.52
N	w	b	T	
0.024 /m²	85 m	9 m	21 %	

68

WAGENINGEN-HOOG
Wageningen

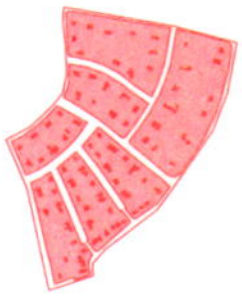

Island				
A	FSI	GSI	OSR	L
12.0 ha	0.18	0.10	5.12	1.84
Fabric				
A	FSI	GSI	OSR	L
15.1 ha	0.14	0.08	6.62	1.84
N	w	b	T	
0.015 /m²	138 m	15 m	21 %	

69

WATERGRAAFSMEER 1
Amsterdam

Island				
A	FSI	GSI	OSR	L
8.8 ha	1.44	0.52	0.33	2.77
Fabric				
A	FSI	GSI	OSR	L
15.7 ha	0.81	0.29	0.87	2.77
N	w	b	T	
0.020 /m²	99 m	25 m	44 %	

70

WATERGRAAFSMEER 2
Amsterdam

Island				
A	FSI	GSI	OSR	L
4.0 ha	1.54	0.63	0.24	2.44
Fabric				
A	FSI	GSI	OSR	L
10.4 ha	0.59	0.24	1.30	2.44
N	w	b	T	
0.021 /m²	96 m	37 m	62 %	

71

WEENA
Rotterdam

Island				
A	FSI	GSI	OSR	L
3.1 ha	6.19	0.72	0.05	8.59
Fabric				
A	FSI	GSI	OSR	L
5.7 ha	3.32	0.39	0.18	8.59
N	w	b	T	
0.017 /m²	116 m	31 m	46 %	

72

WESTERDOK
Amsterdam

Island				
A	FSI	GSI	OSR	L
2.9 ha	5.63	0.84	0.03	6.74
Fabric				
A	FSI	GSI	OSR	L
4.3 ha	3.76	0.56	0.12	6.74
N	w	b	T	
0.020 /m²	99 m	18 m	33 %	

73

WILDEMANBUURT
Amsterdam

Island				
A	FSI	GSI	OSR	L
2.6 ha	1.96	0.22	0.40	8.78
Fabric				
A	FSI	GSI	OSR	L
4.0 ha	1.30	0.15	0.65	8.78
N	w	b	T	
0.021 /m²	97 m	18 m	34 %	

74

WILHELIMINAPLEIN
Amsterdam

Island				
A	FSI	GSI	OSR	L
1.5 ha	1.33	0.11	0.67	12.00
Fabric				
A	FSI	GSI	OSR	L
1.6 ha	1.18	0.10	0.77	12.00
N	w	b	T	
0.010 /m²	193 m	12 m	12 %	

75

WOLVESCHANS 1
Leek

Island				
A	FSI	GSI	OSR	L
4.7 ha	0.41	0.19	1.99	2.15
Fabric				
A	FSI	GSI	OSR	L
6.1 ha	0.31	0.15	2.72	2.15
N	w	b	T	
0.019 /m²	108 m	13 m	23 %	

76

WOLVESCHANS 2
Leek

Island				
A	FSI	GSI	OSR	L
2.8 ha	0.64	0.26	1.17	2.46
Fabric				
A	FSI	GSI	OSR	L
3.7 ha	0.48	0.20	1.67	2.46
N	w	b	T	
0.023 /m²	87 m	11 m	24 %	

77

YPENBURG 1
The Hague

Island				
A	FSI	GSI	OSR	L
2.0 ha	1.07	0.39	0.56	2.72
Fabric				
A	FSI	GSI	OSR	L
2.6 ha	0.83	0.30	0.84	2.72
N	w	b	T	
0.013 /m²	158 m	19 m	23 %	

78

YPENBURG 2
The Hague

Island				
A	FSI	GSI	OSR	L
2.6 ha	1.06	0.43	0.54	2.46
Fabric				
A	FSI	GSI	OSR	L
3.6 ha	0.74	0.30	0.94	2.46
N	w	b	T	
0.020 /m²	101 m	16 m	30 %	

79

YPENBURG 3
The Hague

Island				
A	FSI	GSI	OSR	L
4.5 ha	0.54	0.25	1.40	2.15
Fabric				
A	FSI	GSI	OSR	L
4.9 ha	0.49	0.23	1.59	2.15
N	w	b	T	
0.017 /m²	118 m	5 m	9 %	

80

ZAANHOF
Amsterdam

Island				
A	FSI	GSI	OSR	L
6.5 ha	1.73	0.36	0.37	4.85
Fabric				
A	FSI	GSI	OSR	L
7.9 ha	1.43	0.29	0.49	4.85
N	w	b	T	
0.010 /m²	192 m	18 m	17 %	

81

ZUIDWEST KWADRANT 1
Amsterdam

Island				
A	FSI	GSI	OSR	L
4.0 ha	1.28	0.29	0.56	4.47
Fabric				
A	FSI	GSI	OSR	L
6.9 ha	0.75	0.17	1.11	4.47
N	w	b	T	
0.017 /m²	120 m	28 m	41 %	

82

ZUIDWEST KWADRANT 2
Amsterdam

Island				
A	FSI	GSI	OSR	L
4.9 ha	1.28	0.28	0.57	4.62
Fabric				
A	FSI	GSI	OSR	L
8.0 ha	0.78	0.17	1.06	4.62
N	w	b	T	
0.015 /m²	136 m	30 m	39 %	

83

ZUIDWEST KWADRANT 3
Amsterdam

Island				
A	FSI	GSI	OSR	L
4.0 ha	1.27	0.29	0.56	4.47
Fabric				
A	FSI	GSI	OSR	L
6.9 ha	0.75	0.17	1.12	4.47
N	w	b	T	
0.023 /m²	88 m	21 m	41 %	

SAMPLES FROM GERMANY

1

ARNIMPLATZ
Berlin

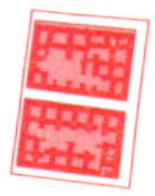

Island				
A	FSI	GSI	OSR	L
5.7 ha	2.97	0.57	0.15	5.23
Fabric				
A	FSI	GSI	OSR	L
8.1 ha	2.09	0.40	0.29	5.23
N	w	b	T	
0.010 /m²	198 m	32 m	30 %	

2

CHAMISSOPLATZ
Berlin

Island				
A	FSI	GSI	OSR	L
3.3 ha	3.21	0.62	0.12	5.22
Fabric				
A	FSI	GSI	OSR	L
4.7 ha	2.24	0.43	0.26	5.22
N	w	b	T	
0.017 /m²	120 m	20 m	30 %	

3

GRAZER DAMM
Berlin

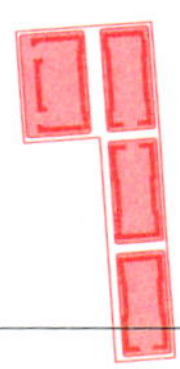

Island				
A	FSI	GSI	OSR	L
8.7 ha	1.21	0.24	0.62	5.00
Fabric				
A	FSI	GSI	OSR	L
11.7 ha	0.90	0.18	0.91	5.00
N	w	b	T	
0.012 /m²	165 m	23 m	25 %	

4

HACKESCHE HÖFE
Berlin

Island				
A	FSI	GSI	OSR	L
3.9 ha	2.84	0.60	0.14	4.70
Fabric				
A	FSI	GSI	OSR	L
4.5 ha	2.45	0.52	0.20	4.70
N	w	b	T	
0.011 /m^2	181 m	13 m	13 %	

5

HUFEISENSIEDLUNG
Berlin

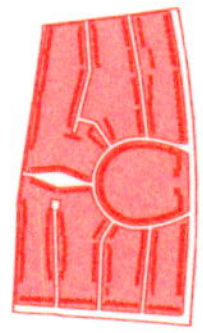

Island				
A	FSI	GSI	OSR	L
16.8 ha	0.59	0.20	1.37	2.98
Fabric				
A	FSI	GSI	OSR	L
20.7 ha	0.48	0.16	1.76	2.98
N	w	b	T	
0.014 /m^2	147 m	14 m	19 %	

6

KARL-MARX-ALLEE II
Berlin

Island				
A	FSI	GSI	OSR	L
9.9 ha	1.28	0.21	0.62	6.03
Fabric				
A	FSI	GSI	OSR	L
14.5 ha	0.87	0.14	0.98	6.03
N	w	b	T	
0.011 /m^2	186 m	32 m	32 %	

7

KLAUSENERPLATZ
Berlin

Island				
A	FSI	GSI	OSR	L
4.3 ha	2.14	0.46	0.25	4.63
Fabric				
A	FSI	GSI	OSR	L
5.9 ha	1.57	0.34	0.42	4.63
N	w	b	T	
0.012 /m^2	165 m	24 m	27 %	

8

LANDSBERGER TOR
Berlin

Island

A	FSI	GSI	OSR	L
2.7 ha	1.52	0.39	0.40	3.92

Fabric

A	FSI	GSI	OSR	L
3.8 ha	1.07	0.27	0.68	3.92
N	w	b	T	
0.018 /m²	110 m	18 m	30 %	

9

MÄRKISCHES VIERTEL
Berlin

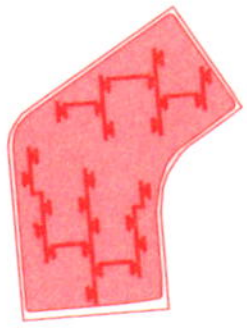

Island

A	FSI	GSI	OSR	L
16.1 ha	2.02	0.14	0.42	14.01

Fabric

A	FSI	GSI	OSR	L
17.9 ha	1.81	0.13	0.48	14.01
N	w	b	T	
0.005 /m²	394 m	21 m	10 %	

10

ONKEL-TOM-SIEDLUNG 1
Berlin

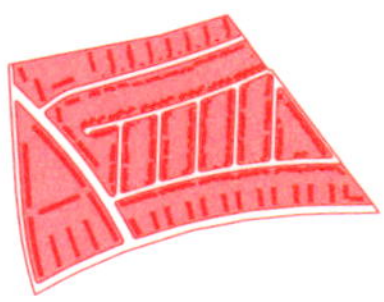

Island

A	FSI	GSI	OSR	L
20.0 ha	0.70	0.23	1.09	2.98

Fabric

A	FSI	GSI	OSR	L
25.0 ha	0.56	0.19	1.45	2.98
N	w	b	T	
0.013 /m²	153 m	16 m	20 %	

11

ONKEL-TOM-SIEDLUNG 2
Berlin

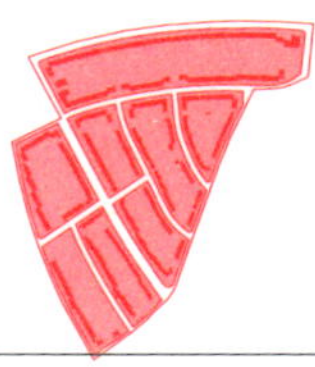

Island

A	FSI	GSI	OSR	L
18.3 ha	0.61	0.20	1.32	3.04

Fabric

A	FSI	GSI	OSR	L
22.8 ha	0.49	0.16	1.72	3.04
N	w	b	T	
0.013 /m²	154 m	16 m	20 %	

12

PARKSIEDLUNG SPRUCH
Berlin

Island				
A	FSI	GSI	OSR	L
4.1 ha	0.86	0.25	0.87	3.52
Fabric				
A	FSI	GSI	OSR	L
4.4 ha	0.80	0.23	0.96	3.52
N	w	b	T	
0.006 /m²	353 m	13 m	7 %	

13

RAUCHSTRASSE
Berlin

Island				
A	FSI	GSI	OSR	L
1.9 ha	1.36	0.28	0.53	4.87
Fabric				
A	FSI	GSI	OSR	L
2.6 ha	1.01	0.21	0.79	4.87
N	w	b	T	
0.014 /m²	143 m	20 m	26 %	

14

RIEHMERS HOFGARTEN
Berlin

Island				
A	FSI	GSI	OSR	L
4.3 ha	2.42	0.52	0.20	4.67
Fabric				
A	FSI	GSI	OSR	L
6.1 ha	1.71	0.37	0.37	4.67
N	w	b	T	
0.008 /m²	244 m	39 m	29 %	

15

RUDESHEIMER PLATZ
Berlin

Island				
A	FSI	GSI	OSR	L
4.8 ha	1.97	0.41	0.30	4.76
Fabric				
A	FSI	GSI	OSR	L
6.3 ha	1.50	0.31	0.46	4.76
N	w	b	T	
0.014 /m²	139 m	18 m	24 %	

16

SIEMENSSTADT
Berlin

Island				
A	FSI	GSI	OSR	L
14.1 ha	0.96	0.22	0.81	4.30
Fabric				
A	FSI	GSI	OSR	L
16.5 ha	0.82	0.19	0.99	4.30
N	w	b	T	
0.008 /m²	254 m	20 m	15 %	

17

STAAKEN
Berlin

Island				
A	FSI	GSI	OSR	L
6.5 ha	0.44	0.24	1.74	1.83
Fabric				
A	FSI	GSI	OSR	L
8.9 ha	0.32	0.17	2.57	1.83
N	w	b	T	
0.014 /m²	143 m	21 m	27 %	

18

TEMPELHOFER FELD
Berlin

Island				
A	FSI	GSI	OSR	L
6.9 ha	0.42	0.20	1.90	2.12
Fabric				
A	FSI	GSI	OSR	L
9.0 ha	0.32	0.15	2.62	2.12
N	w	b	T	
0.013 /m²	151 m	19 m	23 %	

19

THERMOMETERSIEDLUNG
Berlin

Island				
A	FSI	GSI	OSR	L
8.6 ha	1.09	0.19	0.74	5.66
Fabric				
A	FSI	GSI	OSR	L
9.8 ha	0.96	0.17	0.87	5.66
N	w	b	T	
0.008 /m²	262 m	17 m	12 %	

20

TIERGARTEN DREIECK
Berlin

Island				
A	FSI	GSI	OSR	L
2.9 ha	2.35	0.51	0.21	4.63
Fabric				
A	FSI	GSI	OSR	L
4.9 ha	1.37	0.30	0.51	4.63
N	w	b	T	
0.010 /m²	210 m	49 m	41 %	

21

VILLENKOLONIE GRUNEWALD
Berlin

Island				
A	FSI	GSI	OSR	L
9.0 ha	0.57	0.22	1.36	2.59
Fabric				
A	FSI	GSI	OSR	L
11.4 ha	0.45	0.18	1.81	2.59
N	w	b	T	
0.013 /m²	151 m	17 m	21 %	

22

WASSERSTADT SPANDAUERSEE 1
Berlin

Island				
A	FSI	GSI	OSR	L
3.8 ha	1.93	0.34	0.34	5.61
Fabric				
A	FSI	GSI	OSR	L
5.4 ha	1.35	0.24	0.56	5.61
N	w	b	T	
0.020 /m²	100 m	16 m	30 %	

23

WASSERSTADT SPANDAUERSEE 2
Berlin

Island				
A	FSI	GSI	OSR	L
15,7 ha	0.21	0.13	4.25	1.60
Fabric				
A	FSI	GSI	OSR	L
16,4 ha	0.20	0.12	4.45	1.60
N	w	b	T	
0.005 /m²	385 m	8 m	4 %	

SAMPLES FROM SPAIN

1
BARCELONETA
Barcelona

Island				
A	FSI	GSI	OSR	L
1.0 ha	5.12	0.97	0.01	5.27
Fabric				
A	FSI	GSI	OSR	L
2.0 ha	2.55	0.48	0.20	5.27
N	w	b	T	
0.070 /m²	28 m	8 m	50 %	

2
BESOS
Barcelona

Island				
A	FSI	GSI	OSR	L
7.2 ha	1.48	0.35	0.44	4.21
Fabric				
A	FSI	GSI	OSR	L
9.7 ha	1.11	0.26	0.67	4.21
N	w	b	T	
0.011 /m²	174 m	24 m	25 %	

3
BORRELL I SOLIER
Barcelona

Island				
A	FSI	GSI	OSR	L
1.4 ha	1.21	0.24	0.63	4.96
Fabric				
A	FSI	GSI	OSR	L
1.9 ha	0.90	0.18	0.91	4.96
N	w	b	T	
0.016 /m²	122 m	16 m	25 %	

4

CIUTAT VELLA
Barcelona

Island				
A	FSI	GSI	OSR	L
2.0 ha	4.33	0.91	0.02	4.77
Fabric				
A	FSI	GSI	OSR	L
2.3 ha	3.75	0.79	0.06	4.77
N	w	b	T	
0.030 /m²	66 m	5 m	13 %	

5

CONGRES
Barcelona

Island				
A	FSI	GSI	OSR	L
3.5 ha	2.88	0.58	0.15	4.99
Fabric				
A	FSI	GSI	OSR	L
5.8 ha	1.76	0.35	0.37	4.99
N	w	b	T	
0.020 /m²	99 m	22 m	39 %	

6

EIXAMPLE
Barcelona

Island				
A	FSI	GSI	OSR	L
12.1 ha	4.50	0.86	0.03	5.20
Fabric				
A	FSI	GSI	OSR	L
18.8 ha	2.89	0.56	0.15	5.20
N	w	b	T	
0.014 /m²	144 m	29 m	36 %	

7

FINESTRELLES
Barcelona

Island				
A	FSI	GSI	OSR	L
12.3 ha	0.39	0.18	2.10	2.24
Fabric				
A	FSI	GSI	OSR	L
15.7 ha	0.31	0.14	2.80	2.24
N	w	b	T	
0.014 /m²	147 m	17 m	22 %	

8

GOTIC
Barcelona

Island				
A	FSI	GSI	OSR	L
6.0 ha	4.80	0.92	0.02	5.23
Fabric				
A	FSI	GSI	OSR	L
7.2 ha	3.95	0.76	0.06	5.23
N	w	b	T	
0.022 /m²	91 m	8 m	18 %	

9

GRACIA
Barcelona

Island				
A	FSI	GSI	OSR	L
3.0 ha	2.47	0.73	0.11	3.38
Fabric				
A	FSI	GSI	OSR	L
3.8 ha	1.92	0.57	0.22	3.38
N	w	b	T	
0.025 /m²	80 m	9 m	22 %	

10

MAR BELLA
Barcelona

Island				
A	FSI	GSI	OSR	L
1.2 ha	3.11	0.44	0.18	7.03
Fabric				
A	FSI	GSI	OSR	L
2.2 ha	1.73	0.25	0.44	7.03
N	w	b	T	
0.013 /m²	148 m	38 m	44 %	

11

MONTBAU
Barcelona

Island				
A	FSI	GSI	OSR	L
4.7 ha	1.63	0.33	0.41	4.92
Fabric				
A	FSI	GSI	OSR	L
6.3 ha	1.21	0.25	0.62	4.92
N	w	b	T	
0.027 /m²	74 m	10 m	26 %	

12

PEDRALBES
Barcelona

Island				
A	FSI	GSI	OSR	L
2.3 ha	1.42	0.24	0.54	5.92
Fabric				
A	FSI	GSI	OSR	L
2.8 ha	1.13	0.19	0.71	5.92
N	w	b	T	
0.011 /m²	174 m	19 m	20 %	

13

RAVAL
Barcelona

Island				
A	FSI	GSI	OSR	L
1.4 ha	4.47	0.91	0.02	4.89
Fabric				
A	FSI	GSI	OSR	L
1.6 ha	3.83	0.78	0.06	4.89
N	w	b	T	
0.027 /m²	74 m	6 m	14 %	

14

RIBERA
Barcelona

Island				
A	FSI	GSI	OSR	L
1.2 ha	4.88	0.92	0.02	5.33
Fabric				
A	FSI	GSI	OSR	L
1.5 ha	3.94	0.74	0.07	5.33
N	w	b	T	
0.057 /m²	35 m	4 m	19 %	

15

VILA OLIMPICA
Barcelona

Island				
A	FSI	GSI	OSR	L
9.3 ha	2.02	0.40	0.30	5.08
Fabric				
A	FSI	GSI	OSR	L
9.3 ha	1.19	0.23	0.64	5.08
N	w	b	T	
0.013 /m²	159 m	37 m	41 %	

SAMPLES FROM THE UK

1

BARNSBURY
London

Island				
A	FSI	GSI	OSR	L
4.6 ha	1.24	0.40	0.48	3.07
Fabric				
A	FSI	GSI	OSR	L
6.7 ha	0.85	0.28	0.86	3.07
N	w	b	T	
0.021 /m²	94 m	16 m	32 %	

2

CLAPHAM
London

Island				
A	FSI	GSI	OSR	L
3.2 ha	2.08	0.71	0.14	2.92
Fabric				
A	FSI	GSI	OSR	L
4.3 ha	1.57	0.54	0.30	2.92
N	w	b	T	
0.020 /m²	102 m	14 m	25 %	

3

CORNHILL LEADENHALL
London

Island				
A	FSI	GSI	OSR	L
2.2 ha	9.98	0.78	0.02	12.74
Fabric				
A	FSI	GSI	OSR	L
2.9 ha	7.52	0.59	0.02	12.74
N	w	b	T	
0.022 /m²	93 m	12 m	25 %	

4

CORNHILL WOODSTREET
London

Island				
A	FSI	GSI	OSR	L
2.7 ha	7.64	0.98	0.00	7.80
Fabric				
A	FSI	GSI	OSR	L
4.0 ha	5.10	0.65	0.07	7.80
N	w	b	T	
0.028 /m²	71 m	13 m	33 %	

5

HAMPSTEAD GARDEN SUBURBS
London

Island				
A	FSI	GSI	OSR	L
8.0 ha	0.48	0.21	1.65	2.23
Fabric				
A	FSI	GSI	OSR	L
10.1 ha	0.38	0.21	2.21	2.23
N	w	b	T	
0.014 /m²	144 m	16 m	21 %	

6

HIGHBURY EAST
London

Island				
A	FSI	GSI	OSR	L
3.7 ha	0.75	0.19	1.08	3.92
Fabric				
A	FSI	GSI	OSR	L
5.3 ha	0.51	0.13	1.69	3.92
N	w	b	T	
0.019 /m²	104 m	18 m	31 %	

7

NOTTING HILL
London

Island				
A	FSI	GSI	OSR	L
3.6 ha	1.47	0.60	0.27	2.45
Fabric				
A	FSI	GSI	OSR	L
5.1 ha	1.06	0.43	0.53	2.45
N	w	b	T	
0.024 /m²	85 m	13 m	28 %	

8

PUTNEY HAWKESBURY
London

Island				
A	FSI	GSI	OSR	L
2.1 ha	1.17	0.24	0.65	4.87
Fabric				
A	FSI	GSI	OSR	L
3.0 ha	0.84	0.17	0.98	4.87
N	w	b	T	
0.018 /m²	110 m	17 m	28 %	

9

PUTNEY HEALTH
London

Island				
A	FSI	GSI	OSR	L
5.3 ha	0.58	0.29	1.22	2.01
Fabric				
A	FSI	GSI	OSR	L
8.0 ha	0.39	0.19	2.07	2.01
N	w	b	T	
0.026 /m²	77 m	14 m	33 %	

10

SOHO
London

Island				
A	FSI	GSI	OSR	L
1.4 ha	4.24	1.01	0.00	4.19
Fabric				
A	FSI	GSI	OSR	L
2.2 ha	2.67	0.64	0.14	4.19
N	w	b	T	
0.033 /m²	61 m	13 m	37%	

11

WESTMINSTER
London

Island				
A	FSI	GSI	OSR	L
3.0 ha	4.14	0.73	0.07	5.68
Fabric				
A	FSI	GSI	OSR	L
4.2 ha	2.95	0.52	0.16	5.68
N	w	b	T	
0.024 /m²	84 m	13 m	29 %	

SAMPLES FROM SWEDEN

1

HAMMARBY HÖJDEN
Stockholm

Island				
A	FSI	GSI	OSR	L
3.9 ha	0.65	0.21	1.22	3.14
Fabric				
A	FSI	GSI	OSR	L
5.2 ha	0.49	0.16	1.70	3.14
N	w	b	T	
0.020 /m²	101 m	13 m	24 %	

2

HAMMARBY SJÖSTAD
Stockholm

Island				
A	FSI	GSI	OSR	L
4.4 ha	2.62	0.56	0.17	4.69
Fabric				
A	FSI	GSI	OSR	L
8.1 ha	1.42	0.30	0.49	4.69
N	w	b	T	
0.023 /m²	88 m	23 m	46 %	

3

HÖKARÄNGEN
Stockholm

Island				
A	FSI	GSI	OSR	L
5.0 ha	0.92	0.28	0.78	3.32
Fabric				
A	FSI	GSI	OSR	L
6.7 ha	0.69	0.21	1.15	3.32
N	w	b	T	
0.019 /m²	105 m	14 m	25 %	

4

JUNGFRUDANSEN
Stockholm

Island				
A	FSI	GSI	OSR	L
7.5 ha	0.88	0.18	0.93	4.93
Fabric				
A	FSI	GSI	OSR	L
8.3 ha	0.80	0.16	1.05	4.93
N	w	b	T	
0.023 /m²	88 m	4 m	9 %	

5

ÖSTERMALM
Stockholm

Island				
A	FSI	GSI	OSR	L
4.3 ha	3.29	0.64	0.11	5.17
Fabric				
A	FSI	GSI	OSR	L
5.9 ha	2.40	0.46	0.22	5.17
N	w	b	T	
0.019 /m²	105 m	15 m	27 %	

6

SEGELTORP
Stockholm

Island				
A	FSI	GSI	OSR	L
1.7 ha	0.60	0.39	1.02	1.55
Fabric				
A	FSI	GSI	OSR	L
2.2 ha	0.48	0.31	1.44	1.55
N	w	b	T	
0.037 /m²	54 m	6 m	20 %	

7

SKARPNÄCK
Stockholm

Island				
A	FSI	GSI	OSR	L
6.8 ha	1.92	0.50	0.26	3.86
Fabric				
A	FSI	GSI	OSR	L
10.3 ha	1.26	0.33	0.53	3.86
N	w	b	T	
0.022 /m²	91 m	17 m	34 %	

8

SÖDERMALM
Stockholm

Island				
A	FSI	GSI	OSR	L
5.2 ha	3.59	0.67	0.09	5.32
Fabric				
A	FSI	GSI	OSR	L
7.2 ha	2.57	0.48	0.20	5.32
N	w	b	T	
0.018 /m²	110 m	17 m	28 %	

9

SUNDBYBERG
Stockholm

Island				
A	FSI	GSI	OSR	L
4.9 ha	1.76	0.42	0.33	4.17
Fabric				
A	FSI	GSI	OSR	L
6.5 ha	1.33	0.32	0.51	4.17
N	w	b	T	
0.019 /m²	108 m	14 m	24 %	

10

TALLKROGEN
Stockholm

Island				
A	FSI	GSI	OSR	L
4.8 ha	0.23	0.18	3.55	1.24
Fabric				
A	FSI	GSI	OSR	L
6.7 ha	0.16	0.13	5.30	1.24
N	w	b	T	
0.024 /m²	83 m	13 m	29 %	

Mercantile Capitalism (1400–1815)

The majority of Dutch towns were established during this period. Feudal rulers created new towns while, at the same time, other cities arose as a result of economic growth. In the latter case, population growth forced city councils to adopt urban expansion plans. In Amsterdam, population density increased from 110 inhabitants per hectare in 1400 to almost 650 inhabitants per hectare during the Golden Age. At the height of the Golden Age (1650), every citizen of Amsterdam occupied an average of 15 m^2 of city space. In the seventeenth century, urban expansion plans were developed to counter densification and to accommodate economic and population growth. A distinctive feature of two such plans in Amsterdam, the Grachtengordel and the Jordaan, was the increase in the scale of urban planning. This was the first time in the Netherlands that public authorities introduced building regulations and zoning to guide private developments. Through these expansions, the density in Amsterdam fell to around 400 inhabitants per hectare in 1795. By 1815 a further fall in population density to 320 inhabitants per hectare had occurred, following economic stagnation and periods of war in the eighteenth century.

Liberal-Competitive Capitalism (1815–1900)

Following a period of relative stagnation, the Dutch population began to grow once more during the nineteenth century. The population increased from 2.3 million in 1815 to 3.1 million in 1850, and reached 5.1 million by 1900. Industrialization and the agrarian crisis precipitated an even more rapid growth in the cities with a huge migration to them, especially after 1870. In the late nineteenth century this rapid population growth led to problems with overcrowding, ill health and human misery. The population density in Amsterdam reached almost 600 inhabitants per hectare in 1880, comparable to the peak density of 1650. Scientists, urban experts and the state began to recognize the relationship between city form, density and health problems. Influential books about 'better cities' began to focus on both hygiene and aesthetics. Still, plans of the time tended to be little but compromises between ideals and stark economic pragmatism.

State-Managed Capitalism (1900–1979)

The main developments of this period have their origins in the late nineteenth century as capitalism slowly evolved from a liberal-competitive status to a more state-managed and centrally controlled mode. Criticism of the overcrowded and unhealthy industrial city of the nineteenth century led in the Netherlands to the introduction of the Housing Act (Woningwet) in 1901, which had a profound impact on urban planning and design. Central government and municipalities assumed a greater role in city development. During the first half of the twentieth century, Berlage drew up expansion plans for Amsterdam and The Hague, inspired by the work of Sitte. The General Extension Plan of Amsterdam (AUP, 1934), planned by Van Eesteren and Van Lohuizen, represented a unique example of Dutch modern urbanism, while the utopian ideas of Le Corbusier and Gropius contributed to the design of the vertical garden city, a concept that reached its peak in the Netherlands with the realization of the Bijlmermeer in 1973.

Before the Second World War, the new ideals were mostly realized at the city level, leading to a rapid growth of areas of relatively low density. The average population density of Amsterdam decreased from almost 600 inhabitants per hectare at the end of the nineteenth century (1880) to 195 inhabitants per hectare by 1939. After the Second World War, this process of urbanization in ever-lower densities changed into one of suburbanization. The advent of the car in less crowded cities and a rapid colonization of the countryside became synonymous with progress. Population density in Amsterdam continued to decrease to 70 inhabitants per hectare by 1984.

Neoliberal Capitalism (1979–)

The oil crisis of 1973 and a global recession ended an unusually long period of economic growth. This had a great effect on all levels of society. The centralized state-managed planning approach, dominant since the Second World War, gave way to a market-oriented, project- and negotiation-based approach. The basic assumption was that market competition would increase efficiency. Private parties would be forced to be sensitive to the wishes of investors and housing consumers. By being closer to the action, it was assumed that they would be able to respond more quickly to social and economic changes. This was in stark contrast to the image sketched of a preceding period of a bureaucratic, expensive, and inefficient state apparatus that had relied on its planning and housing monopoly to realize top-down developments. Such a collectivist construction was deemed unsuitable for individualized and emancipated postmodern consumers whose postindustrial wealth seemed to be ever increasing. This very affirmative approach to capitalist dynamics paralleled other social and economic reforms of the welfare state that were taking place in the 1980s. The neoliberal TINA stance of the late 1980s expressed this fundamental view on the power of the market: There Is No Alternative (to the market).

During the last decades of the twentieth century, population density in Amsterdam continued to decline and fell to a little more than 60 inhabitants per hectare in 2000. However, the trend of decreasing densities seemed to be slowing down somewhat, probably influenced by the new spatial policy in which the concept of concentrated dispersal was replaced by the concept of the compact city, and the fact that Amsterdam had reached the physical limits of its administrative boundaries. This has resulted in an increase of density of 17 % between 2000 and 2020, mostly due to the extension of Amsterdam with the new island group IJburg. After an annual growth with almost 2 % for the last 100 years, the urban footprint has thus started to decrease again.

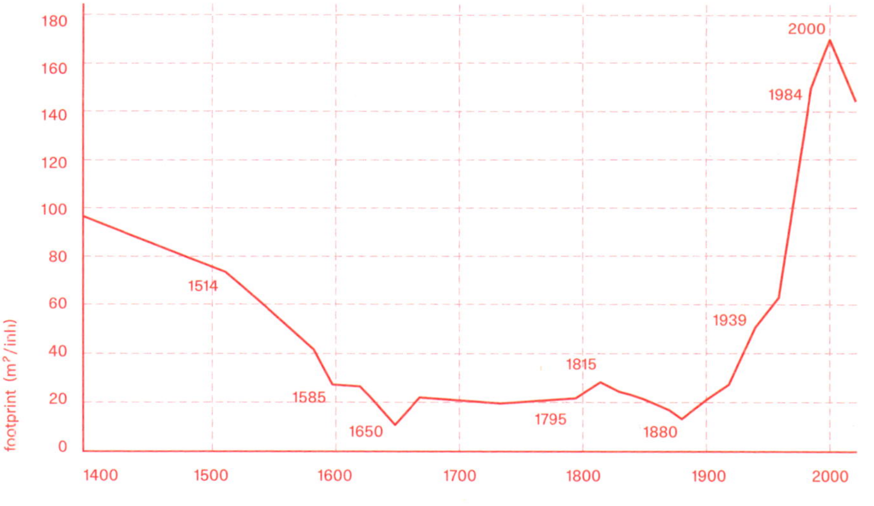

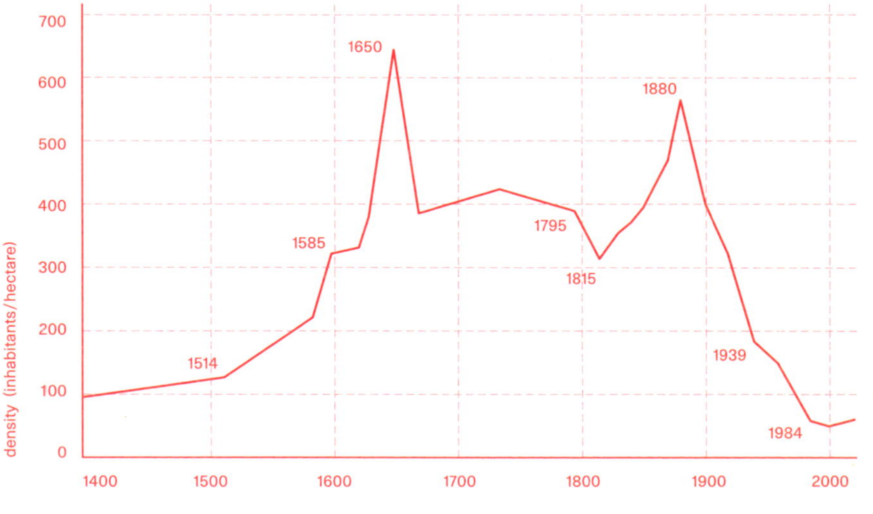

1400

1450

1585

1612

1626

1900

1918

19

1544

1795

1984

2000

2020

1400

⬟ Housing fabrics (Predominately)

1450

⬟ Housing fabrics (Predominately)

1544

⬟ Housing fabrics
(Predominately)

1585

⬟ Housing fabrics
(Predominately)

1612

● Housing fabrics (Predominately)

1626

● Housing fabrics (Predominately)

1795

- Parks
- Housing fabrics (Predominately)

1900

- Industry and offices
- Cemeteries
- Parks
- Housing fabrics (Predominately)

1918

- Industry and offices
- Cemeteries
- Garden allotments
- Parks
- Housing fabrics (Predominately)

1939

- Industry and offices
- Cemeteries
- Garden allotments
- Sports facilities
- Parks
- Housing fabrics (Predominately)

1958
Industry and offices
Cemeteries
Garden allotments
Sports facilities
Parks
Housing fabrics
(Predominately)

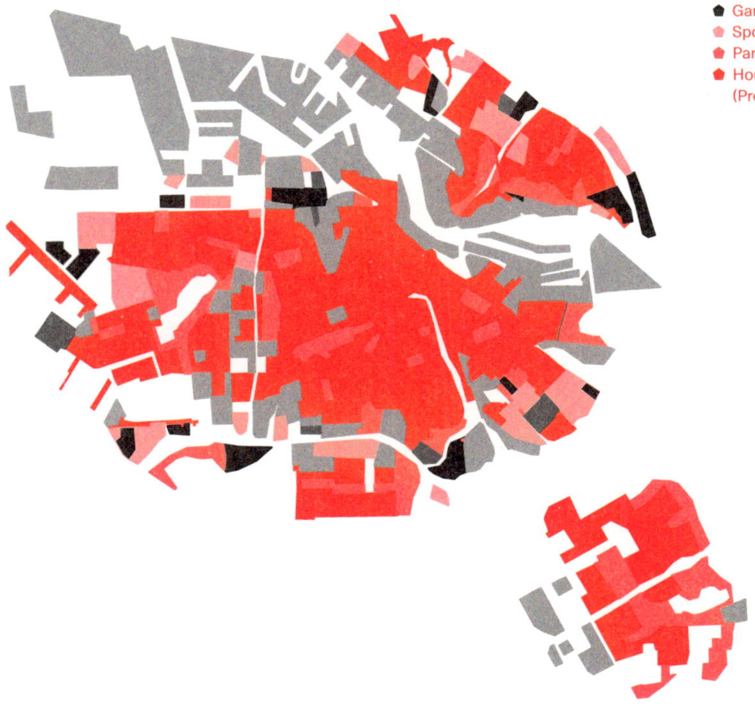
1984
Industry and offices
Cemeteries
Garden allotments
Sports facilities
Parks
Housing fabrics
(Predominately)

2000

- Industry and offices
- Cemeteries
- Garden allotments
- Sports facilities
- Parks
- Housing fabrics (Predominately)

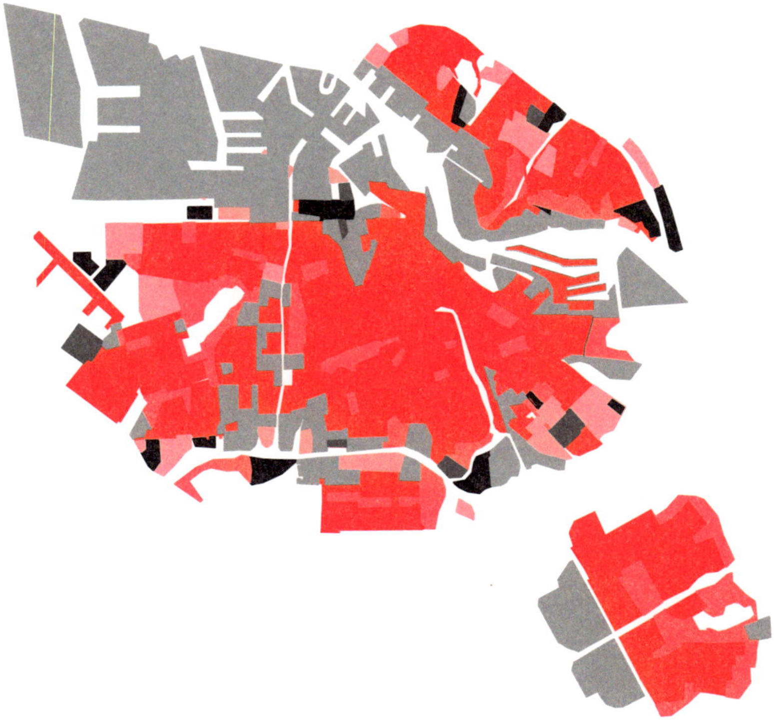

2020

- Industry and offices
- Cemeteries
- Garden allotments
- Sports facilities
- Parks
- Housing fabrics (Predominately)

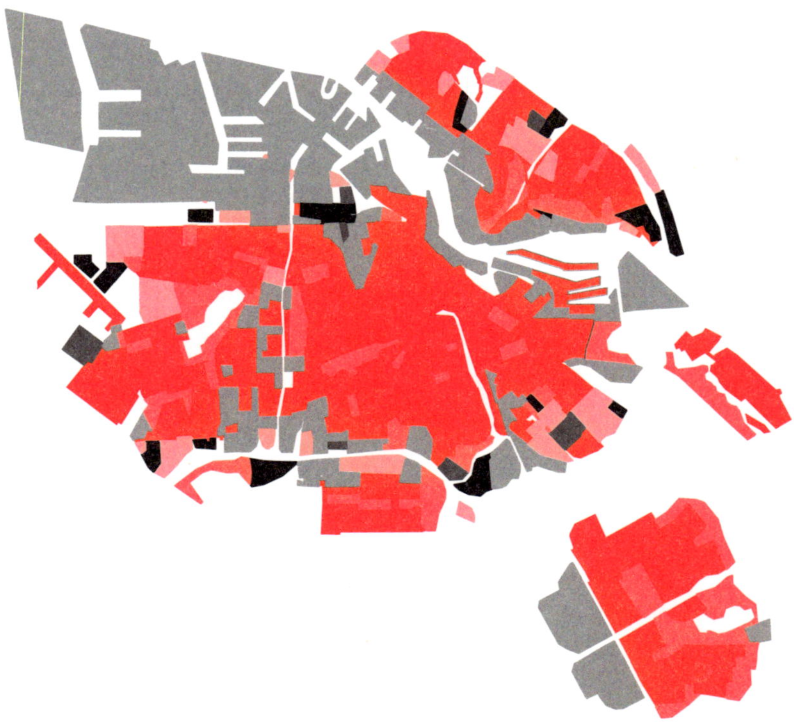

This book was made possible in part by the generous support of the Department of Architecture and Civil Engineering, Chalmers University of Technology and the Swedish Research Council Formas (projects 2017–00914, 2018–00281 and 2019–00226).

This book is a revised edition of the 2010 publication that was made possible in part by the support of the Department of Urbanism, Faculty of Architecture, Delft University of Technology; The Ministry of Housing, Spatial Planning and the Environment (VROM); The Spatial Planning Department – City of Amsterdam (DRO); and Van Eesteren-Fluck & Van Lohuizen Foundation

Authors:
Meta Berghauser Pont and Per Haupt
Copy editor:
D'Laine Camp
Book design:
SJG/ Joost Grootens and Megan Adé
Publisher:
nai010 publishers/ Marcel Witvoet
Printing:
NPN Drukkers
Paper:
Munken Print White 1.5, 115 grs
Typefaces:
Optimo/ Practice
Linotype/ Neue Haas Unica
SJG/ Ceremony XL

Printed and bound in the Netherlands
ISBN 978-94-6208-538-1
NUR 648, 955
BISAC ARC019000, ARC019000
Spacematrix is also available as e-book:
ISBN 978-94-6208-539-8 (pdf)

nai010 publishers is an internationally orientated publisher specialized in developing, producing and distributing books in the fields of architecture, urbanism, art and design.
www.nai010.com

nai010 books are available internationally at selected bookstores and from the following distribution partners:
North, Central and South America:
Artbook | D.A.P., New York, USA
dap@dapinc.com
Rest of the world:
Idea Books, Amsterdam, the Netherlands
idea@ideabooks.nl

For general questions, please contact nai010 publishers directly at sales@nai010.com or visit our website www.nai010.com for further information.

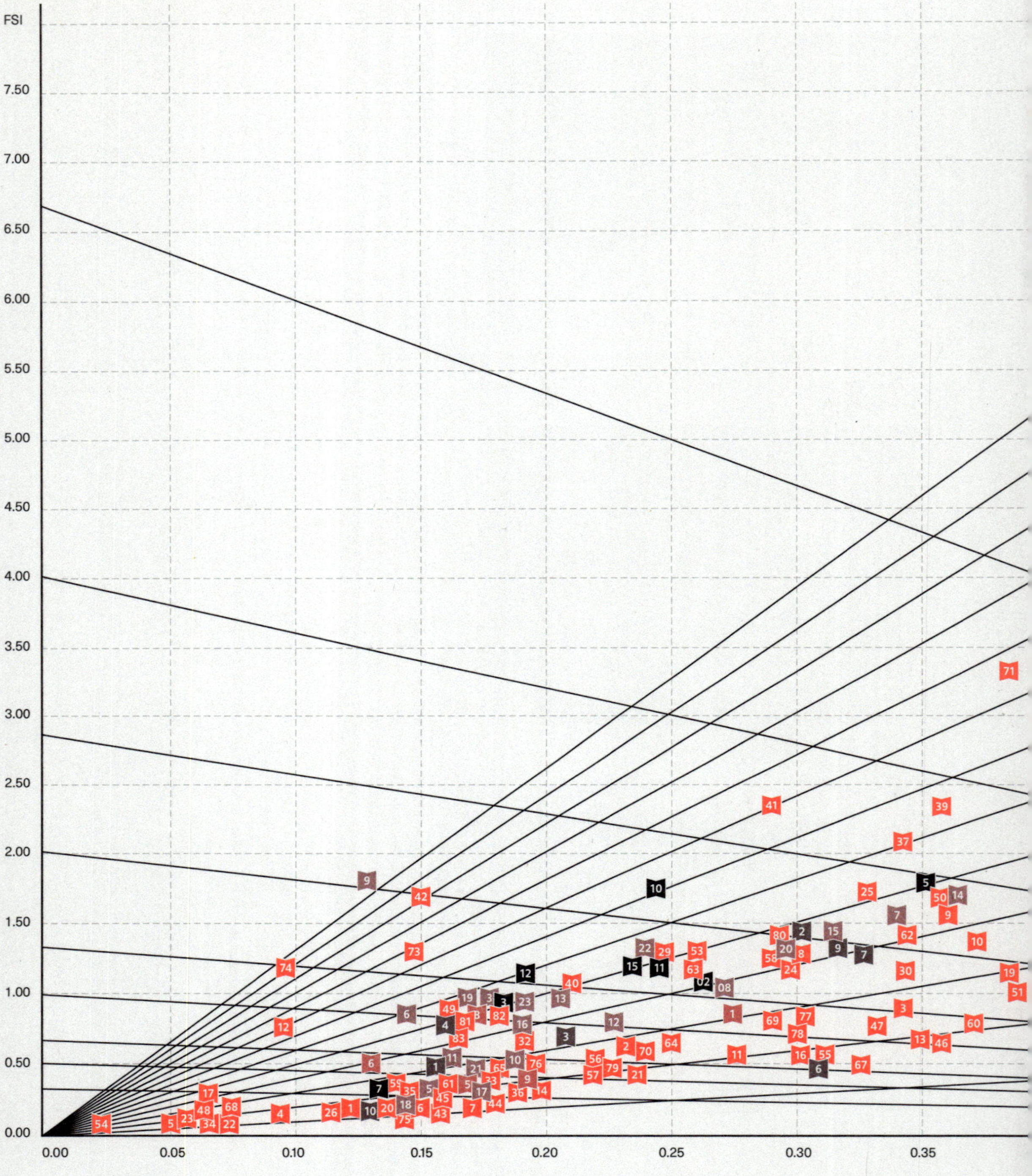

THE NETHERLANDS

1 Achterbos
2 Amsteldorp 1
3 Amsteldorp 2
4 Anloo
5 Balloo
6 Bergen 1
7 Bergen 2
8 Berlage Plan Zuid 1
9 Berlage Plan Zuid 2
10 Berlage Plan Zuid 3
11 Betondorp
12 Bijlmer Oud
13 Blokzijl
14 Borssele
15 Buurt Negen
16 Colijnsplaat
17 De Berg Zuid
18 De Pijp
19 De Veste
20 Douve Weien
21 Dreischor
22 Dwarsgracht
23 Emmer-Erfscheidenveen
24 Feyenoord
25 Funen
26 Gees
27 Goedereede
28 Grachtengordel
29 GWL terrein
30 Heemraadssingel
31 Heveadorp
32 Holendrecht 1
33 Holendrecht 2
34 Hoog Soeren
35 Huisduinen
36 IJlst
37 Java island
38 Jordaan
39 KNSM island
40 Kolenkit
41 Landtong
42 Langswater
43 Molenaarsgraaf
44 Nagele
45 Niehove
46 Nieuwpoort
47 Nieuw Sloten
48 Nimrodpark
49 Nolensstraat
50 Noordereiland
51 Noorderhof
52 Oude Boteringe
53 Peperklip
54 Rosengaarde
55 Sloten
56 Slotermeerlaan
57 Slotermeer Noord
58 Stadstuinen
59 Staphorst
60 Stevensweert
61 Troelstralaan
62 Vaillantlaan
63 Venserpolder
64 Vijfhuizen
65 Vogelwijk
66 Vondelpark
67 Vreewijk
68 Wageningen-Hoog
69 Watergraafsmeer 1
70 Watergraafsmeer 2
71 Weena
72 Westerdok
73 Wildemanbuurt
74 Wilheliminaplein
75 Wolveschans 1
76 Wolveschans 2
77 Ypenburg 1